CHINA'S RETREAT FROM EQUALITY

ACKNOWLEDGMENTS

The household income surveys on which the studies in this book are based, as well as other research expenses, were supported by grants from the Asian Development Bank and the Ford Foundation, to which we express our gratitude. We are also indebted to Marc Eichen, Stephen J. McGurk, Barry Naughton, Scott Rozelle, Terry Sicular, James Wen, Jeffrey Zax, and Zhang Ming, all of whom contributed in one way or another to making this a better book.

—— ASIA AND THE PACIFIC ——

Series Editor: Mark Selden, Binghamton University

Exploring one of the most dynamic and contested regions of the world, this series includes contributions on political, economic, cultural, and social changes in modern and contemporary Asia and the Pacific.

Asia
and the
Pacific

CHINA'S

— INCOME DISTRIBUTION —

RETREAT

— AND —

FROM

— ECONOMIC TRANSITION —

EQUALITY

CARL RISKIN, ZHAO RENWEI, LI SHI, EDITORS

AN EAST GATE BOOK

M.E.Sharpe
Armonk, New York
London, England

An East Gate Book

Library of Congress Cataloging-in-Publication Data

China's retreat from equality : income distribution and economic transition / edited by
Carl Riskin, Zhao Renwei, and Li Shi.
    p.cm.—(Asia and the Pacific)
"An East gate book"
ISBN 0-7656-0690-9 (alk. paper) ISBN 0-7656-0691-7 (pbk. : alk. paper)
    1. Income distribution—China. I. Riskin, Carl. II. Zhao, Renwei. III. Li, Shi. IV. Asia
and the Pacific (Armonk, N.Y.)

HC430.I5 C484 2000   00-052214
339.2′0951—dc21

Printed in the United States of America

BM (c) 10   9   8   7   6   5   4   3   2   1
BM (p) 10   9   8   7   6   5   4   3   2   1

Contents

The Editors and Contributors

The Editors

Carl Riskin is a professor of economics at Queens College, City University of New York, and senior research scholar at Columbia University's East Asian Institute.

Zhao Renwei, a former director of the Economics Institute of the Chinese Academy of Social Sciences (CASS), is one of China's most eminent senior economists.

Li Shi is a professor at the Economics Institute who has specialized in studying income distribution and poverty in China.

The Contributors

Mark Brenner is a research assistant professor in the Political Economy Research Institute, University of Massachusetts, Amherst.

Keith Griffin is Distinguished Professor of Economics at the University of California, Riverside.

Björn Gustafsson is a professor in the Department of Social Work at the University of Göteborg, Sweden.

Azizur Rahman Khan is a professor of economics at the University of California, Riverside.

John Knight is a professor of economics and Head of the Department of Economics at Oxford University.

Lina Song, originally from the Economics Institute in Beijing, is senior lecturer in the Business School, University of Nottingham.

Zhang Ping and **Wang Lina** are both researchers at the Economics Institute, CASS.

Zhu Ling is a professor at the Economics Institute, CASS.

List of Figures and Tables

Figures

Tables

CHINA'S RETREAT FROM EQUALITY

1

Introduction
The Retreat from Equality: Highlights of the Findings

Carl Riskin, Zhao Renwei, and Li Shi

Rising inequality has been a common feature of international economic development in the most recent decades, and China is no exception. One of the world's most egalitarian societies in the 1970s, China in the 1980s and 1990s became one of the more unequal countries in its region and among developing countries generally. This retreat from equality has thus been unusually rapid. The Gini coefficient of inequality in household income rose by 7 percentage points (18 percent), or by 1.0 percentage point per year, between 1988 and 1995.[1] Inequality of rural household per capita income rose an estimated 23 percent over the same seven years; urban inequality increased even faster—by 42 percent.[2] The reason the Gini ratio for overall inequality for China, including both urban and rural households, increased at a lower rate than that of either rural or urban distributions taken separately, is because overall inequality in China is dominated by the large urban-rural income gap that, according to our measurements, remained stable in real terms between 1988 and 1995. This finding contrasts with the official statistics showing the urban-rural gap rising by 20 percent between these years. The principal reason for this difference in findings is that many urban subsidies, which we count as part of urban income but the State Statistical Bureau (SSB) does not, melted away between 1988 and 1995. Thus the SSB overstates the growth of urban income during this period.[3]

Seldom has the world witnessed so sharp and fast a rise in inequality as has occurred in China.[4] Increasing economic and social inequality has therefore been an important subtext in the generally positive story of rapid growth accompanying economic reform and transition, and it calls into question the sustainability of that growth by raising the specter of social instability.

Yet the changes in income distribution are not, in fact, well understood. While there was undoubtedly excessive egalitarianism in some aspects of China's income distribution (such as that of urban wages) before the reform period began, are these the aspects that have changed the most, and do such changes explain the increase in inequality? Can the main sources of increasing inequality be identified and the changes themselves assessed with respect to their impact on efficiency and equity? Are they the product of impersonal economic forces, such as comparative advantage, or have they been helped along by state policies? Do they look like being permanent changes or are they likely to be reversed with further economic development? What implications do they have for such human development objectives as the elimination of abject absolute poverty? These are the kinds of basic questions that the thirteen chapters of this book try to answer.

The Data

These studies are based primarily upon two national surveys of household income that were designed by the authors under the auspices of the Institute of Economics, Chinese Academy of Social Sciences (CASS) in Beijing, and implemented in 1989 and 1996 for the respective years just completed—that is, 1988 and 1995. We believe these surveys, whatever their weaknesses (see below), provide the best data currently available for addressing the income distribution picture in China as a whole. National or quasi national in scope, they provide a great deal of detail missing from the highly aggregated distributional data released by the SSB. Moreover, they make possible the estimation of income according to its standard international definition.[5]

The survey samples were drawn from the national urban and rural samples used by the SSB for its own annual household surveys, and conducted by the provincial branches of the SSB. The surveys of urban and rural China were kept separate because of the very different institutional organization of the two population segments and therefore the need for different questionnaires. Unfortunately it was not possible to include a panel element, since a certain proportion of the SSB sample is changed annually and the entire sample had been changed within the seven years separating our two surveys.

As Table 1.1 shows, the sizes of the samples had to be reduced between 1988 and 1995 for reasons of cost escalation. In addition, the coverage of the rural sample was scaled back. In 1988 this sample included all but two provinces, Tibet and Xinjiang, whereas in 1995 nine others were excluded in addition. The urban sample kept all of its 1988 provinces and gained one, Sichuan, in 1995. We tried to reduce the number of provinces in the rural sample in a way that would not greatly bias our analysis of income for rural China as a whole. Two factors give us some confidence in this regard. First, among China's twenty-nine provinces in 1988, the average rank of the excluded provinces in terms of per capita rural income was 14.9; thus the excluded provinces were evenly distributed among all provinces in terms of per capita rural income. Second, the rural survey instrument contained a

Table 1.1

The 1988 and 1995 National Household Surveys: Details of the Samples

		1988	1995
Urban			
Households		9,009	6,931
Persons		31,827	21,694
Provinces-total		10	11
	-common to both years	10[a]	10[a]
	-included in 1995 but not in 1988		Sichuan
Cities	-total	60	68
	-common	60	60
Rural			
Households		10,258	7,998
Persons		51,352	34,739
Provinces-total		28	19
	-common to both years	19[b]	19[b]
	-included in 1988 but not in 1995	Heilongjiang, Inner Mongolia, Qinghai, Ningxia, Guangxi, Fujian, Hainan, Tianjin, Shanghai	

[a] The urban sample included the following ten provinces (and province-level municipalities) in both years: Beijing, Shanxi, Liaoning, Jiangsu, Anhui, Henan, Guangdong, Yunnan, Gansu, and Hubei.

[b] The rural sample included the following nineteen provinces (including one province-level municipality) in both years: Beijing, Hebei, Shanxi, Liaoning, Jilin, Jiangsu, Zhejiang, Anhui, Jiangxi, Shandong, Henan, Hubei, Hunan, Guangdong, Sichuan, Guizhou, Yunnan, Shaanxi, and Gansu.

question designed to elicit total household income according to the SSB definition; the average figure we obtained for this item is virtually identical to the SSB's own estimate, derived from its larger sample, as reported in the 1996 *Statistical Yearbook of China*.[6]

The chapters in this book investigate various issues that are involved either as causal influences on the income distribution profile (such as urban housing subsidies or the distribution of rural land) or outcomes of it (rural poverty, malnutrition) or both (gender and spatial inequality).

The book is divided into three parts. The first, in keeping with the complexity of the income distribution issue, includes three perspectives on increasing inequality in China. Zhao Renwei presents a political economic analysis, including a discussion of rent-seeking behavior, from the viewpoint of a senior scholar who has long studied China's income distribution and who has personally witnessed the changes as they have occurred. Björn Gustaffson and Li Shi examine changes in distribution using equivalent income—that is, income per household member as adjusted for household size, since some consumption items, such as housing space and furniture, can be easily shared by household members—as their dependent variable, and they seek to pinpoint the relative responsibility of locational and personal characteristics for growing inequality. John Knight and Lina Song attempt to explain inequality in the two benchmark years and the change in inequality between them, and to distinguish in particular the effects of reform policies in causing the change.

The second part deals with urban China. Azizur Rahman Khan, Keith Griffin, and Carl Riskin review and measure the broad trend of increasing income inequality in China's towns and cities, and argue that it is largely responsible for the rise in urban poverty despite extremely fast economic growth. John Knight, Li Shi, and Zhao Renwei investigate urban wages and incomes from a spatial perspective, looking for patterns in the regional distribution of income and its change; Wang Lina investigates the effects of the formerly ubiquitous housing subsidies on urban income distribution; and Björn Gustafsson and Li Shi examine the difference in earnings between men and women.

Part three turns to the rural majority. Zhang Ping analyzes the interregional aspect of rural distribution; Zhu Ling the distribution of food security and nutritional adequacy in the countryside; Mark Brenner the distribution of rural wealth, including land; Lina Song the evidence about rural sex preference provided by consumption structure and the impact on consumption structure of increased bargaining power for women; Li Shi the impact of the "floating population" of rural-urban migrants on rural income distribution; and Carl Riskin and Li Shi the degree to which the rural poor are located within the officially designated poor counties that have been the sole targets of state antipoverty programs.

Before turning to the discussion of rising inequality, we must heed Zhao Renwei's reminder that this increase may not have been quite as dramatic as it looks, because the high degree of equality in the pre-reform period was in some respects illusory. The urban-rural income gap, for instance, was wider than that of other low-income countries in Asia. Connected to this issue was the in-kind supply system that operated in urban areas and, to a much lesser extent, in rural areas; this made for greater inequality in real total income (including income in kind) than in money income alone, because most income in kind went to the already better-off urban population. Moreover, a two-decade policy of keeping wages frozen had produced arbitrary and anomalous inequalities among urban generations. These various sources of inequality temper, but do not reverse, the conclusion that pre-reform income distribution was relatively egalitarian in comparative international context, and in terms of conventional income inequality measures. But they also sensitize us to the complexity of the task of measuring inequality. In some respects (e.g., access to travel opportunities or to the international news media) China was a quite inegalitarian country.

There are biases that lead our surveys both to understate and overstate the true extent of inequality in both years. A principal source of underestimation is that the surveys underrepresent both extremes of the income distribution. On the low end, there is reason to believe that the SSB parent sample, from which our subsample is drawn, underrepresents the poorest villagers, because many of these live in very remote areas that often cannot be reached by motorized transport, and are illiterate as well. At the other end of the distribution, as Zhao points out, the new superrich are almost certainly underrepresented and, even where caught by the sample, are likely to have understated their real incomes. Any substantial income from private business activities is also likely to be understated, since it is poorly documented and subject to the income tax. Zhao cites a survey by the CASS Institute of Sociology that revealed the existence of over 1 million households with incomes of a million yuan or above in 1995. Very few such high-income households were included in our surveys. Nonetheless, our findings do show a sharply increasing gap between the richest (upper 3 percent) and poorest (bottom 10 percent) individuals in China, a gap that rises from a multiple of less than eight in 1988 to one of almost twelve in 1995. This suggests that if the extremes of the distribution had been accurately sampled, our inequality measures would have grown even more rapidly than they did between those two years.

However, one important weakness of the surveys—its treatment of the migrant population—has the opposite effect of causing us to exaggerate overall income inequality. Tens of millions of workers, mostly from poorer rural areas and some with their families, have entered China's towns and cities, mostly in better-off coastal regions, to take or find jobs. These "floating" migrants do not have urban household registration (*hukou*) and are thus excluded from the urban sample. Their incomes are certainly undercounted in their native rural places.[7] Evidence suggests that, on the whole, the migrant population occupies a place in the income distribution between that of their urban host communities and that of their rural native places. That is, they are, on average, poorer than their full-status urban neighbors but richer than the villagers back home. Therefore, their omission (or underrepresentation) from the urban and rural samples widens the distribution. Had they been included in the urban sample, this would have reduced average urban income; putting them in the rural sample would raise rural average income. Either way, the urban-rural income disparity, which is the dominant contributor to income inequality in China, would be smaller. The significance of the migrant population for income distribution is examined in greater detail by Li Shi, whose treatment is discussed below.

Thus there are offsetting biases in the surveys, and we cannot state with any confidence whether the net result is to cause us to overstate or to understate the true absolute degree of income inequality. We are confident, however, that the widespread "retreat from equality" documented in the various studies of this book would survive an elimination of these biases and possibly even grow stronger. The unusual size of the urban-rural gap in China is to a considerable extent a consequence of past and present institutional constraints on market forces (especially constraints on labor mobility and on access to state sector jobs with their many benefits). While market forces have been progressively unleashed, at least by 1995 they had not yet made a serious dent in urban-rural inequality.

Causes of Rising Inequality: Growth or Reform?

How to explain the rapidly rising inequality since the mid-1980s? Some analysts, harking back to Simon Kuznets (1955, 1963), argue that economic growth itself in its early stages is likely to give rise to increasing inequality, because growth tends to occur in a manner that is geographically and sectorally unbalanced; some industries and regions begin growing first, and they grow away from the others. Indeed, China's initial steps toward modernization in the nineteenth and early twentieth centuries were limited to a small number of coastal enclaves—exactly the kind of history from which Kuznets was generalizing. In the first three decades of the People's Republic of China (PRC), from the early 1950s to the late 1970s, on the other hand, central planning was used in part to resist the growth of such inequality through redistributing resources from richer to poorer provinces. After the reform era began in 1979, fiscal decentralization virtually ended such redistribution, while market forces took greater hold. Under these circumstances, did rapid growth itself cause rising inequality?

Zhao Renwei, who engages here in a qualitative analysis of the factors contributing to increased inequality, divides them into three conceptual categories: those associated with economic reform, with policy, and with economic growth. He finds a considerable number of reform and policy factors that have been operating to magnify inequality. An important group of these is what Zhao calls "disorder changes," which include rent-seeking activities, insider appropriation of public assets, monopoly behavior, and cruder forms of corruption. We have little quantitative information about the effects of such activities, but there is a widespread belief in China that they have been pervasive and have had a pernicious effect on the distribution of income. To the extent that this is so, there is nothing inevitably growth-driven about the inequality to which they have given rise.

Moreover, Knight and Song show persuasively that China's rising inequality has had little if anything to do with rising income. Knight, Li, and Zhao (Knight et al.) and Knight and Song both find evidence suggesting, rather, that reform was the primary cause of growing inequality.

Knight et al. fix their attention on what might be called the distribution of urban inequality. That is, while by most measures inequality in general has increased rapidly in China, they ask whether there are discernable patterns to the regional distribution of the increase. They find that urban income inequality within provinces and cities, while generally increasing everywhere, has grown faster in those places that were the most equal to begin with, and slower in those that were initially most unequal. Therefore, the provinces and cities were becoming more alike in their income distributions. Knight et al. trace this trend largely to the behavior of basic wage income, and because wage structure is a good reflection of the progress of economic reform, this leads them to suspect that the timing of reforms may provide the explanation. Cities in which reforms progressed earliest already had more unequal distributions in 1988. As reform spread throughout the country, inequality of provincial urban distributions everywhere caught up with that of the earlier reformers.

Thus it was not growth, per se, that caused increasing inequality, but reform policies, according to these interpretations of the data. Yet one could argue that reform was in fact a prerequisite of the kind of sustained economic growth that China experienced after 1978. Reform policies, after all, were meant to bring into play market forces, which in turn were expected to stimulate faster growth. Some of the kinds of income differentiation discussed in this book clearly indicate the process of market forces taking hold. For instance, Gustafsson and Li show that education, age, and ownership sector of work all greatly increased their impact on earnings between 1988 and 1995; this is just what would be expected when, through a developing labor market, productivity exercises an increasing influence over earnings. Therefore, we do not want to draw too sharp a distinction between the two interacting forces of growth and reform.

Regional Inequality

Average provincial household income and earnings rose in all the provinces studied between 1988 and 1995, but Knight et al. establish that these averages diverged substantially. The richer a province was in 1988, the faster its per capita income and earnings rose. Yet before this period—say, from the beginning of reform in 1978 until 1988—quite the opposite trend appears to have held, that is, there was strong *convergence* of provincial average incomes. Knight et al. attribute this sharp change from an equalizing to a disequalizing regional pattern of growth to the effects of decentralization and the evaporation of planning that attended the acceleration of urban economic reform during the period concerned.[8]

Regional polarization, especially between the advanced provinces of coastal China and those of the less developed west, has been a prime concern of many Chinese, as well as of the government and international organizations such as the World Bank (WB). Many researchers have noted that whatever has happened to interprovincial inequality generally, inequality between coastal and interior regions (especially those in the west) has widened sharply, and this is apparent in our data as well. Gustafsson and Li find that the average income premium received by residents (urban and rural taken together) of eastern coastal regions relative to that received in the more backward west rose from 58 percent in 1988 to 76 percent in 1995.[9] Knight et al. analyze regional differences in urban incomes and find that the disparity between coast and interior is due entirely to differences in the income-generating process, and not at all to differences in the mean income-earning characteristics of workers. In other words, it is not the higher average level of certain characteristics (e.g., education) among coastal workers that explains the income gap, but the higher returns to such characteristics on the coast. But which characteristics in particular? In fact, the researchers show that the role of education has changed dramatically between the two dates. In 1988 almost all of the difference in income between coast and interior came from higher earnings by basic, unskilled labor in the coastal regions. Education had no positive impact on earnings at all. By 1995, however, higher returns to education accounted for half of the difference in income—itself much larger than in 1988—between coast and interior. There was now a premium for education beyond the most basic level in both coastal and interior regions. As Knight and Song's earnings functions reveal, the urban earnings difference between college graduates and those with only a primary school education grew from 9 percent in 1988 to 42 percent in 1995. But the education premium was almost twice as great on the coast as it was in the interior provinces. It seems that rapid growth and technological change on the eastern seaboard was creating shortages of skilled labor and thus differentially driving up coastal wages of skilled and educated personnel.

Regional polarization has also become an issue for the rural population. Most rural income inequality is actually local inequality within individual provinces, rather than among them. That is, inequality within provinces is far greater than that among provincial average incomes, as Zhang Ping shows. Nevertheless, the interprovince component of overall rural inequality has grown much faster than rural inequality overall, its contribution rising from 22 percent of the Theil index of inequality in 1988 to 31 percent in 1995.[10] In the past, rural regional differentiation was closely linked to differences in climate and terrain conditions that determine farm productivity. These differences were noncumulative in nature, so while there might be a large gap between average family income in the Yangzi delta region and that in a dry upland part of Gansu, that gap tended to be relatively stable over time, affected mainly by annual weather fluctuations. What has changed in recent decades, as Zhang Ping shows, is that parts of the countryside have undergone industrial development, and this has in turn affected the nature of rural inequality. The overall income gap between the most developed provinces, on the one hand, and the less developed regions, on the other, comes primarily from differences in industrial income, not from farming. Moreover, Zhang finds that the component of total income that has contributed most to the increase in rural interprovincial inequality is wages, which were responsible for over half of this inequality in 1995. In the countryside, wages are a disequalizing income source.[11]

Rural wages, in fact, accounted for considerably more than the total increase in inequality,[12] as Knight and Song show, and most of this contribution from wages came from a big increase in the share of wages in total income, rather than from increasing inequality of wages themselves. In contrast, the share of household production in total income faded, which reduced overall inequality by 60 percent of the increase in the Gini—thus greatly limiting the rise in inequality. Household production is actually the most equally distributed component of rural incomes, a fact that limited the effect of its falling share in reducing inequality. As Knight and Song state, "The transfer from household-based to individual-based economic activities had a powerful net disequalizing effect on household income per capita."

The responsibility of regionally limited rural industrialization for increasing rural inequality also explains another phenomenon evident in the data, which otherwise would seem perplexing. In much of the world, wealth is distributed less equally than income. But in rural China, Brenner demonstrates, the opposite is true: Inequality of income is much greater than that of wealth and grew much faster between 1988 and 1995. The share of income controlled by richer groups has grown substantially relative to their share of wealth. This is because high incomes in the countryside are the product of off-farm employment opportunities rather than accumulation of income-earning assets. "The situation in rural China," writes Brenner, "is unlike almost any other country in the developing world: rural wage laborers are among the wealthiest residents of the Chinese countryside." Yet Brenner also finds that financial assets grew substantially between 1988 and 1995 to become the third most important component of rural wealth. He surmises that the ongoing development of financial and capital markets will eventually lead to a reversal of the present relation between the wealth and income distributions, causing this relation more closely to resemble that of other countries.

Rural industrialization has a reputation for being an equalizing factor in development. Taiwan's past record of "growth with equity,"[13] for instance, is commonly attributed in part to the spread of labor-intensive rural industries throughout the island. Yet on the mainland it seems that the effects of spreading industry in the form of off-farm wage incomes were powerful propellents of inequality. Why should the mainland's experience be so different? As both Zhang Ping and Knight and Song show, inequality of off-farm wages among China's provinces could not be the answer, because these wages are very equally distributed. Rather, it is inequality of opportunity to gain off-farm employment that is the culprit. Compared to Taiwan, the mainland is so much larger, more populous, and more varied in natural and economic conditions, that diffusion of nonagricultural activities over the population is a much slower task that will take much longer to accomplish. In the meanwhile, unbalanced development of rural industry, and thus of opportunities for lucrative off-farm income, is the principal force promoting income inequality among the provinces—very much in keeping with Kuznets's original suggestions. Still, there is some evidence of diffusion of this opportunity among provinces: Knight and Song's logit analysis reveals that the probability of a rural worker receiving off-farm income exceeded 15 percent in ten provinces out of nineteen in 1995, whereas in 1988 this was true for only three of the provinces. Slowly, it seems, the development of secondary and tertiary activities is spreading to new parts of China.

Housing

We have already noted the apparent paradox, stressed by Brenner, that rural wealth is more evenly distributed than rural income, unlike elsewhere in the world. This paradox of course depends upon the estimated distribution of land—the most important component of rural wealth—and the treatment of the existing usufruct rights to rural land as if they amounted to private ownership. Yet real private ownership of property, suppressed during the era of collectivism, is a new and growing phenomenon in China, as is its corollary, the category of "property income." As Zhao Renwei shows, property income in the urban sector was a small but rapidly growing proportion of urban income, and it was very unequally distributed. Not included in property income and separately calculated is the imputed rental value of owned housing, which has become by far the most important income-yielding asset in urban China. It was also extraordinarily unequal in its distribution, an evident result of an inegalitarian approach to urban housing reform, the workings of which are examined in some detail by Wang Lina.

The picture of housing reform yielded by Wang's study is a disquieting one. On one hand, the ubiquitous policy of work units buying housing from developers or building it themselves and then renting it to their workers at subsidized rents, reveals that at least some of the apparent reform has occurred in name only. It continues an uneconomical approach to housing, propagates rental subsidies that are hard to justify, and discourages proper house maintenance. On the other hand, the impact of an increasingly speculative private housing market dominated by domestic real estate developers, foreign investors, and rent-seeking government officials resulted in unsustainable real estate bubbles. Under these circumstances, it is not hard to see why existing occupiers of state- or unit-owned apartments were encouraged to buy their units at well below market prices. Due to unequal access to such units, Wang writes, urban residents have been differentially favored with "housing welfare," which in turn exacerbates overall inequality.

Sex and Ethnicity

There has been considerable discussion within China about the effects of economic reform on gender inequality.[14] There is no question that women have benefited along with men from many of the new economic opportunities created by the reforms, including the spread of opportunities for off-farm employment. At the same time, however, old and new forms of discrimination have emerged in the freer market-oriented atmosphere. Several of our authors have looked at these issues. Knight and Song, for instance, show that the probability of rural working women receiving off-farm income increased substantially between 1988 and 1995. However, the rate of increase for women was far lower than that for men. Thus, the probability of women receiving nonfarm income actually fell sharply relative to its counterpart for men: In 1988 women were 60 percent as likely as men to receive off-farm income, whereas in 1995 they were only 40 percent as likely. In the cities the income disadvantage of being female almost doubled over the seven years.

Evidence of gender inequality is also examined by Gustafsson and Li, who analyze the gap between the wages of men and women and its change over time. One of their most striking findings is the huge increase in the gender gap for earnings of older people, specifically, people above the general mandatory retirement age of 55 for women. In 1988 women aged 56–65 earned 72 percent as much as men of the same age, whereas by 1995, women earned only 42 percent as much as men. It is possible that this dramatic change was brought about by a combination of rising earnings of men still working after age 55 and fewer opportunities for women than for men to obtain postretirement jobs or start businesses. Indeed, Gustafsson and Li find that about half of the overall earnings gap between men and women can be explained by differences in relevant characteristics for these two groups, among which the difference in average age is the single most important, accounting for 19 percent of the overall gap. Women's forced retirement at 55, and the very low earnings they can expect after retirement, are a major impediment to their lifetime earning ability. Men generally do not retire until age 60, and so have five additional years at the peak of their lifetime earning capacity to compile income.

Much gender inequality originates with differential treatment of boys and girls, and with attitudes that are inculcated within the family and absorbed by children of both sexes at an early age. Our surveys did not directly tackle intrahousehold distribution or attitudes toward gender. Indeed, we estimate our distribution parameters on the dubious assumption that total household income is shared equally among all household members. However, there are indirect inductive ways of using information generated by the surveys to throw light on gender equality and inequality, and Lina Song engages in some virtuoso examples of these methods. She teases from the structure of household consumption evidence of differential attitudes toward—and treatment of—boys and girls in the countryside. Song develops evidence that some 50 percent more is spent on medical care of young boys than of young girls. While boys at a very young age are biologically more susceptible to disease than girls, the difference is not nearly enough to warrant such a large differential in medical spending. The fact that, for our 1995 rural sample, the ratio of boys to girls aged 6 or under is 123:100 strongly suggests differentially poor care for girls.[15]

Song shows that when women's bargaining position in the household is strong—either because they are the head of household or because they have differentially great amounts of education—the share of household spending on their children's education and clothing rises, while the share spent on alcohol and cigarettes falls. Yet, interestingly, she finds no evidence that such high bargaining power for women reduces discrimination against girls. On the contrary, it appears that such a position for women may actually increase the differentially favorable treatment of boys (e.g., the spending differential for medical care rises).

There has also been a substantial gap between the average income of China's Han majority population and that of its various national minorities. Between 1988 and 1995 this gap increased substantially, and in the latter year the average income of the minority population came to no more than two-thirds that of the majority, as shown by Gustafsson and Li. However, they also show that this rise is due solely to the increased negative effects on income of other characteristics, such as having little education and living in western regions—characteristics that pertain especially to minorities. The net deficit in income of being a member of a national minority, itself, after controlling for such other characteristics, actually declined from about 12 percent to about 7 percent of the average majority income. In other words, in 1995 a minority person with characteristics identical to those of a member of the Han majority could expect to receive an income only 7 percent lower. "Pure" antiminority discrimination was therefore rather slight.[16]

Land, Labor Mobility, and the Urban-Rural Gap

Land and labor are the two production factors shaping the rural economy. Land is the single most important asset underlying rural income, and its distribution, along with that of other components of rural wealth, is the subject of Mark Brenner's investigation. Labor earnings depend greatly on mobility, and in this respect the reform period has seen major changes, especially the burgeoning movements of population, mostly people from poorer rural regions moving for part of the year to more developed towns and cities in search of better jobs. Li Shi examines the impact of such temporary migration on the distribution of rural incomes.

Land was the subject of the first major act of economic reform and transition to a market economy. In December 1978 the Third Plenum of the Eleventh Central Committee sent signals that led to the rapid dismantling of the rural commune system throughout China. By and large, the end result of this process was that land farmed collectively in the past was now divided up among the families in each village on an essentially equal per capita basis.[17] This fundamental intralocal equality of the most important component of rural wealth has undoubtedly retarded the growth of inequality in the rural income distribution. It also provides an institutional safeguard against the development of an impoverished class of landless laborers, who comprise the poorest of the poor in other parts of Asia. In China, rural poverty is commonly associated with poor quality land (dry, hilly, infertile), not, as elsewhere, with lack of access to land.

Land—if the villagers' usufruct rights are regarded as quasi ownership—continues to be the dominant component of rural wealth holdings, accounting for more than half of total rural wealth. Moreover, as Brenner shows, land continues to exercise an equalizing effect on overall wealth distribution, because the land itself is so equally distributed. Indeed, while the Gini coefficient for land holdings fell from 0.465 in 1988 to 0.414 in 1995, its *concentration ratio*, which measures its distribution over the population of all income recipients, not just of landholders, actually fell to *zero* in the latter year (from 0.014). In other words, however unequally land was distributed among holders of land, it was perfectly equally accessible to all rural income groups.[18] However, closer examination reveals a somewhat puzzling divergence between the trends of landholdings in physical terms, on the one hand, and in value terms, on the other. In physical terms, landholdings became more equally distributed between 1988 and 1995, as we have seen. In value terms, however, there was a pronounced rise in inequality, the Gini coefficient increasing from 0.323 to 0.393.

The decline in inequality of physical landholdings, Brenner argues, was most likely due to two factors. First, there have been frequent village readjustments of land allocations due to changes in household size because of marriages, births, or deaths, and such reallocations tend to be "dominated by egalitarian considerations." Second, off-farm migration has been concentrated in the more land-constrained regions, lowering household size and reducing the person-to-land ratio in such areas. As for the rise in inequality of land *values*, Brenner notes that this differentiation takes place in the context of values that are compressed relative to the physical distribution of land—values are distributed more equally than physical units. And he argues that the differentiation itself was probably related to growing commercialization in response to rising grain prices.

Unlike land, labor has the propensity to be mobile, and its ability to seek out better income-earning opportunities is a fundamental prerequisite of economic efficiency. This ability was largely suppressed during the collective period for most Chinese. The combination of universal household registration (*hukou*) and strict food rationing had made it virtually impossible for people to leave their native place without permission. One important aspect of the transition period in China has been the relaxation of this rigid control of population movement. Such movement has by and large been tolerated by the government, while the disappearance of food rationing and the emergence of a free market in food has made it possible for people to survive in new venues. The result, as mentioned above, has been a massive migration of people, many from poorer rural regions of central and western China, to the cities and towns of the eastern seaboard in search of lucrative work opportunities.

This phenomenon has a clear impact on income distribution, since large numbers of people in the middle and lower rungs of the distribution ladder are earning larger incomes than they would have without migration. But figuring out exactly how migration has affected distribution is frustratingly difficult, because urban immigrants who still have rural *hukou* are not included in the State Statistical Bureau's urban household sample from which the subsample used by the current study was drawn. As we have already seen, the inclusion of migrants' income in either our urban or (fully in) our rural income estimates would have lowered urban-rural inequality somewhat, and thus reduced overall inequality. This much we can plausibly surmise. But what are the effects of migration on inequality *within* the countryside?

To address this question, Li Shi examines the data generated by our surveys on migration and the receipt of remittances sent home by household members temporarily working away from home. Li shows that out-migration raises household income not only because of the remittances that are sent back by the migrants, but also because migration permits a reallocation of the household labor remaining behind, and this in turn raises labor productivity and thus incomes. But do these effects of migration increase equality or inequality of income distribution? Here, Li Shi remains cautious; whether income distribution is made more or less equal by increases in the incomes of households that have working out-migrants depends upon the location of those households in the income distribution. If they are relatively poor, then their enrichment through migration increases equality. But many migrants come from middle-income rural households, which tend to have strong incentives to increase their incomes, as well as the means to finance travel, subsistence, and risk during the hunt for work, and possibly also existing networks that ensure the availability of better jobs when they do migrate. The success of such households may lead to growing gaps between themselves and the poor and thus to greater intralocal inequality even as it reduces urban-rural inequality. It is possible that the same general income level, sufficient to finance costs of migration but low enough to provide an incentive to migrate, is relatively low in the national perspective but relatively high in that of the poorer provinces. As Li Shi shows, on a national basis and within at least one rich province (Guangdong), migration appears to increase equality of distribution, suggesting that the migrants come from the ranks of the relatively poor. However, within at least one comparatively poor province (Sichuan), migration appears to increase inequality, which suggests that migrants from poorer provinces may come from relatively better-off families.

The appropriate policy response to the disequalizing results of migration within poorer provinces is not to discourage migration, but rather to provide better support for poor would-be migrants, perhaps through encouraging institutional links between their home territories and the dynamic, expanding urban areas seeking cheaper labor, by investing more resources in education in poor areas, or by investing further resources in economic development and diversification in poorer areas.[19] Li Shi calls for a variety of measures to knock down the barriers to a unified national labor market and gradually eliminate the extraordinary urban-rural divide that has characterized China for decades, mostly to the detriment of the rural majority. Moreover, one of his two chapters with Gustafsson (chapter 3, "A More Unequal China?") finds that almost half of the urban-rural income gap is explained by differences in characteristics of the two population groups (e.g., education) other than their location in rural or urban areas—a finding that, upon a moment's reflection, is not surprising and leads us to focus on inequality in access to income-earning characteristics (such as education) as one way of attacking the urban-rural gap. The converse of Gustafsson and Li's finding is that in 1995 a little over half of that gap was pure urban-rural difference in the sense of not being due to urban-rural differences in education or any of the other characteristics for which they control. This is down from the "pure" urban-rural gap in 1988 (138 percent), a finding rather different from the official statistics that show a rising urban-rural gap but do not control for other characteristics.

Rural Poverty and Food Security

During the early part of the reform period—from 1978 up to about 1985—there was a remarkably sharp fall in the rate of absolute rural poverty. Most observers believe that this decline stopped in the late 1980s and then resumed, but in a more irregular and halting fashion, in the 1990s. The estimated number of poor of course depends upon the choice of income poverty threshold and the time trend depends upon how this threshold is updated to account for inflation. While a case can be made that official statistics understate the amount of remaining rural poverty and overstate its rate of decline,[20] the broad record of recent decline was widely accepted. However, Riskin and Li, in their contribution to this volume derive results that throw some doubt on this consensus.

They work here with a definition of household disposable income (and poverty lines) that omits the component of imputed rental value of private housing[21] because, they argue, this income source is likely to be overestimated for the poor population, and they use provincial price indexes rather than the national consumer price index to deflate income.[22] The resulting estimates of the head-count rate of rural poverty, using both official and adjusted poverty thresholds, are considerably higher than the official rate of 6 percent for 1995 and, more important, display no downward trend between 1988 and 1995. In other words, on the basis of Riskin and Li's approach, our surveys reveal at best a constant poverty rate and a growing absolute number of rural poor. This is a very disappointing record to accompany substantial growth that raised average per capita rural income by 38 percent.

Moreover, the plight of the poor in both poor and nonpoor regions deteriorated in some ways between 1988 and 1995. The percentage of poor people with five or more years of education fell substantially, for instance, and the percentage of their total income spent on medical care rose sharply and to very high levels. The fiscal relationship between household and state/collective was very regressive in both years, especially for nonregional poor households, from whom it took over 15 percent of household disposable income.

The poverty reduction record seems to be at least as much the result of broad economic development strategies and their effects on the rural economy, as of specific poverty reduction policies. Until very recently, such policies were entirely aimed at officially designated poor *areas,* often missing many poor families within those areas and entirely missing poor families residing outside of them. By all poverty measures considered here, at least half of the rural poor population lived outside designated poverty areas; on the basis of the official poverty line for 1995, however, more than two-thirds lived outside of such areas.

When adequacy of nutrition is taken as the criterion of well-being rather than income, substantial numbers of Chinese fall below the standard, as Zhu Ling shows, and these are not limited to the very poor. Zhu examines the link between income distribution and China's food security, the latter a subject that has received much attention in recent years.[23] While most of the rural poor, as defined by China's low income–poverty line, are able to obtain enough food to meet minimum standards of nutrition, a substantial minority of them are not. Moreover, undernutrition extends well beyond the absolute poor and afflicts many mid-to-low income people. Zhu Ling argues that such people are under great pressure to accumulate money for their children's marriages or to build new houses, for which purposes they suppress their families' food consumption below a healthy minimum standard.

She holds that China's food relief program "neither reached the poorest, nor was it given to the people who were the most energy inadequate." With regard to poverty and food insecurity, she identifies the most pressing rural problem at present to be the lack of a rural social security system, and she argues that "the existing disaster mitigation and social relief system is far from sufficient to meet the needs of the vulnerable groups during the economic transition period."

Income Distribution and Economic Policy

China's leaders regard the income distribution of the collective era, before reform began in the late 1970s, as having been excessively egalitarian from the perspective of encouraging economic growth, and they have openly promoted greater inequality with the slogan, "Let some get rich first." At the same time, however, they appear to have been taken aback by the strength of centrifugal forces as the more developed eastern coastal regions have grown rapidly away from the much more backward west, and they have accordingly spoken out against polarization. Yet not only was there no pronounced policy agenda dealing with income distribution until quite recently, but quite a few important policies have served to reinforce the polarizing tendencies. These include the extension of special privileges for attracting foreign investment to already advantaged coastal areas, a regressive fiscal interaction between state and households,[24] the fiscal decentralization already mentioned, and a highly disequalizing urban housing reform.

One result of a distribution insensitive policy stance is the disappointing behavior of urban poverty during the period covered by our study. Over these seven years, urban per capita household income rose an estimated 4.5 percent per year; yet what Khan, Griffin, and Riskin (Khan et al.) call the "broad" head-count poverty rate remained virtually unchanged, at best, at around 8 percent of the urban population, while the "deep" head-count rate (reflecting a lower income poverty threshold) actually increased between 56 and 82 percent, depending upon the consumer price index used. Both the proportionate poverty gap (PPA), which measures the average depth of poverty, and the weighted poverty gap (WPA), which is an indicator of the distribution of income among the poor, deteriorated during the period. The importance of growing urban income inequality to this result is indicated by a simulation exercise that showed that the healthy growth of urban per capita income would have reduced the broad urban head-count poverty rate to below 1 percent by 1995, had income distribution remained unchanged from 1988 to that year. Economic reform thus failed to reduce urban poverty in part because of fast growing inequality, and by most measures urban poverty increased. And the deeper was urban poverty, the faster it grew.[25]

The wage structure in 1988 was highly compressed. As Khan et al. argue, this weakened work incentives, impeded labor allocation among firms, and reduced the incentive to acquire knowledge and skills. The rise in wage differentials between 1988 and 1995 (the concentration ratio growing from 0.178 to 0.247) was a necessary step in overcoming these deficiencies. Inequality in the distribution of wages grew to account for 45.6 percent of overall inequality. However, instead of adjusting to compensate for the effects of increased wage inequality, urban public policy further aggravated inequality through a highly disequalizing system of net subsidies, a housing reform that gave rise to an extremely uneven distribution of housing assets and housing services, and the failure to construct an adequate safety net to accommodate the large numbers of layoffs of state sector workers resulting from state enterprise reform. Thus while urban inequality was bound to grow somewhat in the context of market-oriented economic reforms, "regressive social policies made the burdens of transition greater than they need have been,"[26] according to Khan et al.

The end of Zhao Renwei's contribution is also devoted to the need for broad policy improvements. He decries the situation of partial reform that keeps alive many opportunities for rent-seeking and other "disorder" activities, and thus he stresses the need to carry through the reforms systematically and thoroughly. Zhao also would like to see rural development get much more attention from the government, with a view to narrowing the dominant urban-rural income gap, and he emphasizes the importance of improving taxation, education, social security, and labor mobility policies, all of which have an immediate and large bearing on distribution.

A common theme emerging from the chapters in this book is that China's "retreat from equality" has reached the point at which it needs greater and more focused attention from government and society. If undernutrition is a continuing problem, and not only among the poorest; if the under-five mortality rate has actually risen in recent years, despite rapid economic growth;[27] if the poor are losing access even to primary education (see above) and poor rural villages can no longer afford to provide free public schooling;[28] if a new stratum of urban poor is emerging from the reform of state enterprises; then current patterns and levels of inequality threaten not only the health and well-being of many of China's 1.3 billion people, but the very sustainability of China's economic development. Moreover, the hope that breakneck growth could substitute effectively for social policy becomes particularly irrelevant in an era of slower growth, such as has already begun in China. A low-growth environment imposing inequitable burdens on the population is not a recipe for prolonged social stability.

As a continental-sized developing country with a huge population, China must depend primarily on its domestic markets, even while taking full advantage of links with the global economy. From a macroeconomic viewpoint, the disequalizing nature of recent growth has played to and quickly saturated relatively thin urban markets while leaving the vast interior rural market underdeveloped. Healthy increases in the lagging incomes of the rural majority would help to provide a necessary stimulus for an economy that was suffering from low growth and falling prices as the 1990s came to an end.[29]

Thus there are strong arguments pertaining not only to equity but also to sustainability and macroeconomic stability that call for paying renewed attention to inequality in China today. We hope this book will contribute to the growing discussion of income distribution there and help to get this important topic the attention it deserves.

Notes

1. See Chapter 4 by Knight and Song in this volume.
2. See Chapter 5 by Khan, Griffin, and Riskin in this volume; and Khan and Riskin, 1998.
3. See Khan and Riskin, 1998, pp. 250–251.
4. Gustafsson and Li, in Chapter 3 in this volume, suggest that the United Kingdom and Russia in recent years may rival China in speed and extent of increased inequality.
5. For a detailed account of how household disposable income is defined and constructed, and how the definition and estimates differ from those of the SSB, see Khan and Riskin 1998. Some differences remain in Gini ratios estimated by different authors, primarily because of different methods of valuing income and subsidies in kind.
6. See Eichen and Zhang, 1993 for a detailed discussion of the sampling method in 1988. Selection of households was done in basically the same way in 1995.
7. Whether the "floaters'" incomes are included in their home place depends on whether they are listed as members of the household and, if so, on how accurately the respondents record the migrant members' incomes. Household members who have been away for a long time may not be listed at all. Even if listed, their incomes, aside from remittances home, are likely to be ignored or understated.
8. Khan and Riskin (1998, 2001) have attributed this pronounced shift in the mid-1980s to the coastal development strategy and ancillary policies adopted then in order to facilitate China's integration with the global economy.
9. See Chapter 3, "A More Unequal China?" These numbers represent a "pure" interregional difference in the sense that it is the net coastal premium after controlling for a number of other characteristics that affect regional differences in income.
10. The Theil index is a measure of inequality whose chief virtue is that, unlike the more commonly used Gini coefficient, it is directly decomposable in the manner indicated in the text. See note 1 of Chapter 9, by Zhang Ping.
11. This is also reported by Khan and Riskin, 1998.
12. That is, if nothing else had changed except wages, the Gini coefficient for income would have increased by much more than it actually did. Thus something else happened to offset part of the effect of the wage change on the Gini, as the text explains.
13. This is the title of a 1979 book on development in Taiwan; see Fei et al., 1979.
14. A convenient place to look for a summary of information on the impact of reforms on Chinese women is UNDP 1999a. The chapter on the status of women is drawn almost entirely from Chinese sources.
15. As Song points out, this ratio is considerably higher than its official counterpart, which is already higher than would be normally expected. In 1997 the official sex ratio for ages six and below was 118:100 (calculated from *Zhongguo renkou tongji nianjian, 1998*, p. 4).
16. Moreover, it is possible that the addition of other explanatory variables would further reduce the net discrimination coefficient.
17. Villagers were not given formal ownership of the land and could not buy or sell it, but were rather given use rights on a long-term basis.
18. The concentration ratio of land adjusted for irrigation, by counting an irrigated acre as equal to two acres of unirrigated land, was 0.05. See Khan and Riskin, 2001, Chapter 6.

19. The collapse of the redistributive fiscal mechanism that used to benefit poor provinces and localities has made schooling increasingly expensive and beyond the means of many poor families. This was bound to have impacted on their attractiveness to outside employers. See UNDP, 1999a; Rosenthal, 1999.

20. See Khan and Riskin, 2001, Chapter 4, for a detailed discussion of these issues. The authors argue that the disequalizing character of growth in China since the mid-1980s caused the rate of decline of rural poverty to be much slower than it would otherwise have been.

21. In accordance with standard international practice, our measures of income include the imputed value of the services of owned housing, or "imputed rent." For rural income, this is assumed to be 8 percent of the difference between the replacement value of the house and any outstanding debt on the house. Replacement value is estimated by multiplying the floor space in square meters by the provincial average replacement cost per square meter. For urban income, rental value is directly estimated by the household heads, and estimated interest on housing debt is subtracted to obtain the "imputed rent" component of income. See Khan and Riskin, 2001, Chapter 2 for further discussion.

22. It turns out that the rate of price inflation in poor provinces generally exceeded the national average.

23. See Brown, 1995; Riskin, 1996.

24. See Khan and Riskin, 1998.

25. See Khan, Griffin, and Riskin's Chapter 5 contribution to this volume.

26. By the end of 1998 there were an estimated 9 million laid-off workers who had not been reemployed, and a total of 16 million unemployed of all kinds, amounting to about 8 percent of the labor force. See UNDP, 1999b, chapter 4.

27. See WHO, *World Health Report*, Annex Tables for various years, and UNICEF, *The Progress of Nations*, various years. China's State Statistical Bureau has derived similar results from its sample survey on children and women.

28. See Wong et al., 1997; Rosenthal, 1999.

29. See, for instance, UNDP, *China Human Development Report*, 1999b, Chapter 1.

References

Brown, Lester, 1995. *Who Will Feed China? Wake-up Call for a Small Planet*, London: Earthscan.

Eichen, Marc, and Zhang Ming, 1993. "The 1998 Household Sample Survey—Data Description and Availability," in Keith Griffin and Zhao Renwei, eds., *The Distribution of Income in China*, New York: St. Martin's.

Fei, John C.H., Gustav Ranis, and Shirley W.Y. Kuo, eds., 1979. *Growth with Equity: The Taiwan Case*, World Bank research publication, New York: Oxford University Press.

Khan, Azizur Rahman and Carl Riskin, 1998. "Income and Inequality in China: Composition, Distribution and Growth of Household Income, 1988 to 1995," *China Quarterly*, 154.

Khan, Azizur Rahman, and Carl Riskin, 2001. *Inequality and Poverty in China in the Age of Globalization*, Oxford and New York: Oxford University Press.

Kuznets, Simon, 1955. "Economic Growth and Income Inequality," *American Economic Review*, March.

———, 1963. "Quantitative Aspects of the Economic Growth of Nations: VIII. Distribution of Income by Size," *Economic Development and Cultural Change*, January.

Riskin, Carl, 1996. "Unyielding Land of the Dragon" (review of *Who Will Feed China?*), *Times Higher Education Supplement*, London, March 1.

Rosenthal, Elizabeth, 1999. "School: A Rare Luxury for Rural Chinese Girls," *The New York Times*, November 1.

UNDP, 1999a. *The China Human Development Report*, New York and Oxford: Oxford University Press.
UNDP, 1999b. *The China Human Development Report*, 1999. Beijing: Economic and Financial Press for UNDP.
UNICEF. *The Progress of Nations*. New York: UNICEF, various years.
World Health Organization (WHO). *World Health Report*. Geneva: WHO, various years.
Wong, Christine, C. Heady, and L. West, 1997. *Financing Local Development in the People's Republic of China*. Oxford and New York: Oxford University Press.
Zhongguo renkou tongji nianjian (China Yearbook of Population Statistics),1998. Beijing: Statistical Publishing House.

Part I

Perspectives on Increasing Inequality

2

Increasing Income Inequality and Its Causes in China

Zhao Renwei

Introduction

In the nineteen years since China started its economic system reform in 1978, great changes have taken place in the whole economy, including the pattern of income distribution. This chapter tries to describe and examine the changes in the pattern of income distribution in China, especially the increasing inequality of income. Since income distribution is a big issue that covers a wide range, the chapter tries to focus on some significant aspects.

To better understand the changes in income distribution during the transition, the chapter starts with a brief overview and analysis of the characteristics of income distribution prior to the reform. It is necessary to understand the starting point and the background for the changes of the reform period.

China's economic reform is closely linked with economic development or growth. In other words, the transition from a planned economy to a market economy is interwoven with the transformation from a dual economy to a modern economy. Changes in income distribution have happened in all these transitions and transformations. Therefore, the chapter attempts to analyze the underlying causes of increasing inequality resulting from economic development, economic reform, and related economic policies. Finally, some implications for income distribution policy are drawn and some suggestions for its improvement put forward.

The materials and data used in this paper are partly from sample surveys of rural and urban households organized by an international collaborative team associated with the Institute of Economics, CASS (hereafter simplified as Study Group) in 1988 and 1995, partly from the State Statistical Bureau (SSB) and other channels. All unnoted data are from these sample surveys.

Characteristics of Income Distribution in Pre-reform China

Prior to the economic reform (from the setup of the planned economy in 1956 to the start of the economic reform in 1978), China, generally speaking, was an egalitarian society in terms of income distribution, although there were some elements of inequality. What was the evidence of egalitarianism? As a lot of research has shown, the Gini coefficients of income distribution during that period were lower than those in most other countries. In the urban areas, the Gini coefficient was below 0.20, while in the rural areas it was estimated as between 0.21 and 0.24. In contrast, urban Ginis in many developing countries were between 0.37 and 0.43 and rural Ginis between 0.34 and 0.40.[1]

There were many factors contributing to such a high degree of equality in China prior to the reform. First, the institutional arrangement: The socialist system was characterized by public ownership of the means of production. Especially from 1949 to 1956, with the gradual enforcement of public ownership, the people did not have any property income except some interest earnings on a small amount of savings. Second, the policy effect: The policymakers believed that social equity is an important objective of socialism. Therefore, especially during the initial stage of socialist construction, when the policy of more accumulation and less consumption was necessary, even wages had to be kept low and equal. Third, the trammels of traditional ideas: The egalitarian ideology of "worrying about inequality but not about scarcity" had long existed in China's traditional culture. This view separated equality from efficiency, sought distribution without a larger "cake," and mixed up common prosperity and widespread poverty. However, even in such high-equality conditions, some disguised or hidden inequality factors did exist.

1. There was a quite large income gap between rural and urban areas. As World Bank (WB) statistics show, the Chinese urban-to-rural income ratio in 1979 was 2.5:1, higher than in other low-income countries in Asia (where the average ratio was 1.5) and also higher than in middle-income countries (average 2.2).[2]

As in most of the developing countries, the urban-rural income gap was caused by a dual economic structure—the coexistence of a modern industrial sector and a traditional agricultural sector. Unlike in other countries, however, there were peculiar causes for such a big gap in China, namely, the special policies devised by China's decision makers. For instance, low purchasing prices for agricultural products were regarded as a means to accumulate funds for industrialization, and the strict control of urban residents' household registration (*hukou*) prevented the migration of the rural population into the cities. Such policies strengthened the separation of the two sectors.[3] Even in circumstances of relatively high equality, with greater equality in the urban than the rural sector, the farmers still suffered from inequality due to the big gap between urban and rural incomes.

2. In the distribution of consumer goods, the in-kind supply system was emphasized. Under such in-kind distribution, the gap in money income was narrower than that in total real income. In fact, the in-kind distribution system was a hidden or

implicit welfare system with heavy subsidies. The original intention for these subsidies was to use them as a type of compensation to the low-income group in order to reduce inequality. But the results were quite different. First, nearly 80 percent of the rural population did not receive most subsidies that were given to urban residents. Second, the subsidies for some consumer goods such as food, cotton cloth, and edible oil were equally distributed on a per head basis, but some of the others, such as housing, cars, and telephones were distributed based on one's position; therefore, the distribution of subsidies for such consumer goods was quite unequal.

3. The policy of holding wages frozen for a long period of time created an income distribution pattern that had negative effects upon the younger generation. In the twenty years from 1956 to 1976, a policy was followed of keeping wages unchanged. Of course the prices of basic consumer goods in this period were fixed too. From an international perspective, such a long-term policy of frozen wages and prices is quite unusual in peacetime. It seemed on the surface that everyone was equal before frozen wages and prices, but in reality the policy had different effects upon different generations. It led to inequality of income distribution among generations and had a negative impact upon the younger generation in particular.[4] The results of this policy had given rise to an acute social problem by the early 1980s.

In view of experience prior to the reform, it can be concluded that China was an equal society, although there existed some unequal factors, which suggests a certain complexity in China's social economy. The purpose of analyzing such complexity is to have a better understanding of the starting point and background of the changes during the transition.

Some Important Aspects of Increasing Inequality in the Transition

The ideology of egalitarianism sacrificed efficiency and incentives and thus led to a low efficiency level in the economy. In the initial stage of the reform, the policy of "letting some people get rich first" was adopted. It was intended to overcome egalitarianism in income distribution, promote efficiency with strong incentives, and ultimately realize common prosperity based on an enlarged "pie." The experience of economic reform and development since the late 1970s indicates that the general trend was in the right direction. But the changes in income distribution were more complicated than originally expected at the outset of the reform. Here some important aspects of the changes will be described and analyzed.

The General Trend of Changes: A Rapid Increase of Inequality

Table 2.1 presents Gini coefficients calculated from the official SSB data for the years 1978 to 1995. From the table it is clear that income inequality in both rural and urban areas trended upward during this period. The rural Gini rose from 0.21 in 1978 to 0.34 in 1995 while the urban Gini was up from 0.16 in 1978 to 0.28 in 1995.

Table 2.2 shows the Gini coefficients derived from the 1988 and 1995 sample surveys of the Study Group. Although the results differ somewhat from those of

Table 2.1

Gini Coefficients of the Rural and Urban Areas, 1978–1995

Year	Rural	Urban
1978	0.212	0.16
1979	0.237	0.16
1980	0.238	0.16
1981	0.239	0.15
1982	0.232	0.15
1983	0.246	0.15
1984	0.258	0.16
1985	0.264	0.19
1986	0.288	0.19
1987	0.292	0.20
1988	0.301	0.23
1989	0.300	0.23
1990	0.310	0.23
1991	0.307	0.24
1992	0.314	0.25
1993	0.320	0.27
1994	0.330	0.30
1995	0.340	0.28

Source: Li Shi et al., "The Changes of China's Income Distribution During the Transition," dissertation for the International Workshop in Beijing, August 1997.

Table 2.2

Gini Coefficients in 1988 and 1995

Year	Rural	Urban	National
1988	0.338	0.233	0.382
1995	0.416	0.332	0.452

the SSB, the general trend of increasing inequality in both rural and urban areas is similar. The rural Gini coefficient rose from 0.338 in 1988 to 0.416 in 1995, while the urban Gini rose from 0.233 to 0.332; the national Gini coefficient rose from 0.382 to 0.452.

The Urban-Rural Income Gap: An Old Problem

Table 2.3 shows that the income gap between urban and rural residents narrowed in the early 1980s and then widened again from the mid-1980s to the mid-1990s. The ratio of real urban-to-rural income was 2.15:1 in 1983, but by 1987 it had returned to pre-reform levels and it advanced from there to a peak of 2.93 in 1994.

If the combined urban and rural samples in each of the two Study Group sur-

Table 2.3

Urban-Rural Differences in per Capita Income, 1978–1995

Year	Nominal (yuan) Rural	Urban	Real (yuan) Rural	Urban	Urban / Rural ratio Real	Nominal
1978	134	316	134	316	2.36	2.36
1979	—	—	—	—	—	—
1980	191	439	146	401	2.75	2.30
1981	233	458	161	408	2.53	2.05
1982	270	500	191	433	2.27	1.83
1983	310	526	210	451	2.15	1.70
1984	355	608	231	507	2.19	1.71
1985	398	685	238	510	2.14	1.72
1986	424	828	240	577	2.40	1.95
1987	463	916	246	586	2.38	1.98
1988	545	1,119	247	594	2.41	2.05
1989	602	1,261	228	575	2.52	2.10
1990	686	1,387	249	625	2.51	2.02
1991	709	1,544	252	662	2.63	2.18
1992	784	1,826	266	721	2.71	2.33
1993	922	2,337	275	794	2.89	2.54
1994	1,221	3,179	295	864	2.93	2.60
1995	1,578	3,893	325	906	2.79	2.47

Sources: China Statistical Yearbook, 1986 and 1996; Li Shi et al., "The Changes of China's Income Distribution in the Transition," paper prepared for International Workshop in Beijing, August 1997.

veys are divided into income deciles, then in both years the rural population was concentrated in the low-income groups, while the urban population was concentrated in the high-income groups. Table 2.4 shows that, in this respect, there were no remarkable changes between 1988 to 1995. The urban-rural gap for the upper-middle-income groups grew slightly and that for the highest-income groups narrowed slightly. Why? A possible explanation for the latter change is that fast development of township and village enterprises (TVEs) enriched a minority of rural employers, who accordingly entered the highest-income group.

Regional Income Inequality: A Controversial Issue

The issue of regional income inequality includes the question of whether regional gaps are getting larger and how to judge them—issues on which there has been extended debate in academic circles.[5] Here I describe changes in regional income inequality based on the Study Group surveys for 1988 and 1995.

Rural per capita income in all three broad regions examined (east, west and center) increased remarkably from 1988 to 1995 (Tables 2.5 and 2.6). Among them, income in the eastern region grew most rapidly, followed by the central

Table 2.4

Percentage of Rural and Urban Individuals in Combined Income Decile Groups, 1988 and 1995

Decile group	1988 Rural	1988 Urban	1995 Rural	1995 Urban
Lowest	99.24	0.76	99.36	0.64
Second	97.94	2.06	97.41	1.59
Third	95.37	4.63	94.95	5.05
Fourth	89.30	10.70	90.36	9.64
Fifth	77.53	22.47	76.95	23.05
Sixth	56.71	43.29	55.53	44.47
Seventh	36.37	63.63	34.16	65.84
Eighth	24.87	75.13	23.10	76.90
Ninth	20.47	79.53	18.92	81.08
Highest	19.55	80.54	23.78	76.22

Note: 83,179 individuals were covered in the sample survey of 1988, and 56,435 individuals were covered in the survey of 1995.

Table 2.5

Rural Income per Capita and Gini Coefficients in Three Regions, 1988 and 1995 (1988 prices)

Region	1988 (1) Per capita income (yuan)	(2) Gini coeffi- cients	1995 (3) Per capita income (yuan)	(4) Gini coeffi- cients	Change in income (3) − (1) (yuan)	Percent change in income (3)/(1) *100	Income gap among regions (West = 100) 1988	Income gap among regions (West = 100) 1995
East	891	0.34	3,150	0.45	2,260	354	161.7	243.9
Middle	606	0.30	1,599	0.33	993	264	110.0	123.8
West	551	0.29	1,292	0.38	742	235	100	100

Note: The three regions include twenty-eight provinces in the 1988 survey and nineteen provinces in the 1995 survey (italicized), as follows:

Eastern coastal: *Beijing*, Shanghai, Tianjin, *Liaoning, Hebei, Shandong, Jiangsu, Zhejiang*, Fujian, *Guangdong*, Guangxi, Hainan;

Central: *Shanxi*, Inner Mongolia, *Jilin*, Heilongjiang, *Anhui, Jiangxi, Henan, Hubei, Hunan*;

West: *Sichuan, Guizhou, Yunnan*, Shaanxi, *Gansu, Qinghai*, Ningxia.

region, with the western region lagging far behind. Changes in the Gini coefficients of the three regions reveal increasing inequality within each. Moreover, the income gap among regions widened. Perhaps the most remarkable change in regional income inequality was the differential between developed Jiangsu Province

Table 2.6

Rural Income per Capita and Gini Coefficients in Jiangsu and Gansu, 1988 and 1995 (1988 prices)

Region	1988		1995				Income gap between provinces (Gansu = 100)	
	(1)	(2)	(3)	(4)	Growth of income (3) − (1) (yuan)	Percent growth in income (3)/(1) *100		
	Per capita income (yuan)	Gini coeffi- cients	Per capita income (yuan)	Gini coeffi- cients			1988	1995
Jiangsu	834	0.38	3,444	0.394	2,610	413	186.6	334.7
Gansu	447	0.28	1,029	0.338	582	230	100	100

and less-developed Gansu Province. But the changes in the Gini coefficients of the two provinces over the seven years reveal that income inequality within Gansu Province actually increased faster than that within Jiangsu.

Since the coverage of the urban sample survey was quite limited, here we divide it into only two regions (coastal and interior), in order to examine changes in urban regional income inequality.

From Tables 2.7 and 2.8 , we observe that urban per capita income both in the coastal and interior regions increased remarkably fast. The changes in the Gini coefficients show that income inequality increased within both coastal and interior regions. The income gap between regions reveals inequality increasing among the broad regions and also between the selected provinces of Jiangsu (coastal) and Yunnan (interior).

It is obvious from the above data that regional income inequality has increased faster in the rural than in the urban areas.

Inequality of Property Income: A New Problem

As it was mentioned earlier, there was almost no property income for Chinese individuals in the pre-reform period except for some interest earnings from bank savings deposits. Since the reform, however, property income of individuals, especially of urban residents, has increased rapidly and its distribution is quite unequal. This has became a new problem of concern to the public. Property income of urban residents has been closely linked with housing subsidies and imputed rents of private housing.

From Table 2.9, it is clear that the property income of urban residents has increased from 0.49 percent of total individual income in 1988 to 1.3 percent in 1995, and that the housing subsidy for the tenants of public housing and imputed rents of private housing were the two main contributing factors. Among them, the housing subsidy fell sharply, from 18.1 percent in 1988 to 13.9 percent in 1995, a drop of 4.2 percentage points; while imputed rent of private housing rose remarkably, from 3.9

Table 2.7

Urban Income per Capita and Gini Coefficients in Coastal and Interior Areas, 1988 and 1995 (1988 prices)

	1988		1995					
	(1)	(2)	(3)	(4)				
						Percent	Income gap	
	Per		Per		Income	income	between	
	capita	Gini	capita	Gini	growth	growth	areas	
	income	coeffi-	income	coeffi-	(3) − (1)	(3)/(1)	(Interior = 100)	
Region	(yuan)	cients	(yuan)	cients	(yuan)	*100	1988	1995
Coastal	1,584	0.213	2,502	0.277	918	158	134.6	149.0
Interior	1,177	0.220	1,679	0.247	502	143	100	100

Note: Coastal and interior regions are classified as follows: Coastal: Beijing, Guangdong, Jiangsu, and Liaoning; Interior: Shanxi, Henan, Anhui, Sichuan, Hubei, Yunnan, and Gansu. (The survey in 1988 included ten provinces and cities while Sichuan was added in the survey of 1995.)

Table 2.8

Urban Income per Capita and Gini Coefficients in Jiangsu and Yunnan, 1988 and 1995 (1988 prices)

	1988		1995					
	(1)	(2)	(3)	(4)				
						Percent	Income gap	
	Per		Per		Income	income	between	
	capita	Gini	capita	Gini	growth	growth	provinces	
	income	coeffi-	income	coeffi-	(3) − (1)	(3)/(1)	(Yunnan = 100)	
Province	(yuan)	cients	(yuan)	cients	(yuan)	*100	1988	1995
Jiangsu	1,412	0.174	2,251	0.230	839	159	111.4	123.7
Yunnan	1,268	0.198	1,820	0.210	552	144	100	100

percent of total income in 1988 to 10.3 percent in 1995, an increase of 6.4 percentage points. The decrease in housing subsidy for public housing and the increase in imputed rents of private housing were closely related to the housing reform (the commercialization or privatization of public housing), which has been pushed since the late 1980s. Most public housing units were sold to residents at extremely low prices, far below the market price of housing.[6] With the sale of public housing, the burden of subsidy had been reduced or cut off. As a result, the housing commercialization was a transfer of public assets to private property once and for all.[7] If the imputed rent is included in property income, then the total property income of urban residents in 1995 would be around 11.6 percent, or an increase of 7.2 percentage points over the 4.4 percent of 1988.

Table 2.9

Property Income, Subsidies, and Imputed Rent of Private Housing for Urban Residents

Income and its components	1988		1995	
	Ui	Ci	Ui	Ci
1. Property income	0.49	0.437	1.30	0.489
2. Subsidies and income in kind				
a) housing subsidy	18.14	0.331	13.93	0.322
b) income in kind	2.21	0.233	0.99	0.284
c) ration coupon subsidy	5.26	0.130	—	—
3. Imputed rent of private housing	3.90	0.338	10.28	0.371

Source: Li Shi et al., "The Changes of China's Income Distribution During the Transition," paper prepared for International Workshop in Beijing, August 1997.

Notes: Ui = the income share of the i th component; Ci = the concentration ratio of the i th component.

Moreover, property income in the narrow sense had a very high concentration ratio (0.489 in 1995); imputed rent of private housing had a quite high concentration rate too (0.371 in 1995). The concentration ratio of imputed rents of private housing was higher than that of the housing subsidy (0.322 in 1995). Two of the above were disequalizing elements of the urban income distribution in the sense that their concentration ratios were higher than the urban Gini coefficient (0.332 in 1995).

In addition to imputed rents of private housing, other major items of individual property income include interest earnings, dividends, and rents. In 1978 the interest earnings of private savings were only 600 million yuan, or 0.3 percent of total individual income, while by 1995 interest earnings had reached 300 billion yuan, accounting for 7.9 percent of the total individual income.[8]

The inequality in property income is attributable to inequality in distribution of property itself. Tables 2.10 and 2.11 show that since the 1990s the financial assets of the urban households had increased rapidly. Real financial assets per household had grown from 7,869 yuan in 1990 to 14,715 yuan in June 1996, an increase of 87 percent. But financial assets were distributed quite unequally. In June 1996, the financial assets per household owned by the highest quintile of urban households were 12 times those of the lowest quintile.

High-Income Stratum and Rent-Seeking Activities: A Tough Issue

Since the economic reform, the emergence of a high-income stratum has aroused strong reaction in society. How to clarify the scale of the high income stratum and their real income has long been a tough issue. Two kinds of limited materials are available: case studies and our two sample surveys. The former has the defect of

Table 2.10

Financial Assets of Urban Households, 1990 and 1996

	End of 1990			End of June 1996			
	Total 100 mil (yuan)	Per household (yuan)	(%)	Total 100 mil (yuan)	Per household (yuan) nominal	real	(%)
Financial assets:	5,404	7,869	100.0	27,110	30,982	14,715	100.0
Deposits	4,080	5,941	75.5	22,718	25,961	12,331	83.8
Securities	1,052	1,532	19.5	2,467	2,818	1,338	9.1
Cash	272	396	5.0	1,085	1,233	586	4.0
Others	—	—	—	840	970	461	3.1

Source: SSB: Statistical Report, No. 21, November 8, 1996.
Note: The real financial assets per household in 1996 was calculated with the consumer price index of the urban areas given by SSB, and the year 1990 was set as the base year.

Table 2.11

Distribution of Financial Assets of Urban Households Across Quintile Groups, June 30, 1996

Quintile groups	Financial assets per household (yuan)	Percentage owned
Top	74,359	48.0
Second	35,629	23.0
Middle	24,786	16.0
Fourth	13,942	9.0
Bottom	6,192	4.0
All	30,982	100.0

Source: SSB: Statistical Report, No. 21, November 8, 1996.

unclear representativeness. The latter has the defect that high-income individuals are probably underrepresented in the survey and, where captured, probably understated their incomes.

According to case studies carried out in Wenzhou, Zhejiang Province, employers in ordinary private enterprises had incomes averaging 21 times the average income of their employees, whereas in private firms with assets of over 1 million yuan, employers incomes' averaged 79 times those of their employees.[9] In addition, an investigation by the Institute of Sociology, CASS, has revealed that in 1995 there were over 1 million households with an annual income of 1 million yuan or more.[10] These kinds of people are called the new rich in China; most of them are private employers, the rest senior managers of joint ventures and popular entertainers who can command a high price for appearances on stage.

Although the Study Group's two sample surveys did not cover many very high-income individuals, Table 2.12 shows clearly that the ratio between high- and low-income groups increased sharply: The ratio of the top 3 percent to the bottom decile of individuals rose from 7.7 in 1988 to 11.8 in 1995, while the ratio of the top 3 percent to the bottom quintile rose from 4.9 in 1988 to 6.3 in 1995.

As for rent-seeking activities, up to now there are only two studies that have tried to estimate total rents, and these pertain to 1988 and 1992.[11] Although it is very difficult to analyze the distribution of rents in rent-seeking activities, that distribution is universally acknowledged to be extremely unequal.

The above paragraphs have discussed different aspects of the increasing inequality of income distribution in China. However, it is worth noticing that poverty has been reduced during the same period. Official statistics show the poor population falling from 250 million in 1978 to 65 million in 1995.[12] The coexistence of increasing inequality and the reduction in poverty was mainly attributable to the high growth rate of the economy. In other words, increasing inequality during the transition happened on the basis of a "larger pie" due to economic growth.[13]

Evaluation of Increasing Inequality: Causes and Value Judgments

It is very complicated to analyze the causes of increasing inequality since the reform began. In the last several decades, many economists have tried to explain increasing inequality as a natural result of the early stages of economic development, as hypothesized in Simon Kuznets's famous inverted U-shaped time path of distribution. Even if Taiwan was an exceptional case that did not fit the hypothesis, and had achieved high economic growth with a quite equal distribution of income, many economists still adhered to the "Kuznets Curve" as a likely description of a common occurrence.

However, in China's case I believe that there are at least three important elements that together affect income inequality, namely: (1) economic growth; (2) economic reform or institutional changes; and (3) economic policy and its changes (see Table 2.13). Of course, these elements can have either positive or negative effects upon income distribution. Since the mid-1980s, when the negative effect of enlarging inequality played the dominant role, income inequality tended to widen. Moreover, the three elements were interrelated.

Economic Growth or Development

All the facts in the reform indicate that the urban nonstate economy (as compared with the state economic sector) and the rural nonagricultural sector (compared with agriculture) have grown more rapidly and that these were the two strong elements in economic growth that contributed to increasing inequality. From the Study Group survey data shown in Tables 2.14 and 2.15, we can see that the Gini coefficients for wage income of urban employees in the nonstate sector were much

Table 2.12

Mean Wages of Highest 3 percent and Lowest 10 percent and 20 percent of Individuals, 1988 and 1995 (yuan)

	1988	1995 Nominal	1995 Real
1. Top 3%	5,567.4	19,447.70	8,533.3
2. Bottom 10%	724.4	1,644.69	721.6
3. Bottom 20%	1,131.4	3,081.41	1,352.1
Ratio (3%:10%)	7.69	11.82	
Ratio (3%:20%)	4.92	6.31	

Note: The real wage income in 1995 was calculated with the consumer price index of the urban areas given by SSB, and the year 1988 was set as the base year.

Table 2.13

Effects of Economic Growth, Reform, and Policy on Income Inequality

	Effects of inequality	
	Within urban or rural areas	Between urban and rural areas
1. Economic growth or development		
Faster growth of urban nonstate–owned economy	+	+
Faster growth of rural nonagricultural economy	+	−
Development of agriculture	+	−
2. Economic reform or institutional changes		
Order changes		
Price reform in rural areas	−	−
Household responsibility system in rural areas	−	−
Internal migration of rural laborers		−
Commercialization of urban housing	+	+
Disorder changes		
Rent-seeking activities	+	
Insider control	+	+
Monopoly	+	+
Corruption	+	+
3. Economic policy and its changes		
Low purchasing price for agricultural products		+
Taxation on agricultural products		
Extrataxational burden of peasants		+
Personal income tax	−	−
Reduction of urban subsidies		
a) Per head	+	−
b) By position	−	−
Transfer of urban residents' benefits to private property	+	+

Note: "+" represents the increase of inequality; "−" represents the decrease of inequality; some effects of elements on inequality are difficult to judge, so they are left empty.

Table 2.14

Wage Income Gini Coefficients of Urban Employees in State and Nonstate Sectors, 1988 and 1995

	1988	1995
State sector	0.222	0.283
Nonstate sector	0.286	0.347

Table 2.15

Gini Coefficients of Agricultural Income and Nonagricultural Income of Rural Households, 1988 and 1995

	1988	1995
Agricultural income	0.242	0.239
Nonagricultural income	0.390	0.512

higher than those in the state sector, and the Gini coefficients of nonagricultural income were higher than those of agricultural income in the rural areas. Increased inequality flowed directly from the differentially fast development of the urban nonstate and rural nonagricultural sectors. It is obvious that not all kinds of economic growth would lead to increasing inequality. For instance, the rapid development of agricultural production in the period from 1979 to 1984 actually narrowed the income gap between the rural and urban areas, and it was very difficult to judge its comprehensive impact upon income distribution within the rural areas. According to the calculation of Li Shi and others,[14] although inequality within the rural areas had slightly increased in this period, it is hard to attribute this result to the development of agriculture. Perhaps it was caused by the unbalanced development of nonagricultural industry in the rural areas.

Economic Reform or Institutional Changes

China adopted a relatively gradual approach to economic reform, which led to the coexistence of two economic systems (planned and market systems), and especially to the existence of a dual price system (planned prices and market prices). In addition, some noneconomic factors had strong influences on the economy. Therefore, there was a good deal of disorder in the economic reform. I classify the institutional changes into two kinds: order changes and disorder changes.

Starting from the early 1980s, reform of farm product prices and the household contract responsibility system were carried out in the rural areas. These reforms were widely beneficial to rural households and not only decreased income inequality in the rural areas but also, more remarkably, decreased the inequality between the rural and urban areas.

The internal migration of surplus rural laborers also played a remarkable role in reducing the inequality between the rural and urban areas, but its effects on the income distribution within the rural areas were quite complicated, due to the imbalance of the outflow of rural labor as among different regions. Generally speaking, the internal migration of rural laborers has enlarged income differentials within the rural areas as a whole, but it has narrowed the gap in some specific rural regions. So we do not make any mark in Table 2.13 for this element.

Since the late 1980s housing reform has been actively advocated in the cities. Some scholars believe it has been as significant as the household responsibility system in rural areas. Although the housing reform is still going on, its strong effect upon income distribution is quite obvious. As mentioned earlier, the concentration ratio of the imputed rents of private housing was not only higher than the urban Gini coefficient, but also higher than the concentration ratio of the housing subsidy. Obviously, housing reform has enlarged income inequality. No effective measures have been taken in the housing reform up to now to deal with the inequality of in-kind distribution of public housing. For instance, no serious consideration has been given to the differentials between those who have and those who do not have public housing, or between those with good and poor housing or small and large housing. As a result, the housing reform not only increased inequality in urban areas, but also increased inequality between rural and urban areas. In addition, part of the most unequally distributed public housing has not yet been commercialized up to now. It is thus predictable that housing reform will increase inequality further if there is no improvement in policies, especially price policy, in the process of housing commercialization. It should be pointed out that housing reform is a process that manifests the hidden inequality in the old housing system.

The effects of disorder changes on income distribution are the hardest to make clear and also provoke the strongest social reactions. This has been especially true of rent-seeking behavior. As already mentioned, no precise research has been done on the distribution of rents, but it is universally acknowledged that they are distributed quite unequally. There is no doubt that rent-seeking activities have increased inequality and have been major elements in the creation of a high-income stratum.

Insider control[15] is another element of disorder changes in institutional reform. With the decentralization of public assets, various local governments, departments, and enterprises gained control of these assets. Through insider control mechanisms, public assets have been appropriated to serve the interests of particular departments, regions, work units, and individuals. The distribution of such interests is not transparent but is very unequal. More important, insider control has led to the loss of state assets.

Various kinds of monopoly behavior, including department and industry monopoly, were also elements in increasing inequality. To gain sudden big profits by exercising monopoly power has been called rent-creating activities by some econo-mists. Corruption, especially the parlaying of political power into money, has also increased inequality. Bitterly despised by most people, this behavior is neverthe-less difficult to document.

From the above discussion we can confirm that not all elements of institutional change contributed to increasing inequality; some have decreased inequality. It is irrational to blame increasing inequality on the economic reform, per se. Certainly the disorder changes did increase inequality. These and their consequences are to some extent the costs of reform. What is still uncertain is the overall size of neces-sary costs, that is, which costs are unavoidable and which can be avoided. Perhaps it depends on the reform strategy of the next steps: If reform can be expedited, disorder would be lightened.

Economic Policy

In addition to economic growth and institutional changes, economic policy and its changes affect income distribution. Here I would like to elaborate on the effects of economic policy on the inequality between rural and urban areas. As described ear-lier, inequality between rural and urban areas tended to increase from the mid-1980s to the mid-1990s. What were the major contributing factors to this increase? It is unlikely that it was due to economic growth. International experience suggests that urban-rural inequality decreased in most developing countries as their dual econo-mies were transformed into modern economies. In China's own experience, rapid rural industrialization contributed to the decrease in urban-rural inequality. As for the institutional changes, some order changes led to narrowing of the gap, while the consequences of disorder changes are very hard to document using standard avail-able data. In my own view, the main cause of increasing urban-rural inequality is "policy inertia" from the traditional planned economy. The long-term separation of rural and urban areas was a deliberate policy of this system. Low purchasing prices for agricultural products, a high implicit tax upon rural residents, the extratax bur-dens placed on farmers, the strict prohibition on migration from rural to urban areas, the relatively high subsidies and benefits for urban residents, all were important components of policy in China's planned economy.

Since the reform, these policies have to some extent been changed, but many vestiges of them still exist. In the early 1980s and again after 1995, purchasing prices for farm products were raised by a big margin, and this substantially nar-rowed the urban-rural gap, clearly showing the important effects that policy can have on inequality. On the other hand, if the special benefits and subsidies re-ceived by urban residents were transferred into private property (as in the housing reform described earlier), policy would in this case freeze the gap between rural and urban areas into permanent advantage.

Several different value judgments and social responses have been forthcoming in the face of increased inequality. Some consider that, in spite of the increase, income disparities are still within reason and cannot be regarded as "polarization between rich and poor," and that greater income inequality is one of the costs of economic growth. If the income disparity can be kept within a range that preserves social stability, then such inequality would be acceptable.[16] The World Bank's *World Development Report* holds that increasing wage, income and wealth differentials to a certain extent are an essential component of the transition, because market-determined wage differentials create incentives for increased efficiency, and such incentives are of great significance to the success of the reform.[17] Others believe that Gini coefficients between 0.3 to 0.4 represent a medium level of inequality, while China's Gini coefficient has surpassed 0.4. In this view, China has changed from an egalitarian society into a polarized one in a very short period of ten-plus years, and has even surpassed the high level of inequality of the United States.[18]

Here I would like to present my own opinions: First, when Gini coefficients are used to measure inequality in international comparative context, discussion must take account of the particular conditions of different countries. The scale of population, size of territory, and degree of homogeneity of an economic society can all affect the Gini. China is a country of large population and vast territory and with low homogeneity. So it is perhaps natural that China's Gini is higher than that of countries and areas with contrary conditions.

Second, it is necessary to distinguish temporary from long-term phenomena in analyzing inequality. For instance, the Study Group's work indicates that the Gini coefficient of monetary income in the urban private sector fell from 0.49 in 1988 to 0.40 in 1995. If shown to be real by additional research,[19] such change may well have been related to the increase in numbers of private employers and employees, and to the improvement in the competitive environment. If so, we can say that the high Gini coefficient in 1988 was a temporary phenomenon. Future prospects for China's income distribution depend upon the further path of reform. With the establishment of the market mechanism, combined with proper macrocontrols by the government, income inequality should become more rational as the reform deepens. If the disorder elements cannot be overcome in the transition, however, inequality could continue to widen without reaching a turning point, and China would become a more highly polarized society. It is obvious that it is still too early to draw any hasty conclusion based on the temporary phenomena in the transition, but at the same time it is never too early to give close attention to avoiding the bad results of increasing inequality.

Concluding Remarks: Policy Implications and Suggestions

We have analyzed in the foregoing paragraphs the increase in inequality and its causes and consequences during China's transition. Now, finally, we venture a few words on how income distribution in China can be improved.

1. *Carrying the reforms through to the end.* Without deepening the reforms, the problem of increasing inequality caused by disorder elements will not be solved.

Increasing inequality cannot be used as an excuse to deny the direction of reform and return to the old system. Nor can the gradual reform approach followed by China become an excuse to slow down further the progress of reform, for this would increase the costs of the reform and even allow temporary costs of transition to congeal into permanent ones.

2. *Paying more attention to rural development.* Only the relatively high economic growth rate and the larger income pie it brings can provide a solid foundation for decreasing inequality and alleviating poverty. In China's actual conditions, more attention should be given to rural economic development in order to speed up the transformation from the dual economy to the modern one. Only in this way can the prerequisite conditions be created for reducing the urban-rural income gap and interregional inequality. From the viewpoint of strategic development, the rural economy is important not only for safeguarding the food supply and social stability, but also for narrowing income differentials and modernizing the whole nation.

3. *Improving several key policies.* For instance:

(a) *Personal income tax policy.* Personal income taxes are an important means to redistribute income and decrease the inequality between high- and low-income groups. However, a fundamental prerequisite of improved tax policy is that income become much more transparent than it has been.

(b) *Social security policy.* This helps reduce inequality and poverty caused by unemployment, sickness, and old age.

(c) *Labor mobility policy.* Improved labor mobility will provide a precondition for greater equality, namely, more opportunities for individuals—especially rural individuals—to better their conditions.

(d) *Education policy.* It is very important to increase investment in human capital, especially in basic education. Only in this way can the knowledge and skill level of the population be improved; moreover, smaller differentials in educational attainment are a premise for narrowing inequality.

4. *More effective government implementation of income redistribution.* In a mature market economy, taxes and benefits (especially subsidies) are the two principal means used by government in redistributing income. In principle, the use of these regulatory means by government should decrease inequality. But in the time of the planned economy in China, the government carried out a policy of exacting net taxes in the rural areas and net benefits and subsidies in the urban areas, which resulted in greater inequality and a larger urban-rural income gap. Although this situation has improved since the reform, more efforts are still needed to strengthen macrocontrol over taxes and subsidies. More important, the two means should be used together; it is wrong to attend to the one while neglecting the other. For instance, if a progressive income tax is adopted for high-income groups, with the intent of narrowing income inequality, while at the same time high benefits and subsidies are provided to these groups, the redistributive purpose of progressive taxation would be negated.

In sum, the improvement of income distribution is an arduous task. As long as we regard it as an essential part of the cause of economic reform, however, and make unremitting efforts, there is no fundamental reason why China's income distribution cannot be improved in the course of further reform and development.

Notes

Professor Li Shi helped me do the calculations; the Institute of Economics and Statistics, All Souls College, Oxford University, provided good conditions for my writing; the Economic and Social Research Council in the U.K. supported this research; Professors Carl Riskin and John Knight gave very useful comments on the first draft of the chapter. All of these are gratefully acknowledged.

1. The World Bank, 1983; Li Chengrui, 1986; Ren Chaifang and Chen Xuebin, 1996; Adelman and Sunding 1987; A.R. Khan et al., 1993.
2. The World Bank, 1983.
3. Zhao Renwei, 1992.
4. Zhao Renwei, 1985.
5. Liu Shucheng, 1994; Hu Angang, 1994; Yu Gengqian, 1996.
6. The sale price of public housing and the market price of commodity housing are very different in different regions. Generally speaking, the price differentials in small and medium cities are less than in the large cities. In the golden areas of the overlarge cities, the prices are extremely high. In general, the market price is one to two times higher than the sale price of public housing, but in some special cases, the price is twenty times higher (Wang Lina, 1997).
7. In fact, when urban residents buy public housing at the cost price, they have to wait five years to resell it. If they buy public housing at the standard price, which is lower than the cost price, they have to make up the price differentials before they can resell the house.
8. SSB's Income Distribution Study Group, 1996.
9. Zheng Dajiong, 1994.
10. Gao Xiaoyan, 1995.
11. Hu Heli, 1989, and Wan Anpei, 1995.
12. Zhu Fengqi, 1996.
13. However, Khan and Riskin, in a recent study (2001) based on the same two income surveys, argue that poverty is more widespread than indicated by official statistics, and that its rate of reduction slowed considerably after the mid-1980s because of the increase in inequality.
14. Li Shi et al., 1997.
15. Aoki Masahiko and Qiang Yingyi, 1995.
16. Li Peiling, 1995.
17. The World Bank, *World Development Report*, 1996, p. 68.
18. Li Qiang, 1995.
19. The small number of observations of private sector income raises the possibility of high standard error. See Khan and Riskin, 1998.

References

Adelmen, Irma, and David Sunding, "Economic Policy and Income Distribution in China," *Journal of Comparative Economics,* September 1987.
Gao Xiaoyan, "China's Stratum in Changes," *China Industry and Commerce Times,* March 18, 1995.

Hu Angang, *On China Regional Inequality,* Working Paper for Ecology and Environment Research Center, Chinese Academy of Sciences, 1994.

Hu Heli, "Estimated Value of Rents in 1988," *Comparative Study of Social and Economic Systems,* No. 5, 1989.

Khan, Azizur Rahman, et al., "Household Income and Its Distribution in China," in Keith Griffin and Zhao Renwei (eds.), *The Distribution of Income in China*, Macmillan Press, 1993, p. 61.

Khan, Azizur Rahman, and Carl Riskin, "Income and Inequality in China: Composition, Distribution and Growth of Household Income, 1988 to 1995," *China Quarterly*, 154, June 1998.

Khan, Azizur Rahman, and Carl Riskin, *Inequality and Poverty in China in the Age of Globalization*, Oxford and New York: Oxford University Press, 2001.

Kuznets, Simon, "Economic Growth and Income Inequality," *The American Economic Review*, March 1955.

Li Chengrui, "A Statistic Report: The Effects of Economic Policy on Income Distribution and Consumption in China," *Statistic Research*, No. 1, 1986.

Li Peiling, "Transitional Economy: Inequality and Social Fairness," *Studies of Modernization,* Taipei, October 1995.

Li Qiang, "On Inequality in China's Mainland," paper prepared for Beijing International Seminar, June 1995.

Li Shi, Zhao Renwei, and Zhang Ping, "The Changes of China's Income Distribution During the Transition," dissertation for the International Workshop in Beijing, August 1997.

Liu Shucheng (ed.), *Studies on China Regional Development,* China Statistic Press, 1994.

Masahiko, Aoki, and Qiang Yingyi (eds.), *Corporation Management Structure In the Transitional Economy,* China Economic Press, 1995, p.17.

Ren Chaifang, and Chen Xuebin, "The Income Inequality in Urban Areas," *Economic Research Reference,* No. 157, 1996.

Riskin, Carl, *China's Political Economy,* Oxford and New York, Oxford University Press, 1987.

SSB Income Distribution Study Group, "Problems and Countermeasures of Present Income Distribution," *Research Reference,* No. 94, August 20, 1996.

Wan Anpei, "A Study on Value Changes of Rents," *Economic Research*, February 1995.

Wang Lina, "Housing Price and Income Distribution in China," dissertation for the International Workshop in Beijing , August 1997.

World Bank, *China: The Development of Socialist Economy,* Washington DC, 1983, pp. 83–92.

World Bank, *Word Development Report, 1996: From Plan to Market,* China Finance and Economic Press, 1996, p. 68; pp. 69–73.

Yu Gengqian, "Problems of Regional Income Inequality," *Economic Information,* April 19, 1996.

Zhao Renwei, "The Special Phenomena of Income Distribution in China's Transition," *Economic Research*, No. 1, January 1992.

Zhao Renwei, "The Trend of Changes in the Distribution of Workers' Income," *Economic Research,* March 1985. English version in *International Journal of Social Economics,* 18, 8/9/10, MCB University Press Ltd., West Yorkshire, England.

Zheng Dajiong, "Changes of Inequality Based on the Income of Private Employers, Millionaires and Workers," paper prepared for seminar on Equality in the Transition and Countermeasures in Hangzhou, China, December 1994.

Zhu Fengqi, *Research on China Anti-poverty,* China Planning Press, 1996.

3

A More Unequal China? Aspects of Inequality in the Distribution of Equivalent Income

Björn Gustafsson and Li Shi

Introduction

Since the end of the 1980s, nearly all formerly Soviet-type countries have experienced a period of transition toward market economies. The People's Republic of China has not been an exception. The difference between China's transition and those of most other countries is that of so-called gradualism versus "big bang." From the point of view of economic growth, China has achieved a more impressive record than her former "big and little brothers." Thus the average annual growth rate of the gross domestic product (GDP) was as high as 12.2 percent during the period from 1991 to 1994. All indicators of economic performance show that the Chinese economic pie has grown larger and larger. Important sociodemographic indicators also point toward better living conditions on average for the Chinese population. During the transformation period in Russia, life expectancy has decreased, while the opposite is the case for China.

Transformation toward an economy with market allocation, however, is not without problems. One cannot be sure that the tide of rapid economic growth lifts all boats. Looking at how the pie is distributed in a country with fast economic growth, like China, provides us with an alternative criterion to evaluate its performance; this is the topic of this chapter. Has the pie been sliced differently so that the relatively poor receive a smaller proportion? And, if so, do smaller proportions mean smaller absolute portions?

From being a research area plagued with severe data problems the study of Chinese income distribution has recently become a more lively field of research.

Earlier almost all knowledge of the Chinese distribution of income was based on local surveys. However, the official Chinese data published in aggregate form have made possible several recent studies published in the West in which regional issues have attracted particular attention. Examples are Lyons (1991), Tsui (1993, 1996), Knight and Song (1993), Rozelle (1994), Jian et al. (1996), and Yao (1997).

Other studies use microdata. Examples are two studies that cover the second part of the 1980s and two provinces (Aaberge and Li, 1997, who study urban areas, and Tsui, 1998, who investigates rural areas). The coverage is broader in Cheng (1996) who analyzed data from rural areas in five provinces, but only observed income at one point in the mid-1990s. Still another example is an ambitious ongoing research project at the World Bank, utilizing panel data from the second part of the 1980s for four southern provinces (Chen and Ravallion, 1996).

In this chapter we also use microdata to evaluate changes in the distribution of income in China. However, in contrast to the references listed above, our study covers China as a whole. We, like Khan and Riskin (1998) and the other authors in this volume, report and analyze results from the 1988 and 1995 surveys described in the introduction, which make possible meaningful comparisons across time. As in an earlier study of the data for 1988 (Gustafsson and Li, 1998), we follow the present best practice when analyzing the distribution of income in industrialized countries: We work with a target variable of "equivalent income." This means that the disposable income of the household is adjusted for household size. In addition, we use individuals as the unit of analysis.

Our first research question is: Has inequality increased? A very widely held opinion among scholars and others is that income inequality in China has grown ever wider during the transition period (see, for example, World Bank, 1997). This is also apparent in information published by the State Statistical Bureau (SSB) on inequality in household cash income for urban China as well as for rural China. However, we can complement this by analyzing China as a whole, using the broader definition of disposable income.

The second group of questions refers to spatial aspects of income inequality in China. Has the urban-rural income gap widened and can more inequality in China as a whole be attributed to this gap? Are income differentials between eastern, central, and western China increasing and can a larger proportion of inequality in China as a whole be attributed to these differentials?

Finally we ask how the relation has changed among various characteristics at the household and individual levels, such as education, age, and size of household, on the one hand, and income as well as income inequality on the other hand.

Economic Transformation and Industrialization in China and Their Effect on the Distribution of Income

Economic transformation in China goes hand in hand with industrialization. Since the end of the 1980s there have been large changes in the sectoral composition of the economy. According to the national accounts, production in agriculture grew by 25 percent between 1989 and 1994, while the service sector increased by 48 percent and the industrial sector grew by a sensational 102 percent.

Meanwhile, the income gap between urban and rural areas of the People's Republic of China has been large. Figure 3.1, based on the official statistics, indicates an increasing rural-urban gap for cash income during the transition.

An important force preventing the rural-urban income gap from growing even further is migration. Traditionally restrictions on geographic mobility have been considerable in the People's Republic of China. However, during transformation, restrictions have been somewhat relaxed and China is now experiencing rapid urbanization. Thus according to official statistics, the urban part of the population (with urban *hukou*) increased from 25.8 percent in 1988 to 28.6 percent in 1994. This change took place in spite of the natural growth rate of the rural population being 38 percent higher than that of the urban population (SSB, 1995).[1]

A big social issue in contemporary China is the mass rural migration to cities. Persons living in urban China without a *hukou* are thought to number 50 million to 80 million, making up 15 to 25 percent of the total urban population. Urbanization has several effects on income distribution that depend on the characteristics of the migrants, the impact on incomes of the remaining rural population (subsistence income, wages, remittances) as well as the impact on the income of the urban population.

Institutional arrangements for residential housing differ between urban and rural China.

While country people have to provide for housing themselves, urban residents typically have lived in highly subsidized apartments. Although housing reform implying privatization and market-based rents is on the agenda, up until 1995 the system of housing allocation in urban China had not been much changed. This means that housing subsidies have continued to disproportionally benefit the urban population.

Within rural China, economic growth has also provided opportunities for the rural population to move away from farming land to being employed in nonagricultural activities. According to the official statistics, the total labor force in rural areas increased by 6.3 percent in the period from 1990 to 1994, but employment in nonagricultural activities including TVEs (township and village enterprises), private enterprises, and self-employment jumped by 36.9 percent (SSB, 1995). Results from earlier studies point in the direction that shifts away from subsistence farming will lead to increased inequality.[2]

In urban China, employment in the public-owned sector increased modestly by only 7.3 percent from 1988 to 1994, while employment in the nonpublic part such as private, self-employed, and joint-venture and foreign enterprises increased enormously by 206 percent. At the latter point in time, this accounted for nearly 14 percent of the total employment in urban China.

Figure 3.1   **Trend of Difference of Income Between Urban and Rural Households**

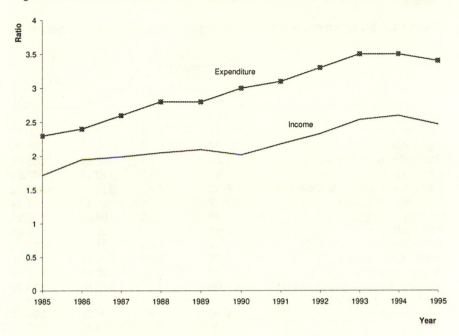

China has been slow in developing labor markets, and labor mobility was still fairly restricted in the middle of the 1990s. Therefore the economic sector becomes an important institutional variable for determining wages of workers. Some workers in a sector with a monopolistic position can share a part of the rents with the enterprises. Table 3.1 presents changes in employment and average wages in different economic sectors in urban China. Changes in the structure of employment are small, but relative wages have varied more. The wage ratio between the sector with the highest and the sector with the lowest average income increased from 1.58 in 1988 to 2.38 in 1994.

Additional reasons for expecting that income inequality has increased are institutional changes within the state-owned sector. State-owned enterprises have been allowed to make more decisions. This means that when wages are set, productivity considerations most likely have become more important than before and earnings differences between workers of different skill levels have increased. However, countering this force, the supply of highly educated workers in urban China has increased rapidly as school-leavers entering the labor force are on average more greatly educated than workers exiting the labor force due to retirement.

Reasons for increased income inequality in China can also be traced to both sides of the public budget. A serious economic problem for present-day China is difficulties with funding public-sector activities. One cause is that during transformation more and more of the state-owned enterprises are taking financial losses.

Table 3.1

Changes in Employment and Wages in Urban China by Economic Sector

	Percentage of employment (%)		Wage as percentage of average (%)	
	1988	1994	1988	1994
Agriculture	5.80	4.58	73.21	62.12
Excavation	6.11	6.09	112.42	103.11
Manufacturing	37.84	36.60	97.88	94.38
Gas, water, electric power	1.30	1.64	112.82	135.69
Construction	7.02	7.22	112.14	107.85
Transportation, communication	6.42	5.62	111.11	129.39
Commerce and trade	12.07	12.34	89.07	77.94
Banking, insurance	1.28	1.76	99.54	147.91
Real estate	0.31	0.49	98.17	138.56
Social services	2.34	3.01	98.40	110.75
Health, sport, welfare	2.76	2.88	100.29	112.96
Education, culture	8.02	8.41	100.00	108.48
Scientific research and technical services	1.06	1.17	110.53	135.79
Government, party, and social organization	6.20	6.85	98.28	109.34
Other	1.75	1.32	115.91	117.20

Sources: China Statistical Yearbook 1995, ed. by SSB. Beijing, China Statistical Publishing House, 1995, pp. 88–89; pp. 114–15.

This provides an additional reason for income differences to appear between enterprises; it is difficult for an enterprise making losses to pay high wages.

Another reason for the increased financial problems of the public sector is the underdeveloped tax-collecting capacity of the central state, that is, only a small proportion of urban workers pay income taxes. Very little of the inequality generated in the productive sphere is thus counterbalanced by income taxes.

The expenditure side of the public sector hardly promotes income equality in China, as the country is not a welfare state. Although systems of social insurance exist, they are organized at the enterprise level, which is an obstacle for labor mobility. Such systems cover the urban population, not the less fortunate rural population.[3]

Economic transformation in China has a very clear regional dimension, as reforms were first institutionalized in the coastal region. The coastal region has attracted a disproportionally large share of foreign investments, and economic growth has been most rapid there. The less populated western part is at the other extreme. In Table 3.2 we report how inequality in (unweighted) average provincial per capita income has developed. The table shows narrowing provincial income inequality during the 1980s but increases thereafter.[4]

Table 3.2

Spatial Inequality in China by Provincial GNP per Capita

	Inequality index			
	1980	1984	1988	1993
Coefficient of variance	0.951	0.753	0.675	0.685
Gini coefficient	0.35	0.304	0.298	0.321
Quintile 1	0.10236	0.10967	0.10606	0.09123
2	0.22254	0.23710	0.23407	0.21521
3	0.36083	0.38511	0.38770	0.36680
4	0.52284	0.57373	0.58887	0.58229
5	1	1	1	1
Number of provinces	30	30	30	30

Data and Assumptions

The data used in this paper are from two surveys, conducted by the Institute of Economics, Chinese Academy of Social Sciences, with assistance from the State Statistical Bureau in Beijing. The first survey of household income in 1988 was implemented in the spring of 1989 and the second refers to the year of 1995 and was conducted during the period of January to March 1996. Similar to the first survey, the second survey had different sample procedures and different instruments for households in rural and urban areas. Both samples were derived from large samples of the State Statistical Bureau. The survey for 1988 covers about 20,000 households and the one for 1995 about 15,000 households.

The questionnaires were designed by members of the research team. Most questions in the questionnaires of the first survey reappeared in the second, and some new questions were added. In the urban questionnaires, income questions were posed with the objective of deriving household disposable income; the households were required to answer questions regarding in-kind income and the market value of housing subsidies as well as imputed rent of privately owned houses. In the rural questionnaires, the present values of private houses were asked for in order to derive their imputed values by adopting a discount rate. Both the rural and urban questionnaires have fairly comprehensive questions about household consumption and its components, as well as about both financial and physical household assets.[5]

The target variable used in this chapter is disposable equivalent income. We use separate scales for imputed rents and other income as presented in Table 3.3 which is based on work done by the State Statistical Bureau. The scale takes the number

Table 3.3

Equivalent Scales for Urban and Rural Households in China

Size of household	Consumption net of housing		Housing expenditure (3)
	Rural (1)	Urban (2)	
1	100	100	100
2	192	188	172
3	288	266	190
4	376	354	207
5	468	429	246
6	561	504	280
7	635	—	327
γ	0.96	0.89	0.56

Note: Figures in columns (1) and (2) are from an index of efficiency of consumption worked out by SSB (see Riskin 1993), which means, for example, only 188 yuan is needed for two persons living together to have same utilities as 200 yuan if they were living separately in urban areas. The figures are used to estimate the parameter γ, with the formula $EY = HY/N^{\gamma}$, in which EY is equivalent income, HY is household income, and N is the number of household members. HY is assumed to be the figures from columns (1) – (3). Taking the form of logarithm for the formula, we derive $\log(HY) - \log(EY) = \gamma\log(N)$. Thus γ can be estimated using ordinary least squares (OLS).

of persons in the household into account but does not attempt to control for characteristics of the person, such as age. We follow today's dominant practice when analyzing the distribution of income in industrialized countries by using individuals as the unit of analysis.[6] This means we assume income in a household is equally shared and we assign the same value to each individual.

Household disposable income consists of individual incomes as well as household incomes not attributed to individuals. The former includes earnings, pensions, monetary and in-kind subsidies. The latter includes household income from farming, family enterprises, and property. As over 70 percent of the urban households were still living in public apartments in 1995, thus paying rents much lower than on the market, housing subsidies for those households were a crucial part of their income. This was calculated as a differential between the respondents' estimate of the market rent and the rents actually paid.[7] It was also considered important to include imputed rent of privately owned houses and apartments. For rural China this was done by applying the discount rate of 8 percent to the present value of the house (as estimated by the respondent).[8]

In all tables here, reported disposable income for 1995 has been expressed in the prices of 1988. This has been done by using price indexes specific to rural and urban parts of each province as published by the State Statistical Bureau (1996).

Table 3.4 shows household size for the two years under investigation. From the national sample it can be seen that on average the household size has decreased. The share of three-member households has increased by 6 percentage points, the share of six-member households has decreased by 3 percentage points, and the share of seven-

Table 3.4

Household Size in National, Rural, and Urban Samples in 1988 and 1995

Number of household members	National sample (%)		Rural sample (%)		Urban sample (%)	
	1988	1995	1988	1995	1988	1995
1	0.7	0.1	0.5	0.1	1.2	0.2
2	4.6	4.7	2.8	2.1	10.2	11.1
3	19.4	25.6	11.8	13.7	43.7	54.9
4	27.4	30.8	26.8	33.7	29.3	23.7
5	22.2	21.6	25.6	27.2	11.3	7.5
6	13.7	10.7	16.9	14.2	3.4	2.1
7 and over	12.1	6.5	15.7	8.9	0.9	0.3

Note: The national sample is weighted in this table and the following tables. The actual ratio of rural population to urban population is 74:26 in 1988, and 71:29 (which is predicted from the ratio of 71.4:28.6 in 1994) in 1995 (SSB, 1995).

Table 3.5

Frequency of Individuals by Age in 1988 and 1995

Age group	National sample (%)		Rural sample (%)		Urban sample (%)	
	1988	1995	1988	1995	1988	1995
–7	11.05	8.47	11.98	9.14	9.01	6.77
8–15	15.45	13.47	16.28	14.49	12.45	10.85
16–25	23.60	19.28	25.47	21.69	17.62	13.55
26–35	13.64	14.87	13.08	14.68	16.87	15.29
36–45	14.95	18.72	13.84	16.94	17.84	23.13
46–55	10.91	13.34	9.52	12.70	14.56	14.57
56–65	6.35	7.07	5.82	5.89	7.35	10.71
66–	4.05	4.78	4.02	4.47	4.40	5.13
Total	100	100	100	100	100	100

and-over-member households has decreased by 5.6 percentage points. The change in household size is larger in the urban sample than in the rural sample.

A notable change in age structure of individuals is reported in Table 3.5 in our sample, which shows that the population of China is aging. This is the outcome of falling birth rates consistent with the official one-child policy[9] and increased life expectancy. The proportion of the population below 25 in China as a whole decreased from 50.1 percent in 1988 to 41.2 percent in 1995. Meanwhile, the proportion of the population over 45 years of age increased from 21.3 percent to 25.2 percent.

Our data do not show more than marginally changed employment rates for China as a whole (Table 3.6). However, when analyzing males and females separately, we find that the employment rate of females has decreased more than that for males. One reason is that younger females, especially in urban areas, have more opportunities for receiving higher education. Another possible reason is that

Table 3.6

Labor Force Participation Rates for China, 1988 and 1995

	National sample (%)		Rural sample (%)		Urban sample (%)	
	1995	1988	1995	1988	1995	1988
Total	81.16	82.46	84.29	84.62	74.05	76.84
Age 16–25	68.88	73.46	74.30	78.31	47.76	53.30
26–35	93.49	96.32	92.60	95.43	95.51	98.02
36–45	93.83	96.06	92.46	95.19	96.72	97.72
46–55	85.11	84.58	89.42	87.88	75.62	78.63
56–65	47.54	49.13	64.41	57.76	25.47	30.39
Male	85.66	86.11	88.53	87.99	78.76	81.07
Age 16–25	69.14	70.99	74.91	75.78	46.50	51.49
26–35	96.63	98.73	96.24	98.44	97.27	99.02
36–45	97.49	99.09	97.04	98.92	98.53	99.52
46–55	95.04	96.14	96.15	96.95	92.13	94.55
56–65	61.44	68.32	78.61	87.01	38.15	47.87
Female	76.63	78.80	79.93	81.20	69.47	72.72
Age 16–25	68.61	75.93	73.69	80.84	49.00	55.16
26–35	90.51	94.11	89.03	92.59	93.94	97.17
36–45	90.37	93.04	88.03	91.46	95.07	96.02
46–55	74.21	71.73	81.81	77.44	58.73	62.07
56–65	30.63	27.13	46.45	35.56	10.85	8.11

female workers have a greater risk of becoming unemployed. Counterbalancing this is an increase in employment rates among persons aged over 55, though there are still few employed females in this age group.

Table 3.7 illustrates that the skill level of the Chinese labor force as measured by the level of education has increased impressively. Unfortunately the progress is strongly concentrated in urban areas. Nevertheless, the proportion having less than primary school education decreased in rural China for both genders.

The Overall Development of Inequality

In Table 3.8 on page 54 based on the two samples, we report mean values of equivalent income for China as a whole, and for urban China and rural China, as well as Lorenz curves for the three distributions. The mean value for China as a whole increased between 1988 and 1995 by 58 percent, which is almost 7 percent on average annual basis. The growth for the urban sample was 62 percent while that for the rural sample was 48 percent. Consistent with what was reported in Figure 3.1 from the official statistics (based on money income) the urban-rural income gap in disposable income increased from 2.58 to 2.83.

Table 3.7

Frequency of Working Members by Education in 1988 and 1995

Education level	National sample (%)		Rural sample (%)		Urban sample (%)	
	1988	1995	1988	1995	1988	1995
Working members						
College	3.64	6.77	0.49	0.54	12.76	23.34
Technical	3.47	5.41	0.90	1.20	10.94	16.65
Upper middle	12.08	12.96	7.77	8.74	24.66	24.22
Lower middle	32.81	38.82	39.9	41.9	38.33	30.13
Primary	27.43	24.09	33.33	31.38	10.34	5.17
Less than primary	20.58	11.95	26.62	20.24	3.01	0.50
Male workers						
College	4.64	8.14	0.41	0.60	16.96	28.43
Technical	3.62	5.50	1.18	1.58	10.72	16.13
Upper middle	14.04	14.89	10.67	12.03	24.06	22.61
Lower middle	37.86	42.97	38.21	48.39	37.00	28.12
Primary	27.07	22.09	33.28	28.75	9.00	4.44
Less than primary	12.77	6.37	16.24	8.65	2.25	0.26
Female workers						
College	2.52	5.22	0.58	0.47	8.14	17.71
Technical	3.29	5.31	0.58	0.77	11.17	17.22
Upper middle	9.92	10.77	4.56	4.98	25.34	25.99
Lower middle	27.23	34.13	22.81	34.48	39.78	32.35
Primary	27.83	26.34	33.37	34.39	11.81	5.98
Less than primary	29.21	18.22	38.10	24.91	3.75	0.75
Head of household						
College	5.97	8.74	0.48	0.55	17.83	26.28
Technical	4.50	6.53	1.22	1.52	11.58	17.37
Upper middle	13.59	15.67	10.46	12.84	20.39	21.39
Lower middle	33.30	38.70	31.82	42.98	36.68	29.58
Primary	28.20	23.34	36.21	32.04	10.95	5.01
Less than primary	14.29	7.01	19.81	10.06	2.57	0.37

The Lorenz curves also illustrated in Figure 3.2 very clearly show income inequality to have increased between the two years under investigation in China as a whole. A good illustration of this is the very different growth rates for the different deciles. While average income for the first decile increased by 18 percent between the two years, growth for the tenth decile was as high as 88 percent. This means that the ratio between the first and tenth decile widened from 1:12 in 1988 to 1:19 in 1995. The Gini coefficient rose from 0.386 to 0.462, an increase of 20 percent.

It is well known that income inequality in urban China is relatively small. Nevertheless, comparisons of Lorenz curves clearly show income inequality in urban China to have been rising. Average income for the first decile increased by 32 percent while for the tenth decile the increase was as high as 80 percent. The ratio between income of the first to the tenth decile increased from 1:4.3 to 1:5.8, and the Gini coefficient increased from 0.228 to 0.276, or by 21 percent.

Table 3.8

Lorenz Curves for China, 1988 and 1995

	National sample		Rural sample		Urban sample	
	1988	1995	1988	1995	1988	1995
Mean value (yuan)	1,161.0	1,838.9	821.7	1,213.8	2,119.9	3,438.7
Cumulative share (%)						
Decile 1	2.282	1.707	2.881	2.288	4.858	3.964
2	6.016	4.505	7.513	5.952	11.213	9.484
3	10.799	8.167	13.339	10.577	18.364	15.942
4	16.571	12.790	20.238	16.148	26.230	23.273
5	23.465	18.568	28.169	22.741	34.817	31.488
6	31.757	25.973	37.224	30.528	44.127	40.612
7	42.201	35.891	47.588	39.736	54.312	50.838
8	55.490	49.239	59.652	50.985	65.705	62.548
9	72.334	67.144	74.662	65.957	79.134	76.852
10	100	100	100	100	100	100
Gini	0.3860	0.4621	0.3247	0.4226	0.2276	0.2762

Figure 3.2a   **Lorenz Curves of National Samples in 1988 and 1995**

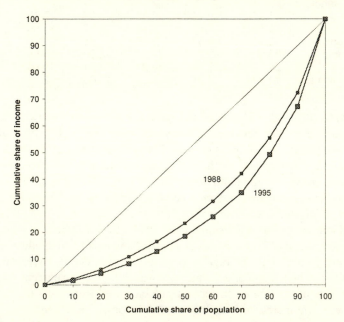

Figure 3.2b   **Lorenz Curves of Urban Samples in 1988 and 1995**

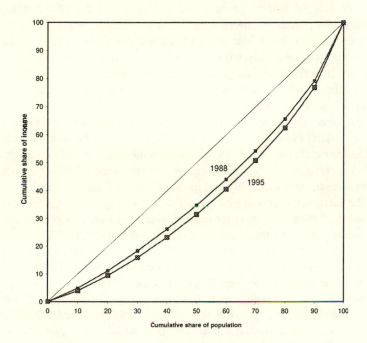

Figure 3.2c   **Lorenz Curves of Rural Samples in 1988 and 1995**

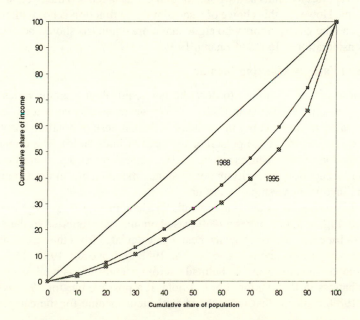

Increases in income inequality in China were most pronounced for rural China. While income of the first decile increased by 17 percent, that of the tenth decile increased by 98 percent—almost three times as much. Compared with growth rates for deciles in urban China we find that income at the bottom of the rural distribution grew more slowly, while the converse was true at the top of the income distribution. In rural China the ratio between the income of the first and tenth deciles increased from 1:9 in 1988 to 1:15 in 1995, while the Gini coefficient rose by 30 percent, from 0.325 to 0.423.[10]

To what extent do our results agree with those reported from the same data by Khan and Riskin (1998) and Khan et al. (1993) based on household income? A general answer is that the direction of change is the same, but the numbers differ. We report a considerably smaller increase in urban inequality but a somewhat larger increase in rural inequality and in the urban-rural income gap.[11]

Are the increases in income inequality in China large by contemporary standards? Although many industrialized market economies have experienced increased income inequality during the last one and half decades, the United Kingdom seems to be the only one that matches China when it come to magnitudes of changes.[12] However, available evidence indicates that income inequality in Russia during the 1990s has widened even more rapidly than in China.[13]

In Figure 3.3 we depict generalized Lorenz curves (Shorrocks, 1983) in order to make a social welfare evaluation, including not only the distribution of income but also its level. For any social welfare function, which is a nondecreasing function of mean income and its distribution, social welfare is larger in 1995 than in 1988. This applies to China as a whole, to rural China taken separately, and also to urban China. However, this choice of a social welfare function is not without controversy, and there are authors who argue that more emphasis should be placed on equity considerations (Tam and Zhang, 1996).

Changes in Factors Affecting Income

The purpose of this section is to describe how equivalent income varies along several dimensions. For China in 1988 and 1995 we investigate variation in equivalent disposable income among individuals in the Chinese population for various dimensions (recorded for the person or the head of household). The dimensions include location (rural-urban, as well as coastal-central-west), age, household size, education, occupation, minority-majority status, membership in the Communist Party, and finally, ownership of work unit.

The analysis has two steps. First, we display how mean values vary after each dimension. Figure 3.4 on pages 59–60 (based on numbers reported in the Appendix) shows for each category how its mean value deviates from the mean value for the entire population. There is one bar for 1988 and one for 1995. This figure allows comparisons of means to be made across categories, as well as comparisons of changes in the relation. For example, if a positive bar for 1995 is larger than for 1988, it means that the average equivalent income for the category has

Figure 3.3a   **Generalized Lorenz Curves of National Samples in 1988 and 1985**

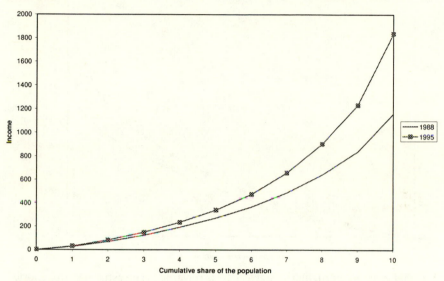

Figure 3.3b   **Generalized Lorenz Curves of Urban Samples in 1988 and 1985**

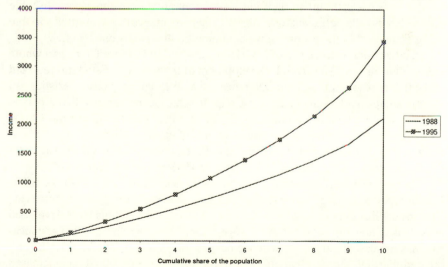

increased more rapidly than for the average person in China as a whole.

The second step is to estimate regression models with a number of explanatory variables using the logarithm of equivalent disposable income as the dependent variable. This makes it possible to investigate net effects ("payoff") for each vari-

Figure 3.3c   **Generalized Lorenz Curves of Rural Samples in 1988 and 1985**

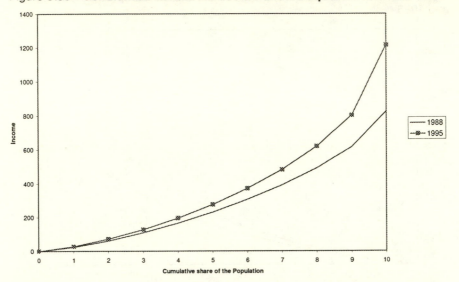

able, that is, how a particular characteristic is rewarded. The estimates are reported in Table 3.9 on pages 61–62, where results from running two different specifications are reported. The difference between the two is that the second allows for interaction between the urban-rural and coastal-central-western dimensions. In Table 3.9 we express all coefficients as differences in percentages of the omitted variable using antilogs.[14] In the following we comment on the results one by one.

An urban-rural income gap of 2.82:1 was reported in 1995 for China as a whole (see section above, "The Overall Development of Inequality"). Estimates reported in the first two columns of Table 3.9 indicate that differences in characteristics can explain somewhat less than half of the gap. It comes as no surprise that a person living in urban China has a much higher income than one living in rural China. However, it is interesting that the "pure" payoff of urban residence (i.e., after controlling for other measured characteristics of the two population groups) actually decreased from a difference of 132 percent in 1988 to 103 percent in 1995.

Why has the payoff from living in urban areas decreased while the gross difference as reported in the previous section and illustrated in Figure 3.4a has increased? The answer lies in how variable values for rural and urban China have developed as well as in how the payoffs have changed. Thus the urban to rural gap in education has increased and (as we will see below) the payoff from education has increased. Further, the negative effect of living in a large household has increased (as will be discussed below), something that has greater consequence in rural China where such households are more prevalent.

People living in eastern China have a higher equivalent income than those living in central regions, who in turn are better off than westerners, although these differences are considerably smaller than the rural-urban disparity (see Figure 3.4b).

Figure 3.4   **Mean Equivalent Income in China in 1988 and 1995 as Percent of Mean Income for all People Living in China in the Same Year, by Categories**

Figure 3.4a

Figure 3.4b

Figure 3.4c

Figure 3.4 *(continued)*

Figure 3.4d

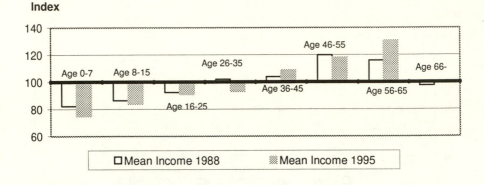

Figure 3.4e

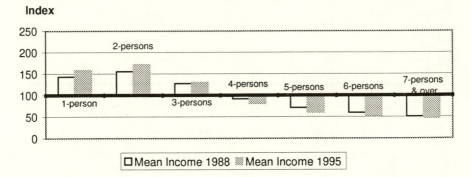

Figure 3.4f

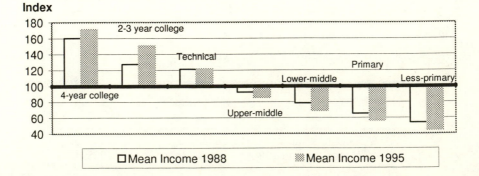

Table 3.9

Results from Multivariate Regression Analysis: Percentage of Coefficients of Variables Relative to Those of Omitted Variables

Variable	Equation 1		Equation 2	
	1988	1995	1988	1995
Area				
Urban	132.12	102.52	—	—
Middle	−27.79	−30.76	—	—
West	−27.93	−40.37	—	—
Sex				
Female	0.73	−1.39	0.73	−1.40
Minority				
Non−minority	13.02	7.35	11.93	6.22
Age				
8–15	5.48	4.63	5.34	4.73
16–25	11.15	14.18	11.15	14.32
26–35	5.90	8.11	5.78	8.11
36–45	7.98	10.06	7.89	10.20
46–55	12.56	13.75	12.56	13.71
56–65	10.34	6.90	10.49	7.54
66 and over	4.67	7.65	4.74	7.98
Number of people per household				
2	−0.03	−6.56	−0.23	−5.73
3	−5.79	−18.58	−6.23	−17.26
4	−17.72	−30.60	−18.18	−29.36
5	−24.41	−37.23	−24.69	−36.01
6	−28.63	−41.90	−28.81	−40.59
7 and over	−32.85	−44.05	−32.87	−42.55
Age of head of household				
26–35	−4.22	5.47	−4.50	4.80
36–45	4.20	16.88	3.93	15.77
46–55	11.97	25.32	11.30	23.95
56–65	12.13	25.47	11.44	24.47
66 and over	9.90	13.14	8.81	12.28
Education				
2–3-year college	−6.49	−6.49	−5.59	−6.74
Technical	−6.34	−11.79	−6.60	−13.38
Upper−middle	−4.03	−8.33	−4.04	−9.44
Lower−middle	−5.19	−10.92	−5.35	−12.01
Primary	−4.75	−14.80	−4.93	−15.68
Less than primary	−14.56	−21.19	−14.34	−21.07
Local−public	−4.15	−6.43	−5.02	−6.39
Ownership				
Collective	−1.38	−13.42	−1.17	−12.69
Private	−4.91	−7.90	−4.39	−6.90
Foreign	60.62	4.95	61.81	7.07
Farm	−6.02	18.96	−5.95	18.91
Other	−14.60	−24.40	−14.91	−23.31

(continued)

Table 3.9 (continued)

Occupational status				
Owner	14.91	22.23	14.91	21.14
Professional	14.68	29.29	15.26	26.94
Manager	20.80	34.41	20.80	33.91
Branch manager	19.24	30.02	19.60	29.63
Office worker	12.08	20.77	12.41	19.18
Skilled worker	5.76	10.17	6.18	9.71
Unskilled worker		8.62		9.06
Other	24.61	29.10	24.11	28.25
Area				
Mid rural	—	—	−27.41	−31.00
West rural	—	—	−31.00	−45.45
East urban	—	—	125.92	91.12
Mid urban	—	—	58.25	32.32
West urban	—	—	86.85	40.10
Adj. R^2	0.50	0.55	0.50	0.55
F–value	2,849.2	2,169.0	2,755.2	2,109.10
Mean of dependent variables	6.798	7.14	6.798	7.14
Number	122,023	77,230	122,023	77,230

Notes: Dependent variables are individual equivalent income and observations are individuals. Omitted variables are: rural, east, east-rural, male, minority, age 0–7, 1-person, H-age 16–25, 4-year college, State-owned, Farmer. All coefficients are statistically significant at 1 percent or 5 percent level except for 2-person, 3-person, collective in 1988 equations; 2-person and foreign in 1995 equations. Percentages (P) are transformed from coefficients (C) by a formula, $P = 100 * \exp(C) - 1$; H is for head of household.

As expected, income has grown fastest in the eastern region, and income differences between the three regions have increased.

Thus, the estimates reported in Table 3.9 show that a person has considerably less income if living in regions other than the east, and that this difference has grown. Westerners in 1995 received an income 40 percent lower than they would have if living in the east. Thus financial incentives to migrate from the west to the east were high, and they have increased. Looking at figures reported in the Appendix we see that in rural areas, especially, growth rates have differed among the three regions. While average equivalent income grew by 20 percent in western rural areas, growth was three and half times as high (71 percent) in the eastern region. This is indeed a very large difference.

Turning to personal characteristics, we find practically no difference in mean income between males and females, but this finding is an artifact of our assumption that incomes of spouses are perfectly pooled within the household so men and women living together have identical well-being.[15] There are very few single person households or households headed by a female, which would give us a window on gender income differences.

Minority members are on average far behind the Han majority in average disposable income. Between 1988 and 1995 average income of the majority increased by 60 percent, and that of minorities by 38 percent. Thus the gap in average income between the Han and minority populations has increased, and in 1995 average income of the minority came to no more than two thirds of that of the majority (see also Figure 3.4c).

However, a striking conclusion from Table 3.9 is that most of the income gap between majority persons and minority persons is attributable to locational and personal characteristics. Most important, the minority population is found disproportionally in rural western regions where the level of education is also lower than elsewhere in China. Only a small part of the minority-majority gap is due to different incomes for persons having the same characteristics, including living in the same region. Interestingly this "net" minority deficit has decreased from 13 percent of the majority income in 1988 to 7 percent in 1995. Those numbers are much smaller than the ones for location reported above, and they suggest that the spread of market forces may have gone some way toward eliminating pure antiminority prejudice in economic activities.

A property of our approach is that we can report equivalent income according to age of each person in a household, thus also for children. If one accepts our choice of equivalence scale, it follows that mean equivalent income increases with age until the mature middle years, after which it drops (Figure 3.4d). The youngest children and the age group 26–35 (including many parents of young children) have had the slowest growth in average equivalent income. At the other extreme is the age class 56–65, which has experienced the highest growth in average equivalent income. Looking at age of household head, those households with a head aged 16–25 lag behind, with a growth of 31 percent compared to 83 percent for those aged 56–65. Thus income turns out to be increasingly strongly related to age in China. This can also be seen from the results of the multivariate analysis (Table 3.9) where coefficients for age of household head are larger in 1995 than in 1988.

In China people in small households are better off than those in large households (see also Figure 3.4e). A major reason for this is the nature of the household formation process. First, larger households are apt to contain one or more children, who do not earn income. Second, old and disabled people who cannot cope for themselves are typically taken in by their relatives, increasing household size without adding to income. Differences in income along this dimension have increased as average equivalent income has grown much faster in small households than in large ones. For example, average equivalent income grew by 62 percent in two-person households but only by 24 percent in five-person households. Results from the regression analysis show increased importance of household size.

There are large differences in average equivalent income among educational groups (Figure 3.4f). The ratio between households headed by someone with four years of college and those headed by one with less than primary education grew from 3.0:1 in

1988 to 3.8:1 in 1995. However, many of these differences are due to differences in where the family lives, where its working members work, and the size of the household. Controlling for a number of characteristics, the net differences due to education shown in Table 3.9 are much smaller. Still, all reported coefficients on education are estimated with a high degree of statistical significance. The net gap between having four years of college and having less than primary school education amounted to only 15 percent in 1988 but had grown to 21 percent in 1995. These results are consistent with some recent studies arguing that the earnings premium of education has increased in China during the reform process.[16]

The breakdown of occupation and of ownership sector of household head overlaps considerably with the urban-rural breakdown, as most rural residents are classified as farmers, a category of ownership as well as of occupation.[17] Turning to occupation, the low average income of farmers is obvious. High-income occupations, not surprisingly, are manager and professional. The regression analysis shows that the income premium of having an occupation other than farming has increased between the two years. The gap between households with a head working in state-owned enterprises and those whose heads worked on farms grew from 1:2.8 in 1988 to 1:3.1 in 1995. However, much of these differences disappears in the regression analysis of Table 3.9, which assigns them to other relevant characteristics.

Decomposition by Subgroups

In this section we decompose the population into mutually exclusive subgroups according to alternative breakdowns of the sample. Using additively decomposable inequality indices, we investigate inequality in various subgroups at the two points in time and analyze change in total inequality. An inequality index is adaptively decomposable when it fulfils the following requirement:

Aggregated inequality = inequality within groups + inequality between groups.

The first item on the right side of the equation—within group or intragroup inequality—is a weighted sum of the inequality indexes of the individual groups into which the population is divided. The second component—between-group or intergroup inequality—is the inequality that would exist if people received the average income of the group to which they belonged rather than their actual income. It thus represents the amount of inequality that would remain if there was no inequality within each group.

The Theil index is defined as

$$T(Y;N) = \frac{\sum_i \left(\frac{y_i}{\mu}\right)\log\left(\frac{y_i}{\mu}\right)}{N} \tag{3.1}$$

and the mean logarithmic deviation (MLD) defines as

$$MLD(y;N) = \frac{\sum_i \log\left(\frac{\mu}{y_i}\right)}{N}$$

(3.2)

where μ is the mean equivalent income and N the total number of individuals.

The Theil index decomposes as

$$T(y;N) = \sum_k T(y^k, N_k)\left(\frac{\mu_k N_k}{\mu N}\right) + \frac{1}{\mu N}\sum_k \mu_k N_k \log\left(\frac{\mu_k}{\mu}\right)$$

(3.3)

The MLD index decomposes as

$$MLD(y;N) = \sum_k MLD(y^k, N_k)\left(\frac{N_k}{N}\right) + \frac{1}{N}\sum_k N_k \log\left(\frac{\mu}{\mu_k}\right)$$

(3.4)

The Theil index thus uses income as weights for the various groups when obtaining the between-group component; this role is taken by the population for MLD. We use both alternatives and present the results in the Appendix. It turns out that the overwhelming majority of results are similar for the two indices, and therefore we will concentrate our comments on results obtained using the MLD index.

Results on the size of within-group inequality in 1988 and 1995 for various categories presented in the Appendix show that, rather generally, income inequality within a category is larger the second year. Table 3.10 shows the size of the within and between components for both years when the sample is divided by individual characteristics, while Table 3.11 shows results from breakdowns made according to characteristics of the household head. (Tables 3.10 and 3.11 are on pages 66–69).

Starting with the *rural-urban* divide, we see that almost two-fifths of inequality in China as a whole in 1988 can be attributed to differences in mean income between the two parts. As discussed above, inequality within each part, and especially within rural China, has increased a great deal (see also Figure 3.5). Thus, even though the rural-urban income gap has widened, the proportion of total inequality that can be attributed to that gap in 1995 is down to one-third.[18]

Turning to the dimension *west-middle-east*, we see from Figure 3.6 that in 1988 inequality in western China was as large as that in the coastal region, and that it became the largest in 1995. This is a disturbing result as mean income has increased modestly in western China. We cannot rule out the possibility that living standards in the west have deteriorated at the lower end of the income distribution, something that deserves further investigation. However, looking at 1995, this dimension continues to be much less important than the rural-urban dimension for Chinese inequality as the between-group component reported in Table 3.10 is much smaller than that for the rural-urban dimension.

The interaction of the *rural-urban* categories with those of *west-middle-east* yields a total of six classes. Largest is inequality within the rural-east, which in-

Table 3.10

Decomposition of Within-Group and Between-Group Inequality in 1998 and 1995, by Individual Characteristics

Sample partition	Year	1000 MLD index			1000 Theil index		
		Total inequality	Within-group inequality	Between-group inequality	Total inequality	Within group inequality	Between group inequality
Rural-urban	1988 (%)	258.31 (100)	159.6 (61.8)	98.7 (38.2)	253.3 (100)	145.6 (57.5)	107.7 (42.5)
	1995 (%)	378.41 (100)	255.9 (67.6)	122.5 (32.36)	373.2 (100)	242.3 (64.9)	130.9 (35.1)
Three "belts"	1988 (%)	258.31 (100)	238.8 (92.5)	19.5 (7.5)	253.3 (100)	233.6 (92.2)	19.7 (7.8)
	1995 (%)	378.45 (100)	343.1 (90.7)	35.4 (9.3)	373.14 (100)	336.9 (90.3)	36.2 (9.7)
Six regions	1988 (%)	258.31 (100)	138.4 (53.6)	119.9 (46.4)	253.3 (100)	125.8 (49.7)	127.5 (50.3)
	1995 (%)	378.41 (100)	206.6 (54.6)	171.8 (45.4)	373.14 (100)	202.7 (54.3)	170.4 (45.7)
Age group of individual	1988 (%)	258.34 (100)	251.5 (97.4)	6.9 (2.6)	253.3 (100)	246.3 (97.3)	6.9 (2.7)

	1995 (%)	378.41 (100)	351.9 (93)	26.5 (7)	373.14 (100)	361.3 (96.8)	11.9 (3.2)

Sex group of individual	1988 (%)	258.31 (100)	258.3 (100)	0.0 (0)	253.2 (100)	253.3 (100)	0.0 (0)
	1995 (%)	378.41 (100)	378.0 (100)	0.4 (0)	373.14 (100)	373.1 (100)	0.0 (0)
Minority status	1988 (%)	258.31 (100)	256.0 (99.1)	2.3 (0.9)	253.2 (100)	251.1 (99.2)	2.1 (0.8)
	1995 (%)	378.41 (100)	373.2 (98.6)	5.2 (1.4)	373.14 (100)	368.5 (98.8)	4.6 (1.2)
Personal status	1988 (%)	258.31 (100)	n.a.	n.a.	253.3 (100)	n.a.	n.a.
	1995 (%)	378.41 (100)	357.0 (94.3)	21.4 (5.7)	373.2 (100)	348.7 (93.4)	24.5 (6.6)
Household size	1988 (%)	258.31 (100)	205.6 (79.6)	52.7 (20.4)	253.3 (100)	199.2 (78.7)	54.1 (21.3)
	1995 (%)	378.41 (100)	303.7 (80.3)	74.7 (19.7)	373.14 (100)	297.4 (79.7)	75.7 (20.3)

Notes: 1. Income is individual equivalent disposable income. Subgroups are defined as follows: Rural-urban: Rural, Urban. Three-belts: East, Middle, West. Six-regions: Rural-East, Rural-Middle, Rural-West, Urban-East, Urban-Middle, Urban-West. Age group: 0–7, 8–15, 16–25, 26–35, 36–45, 46–55, 56–65, 65–. Sex: male, female. Minority status: ethnic minorities, Han majority. Personal status: worker, pensioner, unemployed, housewife, disabled person, student, pre-school child, other. Household size: 1 person, 2, 3, 4, 5, 6, 7 and over.

Table 3.11

Decomposition of Within-Group and Between-Group Inequality in 1988 and 1995, by Characteristics of Household Head

Sample partition	Year	1000 MLD index			1000 Theil index		
		Total inequality	Within-group inequality	Between-group inequality	Total inequality	Within-group inequality	Between-group inequality
Age group of head	1988	258.31	256.2	2.1	253.3	251.4	1.9
	(%)	(100)	(99.2)	(0.8)	(100)	(99.3)	(0.7)
	1995	378.41	371.4	7.0	373.14	366.1	7.0
	(%)	(100)	(98.1)	(1.9)	(100)	(98.1)	(1.9)
Education of head	1988	258.31	226.0	32.3	253.3	218.3	35.0
	(%)	(100)	(87.5)	(12.5)	(100)	(86.2)	(13.8)
	1995	378.41	322.6	55.8	373.14	311.3	61.8
	(%)	(100)	(85.3)	(14.7)	(100)	(83.4)	(16.6)
Party membership of head	1988	258.31	242.8	15.5	253.3	236.6	16.7
	(%)	(100)	(94.0)	(6.0)	(100)	(93.4)	(6.6)
	1995	378.41	359.6	18.8	373.14	353.1	20.0
	(%)	(100)	(95.0)	(5.0)	(100)	(94.6)	(5.4)
Employment status of head	1988	258.6	256.7	1.6	253.3	251.6	1.7
	(%)	(100)	(99.4)	(0.6)	(100)	(99.3)	(0.7)
	1995	378.41	361.7	16.7	373.14	353.4	19.7

	(%)	(100)	(95.6)	(4.4)	(100)	(94.7)	(5.3)
Work unit's ownership of head	1988	258.31	159.2	99.4	253.3	149.5	103.8
	(%)	(100)	(61.6)	(38.4)	(100)	(59.0)	(41.0)
	1995	378.41	241.2	137.2	373.14	233.2	139.9
	(%)	(100)	(63.7)	(36.3)	(100)	(62.5)	(37.5)
Occupation of head	1988	258.31	160.4	97.9	253.3	150.8	102.4
	(%)	(100)	(62.1)	(37.9)	(100.2)	(59.6)	(40.6)
	1995	378.41	237.5	140.9	373.14	229.3	143.8
	(%)	(100)	(62.8)	(37.2)	(100)	(61.5)	(38.5)

Notes: Income is equivalent household disposable income per capita. Unit of analysis is individual. Definitions of subgroups are as follows: Age group of head: 16–25, 26–35, 36–45, 46–55, 56–65, 65–. Education of head: 4-year college or above, 2–3-year college, technical or professional school, upper-middle school, lower-middle school, primary school, less than primary school. Party membership: Communist Party member, non-Communist Party member. Employment status of head: worker, pensioner, unemployee, housewife, disabled person, other. Work unit's ownership: state-owned public, other public, urban collective, private and self-employed, foreign and joint venture, family farming, other (such as TVEs). Occupation of head: owner of private enterprise, professional, manager or director of enterprise, branch manager or director of enterprise, office worker, skilled worker, unskilled worker, rural cadre, farmer.

Figure 3.5   **Within-Group Inequality for Urban and Rural China According to the MLD Index, 1988 and 1995, by Characteristics of Individuals**

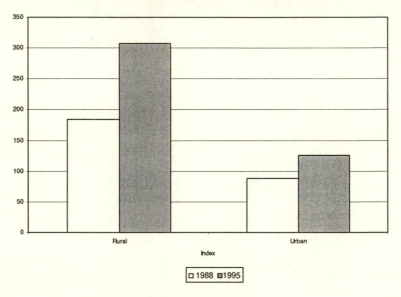

Figure 3.6   **Within-Group Inequality for Region (Three Levels) According to the MLD Index, 1988 and 1995, by Characteristics of Individuals**

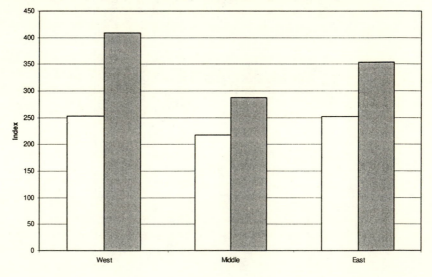

Figure 3.7   **Within-Group Inequality for Region (Six Levels) According to the MLD Index, 1988 and 1995, by Characteristics of Individuals**

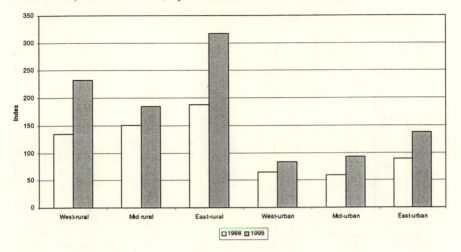

creased considerably between 1988 and 1995 (see Figure 3.7). Inequality also increased a great deal in the rural west, becoming larger than in the rural center. If mean incomes of the six regions were set to be equal, and only inequality within each region were to remain, inequality in China as a whole would shrink by almost one-half. Thus Chinese income inequality has a very clear locational dimension.

The breakdowns by *occupation of household head* and *ownership of work units* both overlap with the rural-urban breakdown and thus give a similar picture. Therefore, about two-fifths of total inequality is attributed to that between the two groups.

Compared to locational dimensions, several individual dimensions are less important. Average equivalent income in China is not very different for different groups defined by *age* of the person or the head of the household. No more than 3 percent of total inequality in China would vanish in 1988 if mean income of persons belonging to various age groups were to disappear. However, this proportion has increased.[19]

Using our definition of equivalent income, we find that one-fifth of the total inequality is due to differences in mean income between *households of different sizes.* Turning to *gender,* the remarkable finding is the lack of a relation to inequality. If the mean income of *minorities* were to be equal to the mean income of the majority population (and inequality in each category kept constant), income inequality in China as a whole would decrease by not more than 1 percent.

Inequality within the category *persons living in households headed by a party member* is smaller than among those living in other households. If the mean income of the two categories were to be identical, total inequality in China would decrease by 6 percent in 1988 and 5 percent in 1995.

There is an interesting change in the relation between *education of household head* and inequality. Inequality is largest among those with limited education,

Figure 3.8 **Within-Group Inequality for Education Level According to the MLD Index, 1988 and 1995**

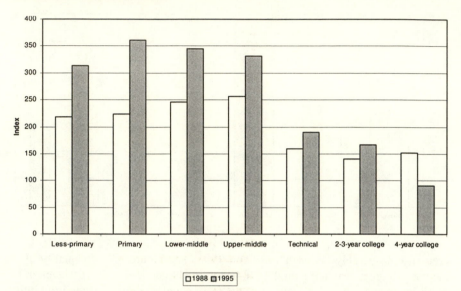

smallest among those with higher educations (see also Figure 3.8). Inequality has also grown fastest among those with limited education. A growing proportion of total inequality in China can be attributed to a different mean income for categories defined by the education of the household head. In 1995 almost one-sixth of total inequality in China as a whole would vanish if the mean income of categories formed according to education of household head were to disappear.

Accounting for Changes in Inequality

We now turn to the question of changes in income inequality in China as a whole. The change in MLD between two periods, t and t + k, may be written as:[20]

$$\Delta L = L_{t+k} - L_t = \sum_k \overline{v_k} \Delta L_k + \sum_k \overline{L_k} \Delta v_k - \sum_k \left(\overline{\ln \lambda_k}\right) \Delta v_k - \sum_k \overline{v_k} \Delta \ln \lambda_k$$

$$\approx \sum_k \overline{v_k} \Delta L_k + \sum_k \overline{L_k} \Delta v_k + \sum_k (\overline{\lambda_k} - \overline{\ln \lambda_k}) \Delta v_k + \sum_k (\overline{\theta_k} - \overline{v_k}) \Delta \ln \mu_k \quad (3.5)$$

where μk = mean value of group k, $\lambda_k = \mu_k / \mu$, v_k = share of group observations in total, and $\theta_k = v_k \cdot \lambda_k$, Δ represents the change in the relevant variable from period t to period $t + k$. A bar over a variable represents an average for the two period values. The approximation is more useful than the exact decomposition as it relates inequality changes to changes in subgroup inequalities, shares, and means.

The four terms can be interpreted as: (a) the effect of intertemporal changes on within-group inequality, (b) the effect of changes in population shares on within-group inequality, (c) the effect of changes in population shares on the relative mean income of the population groups, and (d) the relative mean income of the population groups. The overall effect of demographic changes is given by the sum of the second and third term.

A general finding of our work is that effects of demographic changes are very small. Income inequality has increased in almost all categories studied, and there is no clear exception. Another general result is that changes in within-group inequality dominate increases in between-group inequality.

From Table 3.12 it can be seen that one-sixth of the increase in inequality in China as a whole is due to the increased income gap between rural and urban China. This is only marginally more than the 13 percent that can be attributed to increased differences in means for eastern, middle, and western China. Turning to the division of China into six regions, Table 3.12 shows that rising differences in means account for 38 percent of the growth of inequality in China as a whole. Thus while increased income gaps among the regions are definitely important, most of the increase in income inequality is within each of the six regions. As the dimensions *work unit ownership* and *occupation of household head* strongly coincide with the locational variables, it is understandable that increases in differences in mean values among categories formed by those dimensions account for similar proportions (29 percent and 36 percent respectively).

About one-fifth of the growth of inequality in China as a whole can be attributed to the growth of differences in mean income by education level of household head. Results for households of different sizes are rather similar. Somewhat smaller (16 percent) is the proportion of inequality stemming from employment status of household head.

Turning to other breakdowns, we find several examples where changes in mean values for the categories account for very little of the total increases in income inequality in China as a whole. The examples are age of household head (4 percent), age of person (3 percent), party membership of household head (3 percent), minority status of individual (3 percent), and finally gender of the person (less than 1 percent).

Conclusion

In the foregoing analysis we have worked with equivalent disposable income and taken individuals as the unit of analysis. We have estimated income functions for 1988 and 1995 and analyzed the results using additively decomposable inequality indices. From our analysis a number of conclusions can be drawn regarding how inequality in equivalent income has changed during industrialization and transition toward a market economy.

Table 3.12

Subgroup Decompositions of Changes in Income Inequality (MLD), 1988 and 1995

		Percent change in MLD accounted for by changes in:			
Subgroup partition	Percent change in aggregate inequality	Within-group inequality (term 1)	Population shares (term 2)	(term 3)	Subgroup mean income (term 4)
Rural-urban	46.5	38.6	−1.2	1.4	7.7
	(100)	(83.0)	(−2.5)	(3.1)	(16.5)
Three "belts"	46.5	39.8	0.5	−0.1	6.3
	(100)	(85.6)	(1.1)	(−0.2)	(13.5)
Six regions	46.5	28.0	−1.6	2.3	17.8
	(100)	(60.3)	(−3.5)	(4.9)	(38.3)
Age group of individual	46.5	44.1	0.4	0	2.0
	(100)	(94.8)	(0.9)	(0)	(4.3)
Sex of individual	46.5	46.4	0	0	0.1
	(100)	(99.8)	(0)	(0)	(0.2)
Minority status of individual	46.5	45.3	0	0	1.2
	(100)	(97.5)	(0)	(0)	(2.5)
Household size	46.5	37.1	0.9	−0.8	9.3
	(100)	(79.8)	(2.0)	(−1.8)	(19.9)
Age group of household head	46.5	44.4	0.2	−0.2	2.1
	(100)	(95.4)	(0.5)	(−0.5)	(4.6)
Education of household head	46.5	38.5	−1.1	0	9.1
	(100)	(82.7)	(−2.3)	(0)	(19.6)
Party membership of household head	46.5	45.2	0	−0.2	1.5
	(100)	(97.1)	(0.1)	(−0.4)	(3.2)
Employment status of household head	46.5	41.0	−3.9	2.1	7.3
	(100)	(88.2)	(−8.3)	(4.5)	(15.6)
Work unit's ownership of head	46.5	32.7	−1.2	1.4	13.6
	(100)	(70.3)	(−2.5)	(3.1)	(29.2)
Occupation of head	46.5	28.2	1.6	−0.2	16.9
	(100)	(60.7)	(3.4)	(−0.3)	(36.3)

A first, uncontroversial result is that income inequality increased. The increase is large by contemporary standards. We report that the Gini coefficient of equivalent income increased from 0.386 to 0.462. Further, the growth of Chinese income inequality is rather general and not limited to a particular region or population group. (See Appendix 3.1 and 3.2 on pages 76–79.)

A rather large proportion of Chinese income inequality is due to location. The urban to rural income gap is great and has widened. However, inequality within urban China and particularly within rural China has also widened, and therefore in the middle of the 1990s a somewhat reduced proportion of inequality in China as a whole can be attributed to the rural to urban income gap. Although part of this gap can be ascribed to different characteristics of the two groups—for example, to the urban population being more highly educated and living in smaller households—most of it cannot be attributed to such differences at the household level.

Households situated in the better-off eastern part of China have on average experienced a much larger income growth than households living elsewhere. At the other extreme, the income of low-income people in the west might even have decreased. Linked to the west's difficulties is the relative underdevelopment of the income of minorities, who are located disproportionately in the rural parts of western China. While starting small, a growing proportion of Chinese inequality can be attributed to differences in mean income between east, middle, and west China. The incomes of people having the same personal characteristics are increasingly differentiated according to which of the three regions they reside in.

The relation between education and income in China has become stronger. Income of the growing numbers of more highly educated has increased rapidly, while the declining population with very limited education has experienced a slow development in average income as well as a rapid increase in income inequality. However, much of the relation between education and income is due to where the person lives and works and to the size of household, not to education, per se.

For the increased proportion of small households income has increased most rapidly. The decreasing proportion of large households has had a less favorable development in average income. Also, differences in income due to age have increased, as have differences between households with and without party members. However, very little of the increase in income inequality in China as a whole can be attributed to these widening differences.

We have found many reasons for answering yes to the question in our chapter title, "A more unequal China?" There is, however, one exception. Differences in equivalent income between men and women have not grown. The reason for this is that in China there are very few households with only one man or one woman. However, the reader should remember that we have assumed that in all households income is evenly distributed among the members.

Appendix 3.1

Mean Equivalent Income, Education of Population, and Inequality of Subgroups: by Characteristics of Head of Household

Variable	1995				1988			
	Mean income	Share of sample	MLD	Theil	Mean income	Share of sample	MLD	Theil
Age 16–25	1,360	0.011	335.1	330.0	1,041	0.036	251.7	257.8
Age 26–35	1,536	0.195	358.7	361.2	1,097	0.201	263.3	257.8
Age 36–45	1,789	0.354	355.1	352.8	1,104	0.338	236.4	234.3
Age 45–55	1,924	0.280	386.0	382.7	1,253	0.278	257.6	248.9
Age 56–65	2,272	0.124	418.5	384.9	1,243	0.117	293.5	284.9
Age 66–	2,039	0.036	335.0	314.3	1,217	0.029	281.3	272.3
4-year college	4,203	0.026	152.4	156.0	2,432	0.023	91.2	104.0
2–3-year college	3,693	0.044	166.3	182.9	1,936	0.024	140.8	115.1
Technical	2,979	0.056	190.3	166.4	1,842	0.038	159.0	143.2
Upper-middle	2,100	0.145	331.1	312.5	1,405	0.119	256.5	240.2
Lower-middle	1,690	0.382	345.0	351.9	1,193	0.315	245.4	237.2
Primary	1,388	0.253	361.1	399.7	993	0.295	223.8	233.3
Less-primary	1,094	0.094	313.4	351.8	823	0.186	218.3	226.0
Party-member	2,615	0.202	331.8	311.3	1,589	0.210	218.6	204.1
Nonparty-member	1,646	0.798	366.6	369.9	1,047	0.790	249.2	250.0
Working	1,760	0.905	375.8	377.6	1,149	0.936	254.6	250.2
Pensioner	3,496	0.055	139.9	142.3	944	0.004	187.9	194.1
Unemployee	2,084	0.001	240.6	211.9	0	0.000	0.0	0.0
Housewife	1,216	0.014	285.1	299.5	945	0.004	153.7	155.8
Disabled	1,190	0.005	214.6	228.3	777	0.003	226.8	246.0

Other	1,595	0.020	431.4	472.7	1,429	0.053	308.5	278.8
State-owned	3,379	0.103	181.1	183.9	2,156	0.108	105.4	114.5
Local-public	3,390	0.148	124.9	134.0	1,946	0.109	100.6	95.7
Collective	2,757	0.045	196.9	190.8	1,678	0.066	185.9	176.8
Private	1,797	0.041	305.8	325.3	1,181	0.026	246.9	234.5
Foreign	3,388	0.002	310.3	291.2	4,393	0.001	197.0	142.6
Farm	1,092	0.620	273.1	314.4	769	0.639	166.0	166.7
Other	2,667	0.041	309.6	326.4	1,555	0.052	231.2	217.4
Owner	2,068	0.032	295.3	312.3	1,366	0.016	228.4	209.3
Professional	3,747	0.067	141.6	151.4	2,124	0.046	105.7	102.8
Manager	4,088	0.016	130.2	145.6	2,166	0.024	123.6	113.2
Branch-manager	3,417	0.040	211.8	217.4	2,170	0.012	198.1	190.9
Office worker	3,305	0.058	134.3	148.6	2,010	0.075	123.6	124.2
Skilled worker	2,935	0.065	151.6	151.6	{ 1,777	0.163	143.1	144.7
Unskilled worker	2,751	0.087	213.2	207.6				
Rural cadre	1,759	0.030	243.8	255.2	1,182	0.022	228.2	221.3
Farmer	1,074	0.606	271.8	314.2	774	0.642	170.0	172.4

Notes: (1) Private includes self-employed. (2) Foreign includes joint-venture firms. (3) Owner means owner of private firm or self-employment. (4) There is no classification between skilled and unskilled workers in the 1988 sample.

Appendix 3.2

Mean Equivalent Income, Shares of Population, and Inequality of Subgroups: by Characteristics of Individuals

Variable	1995				1988			
	Mean income	Share of sample	MLD	Theil index	Mean income	Share of sample	MLD	Theil index
Rural	1,218	0.719	307.4	358.8	822	0.741	184.4	188.4
Urban	3,439	0.281	125.8	136.6	2,131	0.259	88.7	98.5
East	2,508	0.364	354.2	344.7	1,449	0.389	251.9	247.7
Middle	1,486	0.376	287.1	285.0	1,011	0.385	217.2	201.2
West	1,423	0.260	408.4	396.1	920	0.226	252.9	255.6
East-rural	1,786	0.260	317.4	350.6	1,044	0.287	188.1	193.8
Mid-rural	981	0.274	185.5	207.5	708	0.272	151.2	141.5
West-rural	770	0.185	233.0	289.1	641	0.182	134.7	130.5
East-urban	4,322	0.104	137.7	146.7	2,587	0.102	89.8	100.9
Mid-urban	2,841	0.102	92.9	93.4	1,744	0.113	59.9	64.3
West-urban	3,032	0.075	84.1	91.0	2,065	0.044	64.8	67.0
Male	1,851	0.506	380.8	376.2	1,163	0.503	257.5	253.1
Female	1,833	0.494	376.0	364.0	1,158	0.497	259.1	253.5
Minority	1,227	0.068	393.5	413.1	890	0.068	262.0	271.5
Non-minority	1,887	0.932	371.7	366.4	1,181	0.932	255.6	250.0
Age 0–7	1,397	0.083	350.1	353.0	976	0.108	254.7	252.9
Age 8–15	1,563	0.153	356.1	363.1	1,025	0.169	233.5	237.8
Age 16–25	1,696	0.191	363.4	374.2	1,096	0.223	241.7	237.9
Age 26–35	1,732	0.145	365.4	359.6	1,212	0.135	266.1	256.3
Age 36–45	2,027	0.183	349.0	335.4	1,233	0.147	239.1	229.9
Age 46–55	2,203	0.130	389.5	374.9	1,423	0.106	268.4	253.4

Age 56–65	2,435	0.069	413.4	365.6	1,375	0.061	290.7	276.2
Age 66–	1,874	0.046	384.1	381.6	1,158	0.041	266.1	261.5
1–person	3,325	0.001	400.1	355.1	2,057	0.002	293.7	269.5
2–person	3,615	0.046	294.1	259.5	2,231	0.024	239.4	209.2
3–person	2,744	0.252	263.2	238.1	1,829	0.147	172.8	159.2
4–person	1,692	0.304	346.0	365.9	1,316	0.245	236.5	221.2
5–person	1,270	0.220	299.0	327.3	1,023	0.232	226.5	232.5
6–person	1,095	0.109	306.1	327.8	856	0.165	201.3	197.4
7–person and over	982	0.068	280.6	295.3	727	0.186	163.4	164.1
Working	1,886	0.595	380.6	376.6				
Pensioner	3,795	0.040	136.1	143.0				
Unemployed	2,406	0.007	208.7	201.1				
Houseworking	1,355	0.041	315.0	338.3				
Student	1,673	0.206	349.1	349.9				
Pre-school	1,404	0.059	365.9	371.5				
Disabled	1,225	0.013	290.9	310.3				
Other	1,326	0.040	342.6	372.9				

Notes

This work has been financially supported by the Swedish Council for Research in the Humanities and Social Sciences and the Swedish Council of Social Research. An earlier version of the chapter was presented at the Workshop of Income Distribution in China, Beijing, August 1997, and we thank participants for useful comments.

1. For a more extensive discussion see, for example, Kojima (1995).

2. See Khan et al. (1992) and Zhu Ling (1994) who studied nonagriculture income, and Gustafsson and Li (1997) who studied money income.

3. Gustafsson and Li (1997) showed that in 1988 public sector transfers, while decreasing inequality within urban China, increased income inequality in China as a whole.

4. The figures might overestimate real development due to migration. In Chinese statistics, migrants are usually included in the population of the provinces of origin, not in the provinces of destination. Moreover migrants' remittances are included in total GDP for the provinces of destination, not the provinces of origin. However, it is difficult to have a view on the size of the bias.

5. More information on the first survey can be found in Eichen and Zhang (1993) and on the second survey in Khan and Riskin (1998).

6. See, for example, Gottschalk and Smeeding (1997) or Gottschalk, Gustafsson, and Palmer (1997).

7. The question in the urban questionnaire was phrased: "If you could rent out your house or apartment, estimate the rent per month."

8. Our definition is very similar to the one used by Khan et al. (1993). The only difference concerns on which housing-value imputed rents in the rural sample are based, as a present market value is not recorded in the questionnaire. We used the original values as reported by the respondents, while Khan et al. (1993) applied an algorithm to arrive at present values. Thus our variable disposable income has a somewhat lower mean value.

9. The birth rate decreased from 2.24 percent in 1988 to 1.71 percent in 1995.

10. One might ask how our estimates of Gini coefficients relate to those based on household income unadjusted for household size. The answer is that the strong increase in inequality is also clearly shown in that case as well. However, the increase in rural China is somewhat smaller than our findings, while the reverse is true for urban China. The Gini coefficient for China as a whole presented in Table 3.8 is higher than for unadjusted household income. The estimates of Gini coefficients for household income are as follows for 1988/1995: China as a whole 34.61/41.86, rural China 34.89/42.46, and urban China 23.93/27.55.

11. Comparing Khan et al. (1993) and Khan and Riskin (1998), one finds an urban to rural income gap increasing as little as from 1:2.42 in 1985 to 1:2.47. Khan and Riskin (1998) report the following Ginis for 1988/1995: China as a whole, 38.2/45.2; urban China, 23.3/33.2; rural China, 33.8/41.6.

Our point estimates of inequality can be supposed to depend on choice of equivalence scale. To investigate this we made a sensitivity analysis (for rural China 1995) by varying the parameter γ defined in a note to Table 3.3 as measuring efficiency in consumption. It turns out that varying γ affects the estimate only marginally. Thus for γ equal to 0.1 the Gini is 42.0 percent, and it decreases for increasing values of γ down to 41.7 (when γ equals 0.3 to 0.5) to increases up to 42.7 (when γ equals 1.0).

12. Gottschalk and Smeeding (1997) survey the literature. Johnson and Webb (1993) report increases in Gini coefficients from 23.81 in 1979 to 31.04 in 1988. Expressed as a difference, this is smaller than that experienced by China as a whole (7.23 percentage points compared with 7.61 for China, but for a period of nine years). However, in percentage terms the increase in China as a whole was smaller.

13. According to Doyle (1996), the Gini for Russia (household income per household) jumped from 22.8 percent in March 1992 to 32.0 in August 1992, while other changes during 1992 were much smaller. However, when interpreting those numbers, one should keep in mind that they are based on official data that can be questioned because of sampling problems and undercoverage.

14. See for example Halvorsen and Palmquist (1980).

15. In Chapter 8 we show that the gender earnings gap in urban China has increased somewhat from 1988 to 1995.

16. Li and Zhang (1998) and Meng and Wu (1998); see also Liu (1998).

17. The ownership status of family farms in China is ambiguous. Farmers have long-term use rights to their land, but cannot freely buy or sell land, which is still regarded as owned by the state or collective. Hence, "family farm" is given its own ownership status, along with state-owned, private, foreign, and so forth.

18. The World Bank (1997) p. 16 shows that the proportion of total inequality attributed to the difference in mean income between rural and urban areas is rather sensitive to how disposable income is defined. Thus by applying various assumptions for 1990, the percentage changes from 21 percent to 52 percent. In the results highlighted in the publication, the "between" components are considerably greater than what we are reporting. Similarly, larger proportions of the changes in total inequality between years are attributed to the between-groups component than in our study.

19. Here is one of the few examples where choice of the inequality index is critical to the conclusion. According to the MLD, the increase is large, while it is very small when applying the Theil index. The reader should also remember that intrahousehold distribution is assumed equal—everyone in a household is assumed to get the household average per capita equivalent income. Further, we have computed equivalent income for one specific equivalence scale.

20. See, for example, Mookherjee and Shorrocks (1982), Tsakloglou (1993), or Jenkins (1995).

References

Aaberge, R., and Li, X. (1997) "The Trend in Urban Income Inequality in Two Chinese Provinces, 1986–1990," *Review of Income and Wealth*, 43, 335–355.

Chen, S., and Ravallion, M. (1996) "Data in Transition: Assessing Rural Living Standards in Southern China," *China Economic Review*, 7, 23–56.

Cheng, Y. (1996) "A Decomposition Analysis of Income Inequality of Chinese Rural Households," *China Economic Review*, 7, 155–167.

Doyle, C. (1996) "The Distributional Consequences During the Early Stages of Russia's Transition," *Review of Income and Wealth*, 42, 493–505.

Eichen, M., and Zhang, M. (1993) "The 1988 Household Sample Survey—Data Description and Availability" in Griffin, K., and Zhao, R. (eds.) *The Distribution of Income in China*, London: Macmillan.

Gottschalk, P., Gustafsson, B., and Palmer, E. (1997) *Changing Patterns in The Distribution of Economic Welfare: An International Perspective*, Cambridge: Cambridge University Press.

Gottschalk, P., and Smeeding, T. (1997) "Cross National Comparisions of Earnings and Income Inequality," *Journal of Economic Literature*, 35, 633–687.

Gustafsson, B., and Li, S. (1997) "Types of Income and Inequality in China at the End of the 1980s," *Review of Income and Wealth*, 43, 211–226.

Gustafsson, B., and Li, S. (1998) "Inequality in China at the End of the '80s–Locational Aspects and Household Characteristics," *Asian Economic Journal*, 12, 35–63.

Halvorsen, R., and Palmquist, R. (1980) "The Interpretation of Dummy Variables in Semi-logarithmic Equations," *American Economic Review*, 70, 474–475.

Jenkins, S. (1995) "Accounting for Inequality Trends: Decomposition Analysis for the UK, 1971–86," *Economica*, 62, 29–63.

Jian, T., Sachs, J., and Warner, A. (1996) "Trends in Regional Inequality in China," *China Economic Review*, 7, no. 2, 1– 21.

Johnson, P. and Webb, S. (1993) "Explaining the Growth in UK Income Inequality: 1979–1988," *Economic Journal*, 103, 429–435.

Khan, A.R., Griffin, K., Riskin, C., and Zhao, R. (1992) "Household Income and its Distribution in China," *China Quarterly*, 132, 1029–1061.

Khan, A.R., Griffin, K., Riskin, C., and Zhao, R. (1993) "Sources of Income Inequality in Post-Reform China," *China Economic Review*, 4, 19–35.

Khan, A. R. and Riskin, C. (1998) "Income Inequality in China: Composition, Distribution and Growth of Household Income, 1988 to 1995," *China Quarterly,* 154, 221–253.

Knight, J., and Song, L. (1993) "The Spatial Contribution of Income Inequality in Rural China," *Cambridge Journal of Economics*, 17, 195–213.

Kojima, R. (1995) "Urbanization in China," *The Developing Economies*, 33, 121–154.

Li, T., and Zhang, J. (1998) "Returns to Education Under Collective and Household Farming in China," *Journal of Developing Economics*, 26, 338–357.

Liu, Z. (1998) "Earnings, Education, and Economic Reforms in Urban China," *Economic Development and Cultural Change*, 697–725.

Lyons, T. (1991) "Interprovincial Disparities in China: Output and Consumption, 1952–1987," *Economic Development and Cultural Change*, 39, 471–506.

Meng, X., and Wu, H. (1998) "Household Income Determination and Regional Income Determination in Rural China," *Asian Economic Journal*, 12, no. 1, 65–88.

Mookherjee, D., and Shorrocks, A.F. (1982) "A Decomposition of the Trend in UK Income Inequality," *Economic Journal*, 92, 886–902.

Riskin, C. (1993) "Income Distribution and Poverty in Rural China" in Griffin, K. and Zhao, R. (eds.) *The Distribution of Income in China*, London: Macmillan.

Rozelle, S. (eds.) "Rural Industrialization and Increasing Inequality: Emerging Patterns in China's Reform Economy," *Journal of Comparative Economics*, 19, 362–391.

Shorrocks, A.F. (1983) "Ranking Income Distributions," *Economica*, 50, 3–17.

State Statistical Bureau (1995) *China Statistical Yearbook, 1995*, Beijing: China Statistical Publishing House.

State Statistical Bureau (1996) *China Regional Economy: A Profile of 17 Years of Reform and Opening-up,* Beijing: China Statistical Publishing House.

Tam, M-Y, and Zhang, R. (1996) "Ranking Income Distributions: The Tradeoff between Efficiency and Equality," *Economica*, 63, 239–52.

Tsakloglou, P. (1993) "Aspects of Inequality in Greece," *Journal of Development Economics*, 40, 53–74.

Tsui, K.Y. (1993) "Decomposing of Chinas Regional Inequalities," *Journal of Comparative Economics*, 17, 600–627.

Tsui, K. Y. (1996) "Economic Reform and Interprovincial Inequality in China," *Journal of Development Economics*, 50, 353–368.

Tsui, K.Y. (1998) "Factor Decomposition of Chinese Rural Inequality: New Methodology, Empirical Findings, and Policy Implications," *Journal of Comparative Economics*, 26, 502–528.

World Bank (1997) *Sharing Rising Incomes*, China 2020 Series, Washington DC: World Bank.

Yao, S. (1997) "Industrialization and Spatial Income Inequality in Rural China, 1986–92," *Economics of Transition,* 5, 97–112.

Zhu, L. (1994) "The Impact of Growth of Non-agricultural Income on Income Distribution in Rural China" in Zhao Renwei and Keith Griffin (eds.) *Studies on Income Distribution of Households in China*, Beijing: Press of Chinese Social Sciences (in Chinese).

4

Economic Growth, Economic Reform, and Rising Inequality in China

John Knight and Lina Song

Introduction

Rising income inequality in many countries is "bringing income distribution in from the cold" as a research topic (Atkinson, 1997, p. 297). In the United Kingdom, for instance, the Gini coefficient of inequality in household income per equivalent adult rose by 9 percentage points, from 25 to 34 percent, between 1979 and 1991, or by 0.75 percentage points per annum (Goodman and Webb, 1994, p. A3). China has similarly undergone an increase in income inequality. The Gini coefficient of household income per capita rose by 7 percentage points, from 38 to 45 percent, between 1988 and 1995, or by 1.0 percentage points per annum. This rising inequality in China, as in many other countries, deserves explanation.

In the United States "a large descriptive literature has documented the rise in inequality, while a smaller behavioral literature has sought to delineate the causes of this rise" (Gottschalk, 1997, p. 21). Although inequality has grown both at the household and at the individual level, the literature has focused on wage inequality. It is more difficult to model inequality at the household level—involving as it does interaction among household members—but it is more directly relevant to economic welfare. Our concern in this chapter is with the inequality of both household income per capita and individual wages; our emphasis is on explanation rather than description.

The weight of empirical evidence for developed countries suggests that the rising inequality of wages is demand-driven: Technical progress has favored skilled labor in production, and the supply of skills has not kept pace with the rising demand (Topel, 1997, p. 72). This is an explanation of movement from one market equilibrium to another. In China, by contrast, there has been movement from market disequilibrium toward equilibrium. There are two obvious explanations for the rise in income inequality in China: economic growth and economic reform policies. Over the seven years from 1988 to1995, real GDP in China nearly doubled, growing by 88 percent. This rapid growth was inevitably accompanied by much structural change in the economy. Over the same period, economic reforms—which had begun in the late 1970s—proceeded rapidly, with the diminution of physical planning, the decentralization of decision making, the creation and liberalization of factor and product markets, and the move toward market prices. We wish to distinguish the relative contributions of growth and of reform policies to rising inequality. However, this can be done only in a proximate sense because economic reforms contributed to economic growth and economic growth encouraged and permitted economic reforms.

Economists studying income distribution in poor countries have been much drawn to the Kuznets hypothesis (Kuznets, 1955). This is the notion that, as an economy develops, income inequality initially increases but eventually peaks and thereafter declines. An increase can occur because of the enclave nature of initial economic development: the relative expansion of the small, high-income sector raises the inequality index. Moreover, there may be greater inequality in the high-income than in the low-income sector. Eventually the further relative expansion of the high-income group lowers the inequality index, and intersectoral transfer depresses the sectoral income gap that contributes to inequality. Thus beyond a certain point, the equalizing forces may outweigh the disequalizing forces, and inequality declines.

There has been much empirical testing of the Kuznets hypothesis, using cross-sectional and time-series data. The data sets and methodologies are of varied quality. In their survey of this topic, Anand and Kanbur questioned the theoretical basis of the inverted-U shape (1993a) and, after an exhaustive set of tests, concluded that the inverse-U hypothesis is not supported by the evidence (1993b, pp. 41–42). Economic development may well affect inequality but there appears to be no stable relationship across countries: initial conditions and government policies are important. Kanbur (1997, p. 84) accordingly argued that individual country case studies, over time—which examined the various influences on inequality, including government policies—would provide a richer and more informative explanation of the relationships between development and inequality. We adopt this approach by examining the growth in inequality in China between 1988 and 1995. We draw on the 1988 and 1995 national surveys of household incomes that provide the principal empirical foundation for the studies in this book.

The Rise in Rural Inequality

We exploit the fact that each Chinese province (with a mean population of 41 million in 1995) is equivalent in size to a substantial country elsewhere in the developing world. Our cross-province analysis is therefore like a cross-country analysis. Where I_{jt} is an index of income inequality in province j in year t, we analyze the relationship between inequality and constant price income per capita Y_{jt}, using various functional forms. For instance, we can estimate a cross-section for each year:

$$I_j = a + b\, Y_j + c\, Y_j^2 + u_j \tag{4.1}$$

Here the coefficients b and c reflect the influence of income level on inequality. Alternatively, we can pool the samples and, where D_1 is a dummy variable indicating that $t = 1$ ($t = 0$ being the omitted category), estimate

$$I_{jt} = a + b\, Y_{jt} + c\, Y_{jt}^2 + d\, D_1 + u_{jt} \tag{4.2}$$

The coefficients b and c again show how income affects inequality. The residual influence, associated with the passage of time but arguably reflecting the effect of the economic reforms, is shown by the coefficient d.

Table 4.1 shows cross-section estimates of equation (4.1), using the Gini coefficient of income per capita, for the nineteen provinces common to the two rural samples. Over our period the average value of the Gini coefficient rose from 29.6 to 37.6 percent, that is, by 8.0 percentage points. In both cases the curve is slightly U-shaped but the curvature is not statistically significant. The simple linear relationship is therefore also shown. In both years the relationship is upward sloping, but significantly so only in 1995. We pose the counterfactual question: What is the effect on inequality in each year of substituting the mean income per capita of the other year? Using first the 1988 equation and then the 1995 equation, the difference in the Gini coefficient that is attributable to income is 0.8 and 1.2 percentage points respectively. On this basis the growth in income can account for no more than 15 percent of the growth in inequality.

Table 4.2 shows the estimate based on equation (4.2), using the pooled sample, where the dummy variable D_1 represents 1995 observations. The pooled sample generates an inverted U-shaped curve, but again the curvature is not significant; a linear specification is therefore also shown. A set of province dummy variables is added to both equations. By thus allowing for fixed effects, we obtain a better estimate of the independent effect of time. The coefficient on D_1 is positive and significant, having values ranging from 6.8 to 7.9. Standardizing for income, the Gini coefficient was thus considerably higher in 1995 than in 1988. Again, the growth in income can explain no more than 15 percent of the growth in inequality, and since none of the income terms is significantly different from zero, the growth of income may contribute nothing at all.

Knight, Li, and Zhao in Chapter 6 below have found evidence of cross-province convergence in intraprovince inequality for the urban samples of the 1988 and 1995 surveys. Is similar convergence to be found in the rural samples? To answer this question we estimate the equation

Table 4.1

The Cross-Section Relationship between the Gini Coefficient of Household Income per Capita and Household Mean Income per Capita in 1995 prices, by Province in Rural China, 1988 and 1995

	1988		1995	
	Curvilinear	Linear	Curvilinear	Linear
Intercept	31.139**	26.863***	38.103***	32.386***
Income (Y)	−0.003	0.002	−0.003	0.003**
Income squared (Y^2)	0.000006		0.000001	
Adj. R^2	−0.061	−0.006	0.201	0.028
F-value	0.486	0.898	3.266*	5.810**
Mean value of G	29.468	29.468	37.588	37.588
Mean value of Y	1,612.059	1,612.059	2,080.842	2,080.842
Number of provinces	19	19	19	19

Notes: The dependent variable in each case is the Gini coefficient (G), expressed as a percentage. * denotes significance at the 10 percent, ** at the 5 percent, and *** at the 1 percent level. The 1988 incomes are adjusted by the increase in the rural consumer price index over the period 1988–1995 (by 120.09 percent).

Table 4.2

The Cross-Section Relationship between the Gini Coefficient of Household Income per Capita and Household Mean Income per Capita in 1995 Prices, by Province in Rural China, Pooled 1988 and 1995 Sample

	Without province dummies		With province dummies	
	Curvilinear	Linear	Curvilinear	Linear
Intercept	26.663***	27.922***	34.831***	36.708***
Income (Y)	0.002	0.001	0.0001	−0.0008
Income squared (Y^2)	−0.0000002		−0.0000001	
1995 observation (D_1)	7.415***	6.889***	7.906***	7.770***
Adj. R^2	0.388	0.402	0.500	0.528
F-value	8.819***	13.447***	2.759**	3.069**
Mean of G	33.301	33.301	33.301	33.301
Mean of Y	1,846.371	1,846.371	1,846.371	1,846.371
Number of observations	38	38	38	38

Notes: The dependent variable is the Gini coefficient, expressed as a percentage. *** denotes statistical significance at the 1 percent and ** at the 5 percent level. The 1988 incomes are adjusted by the increase in the rural consumer price index over the period 1988–1995 (by 120.09 percent). The omitted category (D_0) is a 1988 observation. The last two columns report results of equations containing eighteen unreported province dummies that are significant as a set, but only a few are significantly different from the omitted province, Jiangsu.

$$I_{j1} - I_{j0} = a + b\,I_{j0} + u_{ji} \tag{4.3}$$

for the nineteen provinces common to the two rural samples (Table 4.3). The estimate indicates powerful and statistically significant convergence. For instance, if the Gini coefficient of a province was 10 percentage points lower in 1988, the subsequent increase in the Gini would be higher by 6.4 percentage points.

The evidence of Tables 4.1 and 4.2 suggests that rural inequality rose substantially in the provinces of China for reasons other than the growth of income. If this increase is not due to economic growth as reflected in rising incomes, the other likely explanation is economic reform policies and their effects. Table 4.3, showing that initial high inequality curbs its subsequent rise, also points the finger of suspicion at economic reforms. It is possible that those provinces that had introduced rural economic reforms earlier, or had responded to those reforms earlier, reported higher inequality in 1988. The late starters, by contrast, still had low income inequality in 1988 but experienced larger increases in inequality over the subsequent seven years.

In order to explore and isolate the role of economic reform policies and their effects, we need to have proxy measures for the extent of rural economic reform in a province. We also need to include other possible determinants of inequality that are unrelated to reform policies. One of the most important rural reforms was to permit and encourage rural industrialization. Knight and Song (1993, 1997) have shown that nonagricultural development tends to raise rural income inequality. Accordingly, we introduce the degree of nonagricultural development—measured by $\pi = Y_n / Y$, where Y_n is household nonagricultural income per capita and Y the equivalent total income—as an explanatory variable. It is generally considered that the coastal provinces (C_1) proceeded faster and further with their rural economic reforms. We introduce C_1 as a proxy for greater reform and marketization. We also take account of the sheer size of a province, as measured by population (P), as larger size can mean greater diversity and weaker internal mobility of resources.

Our extended equation is therefore:

$$I_{ji} = a + b\,Y_{ji} + c\pi_{ji} + dC_{ij} + e\,P_{ji} + u_{ji}. \tag{4.4}$$

The coefficients c and e are expected to be positive, whereas d<or>0 as the effect of greater reform and marketization is ambiguous: The response to profitable new opportunities can raise inequality but greater resource mobility can lower it.

The results for 1988 and 1995 are very similar (Table 4.4.) The dummy variable representing the coastal region has a high and significant coefficient. In both years the coastal provinces have Gini coefficients about 7.5 percentage points higher than the interior provinces, other things being equal. The introduction of this regional dummy turns the coefficient on income per capita slightly negative. The two variables are collinear but the regional dummy appears to be a better discriminator. This could reflect the greater extent and success of the rural reforms in the

Table 4.3

Testing for Cross-Province Convergence in Intraprovince Inequality, Rural China, 1988–1995

	Increase in Gini coefficient
Intercept	26.330**
Initial inequality (G_0)	−0.640**
Adj. R^2	0.148
F-value	4.116*
Mean of dependent variable (ΔG)	7.738
Number of observations	19

Notes: The dependent variable is the change in the Gini coefficient of household income per capita in each province ($\Delta G = G_1 - G_0$). * denotes statistical significance at the 10 percent and ** at the 5 percent level.

coastal provinces. The coefficient on the share of nonagricultural income is positive, as expected, but not statistically significant. A 10 percent higher share would raise the Gini coefficient by 3.2 percent in 1988 and by only 0.6 percent in 1995. Contrary to expectations, larger provinces have lower inequality, but the effect is neither significant nor substantial.

Our other exercise is to explain the change in inequality over the seven years. We consider the same proxy variables as before. The relative increase in nonagricultural income ($\Delta \pi$) is hypothesized to raise the growth of inequality. C_1 might equally well represent the pace of reform and marketization over the period, as its extent. It is appropriate to enter the population term as a rate of growth ($\Delta p = \ln P_1 - \ln P_0$), reflecting the possible depressing effect on some household incomes of expanding population with limited resources (Howes and Hussain, 1994). We also include ($\Delta y = y_1 - y_0$, where y_i is the logarithm of income per capita in year i, as the dynamic income term. Finally, we include I_0, the initial value of inequality, to test for "conditional convergence," that is to discover whether our additional variables can fully explain the convergence found in Table 4.4. The interprovince equation is therefore:

$$I_{j1} - I_{j0} = a + b\Delta \pi_j + c\, C_{1j} + d\Delta\, p_j + e\Delta y_j + fI_{j0} + u_j \qquad (4.5)$$

The estimated equation is presented in Table 4.5. The coastal region dummy raises the growth in inequality by 6 percentage points, and the coefficient on income growth is negative. Faster growth of population raises the growth in inequality. For instance, 10 percent faster growth over the 7 years increases ΔI_j by some 7 percentage points. This suggests that the one-child family policy may have been important in containing the growth in inequality. However, none of these coefficients is statistically significant.

The only significant coefficient is that on initial inequality: an initial Gini coef-

Table 4.4

Explaining Interprovince Inequality in Rural China, 1988–1995

	Mean value		Coefficient	
	1988	1995	1988	1995
Intercept			31.669**	*38.348***
Income per capita (Y)	1,612.059	2,080.842	–0.004*	–0.001
Percentage of nonagricultural income (π)	10.163	14.184	0.323	0.059
Coastal region (C_1)	0.316	0.316	7.410***	7.802
Population of province (P)	47.973	48.669	–0.033	–0.058
Adj. R^2	0.305	0.303		
F-value			2.973**	2.959**
Mean of dependent variable (G_j)	29.468	37.588		
Number of observations	19	19		

Notes: The dependent variable is the Gini coefficient of rural household income per capita in each province (G_j). *** denotes statistical significance at the 1 percent, ** at the 5 percent, and * at the 10 percent level. Income per capita in 1988 is expressed in 1995 prices. The coastal region is defined to comprise Beijing, Liaoning, Jiangsu, Zhejiang, Shandong, and Guangdong. In the absence of data on rural population in 1988, the total population (in millions) of the province is used in both years.

Table 4.5

Explaining the Change in Interprovince Inequality in Rural China, 1988–1995

	Mean value	Coefficient
Intercept		29.320**
Proportionate growth of income (Δy)	0.196	–0.540
Coastal region (C_1)	0.316	6.111
Change in share of nonagricultural income ($\Delta \pi$)	4.016	0.043
Percentage growth of population (Δp)	1.226	1.543
Initial Gini coefficient (G_0)	29.611	–0.872**
Adj. R^2	0.200	
F-value	1.898	
Mean of dependent variable (ΔG)	7.380	
Number of observations	19	

Notes: The dependent variable is the change in the Gini coefficient in each province (ΔG_j). The notes of Table 4.4 again apply.

ficient that is lower by 10 percentage points raises the subsequent growth of the Gini by nearly 9 percentage points. Not only is the result of Table 4.4 confirmed but conditional convergence is slightly stronger than simple convergence. The new variables added to help explain the observed convergence in inequality across provinces have entirely failed to do so.

The Gini coefficient of income per capita rose sharply in rural China over the seven years. This occurred in almost all provinces, although the inequality of inequality among provinces declined. What happened to the inequality among provinces of mean rural income per capita? We answer this question by conducting two tests of divergence (or convergence) of the means: So-called β-divergence and σ-divergence. β-divergence is tested using the equation

$$y_1 - y_0 = a + by_0 \tag{4.6}$$

where y_i is the logarithm of province mean rural income per capita in year i ($i = 0$, 1 representing 1988 and 1995 respectively). If $b < 0$, there is convergence of the means over time; $b > 0$ indicates divergence. σ-divergence requires that the standard deviation of y_i rises ($\sigma_1 > \sigma_0$). Our results suggest divergence on both tests: The coefficient on y_0 is 0.287 (but significant only at the 15 percent level), and the standard deviation of y_i rises, from 0.306 to 0.458. The growth in rural inequality does indeed appear to have a spatial element. The underlying mechanisms of increasing spatial dispersion can be explored by means of the decomposition analyses below.

Explaining Increased Rural Inequality

Our object in this section is to explore the reasons for the increase in income inequality that occurred in the rural areas of almost all the provinces in our rural samples. Our approach is to decompose the increase in various ways. There are two main questions. First, to what extent was the increase in inequality due to changes in the sources of income and in the extent of inequality within each source? In particular, was it due to the growth of nonagricultural incomes—township, village, and private enterprise (TVP) wages, business income, and migrant wages—that had been permitted and encouraged by the rural reforms? Secondly, were changes in household structure responsible for the rise in inequality? In particular, did family planning policies and practices cause income per capita to diverge among households?

Decomposition by Income Source

The methodology involves the decomposition of the Gini coefficient into the contributions made by the various income components, using the property

$$G = \Sigma \pi_i = \Sigma u_i C_i \tag{4.7}$$

where G = the Gini coefficient of income inequality

u_i =   the ratio of the i th component of income to total income, that is, its share of the total

C_i =   the concentration ratio of the i th component of income

π_i =   the contribution of the i th component to the Gini coefficient.

The concentration curve $C_i(x)$ represents the share of component i received by the lowest x proportion of recipients of *total* income. The concentration ratio C_i is then derived from the concentration curve in exactly the same way as the Gini coefficient is derived from the Lorenz curve. The contribution made by each component of income to the Gini coefficient is given by $\pi_i = u_i C_i$.

The inequality of household income per capita in 1988 and 1995 will first be decomposed into the contributions of the various income components. The change in inequality over that period (ΔG) will then be decomposed into the changes of the component contributions:

$$G_1 - G_0 = \Sigma \pi_{i1} - \Sigma \pi_{i0} \tag{4.8}$$

where the subscripts 0, 1 refer to 1988 and 1995 respectively. Finally, a simulation exercise is conducted to answer the question, What part of the increase in inequality is due to the change in component shares, and what part to the change in component concentration ratios?

$$G_1 - G_0 = \Sigma C_{i1} (u_{i1} - u_{i0}) + \Sigma u_{i0} (C_{i1} - C_{i0}) \tag{4.9}$$

Alternatively,

$$G_1 - G_0 = \Sigma C_{i0} (u_{i1} - u_{i0}) + \Sigma u_{i1} (C_{i1} - C_{i0}) \tag{4.10}$$

where, in each case, the first term represents the effect of changes in shares and the second that of changes in concentration ratios. The underlying hypothesis is that the increasing opportunities for obtaining nonfarm income were unequally distributed and therefore contributed to the rise in rural inequality.

The inequality of household income per capita in rural China, as measured by the Gini coefficient, rose by no less than 8.6 percentage points between 1988 and 1995, from 35.4 to 44.0 percent. This increase is decomposed into the contribution of each income source in Table 4.6, and further decomposed into the contribution of the changing shares and concentration ratios of each source in Table 4.7.

Table 4.6

Rural Income Inequality: Decomposition by Income Source, 1988 and 1995

	Income share (100u_i)		Concentration ratio (100C_i)		Contribution to inequality (100π_i)		Change 1988–1995		
	1988	1995	1988	1995	1988	1995	$\Delta100\,u_i$	$\Delta100C_i$	$\Delta100\pi_i$
Wages	10.48	26.20	71.33	74.15	7.48	19.43	15.72	2.82	11.95
Income from TVPs	2.79	6.50	47.20	53.63	1.32	3.49	3.71	6.43	2.16
Household production income	80.93	62.51	28.81	29.08	23.32	18.18	18.42	0.27	–5.14
Farm		51.54		24.76		12.76			
Nonfarm		10.97		49.38		5.42			
Property income	0.20	0.52	46.96	55.84	0.09	0.2	0.32	8.88	0.20
Net public transfer	–2.07	–0.18	5.86	–596.36	–0.12	1.07	.89	602.22	1.19
Net private transfer	7.67	4.46	43.24	34.31	3.32	1.53	3.21	–8.93	–1.79
Total income	100.00	100.00	35.39	43.99	35.39	43.99	0.00	8.60	8.60

Table 4.7

The Contribution of Each Income Component to the Change in the Inequality of Rural Household Income,1988–1995, Actual and Counterfactual Simulations

		Percentage contribution of income component *i* to the change in the Gini coefficient $(100 \, \Delta \pi / \Delta G)$			
		Contribution due to change in:			
		Decomposition 1		Decomposition 2	
	Actual	C_i	u_i	C_i	u_i
Wages	139.4	3.4	135.9	8.7	130.8
Income from TVPs	25.2	2.0	23.2	4.8	20.4
Household production income	−60.0	2.5	−62.5	2.0	−62.0
Property income	2.3	0.3	2.1	0.5	1.8
Net public transfer	13.9	145.4	−131.6	12.6	1.3
Net private transfer	−20.9	−8.0	−12.9	−4.6	−16.2
Total income	100.0	145.6	−45.8	24.0	76.1

Note: Decomposition1 involves standardizing u_i on year 0 (1988) to show the contribution of the change in C_i, and C_i on year1 (1995) to show the contribution of the change in u_i; decomposition 2 involves standardizing shares on 1995 and concentration ratios on 1988.

The main contribution (12 percentage points), accounting for 139 percent of the total increase, came from individual wages. Although the concentration ratio for individual wages was very high, it barely increased over the seven years. Rather, the contribution of wages rose because the share of wages rose, from 10.5 to 26.2 percent of total income. Table 4.7 confirms that the contribution of wages was overwhelmingly due to their rising share. A very similar story can be told for individual income from TVPs. Its contribution was much smaller than that of wages (accounting for 25 percent of the increase in the Gini coefficient), but that was again almost entirely due to the growing importance of this source of income.

The share of household production income fell from 80.9 to 62.5 percent of total income. Although its low concentration ratio limited the impact on inequality, the sharp decline in the share of household production reduced inequality by 60 percent of the net increase in the Gini coefficient. The transfer from household-based to individual-based economic activities had a powerful net disequalizing effect on household income per capita. This symbol of modernization is also a harbinger of inequality.

The effect of property income was minor, basically because its share was small and remained small. Net private transfers became both equalizing and less important: Both changes reduced the contribution to inequality. Net public transfers were actually negative in both years: Local governments raised net taxes from households. The sign of C_i changed, being positive in 1988 and negative in 1995. However, the inegalitarian intervention in 1995—probably reflecting the disbursement to households of communal income, such as TVP profits, within rich villages or townships—was offset by much smaller net taxation of households.[1]

The rural sample can be divided into three categories, households with only farm income, those with both farm and nonfarm income, and those with only nonfarm income. The third category is both very small and biased: Households that have not been allocated land are excluded from our sampling frame, that is, the rural sample survey of the State Statistical Bureau. We compare the other two, farming only and mixed activity households, examining the sources of rising inequality within each group.

The Gini coefficient of the pure farmers changed very little, increasing from 35.1 to 36.2 percent (Table 4.8). The increased inequality due to production income (by 3.0 percentage points) was offset by a decline due to nonproduction income (by 1.9 percentage points). By contrast, the incomes of mixed activity households diverged: Their Gini coefficient started at roughly the same level as the farmers' (33.5 percent) but rose to 44.0 percent. The two individual income sources (wages and income from TVPs) together accounted for more (15.2 percentage points) than the total increase in inequality. Above all, the growth of wage employment opportunities is responsible for the rise in rural income inequality.

We see the importance of wage income for rural inequality in Table 4.9. The poorest 50 percent of rural households (in terms of income per capita) obtained 6 percent of wage income in 1988 and 5 percent in 1995. The top 10 percent obtained 62 and 65 percent respectively. These concentration curves generated the highest concentration ratios (71 and 74 percent respectively), the next highest being income from enterprises. Hence the important contribution of these two components to the growth in inequality as wage and TVP activities grew. The share of wages increased from 9 to 22 percent of rural income over the seven years. Clearly the growth of wage employment is crucial to the growth of rural inequality.

Decomposition by Income Group

Whereas it is possible to decompose the Gini coefficient of income inequality according to the contribution of various income components (where income is the sum of these components), it is not possible to decompose the Gini coefficient according to the contribution of various subsamples (where the sample is the sum of these subsamples). However, such between-group decomposition is possible for the Theil entropy index of inequality and for the variance of log income. Both of these inequality measures can separate inequality into within-group and between-group components.

Table 4.8

Rural Income Inequality of Farming-Only Households and Mixed Activity Households: Decomposition by Income Source, 1988 and 1995

	Income share (100 u_i)		Concentration ratio 100 C_i		Contribution to inequality (100 π_i)		Change 1988–1995		
	1988	1995	1988	1995	1988	1995	$\Delta100\,u_i$	$\Delta100\,C_i$	$\Delta100\,\pi_i$
Farming-only households									
Household production income	93.52	95.83	33.04	35.42	30.90	33.94	2.31	2.38	3.04
Property income	0.13	0.33	32.57	38.16	0.04	0.13	0.20	5.58	0.08
Net public transfer	−2.96	−1.71	8.84	−12.07	−0.26	0.21	1.25	−20.91	0.47
Net private transfer	9.31	5.55	47.28	34.80	4.40	1.93	−3.76	−12.48	−2.47
Total income	100.00	100.00	35.08	36.20	35.08	36.20	0.00	1.12	1.12
Mixed activity households									
Wages	12.31	30.48	68.13	70.17	8.39	21.39	18.17	2.03	13.00
Income from TVPs	3.32	7.73	43.49	47.58	1.44	3.68	4.41	4.09	2.23
Household production income	78.85	56.92	26.09	28.08	20.57	15.98	−21.93	1.99	−4.59
Property income	0.21	0.52	50.55	53.31	1.06	2.77	0.31	2.76	1.71
Net public transfer	−1.86	0.07	6.49	1,818.30	−1.21	1.27	1.93	1,811.81	1.39
Net private transfer	7.16	4.27	43.04	33.83	3.09	1.44	−2.89	−9.21	−1.64
Total income	100.00	100.00	43.04	44.04	33.47	44.04	0.00	10.57	10.57

Note: "Farming-only" households have no individual wage income, individual income from TVPs, or household nonfarm production income; "mixed activity" households have income from at least one of these sources.

The Theil index can be decomposed into within-group and between-group terms:

$$T = T_w + T_b \tag{4.11}$$

$$T_w = \sum_i \pi_i T_i \tag{4.12}$$

$$T_b = \sum_i \pi_i \log \tag{4.13}$$

where T_w is the average of the within-group Theil indices T_i, weighted by income shares (π_i), and T_b is the between-group Theil index, p_i being the proportion of households in group i.

Taking the variance of log income as an example, consider the uses to which the decompositions can be put:

$$V = V_w + V_b$$

$$= \sum_i p_i V_i + \sum_i p_i (x_i - x)^2 \tag{4.14}$$

where V_w is the (population-share) weighted average of within-group variances V_i, and V_b is the between-group variance of group mean values of log income (x_i).[2] In the case of the log variance measure, it is simple to distinguish between the change in inequality due to change in the within- and between-group indices and that due to change in the relative importance of the different groups. For instance, given that

$$V'_1 = \sum_i p_{io} V_{i1} + \sum_i p_{io} (x_{i1} - x_1)^2 \tag{4.15}$$

The term ($V'_1 - V_0$) represents the effect of changing within- and between-group variances, and the residual ($V_1 - V'_1$) shows the effect of changing group shares.

Over the seven years the Theil index rose by 0.176, from 0.206 to 0.382, and the log variance by 0.228, from 0.468 to 0.696. To what extent was this rise due to changes in household activities or composition? Four groupings were decomposed. In two cases (a division into farming-only, nonfarming only, and mixed activity, and a division into one-, two-, and three- or more generation households) the between-group inequality was negligible, as was its contribution to the rise in inequality. The more interesting groupings are those of households with and without sources of individual income (wages or individual businesses), and households by size (one, two, . . . eight or more members). Table 4.10 accordingly presents the decomposition of inequality into within- and between-group components in each year, and Table 4.11 the relative contributions of within- and between-group components to the rise in inequality between the two years.

Comparing households with and without individual income sources, the between-group contribution to inequality ranged from 10.7 to 14.4 percent of the total. Within-group inequality rose sharply over the seven years, especially for the group with individual incomes. The contribution of between-group inequality to the increase was therefore minor (at most 22 percent). The proportion of households with individual income sources grew from 30.3 to 51.9 percent. Rural inequality was affected by this development: Had population shares remained constant, the log variance index would have risen by 14 percent less. Nevertheless, our analysis of groups is clearly a blunter instrument than our analysis of income sources above.

Table 4.9

The Percentage Distribution of Each Income Source Among Deciles of Rural Household Income per Capita, 1988 and 1995

Share of income source accruing to each decile of households ranked by income per capita

Decile	Total income		Wage income		Individual business income	
	1988	1995	1988	1995	1988	1995
Richest	26.41	35.40	61.46	64.59	38.93	37.81
Second	15.41	15.04	14.93	13.91	13.93	19.38
Third	12.29	11.13	7.42	7.16	11.32	14.58
Fourth	10.46	9.06	5.38	4.97	8.57	7.72
Fifth	9.07	7.57	3.28	3.28	6.81	5.53
Sixth	7.88	6.42	2.96	2.37	6.94	4.77
Seventh	6.79	5.41	1.77	1.42	4.82	4.67
Eighth	5.66	4.47	1.46	1.04	2.91	2.93
Ninth	4.36	3.53	0.06	0.09	3.83	1.77
Poorest	1.68	1.96	0.08	0.04	1.93	0.08

There is a consistent empirical regularity in many countries: Household income per capita varies inversely with household size. Accordingly, changes in the mean and variance of household size can have substantial effects on the distribution of income (Lam, 1997, pp. 1032, 1053). Table 4.12 highlights the relevant features of household composition and inequality in China. In seven of the eight household sizes, within-group inequality rose sharply over time. Within-group inequality was therefore dominant: The growth of between-group inequality contributed at most only 11 percent to the total increase in inequality (Table 4.11). In 1988, 15 percent of the households had no more than three members and 42 percent no more than four. In 1995 the corresponding figures were 24 and 60 percent respectively. The main reason for the decline in household size (the mean fell from 5.0 to 4.3 members) was the delayed effects on household membership of the one-child family policy, introduced in 1979. In both years mean income per capita declines almost monotonically as household size increases. This may reflect a dependency ratio rising with size, particularly if household composition is endogenous, that is, economically insecure individuals combine to provide mutual support. In both years, also, within-group inequality of household income per capita declines almost monotonically as household size increases. This may reflect the equalizing effect of income-sharing within the household. It is predictable, therefore, that the effect of households becoming smaller was to disequalize incomes.

This effect proved to be less powerful than expected. The change in household structure on its own could explain only 8 percent of the rise in the log variance of rural household income per capita. However its effect on the mean was more pronounced. Real income per capita rose by 34.8 percent over the seven years. It would have risen only 24.4 percent had household composition remained unaltered, that is, 30 percent of the increase can be accounted for by the shrinking of rural households.

Table 4.9 *(continued)*

Share of income source accruing to each decile of households
ranked by ir   e per capita

Household production		Property income		Net public transfer		Net private transfer	
1988	1995	1988	1995	1988	1995	1988	1995
20.65	28.53	38.73	39.29	13.73	−455.95	36.66	24.77
15.72	15.47	17.31	22.07	10.64	−31.11	14.54	16.91
13.21	12.20	10.53	10.69	10.68	36.89	10.21	12.51
11.37	10.14	7.08	9.27	10.68	55.18	8.94	10.03
10.03	8.39	5.36	6.86	9.18	93.39	7.56	9.80
8.71	7.29	9.19	3.66	8.93	93.45	5.70	7.50
7.64	6.03	1.09	2.96	8.68	86.34	5.02	6.97
6.34	5.31	2.41	1.73	8.56	78.65	4.56	4.32
4.87	4.19	1.23	2.14	7.56	67.81	3.41	4.22
1.46	2.46	7.05	1.33	11.36	75.3	3.40	2.98

Table 4.10

Decomposition into Within- and Between-Group Inequality of Household Income per Capita, 1988 and 1995: Percentage Contribution

Grouping	Index	1988		1995	
		Within-group	Between-group	Within-group	Between-group
Households with and without individual incomes	Theil	88.4	11.6	87.4	12.6
	log variance	89.3	10.7	85.6	14.4
Households by size	Theil	95.3	4.7	95.0	5.5
	log variance	96.4	3.6	94.1	5.9

Table 4.11

Within- and Between-Group Percentage Contributions to the Growth in Inequality of Household Income per Capita, 1988–1995

Grouping	Index	Within-group	Between-group
Households with and without individual incomes	Theil	86.1	13.9
	log variance	78.0	22.0
Households by size	Theil	94.5	5.5
	log variance	89.4	10.6

Table 4.12

Characteristics of Rural Households by Size, 1988 and 1995

Number of household members	Percentage of sample		Mean income per capita (yuan per annum)		Log variance of income	
	1988	1995	1988	1995	1988	1995
1	0.51	0.33	983.0	2,596.5	1.359	1.325
2	2.79	4.57	903.0	2,882.9	0.568	0.753
3	11.71	19.39	919.0	2,759.0	0.499	0.751
4	26.81	35.99	776.5	2,178.4	0.478	0.677
5	25.68	23.91	701.9	1,850.7	0.467	0.563
6	16.84	10.39	647.8	1.661.0	0.377	0.630
7	8.46	3.51	583.5	1,660.2	0.396	0.539
8–	7.20	1.12	591.3	1,390.8	0.345	0.672
Total	100.00	100.00	727.3	2,158.4	0.468	0.696

Access to Individual Labor Income

We saw earlier that the most important reason for the rise in rural inequality is the greater access of households to wage employment and individual self-employment, and the high incomes that they provide. Together these activities contributed 150 percent of the total increase in the Gini coefficient. In 1988 they accounted for 13 percent of household income, and in 1995 for 33 percent. What are the characteristics that help some people—still only a minority—to grasp such employment opportunities?

We conduct a logit analysis, identical for 1988 and 1995, to investigate this question. The dependent variable is whether a worker received individual labor income, that is, local or migrant wage income, or income from nonfarm self-employment. Three types of explanatory variable are considered: Worker characteristics, household characteristics, and locational characteristics. The coefficients in the logit regressions are reported in Table 4.13, and the standardized probabilities, based on these parameters, in Table 4.14. The coefficients are generally significant, and the goodness-of-fit is high. The most important personal characteristic is the education of the worker, which greatly assists access in both years. Next most important, particularly in 1995, is being of the male gender. The fact that minority status became a handicap in 1995 also suggests increased labor market discrimination.

In both years household access to more farming land reduces the probability of wage- or self-employment. This might merely indicate that densely populated, developed areas have little land per household. It might, however, be because land scarcity pushes workers into nonfarm activities. Only in one case—the number of workers in the household—does the sign of the coefficient change significantly over time. In both years the relationship is curvilinear. In 1988 the probability rises to a peak when there are three household workers. This rise is to be expected if additional adults are freer to leave the farm or if they receive priority in TVP recruitment.

Table 4.13

The Determinants of Access to Individual Labor Income: Logit Analysis of Rural Workers, 1988 and 1995

	1988	1995
Intercept	−0.462**	−0.174
Personal variables		
Post-secondary education (E_1)	0.858**	0.677**
Upper–middle school (E_2)	0.580**	0.206**
Primary years 4–6 (E_4)	−0.521*	−0.426**
Primary years 1–3 (E_5)	−1.188**	−0.403**
Illiterate (E_6)	−1.673**	−1.574**
Male sex (S_1)	0.490**	1.085**
Minority status (M_1)	−0.061	−0.420**
Not party member (CP_2)	−0.739**	−0.015
Household variables		
Household workers (W)	0.248**	−0.234**
Household workers squared (W^2)	−0.037**	0.024**
Farming land (L)	−0.020**	−0.066**
Farming land squared (L^2)	0.00002**	0.001**
Location variables		
Suburb area (SB_1)	0.941**	0.763*
Hilly terrain (T_2)	−0.402**	0.040
Mountainous terrain (T_3)	−0.738**	−0.030
Beijing (P_1)	0.897**	0.348*
Hebei (P_2)	−1.474**	−0.792**
Shanxi (P_3)	−1.243**	−0.525**
Liaoning (P_4)	−1.451**	−1.015**
Jilin (P_5)	−2.052**	−1.633**
Zhejiang (P_7)	−0.040	1.223
Anhui (P_8)	−2.384**	−0.368**
Jiangxi (P_9)	−1.684**	−0.146
Shandong (P_{10})	−2.733**	−0.939**
Henan (P_{11})	−2.535**	−1.056**
Hubei (P_{12})	−2.176**	−1.723**
Hunan (P_{13})	−2.375**	−0.739**
Guangdong (P_{14})	−0.703**	−0.326**
Sichuan (P_{15})	−1.567**	−1.117**
Guizhou (P_{16})	−2.061**	−0.332**
Yunnan (P_{17})	−2.481**	−0.971**
Shaanxi (P_{18})	−2.055**	−0.893**
Gansu (P_{19})	−2.378**	−0.941**
Other provinces (P_{20})	−1.083	−2
Log likelihood	2,681.7**	3,523.6**
Number of observations	29,546	23,908

Notes: The dependent variable is whether the worker has individual labor income ($p = 1$). The proportion of workers with $p = 1$ is 7.4 percent in 1988 and 21.3 percent in 1995. **denotes statistical significance at the 1 percent and * at the 5 percent level. The omitted categories in the dummy variable analysis are lower-middle school (E_3), female (S_2), Han (M_2), party member (CP_1), non-suburb area (SB_2), plain terrain (T_1), and Jiangsu (P_6).

Table 4.14

The Standardized Percentage Probabilities of Access to Individual Labor Income: Logit Analysis of Rural Workers, 1988 and 1995

	1988	1995
Mean values	3.9	16.7
Post-secondary education (E_1)	14.1	36.0
Upper-middle school (E_2)	11.0	26.0
Lower-middle school (E_3)	6.5	22.2
Primary years 4–6 (E_4)	4.0	15.7
Primary years 1–3 (E_5)	2.1	16.0
Illiterate (E_6)	1.3	5.6
Male sex (S_1)	5.0	25.5
Female sex (S_2)	3.1	10.4
Minority status (M_1)	3.7	11.9
Han (M_2)	4.0	17.1
Party member (CP_1)	7.5	16.9
Not party member (CP_2)	3.7	16.6
Household workers		
($W = 1$)	3.6	20.4
($W = 2$)	4.0	18.3
($W = 3$)	4.3	16.6
($W = 4$)	4.2	15.7
Farming land		
($L = 3$ mu)	4.6	19.8
($L = 6$ mu)	4.3	17.3
($L = 9$ mu)	4.1	15.3
($L = 12$ mu)	3.9	13.8
($L = 15$ mu)	3.7	12.7
($L = 18$ mu)	3.5	11.9
Suburb area (SB_1)	9.4	29.3
Not suburb area (SB_2)	3.9	16.2
Plain terrain (T_1)	5.1	16.6
Hilly terrain (T_2)	3.5	17.2
Mountainous terrain (T_3)	2.5	16.2
Beijing (P_1)	34.0	37.1
Hebei (P_2)	4.6	15.9
Shanxi (P_3)	5.7	19.8
Liaoning (P_4)	4.7	13.1
Jilin (P_5)	2.6	7.5
Jiangsu (P_6)	17.3	29.4
Zhejiang (P_7)	16.8	32.0
Anhui (P_8)	1.9	22.4
Jiangxi (P_9)	3.7	26.5
Shandong (P_{10})	1.3	14.0
Henan (P_{11})	1.6	12.7
Hubei (P_{12})	2.3	6.9
Hunan (P_{13})	1.9	16.6
Guangdong (P_{14})	9.4	23.1
Sichuan (P_{15})	4.2	12.0
Guizhou (P_{16})	2.6	23.0
Yunnan (P_{17})	1.7	13.6
Shaanxi (P_{18})	2.6	14.6
Gansu (P_{19})	1.9	14.0

Note: The estimates are based on Table 4.13 and on mean values other than the variable in question.

In 1995 the probability falls monotonically as the number of workers rises over the relevant range. This unexpected result might reflect the endogeneity of the household, that is, adult sons form a separate household only when they are gainfully employed. Alternatively, in 1995, when more people could find nonfarm activities, workers in small households might have been less prone to engage only in farming.

The place of residence, and therefore of birth, is clearly important for access to individual labor income. Residence in suburban areas improves access, and in mountainous areas worsens it. In 1988 the probability of having individual labor income exceeded 15 percent in only three of the nineteen common provinces and was below 8 percent in fifteen provinces; in 1995 the corresponding numbers were ten and two provinces respectively.

The most important variable explaining the rise in rural inequality was the growth in the number of wage jobs and self-employment activities available to rural workers. Our analysis of household characteristics provides mixed signals as to whether these jobs were freely chosen or in effect rationed. However, since the great majority of workers have an economic incentive to take up wage employment or set up businesses, it is likely that many wanted such work but failed to obtain it. Location, productive personal characteristics, and nonproductive personal characteristics giving rise to discrimination, all contributed to the rationing process.

The Rise in Urban Inequality

In this section we apply the methods used above in the analysis of intraprovincial inequality in rural China to examine the differential growth in inequality among provinces. The analysis is based on the ten provinces common to the urban samples of 1988 and 1995. Table 4.15 presents cross-province estimates of equations (4.1) and (4.3). The coefficients on Y and Y^2 are significant and imply a U-shaped relationship in both years.

The province mean Gini coefficient rose by 4.4 percentage points, from 19.5 to 23.9 percent, over the seven years. However, that part of the change that could be attributed to the rise in income was −0.4 percentage points (using the 1995 equation). Thus none of the increase in inequality was due to economic growth in the form of rising incomes. Similarly, the pooled regressions imply that factors other than income, captured by the time dummy, accounted for 3.9 percentage points, or, allowing for province-fixed effects, for 4.8 percentage points, that is, for more than the actual increase in the mean Gini coefficient.

Again, we need to consider the effect of various proxies for reform. One such proxy is a dummy variable representing the four coastal provinces (C_1), on the assumption that urban reforms started earlier and went further in these provinces. Another is the proportion of workers employed in the nonstate sector (N), as a measure of the degree of enterprise autonomy and market freedom.

Table 4.16 shows the effects of the inclusion of these variables in the regression equations of Table 4.15. In 1995 the proxies for reform both have the expected

Table 4.15

The Cross-Section Relationship Between the Gini Coefficient of Household Income per Capita and Household Mean Income per Capita in 1995 Prices, by Province in Urban China, 1988, 1995, and Pooled

	1988	1995	Pooled	Pooled
Intercept	45.985***	46.646***	35.263***	6.054
Income (Y)	−0.012*	−0.009**	−0.007**	0.005
Income squared (Y^2)	0.000001**	0.0000008**	0.0000007	0.0000004
1995 observation (D_1)			3.931***	4.779***
Beijing				0.888
Shanxi				4.307
Liaoning				−0.831
Anhui				1.460
Henan				4.731*
Hubei				−0.599
Guangdong				9.542*
Yunnan				0.075
Gansu				−2.290
Adj. R^2	0.556	0.465	0.593	0.744
F-value	6.629**	4.910**	10.212***	5.595**
Mean of *G*	19.462	23.932	21.697	21.697
Number of provinces	10	10	20	20

Notes: The omitted categories in the dummy variable analysis are Jiangsu and 1988 observations. ***denotes statistical significance at the 1 percent, ** at the 5 percent, and * at the 10 percent level.

sign but neither coefficient is significantly different from zero. The Gini coefficient is higher in the coastal provinces, *ceteris paribus*, and if the proportion of nonstate employed rises by ten percentage points, the Gini coefficient rises by 0.6 percentage points. The contrast is with 1988: Both coefficients were then unexpectedly negative, and significantly so.

It is dangerous to build a story on a sample of ten observations and collinear explanatory variables. Nevertheless, we have a possible explanation for this puzzle. For exogenous reasons, the provinces that reformed early—the coastal provinces and those with large nonstate sectors—had lower inequality in 1988, standardizing for income level. By 1995 the economic reforms had made sufficient impact to neutralize those exogenous effects and even to reverse the inequality rankings.

Table 4.17 examines the determinants of the change in the Gini coefficient. Again we find that the initial value of the Gini (G_0) has a negative and significant effect: There is interprovince convergence in the inequality of urban income per capita over the seven years. Moreover, there is also conditional convergence: The relationship holds even when other explanatory variables are introduced. The coastal dummy (C_1) has a positive, albeit not significant, coefficient. The proportionate change in

Table 4.16

The Effect of Proxies for Economic Reform on Inequality of Household Income per Capita, Urban China, 1988, 1995

	1988		1995	
Intercept	35.650**	51.182***	49.786***	44.524**
Income (Y)	−0.008*	−0.013**	−0.010**	−0.009**
Income squared (Y^2)	0.000001**	0.000001**	0.000001**	0.000001**
Coast (C_1)	−3.449**		1.277	
Percentage of nonstate employees (N)		−0.152*		0.057
Adj. R^2	0.776	0.714	0.431	0.418
F-value	11.400***	8.504**	3.270*	3.159*
Mean of dependent variable	19.462	19.462	23.932	23.932
Number of observations	10	10	10	10

Notes: The coastal provinces (C_1) comprising Beijing, Liaoning, Jiangsu, and Guangdong; the six remaining interior provinces (C_0) are the omitted category. *** denotes statistical significance at the 1 percent, ** at the 5 percent, and * at the 10 percent level.

income also has a positive coefficient: More rapid growth is disequalizing. However, the effect is negligible and could have risen by chance. Our tentative inference, therefore, is that urban inequality grew faster in the provinces that began with lower inequality and in the more rapidly growing and reforming provinces.

Explaining Increased Urban Wage Inequality

Comparing the urban individual samples, we find that the mean real wage increased by 52 percent (6.1 percent per annum) over the period from 1988 to 1995 (Table 4.18). The table also shows what happened to the inequality of earnings over the seven years. Two types of inequality measure are used: Measures that embody all the data in one statistic (the Gini coefficient, the coefficient of variation, and the variance of log earnings) and measures of the dispersion of earnings structure (the ratios of the ninetieth and the tenth percentile, of the ninetieth to the

Table 4.17

The Determinants of the Increase in the Gini Coefficient of Household Income per Capita, by Province in Urban China, 1988–1995

Equation:	1	2	3	4
Intercept	14.074**	3.227	3.947***	12.879
Initial value of Gini (G_0)	–0.493*			–0.478
Proportionate change in income (y_1-y_0)		1.440		0.574
Coastal region (C_1)			1.308	1.021
Adj. R²	0.278	–0.118	–0.338	0.115
F-value	4.457*	0.053	0.667	1.388

Notes: *** denotes statistical significance at the 1 percent, ** at the 5 percent, and * at the 10 percent level. The mean of the dependent variable ($\Delta G = G_1-G_0$) is 4.470 and the number of observations is 10 in each case.

median, and of the median to the tenth). Not only did inequality increase on all three measures but structure widened on all three measures. Whereas the median increase in real earnings was 48 percent, the pay of the tenth percentile (the worker ranked 10 percent from the bottom) rose by only 6 percent, and that of the ninetieth percentile by 75 percent. The ratio of the ninetieth to the tenth percentile earnings rose by 66 percent; this widening was greater below the median than above it.

We estimate earnings functions of the form $Y = F(X)$ where Y is individual earnings and X is a vector of characteristics. Table 4.19 (pages 108–109) presents estimates for both 1988 and 1995, using the urban individual samples. The specifications are identical to facilitate comparisons, and earnings in both years are expressed in 1995 prices. The explanatory variables that might represent discrimination are gender, minority status, and Communist Party membership; those that might reflect segmentation are ownership and province; and the potential human capital variables are educational level, age group, and skill-based occupation.

Whether we consider the equations in levels or in logarithms, there are important differences in the coefficients for the two years. Consider the variables that might represent discrimination. The coefficient on female sex, small in 1988, became larger, while the disadvantage of minority status and the advantage of Communist Party membership increased sharply in absolute terms. It appears that the decentralization of wage setting and recruitment made it possible for employers to discriminate more on noneconomic grounds. The relative wage advantage of employees in state-owned enterprises and institutions generally increased, especially in relation to the private and individually owned sector: Only foreign-owned enterprise pay rose relative to

Table 4.18

Measures of Central Tendency and Dispersion of Earnings per Worker, 1988 and 1995, Urban China

	1988	1995	1995 minus 1988	1995 (1988=100)
Mean	4,151	6,294	2,143	152
Median	3,793	5,598	1,805	148
10th percentile	2,343	2,479	136	106
90th percentile	6,045	10,596	4,551	175
Ratio of 90th to 10th percentile	2.58	4.27	1.69	166
Ratio of 90th percentile to median	1.59	1.89	0.30	119
Ratio of median to 10th percentile	1.62	2.26	0.64	140
Gini coefficient (percent)	22.9	30.7	7.8	134
Coefficient of variation (percent)	57.2	62.2	5.0	109
Log variance	0.179	0.484	0.0305	270

state pay. This growing segmentation suggests that a large part of the urban economy remained immune to labor market forces. The spatial dispersion of wages increased considerably: The standard deviation of the province coefficients increased by 7.1 times in the equation with the dependent variable expressed in yuan, and by 2.3 times in the logarithmic equation. The growing wage segmentation among provinces was not offset by equilibrating labor mobility.

By contrast, there is also some evidence to suggest that market forces have become more important in certain respects. In particular, the returns to education rose sharply. For instance, the earnings difference between college graduates and primary school-leavers, *ceteris paribus,* was 9 percent in 1988 and 42 percent in 1995. Moreover, the coefficients of the occupation terms indicated some increase in the earnings premium on occupation-specific skills. This is best seen by comparing the omitted category, production workers, with cadres and professional and technical workers: The percentage skill premium rose from some 4 percent to 17 percent in each case. The owners, or owners and managers, of private or individual enterprises, whose importance and income might have been expected to grow over the seven years, are poorly represented in the sample, and it is likely that the more successful businesspeople did not respond, or hid income.

The age-earnings profile changed in an interesting way. The earnings of those

Table 4.19

Earnings Functions for Individual Workers in Urban China, 1988 and 1995

		Mean value		Log of earnings		Earnings (yuan per annum)	
		1988	1995	1988	1995	1988	1995
Intercept		1.000	1.000	7.939**	8.230**	3,719.296**	4,236.040**
S_2	Female sex	0.476	0.472	−0.093**	−0.148**	−391.722**	−678.328**
E_1	College or above	0.061	0.079	0.150**	0.401**	787.206**	2,315.073**
E_2	Professional school	0.067	0.156	0.099**	0.328**	498.866**	1,841.764**
E_3	Middle level professional, technical, Vocational school	0.110	0.165	0.091**	0.309**	462.503*	1,676.508
E_4	Upper–middle school	0.247	0.247	0.101**	0.251**	544.521**	1,313.461**
E_5	Lower–middle school	0.385	0.300	0.099**	0.181**	543.345**	1,068.058**
E_6	Primary school	0.104	0.048	0.064**	−0.021	430.143**	1.280
M_2	Minority status	0.038	0.047	−0.015	−0.065*	20.955	−431.696**
OW_1	State-owned	0.388	0.271	0.131**	0.239**	−491.753**	1,303.086**
OW_2	Local publicly owned	0.387	0.529	0.062*	0.072*	−817.645**	361.540*
OW_3	Urban collective	0.202	0.149	−0.017	−0.076*	−883.457**	−314.480
OW_5	Sino-foreign joint venture	0.003	0.011	0.324	0.298**	916.668**	1,449.738**
OW_6	Foreign-owned	0.001	0.001	−0.153	0.726**	−1580.072*	7,877.144**
OW_7	Other	0.005	0.006	0.148**	−0.016	−606.685*	−535.845**
A_1	–20	0.054	0.022	0.210**	−0.545**	−550.531**	1,722.617**
A_2	21–25	0.109	0.089	0.081**	−0.217**	192.271**	−942.082**
A_4	31–35	0.174	0.153	0.117**	0.152**	483.494**	629.088**
A_5	36–40	0.178	0.192	0.186**	0.233**	640.165**	1058.335**
A_6	41–45	0.128	0.199	0.272**	0.290**	1,042.170**	1,366.199**
A_7	46–50	0.123	0.117	0.314**	0.250**	1,231.403**	1,320.373**
A_8	51–55	0.077	0.069	0.334**	0.188**	1,337.380*	1,303.235**

A_9 56–60	0.034	0.040	0.336**	0.110**	1,291.234**	1,142.481**
A_{10} 61–65	0.005	0.008	0.330**	−0.635**	1,315.789**	−1,750.813**
A_{11} 66–	0.002	0.002	0.135*	−0.606**	544.076	−1,888.963**
P_{11} Beijing	0.049	0.082	0.160**	0.119	774.943**	1,046.182**
P_{14} Shanxi	0.108	0.107	−0.059**	−0.405**	−148.691*	−2,162.792**
P_{21} Liaoning	0.104	0.119	0.012**	−0.249**	11.486	−1,367.088**
P_{34} Anhui	0.099	0.081	−0.095*	−0.321**	−267.210**	−1,860.150**
P_{41} Henan	0.118	0.095	−0.149**	−0.409**	−531.744**	−2,160.304**
P_{42} Hubei	0.109	0.119	0.098**	−0.209**	−390.489**	−1,237.002**
P_{44} Guangdong	0.119	0.097	0.239**	−0.437**	1386.700**	4,292.917**
P_{53} Yunnan	0.102	0.109	0.074**	−0.216**	334.503**	−1,349.157**
P_{62} Gansu	0.066	0.063	0.005	−0.440**	−37.985	−2,411.717**
CP_1 Communist Party member	0.235	0.251	0.041**	0.086**	230.895**	515.794**
OC_1 Owner of private or individual enterprise	0.011	0.013	−0.168**	−0.063	2,063.906**	877.224**
OC_2 Owner and manager of private enterprise	0.002	0.002	0.043	0.057	543.024	−142.800
OC_3 Professional or technical worker	0.157	0.213	0.043**	0.162**	138.750*	726.628**
OC_4 Cadre	0.064	0.117	0.057**	0.155**	203.626*	929.910**
OC_5 Office worker	0.234	0.204	0.010	0.065**	13.815	268.100**
Adj. R^2			0.313	0.352	0.169	0.386
F-value			209.253**	148.812**	94.039**	171.975**
Dependent mean			8.240	8.563	4,155.569	6,295.685
Number of observations	17,830	10,627	17,830	10,627	17,830	10,627

Notes: ** denotes statistical significance at the 1 percent and * at the 5 percent level. The omitted categories in the dummy variable analysis are S_1 (male sex), M_1 (Han), E_7 (no education), OW_4 (private or individually owned), A_3 (age 26–30), P_{32} (Jiangsu province), CP_2 (not a Communist Party member), and OC_6 (production worker).

under 26 fell drastically relative to the omitted category (age 26–30). In 1995 the profile peaked earlier (at age 41–45 instead of 51–60) and fell dramatically after age 60. This is consistent with a move to a more productivity-based and a less bureaucratically based earnings structure. The age groups that suffered a relative fall were young people—lacking skills and having to compete for jobs—and older people—becoming less productive.

Using the earnings functions of Table 4.19, the growth of earnings between 1988 and 1995 can be decomposed as

$$\overline{Y}_1 - \overline{Y}_0 = F_1(\overline{X}_1 - \overline{X}_0) + (F_1 - F_0)\overline{X}_0 \tag{4.16}$$

where the first term reflects the effect of differences in characteristics and the second the effect of differences in coefficients. The alternative decomposition is

$$\overline{Y}_1 - \overline{Y}_0 = F_0(\overline{X}_1 - \overline{X}_0) + (F_1 - F_0)\overline{X}_0 \tag{4.17}$$

Decompositions of this sort can help us to understand why the average real wage rose by some 50 percent over the seven years.

Table 4.20 presents a decomposition of the growth in mean real wages over the seven years, using the two alternative decomposition formulae and the earnings functions with the dependent variable in absolute form. When the coefficients of 1988 are used to measure the effect of the change in mean characteristics, the effect is slight: 94 percent of the growth in wages is due to the change in the income-generation mechanism. Using the coefficients of 1995—when education was better rewarded—the improved characteristics of the labor force account for 18 percent of the wage increase and increased education alone for 10 percent.

The table shows that some changes in the earnings function raised the mean wage and some lowered it. The contribution of a variable or set of variables is arbitrary because the choice of omitted category in a dummy variable analysis alters the relative contributions of the intercept and the dummies. The intercept term rose by 14 percent over the seven years. That implies a relative stagnation in the pay of those possessing the characteristics of the omitted categories (uneducated, male, Han, 26–30 year old, production worker, in the private sector, in Jiangsu). This might be thought of as the unskilled market wage. It is, however, better measured as the change in all the provinces rather than in prosperous Jiangsu.[3] At the national level the unskilled market wage actually fell in real terms, by 7 percent. On the one hand, the greater discrimination against women and the fall in wages elsewhere relative to Jiangsu pulled down the wage. On the other hand, the higher returns to education can explain roughly a third of the entire increase in the wage, and the greater payment to workers in the public, collective, and foreign-owned sectors relative to the private sector can explain even more of the increase. The most interesting conclusion to be drawn from this decomposition analysis

Table 4.20

Decomposition of the Increase in Mean Real Wages: Urban China, 1988–1995

	Using coefficients of:	
	1988	1995
Percentage due to difference in:		
Coefficients	93.6	82.5
Gender	−6.3	−6.4
Education	40.2	31.2
Ownership	55.5	64.4
Province	−37.1	−35.9
Age	2.2	0.9
Mean characteristics	6.4	17.5
Education	0.7	9.7
Ownership	−0.3	−9.3
Province	0.5	−0.8
Age	4.4	7.5

Notes: The difference in mean wages (in 1995 prices) that is to be explained is 2,139.9 yuan per annum (= 100.0 percent). The decomposition is based on columns 1, 2, 5, and 6 of Table 4.19.

returns—in raising the mean real wage of urban workers between 1988 and 1995.

Owing to the potential bias arising from truncation of the subsamples, we estimate the earnings functions using maximum likelihood rather than ordinary least squares (OLS) methods. A decomposition exercise cannot be conducted because the products of characteristic mean values and maximum likelihood estimate (MLE) coefficients do not sum to the mean value of the dependent variable. It is nevertheless possible to pose economically meaningful counterfactuals. Where $i = 1, 2, 3, 4$ indicates the quarter, the change in (geometric) mean earnings attributable to the change in coefficients is

$$\hat{Y}_{i_1} - \hat{Y}_{i0} = (F_{i_1} - F_{i0})\overline{X}_{i0} \tag{4.18}$$

$$\text{or } \hat{Y}_{i_1} - \hat{Y}_{i0} = (F_{i_1} - F_{i0})\overline{X}_{i_1} \tag{4.19}$$

according to whether the 1988 or 1995 mean characteristics are employed. For instance, the counterfactual in equation (4.18) is: What would have happened to earnings by quarter had each 1988 subsample been paid according to its 1995, instead of its 1988, earnings function?

The two counterfactual exercises cannot explain much of the growing wage divergence among the quarters (Table 4.21). Both show a simulated increase of nearly one third for the bottom quarter and about one-half for the top quarter.

nearly one third for the bottom quarter and about one-half for the top quarter. Growth in labor market discrimination lowers earnings at the bottom of the earnings distribution, as does the changing wage structure by province. The omitted category, private ownership, falls relative to other categories as we move up the quarters: The changing pattern of rewards by ownership makes the largest contribution to the simulated wage divergence. The bottom quarter gains, however, in its unskilled market wage (using the weighted average for the provinces). The inference to be drawn from this analysis is that the growth of discrimination and of spatial and enterprise segmentation contributed to the dispersion of earnings by helping well-paid and harming poorly paid workers.

How far did the different mean characteristics of employees in the four quarters of the earnings distribution contribute to the rise in earnings inequality? We explore this question by posing the counterfactual: What would be the effect on (geometric) mean earnings of paying workers with the mean characteristics of each quarter according to the 1995, instead of the 1988, earnings function estimated for the sample as a whole? There are two equations, according to whether the 1988 or the 1995 characteristics are used:

$$\hat{Y}_{i1} - \hat{Y}_{i0} = (F_1 - F_0)\overline{X}_{i0} \qquad (4.20)$$

$$\text{or } \hat{Y}_{i1} - \hat{Y}_{i0} = (F_1 - F_0)\overline{X}_{i1} \qquad (4.21)$$

Table 4.22 presents the results of this exercise. Whereas the (geometric) mean earnings of the top and bottom quarters diverged by 56 percentage points, the simulations account for a divergence of 20 or 36 percentage points (using the mean characteristics of 1988 and 1995 respectively). In other words, the income-generation process changed in such a way as to help workers with high-earning characteristics, and harm those with low-earning characteristics. The patterns yielded by equations (4.20) and (4.21) are similar. Using the latter, we find a monotonic positive relationship across the quarters in the case of the province-weighted unskilled market wage, human capital (both education and occupation), and market imperfections (especially via growing spatial segmentation). The payments attributable to all these components—raw labor, productive characteristics, labor market discrimination, and segmentation—evolved in such a way as to help workers who possessed favorable characteristics and harm those who did not.

A second approach to understanding the rise in earnings inequality is to examine the contribution of particular characteristics, or sets of characteristics, to the change in a summary measure of inequality. We choose the Gini coefficient, which rose sharply over the seven years—from 22.9 to 30.7 percent. Can this increase be decomposed into the contributions of the various characteristics that enter the earnings function?

Consider the income sources of individual

$$i : y_i = \sum_k {}_{ik} .$$

Table 4.21

The Actual Increase in Mean Real Earnings per Worker in Each Quarter of the Earnings Distribution in Urban China, 1988–1995, and the Counterfactual Increase Arising from Differences in Mean Characteristics Among Quarters

Percentage increase in mean real earnings	Quarter			
	Bottom	Second	Third	Top
Actual:				
Arithmetic mean	9.6	40.2	55.4	70.4
Geometric mean	−1.8	33.5	43.8	54.1
Counterfactual based on eq. (4.18)	30.6	30.5	35.2	44.7
due to:				
Unskilled market wage (Jiangsu)	75.1	32.6	24.0	21.8
Unskilled market wage (weighted				
average)	46.7	16.5	9.0	6.7
Human capital	10.4	18.3	18.3	10.9
Education	13.5	16.9	18.9	19.4
Occupation	4.3	2.1	1.8	3.1
Age	−7.3	−0.7	−2.5	−11.7
Market imperfections	−55.0	−10.4	−7.0	11.9
Discrimination	−9.7	−1.0	0.7	1.0
Ownership	−16.8	−3.3	7.2	26.1
Province	−28.5	−16.1	−14.9	−15.1
Counterfactual based on eq. (4.19)	30.5	33.3	38.9	57.7
due to:				
Unskilled market wage (Jiangsu)	75.1	32.6	24.0	21.8
Unskilled market wage (weighted				
average)	42.3	13.7	8.9	14.1
Human capital	16.6	22.4	22.4	16.5
Education	16.2	20.0	21.9	23.1
Occupation	5.4	2.8	2.3	3.9
Age	−5.0	−0.4	−1.8	−10.4
Market imperfections				
Discrimination	−9.5	−1.0	0.7	1.0
Ownership	−19.0	−3.8	6.9	25.9
Province	−32.7	−19.0	−15.1	−7.7

Shorrocks (1982) has shown, for a large class of inequality measures, that the share of inequality contributed by income source k is given by

$$\pi_k = \frac{\text{cov}(y_k, y)}{\text{var}(y)}$$

$$= r_k s_k / s \tag{4.22}$$

Table 4.22

The Actual Increase in Mean Real Earnings per Worker in Each Quarter of the Earnings Distribution in Urban China, 1988–1995, and the Counterfactual Increase Arising from Differences in Mean Characteristics Among Quarters

Percentage increase in mean real earnings	Quarter			
	Bottom	Second	Third	Top
Actual:				
Arithmetic mean	9.6	40.2	55.4	70.4
Geometric mean	−1.8	33.5	43.8	54.1
Counterfactual based on eq. (4.20)	11.6	23.5	27.3	31.6
due to:				
Unskilled market wage (Jiangsu)	29.1	29.1	29.1	29.1
Unskilled market wage (weighted average)	9.7	10.9	12.1	17.0
Human capital	4.5	12.5	12.9	10.6
Education	10.6	11.3	11.9	11.8
Occupation	2.0	3.4	4.4	4.9
Age	−8.2	2.1	−3.5	−6.0
Market imperfections	−21.9	−18.1	−14.6	−8.1
Discrimination	3.3	−2.3	−1.3	−0.6
Ownership	0.7	2.4	3.6	4.5
Province	19.3	−18.1	−16.9	−12.1
Counterfactual based on eq. (4.21)	10.5	24.5	32.7	46.2
due to:				
Unskilled market wage (Jiangsu)	29.1	29.1	29.1	29.1
Unskilled market wage (weighted average)	6.4	7.5	11.8	23.6
Human capital	7.4	17.5	19.1	19.2
Education	12.2	14.7	15.9	16.8
Occupation	2.5	4.6	5.4	6.2
Age	−7.3	−1.7	−2.2	−3.8
Market imperfections	−26.0	−22.0	−10.5	−2.1
Discrimination	−3.3	−2.2	−1.3	−0.6
Ownership	−0.0	1.7	8.1	4.0
Province	−22.7	−21.6	−17.3	−5.5

where r_k and s_k are respectively the correlation coefficient and the standard deviation of source k, s is the standard deviation of income, and

$$\sum_k \pi_k = 1.$$

The contribution of the source k thus depends on its degree of correlation with income and its relative degree of inequality. In fact, $_k$ is simply the ordinary least squares regression of y_k on y.

Fields (1996) and Ravallion and Chen (1999) adapt this formula to calculate the contribution of income source k to the change in inequality over time:

$$\mu_k = \frac{\pi_{k1}I_1 - \pi_k I_0}{I_1 - I_0}$$

(4.23)

where I_j ($j = 1,0$) is a measure of inequality and

$$\sum_k \mu_k = 1.$$

How can this equation be applied when characteristics determine income through a stochastic process? We have

$$y_i = \sum_k \beta_k x_{ik}$$

where x_k is characteristic k (one of this set being an error term, for which $\beta_k = 1$). As Fields (1996) has shown, the contribution of characteristic k to inequality of income is

$$\pi_k = \frac{\beta_k \mathrm{cov}(X_k, y)}{\mathrm{var}(y)}$$

(4.24)

This is equivalent simply to the partial regression coefficient of income on characteristic k (holding all other variables constant) multiplied by the total regression coefficient of characteristic k on income (holding nothing else constant).[4]

The decomposition is based on the semilogarithmic specifications in Table 4.19. Table 4.23 shows the contribution of each variable to inequality in 1988 and in 1995, and its contribution to the increase in inequality over the seven years. It also provides corresponding information for the sets of variables representing productive characteristics and market imperfections. Only a third of earnings inequality can be explained: The unexplained residual is important in each case. It might represent measurement error or individual characteristics such as unobserved ability or employer characteristics such as profitability and locality.

Given that women were less well paid than men initially, their enlarged negative coefficient contributed little to the increase in inequality, as measured by the Gini coefficient. However, the discrimination variables as a group could explain only 3 percent of the increase in inequality. The segmentation variables accounted for 10 percent of inequality in 1988 but for as much as 17 percent in 1995, mainly because of the more dispersed province coefficients. Although ownership form also contributed, province alone accounted for 33 percent of the growth in inequality. Insofar as provincial differences in wages represented differences in the marginal product of labor, they were efficient market signals to which the immobility of labor had prevented an equilibrating response; insofar as they represented rent sharing by employers, they were a new form of market segmentation.

The human capital variables are the second-most important identifiable disequalizing force. Education contributed 11 percent and skill-based occupation 7 percent. By contrast, age had an equalizing effect overall. The relative fall in the earnings of well-paid prime-age workers (aged 45–60) reduced inequality consid-

Table 4.23

Decomposition of Earnings Inequality by the Determinants of Earnings: 1988, 1995, and 1988–1995

			1988–1995	
	1988	1995	Total increase	Explained increase
Human capital	18.0	14.8	5.2	8.6
Education	0.3	3.0	10.7	24.0
Age	16.5	9.1	−12.7	−28.5
Occupation	1.2	2.7	7.2	16.2
Disequalizing components	6.8	11.1	29.4	64.6
Discrimination	3.2	3.2	2.9	6.4
Gender	2.2	1.9	1.0	2.2
Communist Party membership	1.0	1.2	1.7	3.7
Minority status	0.0	0.1	0.2	0.4
Segmentation	10.3	16.9	36.4	79.9
Ownership form	2.2	2.6	3.8	8.3
Province	8.1	14.3	32.6	71.6
Residual	68.5	65.1	55.5	

Notes: The decomposition of the change in inequality is based on the Gini coefficient. The disequalizing components of human capital are education beyond secondary school; the professional, technical, and administrative occupations; and age below 26 and above 60. The third column shows the contributions of each component to that part of the increase in inequality that can be explained by the measured determinants of earnings.

erably, whereas the relative fall in the earnings of workers under 25 and over 60 raised it. This last effect plus the relative rise in the earnings of those with more than secondary education and those in professional, technical, and administrative occupations together accounted for 29 percent of the increase in inequality. These particular changes are very likely to represent the stirring of labor market forces and a move toward efficiency-based pay determination. This decomposition analysis suggests that there is indeed an efficiency-equity trade-off to be made.

Conclusion

The inequality of household income per capita increased sharply in both rural and urban China over the seven-year period from 1988 to 1995. This is hardly surprising for an economy in rapid transition from a centrally planned to a market system over a period in which GDP increased by 88 percent. Nevertheless, it is worth analyzing the processes by which inequality increased, and in particular the roles of various economic reform policies and of economic growth itself. This is perhaps the central issue in the analysis of the 1988 and 1995 household income surveys. It is not easy to isolate the effects of various changes in the economy and of various economic reform policies on the inequality of income: There is no well-established methodology available. Our approach was twofold. First, we attempted to distinguish the effects of growth and reform by means of spatial analysis, using interprovince data. Second, we attempted to explain the increase in inequality, relating it to economic and policy changes, by means of decomposition analysis, including decomposition by income sources, income groups, and income-determining characteristics. The sharp economic and institutional rural-urban divide required that the rural and urban samples be analyzed separately.

We first examined the burgeoning inequality of income in rural China. The object was to explain the 8 percentage point increase in the Gini coefficient over the seven years. Our quest for the conventional inverse U-shaped Kuznets curve relating inequality and income per capita, using cross-province data, generated an upward-sloping relationship but without significant curvature. Moreover, the growth in income over the period could itself explain no more than 15 percent of the growth in inequality. The economic reform policies were the most likely explanation for the remainder. A dummy variable representing the coastal provinces indicated that their Gini coefficients were substantially higher, *ceteris paribus*, and their increase in inequality over the seven years was also higher. Insofar as this variable represents earlier and further economic reform, it provides powerful evidence of the disequalizing effect of the reform policies in rural China. Population growth was also found to accelerate the growth in inequality, possibly through its depressing effect on some incomes. There was powerful evidence of convergence in inequality across provinces: Inequality rose in all provinces but particularly in those that started with low inequality. Moreover, convergence was "conditional" as well as "absolute," as it remained even after other explanatory variables were introduced into the equation. The disequalizing effect of economic reform appeared to be most powerful initially and thereafter to diminish.

We explored the reasons for rising rural inequality by decomposing the increase in various ways. Decomposition by income source revealed that the rise was more than fully explained (over 150 percent) by the increased importance of wage income and individual business income in total rural income. Their share in the total rose remarkably, from 13 to 33 percent. The returns to labor from these sources were higher than the returns from other sources, and they accrued largely to high-income households. Because they remained minority activities, their relative growth increased inequality—a process that has been studied in other contexts (Kuznets, 1955; Knight and Sabot, 1983).

Who were the beneficiaries of the growth in rural inequality? Our analysis suggested that certain characteristics improve the chances of obtaining wage employment or individual self-employment. Among the personal characteristics, more education, male gender, and Han nationality all help. The notion that households with too much labor in relation to land choose these jobs is supported by the negative relationship with farming land, but is contradicted by the negative relationship, in 1995, with the number of household workers. It is clear that locality—where a household lives and, thus, in China, where it originated—is very important to the process of income polarization.

We also examined the effect of demographic changes on rural inequality. The average size of rural households diminished by 14 percent over the seven years, associated with the one-child-family policy. Given the inverse correlation between household size and both the mean and the dispersion of household income per capita, we expected this contraction to increase inequality. However, the effect proved to be minor: The change in household composition could explain only 8 percent of the rise in rural inequality. On the other hand, it could explain 30 percent of the real increase in rural income per capita.

None of the increase in the inequality of urban income per capita can be attributed to rising incomes. The U-shaped relationship between the level and inequality of income, although weak, implies that the rise in income actually reduced inequality a little over the seven years. There was strong convergence of inequality, that is, low initial inequality assisted its growth. The spatial analysis suggests a role for two proxies for economic reform: Coastal location and the size of the nonstate sector. Standardizing for income, coastal provinces and those with larger nonstate sectors appeared to have low urban inequality near the start of the urban reforms, possibly for exogenous reasons. However, their effects on inequality were each positive, albeit insignificantly so, by the mid-1990s. It appears from our analysis of the differential timing and extent of economic reform across ten provinces that reform has indeed raised urban inequality.

The urban wage structure changed in interesting ways over our period. On the one hand, the altered returns to education, occupation-based skills, and age suggest that wages became more responsive to worker productivity. Another indication that market forces became more important was the decline in our proxy for the unskilled market wage. On the other hand, there were signals of greater labor market discrimination and segmentation, involving gender, ownership, and province. Overall, labor earnings became much more unequally distributed—the Gini coefficient rose by 8 percentage points—with the earnings of low-paid workers actually rising very little in real terms.

Our analysis of earnings by quarters showed that the growth in labor market discrimination and segmentation contributed to the dispersion of earnings by helping well-paid and harming poorly paid workers. Moreover, the income-generation process changed in such a way as to help workers possessing high-earning characteristics and to harm those without such characteristics. The increased rewards for human capital were found to raise earnings generally, but least in the bottom quarter of the wage distribution.

Our decomposition of the increase in wage inequality by income-earning characteristics showed that the disequalizing components of the human capital variables made the most important observable contribution to the increase in inequality. These changes were very likely to represent the stirring of labor market forces and a move toward efficiency-based pay determination. The discrimination variables accounted for only a small part of the increase, whereas increased wage dispersion among provinces was powerfully disequalizing.

Although we have not examined whether, and how much, the incidence of poverty has fallen, our evidence is generally consistent with the great majority of households becoming better off over the seven years. The main exception that we have uncovered is the stagnation or decline in the real wages of workers with low pay and few productive characteristics. That raises the basic question: How far should we be concerned with rising inequality if household incomes are rising generally albeit at different rates?

The concept of "relative deprivation" may be helpful, although its value implications are ambiguous. Gurr (1970, chapter 3) hypothesized that, because poor people make comparisons with others like themselves, their expectations—and consequently their feelings of relative deprivation—are greater the larger the gain of the most successful group of similar socioeconomic status. Hirschman (1973) argued that the success of the poor who achieve upward mobility has two, contrary, effects on the welfare of those remaining poor. On the one hand, it strengthens subjective expectations that they will in turn succeed; on the other hand, it strengthens feelings of failure and relative deprivation. With time the former feelings may give way to the latter. This is terrain unfamiliar to economists yet potentially relevant to the formulation of value judgments about the growth of measured inequality.

It is arguable that subjective perceptions should be irrelevant to value judgements. The central concern should be peoples' absolute deprivation in terms of their capabilities to lead good lives (Sen, 1983). The welfare of the poor should receive no less weight in the social welfare function, relative to the rich, simply because the poor do not feel dissatisfied or deprived. It is difficult to disagree with this value judgment, but it raises the underlying question: Who is to determine the social welfare function? If we respect the government's social welfare function, we should recognize that perceptions, and feelings of relative deprivation, give rise to pressures. Such pressures generally influence the social welfare function implicitly formulated by government.

There are two concepts of intergroup mobility: one is the mobility of individuals without changes in relative group sizes, and the other is the mobility that results from such changes. The extent of the former has no effect on measures of inequal-

ity, yet it may influence value judgments about inequality. Thus inequality of outcomes may be more acceptable if there is equality of opportunities. A relative
increase in the high-income group may well be found to increase measured inequality, yet it is a pervasive and possibly inevitable characteristic of a stage of
economic development.

Consider the relevance of these points to Chinese policy. This chapter throws
light on two basic questions. What were the relative roles of economic growth
and economic reform in raising income inequality? Our interprovince analyses
indicate that the role of economic growth has been, at most, negligible. However, this is misleading for two reasons. First, the most important contribution to
rising rural inequality—the growing importance of income from wage-employment and individual businesses—required growth as well as reform: It could not
have occurred to such an extent without rapid economic growth. The rise in the
returns to human capital in the urban sector probably reflects both a move toward market equilibrium returns and a rise in market equilibrium returns: Economic growth generated a rapid growth of demand for human capital relative to
the growth in supply. Second, growth encouraged reform, and reform generated
growth: The two were intertwined.

Did the rise in inequality involve a trade-off between efficiency and equity
objectives? Some of the new inequalities appear justifiable in terms of the greater
incentives or efficiency to which they give rise. In particular, it is likely that initially the urban returns to education and to occupational skills were too low, and
that the pattern of returns to age did not adequately reflect the age-productivity
relationship. Other emerging disparities are more difficult to justify in terms of
output objectives. For instance, the greater discrimination by gender and sharper
segmentation by ownership form and by province suggest new sources of economic inefficiency. The confrontation of these new inefficiencies requires more
competition based on greater labor mobility, and thus the development of a full-
fledged urban labor market in China. Yet other sources of increased inequality
appear to be an unavoidable consequence of the economy having reached a partial
and incomplete stage of development and marketization. For instance, the relative
growth of income from wage-employment and individual self-employment has
necessarily raised income inequality among rural households. The only policy
leverage in this case would be to address the reasons why the returns to rural labor
are higher in these activities.

In the post-Mao period the Chinese government reacted to the situation that
prevailed under central planning and control. In adopting its reform policies, the
government espoused output objectives above all. It eschewed egalitarianism in
favor of allowing some areas and some people to prosper, with the expectation that
their prosperity would assist others and be spread: "Prosperity to some, to most,
then to all (Du, 1989, p. 192). Indeed, the government promoted inequality in
various ways, for instance by giving special privileges to coastal cities and Special
Economic Zones. Two decades after the economic reforms began, there is now a

good case for reconsidering priorities. We have shown that the Gini coefficient has risen strongly—by about one percentage point per annum—over the seven years of our study. The rising inequality may well generate perceptions of relative deprivation, for instance among farming households left behind, migrant workers, and redundant urban workers. The pressures to which this discontent gives rise are likely to influence policy objectives, whether before or after they begin to threaten political stability. Our research can be useful for policy making if it alerts government to the trends in inequality and the nature of the trade-offs between efficiency and equity objectives.

Notes

1. The alternative decompositions into the contributions of concentration ratios and shares produce very different results because of the sign change on C_i (Table 4.7).
2. For an account of the definition, properties, and decomposition of these inequality indices, see, for instance, Anand (1983, Appendices A–C).
3. In each year the intercept is adjusted by the weighted average of the province coefficients.
4. All this is well explained in Ravallion and Chen (1999).

References

Anand, Sudhir (1983). *Inequality and Poverty in Malaysia: Measurement and Decomposition*, New York: Oxford University Press.
Anand, Sudhir, and S.M.R. Kanbur (1993a). "The Kuznets process and the inequality-development relationship," *Journal of Development Economics*, 40, 25–52.
Anand, Sudhir and S.M.R. Kanbur (1993b). "Inequality and Development: A Critique," *Journal of Development Economics*, 41, 19–43.
Atkinson, A.B. (1997). "Bringing Income Distribution in from the Cold," *Economic Journal*, 107, 441, 297–321.
Du Runsheng (1989). *China's Rural Economic Reform*, Beijing: Foreign Languages Press.
Fields, Gary S. (1996). "Accounting for Differences in Income Inequality," Cornell University, wordprocessed.
Goodman, A., and S. Webb (1994). *For Richer, For Poorer*, London: Institute of Fiscal Studies, Commentary No. 42.
Gottschalk, Peter (1997). "Inequality, Income Growth and Mobility: The Basic Facts," *Journal of Economic Perspectives*, 11, 2, Spring, 21–40.
Gurr, Ted Robert (1970). *Why Men Rebel*, Princeton: Princeton University Press.
Hirschman, Albert O. (1973). "The Changing Tolerance for Income Inequality in the Course of Economic Development," *Quarterly Journal of Economics*, 87, 544–66.
Howes, Stephen, and Athar Hussain (1994). "Regional Growth and Inequality in Rural China," STICERD, London School of Economics, wordprocessed.
Kanbur, Ravi (1997). "Income Distribution and Development," World Bank, wordprocessed, January, 1–100.
Knight, John, and Richard Sabot (1983). "Educational Expansion and the Kuznets Effect," *American Economic Review*, 73, 5, December, 1132–1136.
Knight, John, and Lina Song (1993). "Workers in China's Rural Industries," in Keith Griffin and Zhao Renwei (eds.), *The Distribution of Income in China*, London: Macmillan.
Knight, John, and Lina Song (1997). "Chinese Peasant Choices: Farming, Rural Industry or

Migration," Institute of Economics and Statistics, University of Oxford, Discussion Paper No. 188, January, 1–29.

Kuznets, Simon (1955). "Economic Growth and Income Inequality," *American Economic Review*, 45, March, 1–28.

Lam, David (1997). "Demographic Variables and Income Inequality," in M.R. Rosenzweig, and O. Stark (eds.) *Handbook of Population and Family Economics*, Volume 1B, Amsterdam: Elsevier.

Ravallion, Martin, and Shaohua Chen (1999). "When Economic Reform is Faster than Statistical Reform: Measuring and Explaining Inequality in Rural China," *Oxford Bulletin of Economics and Statistics*, 61, 1, February, 33–56.

Sen, Amartya (1983). "Poor, Relatively Speaking," *Oxford Economic Papers*, 35, 2, July, 153–69.

Shorrocks, Anthony F. (1982). "Inequality Decomposition by Factor Components," *Econometrica*, 50, 193–211.

Topel, Robert H. (1997). "Factor Proportions and Relative Wages: The Supply-side Determinants of Wage Inequality," *Journal of Economic Perspectives*, 11, 2, Spring, 55–74.

Part II

Urban China

5

Income Distribution in Urban China During the Period of Economic Reform and Globalization

Azizur Rahman Khan, Keith Griffin, and Carl Riskin

This chapter addresses three issues that are central to understanding the effects of the transition in China from central planning to a more market-oriented economic system. First, what have been the consequences of the economic reforms for the distribution of income in urban areas? Second, what has happened to the incidence of urban poverty? Third, have government policies helped to diminish or accentuate urban poverty and inequality? Answers to these questions are based upon a comparison of the two national sample surveys, conducted in 1988 and 1995, which form the main empirical basis for this book.

Changes in Urban Inequality

The distribution of income in urban China in 1988, ten years after the economic reforms began, was remarkably egalitarian. True, urban inequality had increased, but the Gini coefficient continued to be lower than in any other country for which data are available.[1] It is now possible, for the first time, to measure changes in the degree of income inequality in urban areas using internationally comparable concepts of income. It is also possible to use the two surveys to determine which components of total income have contributed most to the change in inequality. Both of these tasks are carried out here, and the basic data are presented in Table 5.1.

Between 1988 and 1995 the Gini coefficient for the distribution of household income per capita increased from 0.233 to 0.332, or by 42.5 percent (row 1 of the table). Although the degree of inequality still is low in comparison with other devel-

Table 5.1

Urban Income Inequality in China and Its Sources,1988 and 1995

	Share of total income (%)		Gini or concentration ratio		Contribution to overall inequality (%)	
	1988	1995	1988	1995	1988	1995
1. Total income	100.0	100.0	0.233	0.332	100.0	100.0
2. Cash income from employment	44.42	61.30	0.178	0.247	33.9	45.6
3. Pensions, etc.	6.83	11.69	0.335	0.316	9.8	11.1
4. Income from private and individual enterprises	0.74	0.53	0.413	0.042	1.3	0.1
5. Property income	0.49	1.27	0.437	0.484	0.9	1.9
6. Rental value of owned housing	3.90	11.39	0.338	0.639	5.7	21.9
7. Housing subsidy	18.14	9.74	0.311	0.516	24.2	15.1
8. Other net subsidies	20.94	1.25	0.188	0.296	16.9	1.1
9. Private transfers, etc.	4.53	2.84	0.383	0.371	7.4	3.2

Source: Khan and Riskin,1998.

oping countries, the sharp increase in inequality in only seven years is remarkable. Equally remarkable is the change in the composition of income that occurred during that period, notably, the rise in cash income from employment from 44.4 to 61.3 percent of total income (row 2), the rise in the relative importance of pensions (row 3) and of the rental value of owned housing (row 6) combined with the fall in the importance of housing subsidies (row 7) and the virtual disappearance of other subsidies net of direct taxes and fees (row 8). In 1988 urban households were dependent on subsidies from their "work unit" and the government for 39 percent of their income; by 1995, subsidies accounted for only 11 percent of household income.

In the middle columns of Table 5.1 we report the concentration ratios for each of the nine components of income. These concentration ratios are calculated in the same way as Gini coefficients except that households are ranked in order of per capita income rather than in order of income received from each source of income. The concentration ratio for a particular source, say, wages, measures the distribution of wage income over all income recipients, not over wage recipients. The Gini coefficient is simply a weighted average of the concentration ratios, where the weights are the shares of each source of income in total income.

The final two columns of Table 5.1 contain information on the contribution of each source of income to overall inequality in the distribution of income. The contribution of any particular source to the overall Gini ratio is given by the share of that source in total income multiplied by its concentration ratio. We can regard a source as "equalizing" or "disequalizing" according to whether its concentration ratio is lower or higher than the overall Gini. If lower, an increase in that source's share of income would lower the Gini, *ceteris paribus;* if higher, it would raise the Gini. In 1988 only wage income and net subsidies other than housing were equalizing, in this respect; all other components of total income were disequalizing. In 1995 wage income, net subsidies other than housing, pensions, and income from private and individual enterprises were equalizing; the other four sources of income were disequalizing. However, only pensions, income from private and individual enterprises,[2] and private transfers were more equally distributed in 1995 than in 1988. All other components of total income were less evenly distributed, particularly the rental value of owned housing and housing subsidies.

Four sources of income—wages (row 2), pensions (row 3), the rental value of owned housing (row 6), and housing subsidy (row 7)—account for 93.7 percent of overall inequality. In the case of wages and the rental value of owned housing, both the concentration ratio and the share in total income rose. In the case of housing subsidies, the concentration ratio rose dramatically (from 0.311 to 0.516) but their share of total income fell by nearly a half (from 18.14 to 9.74 percent of total income). The opposite occurred in the case of pensions. The share of pensions in total income rose, but the concentration ratio fell slightly.

Despite changes in the composition of income, virtually all of the increase in urban income inequality in China was due to the increase in inequality of individual income components, and none was due to the change in the composition of income. The change in the composition of sources of income played no role in explaining the increase in urban inequality. Had the composition of income in 1995 remained the same as in 1988 and only the distribution within individual components changed as it did, the Gini ratio of urban income distribution in 1995 would have been exactly the same as its actual value.[3]

Urban Poverty

The real income of urban households increased 4.48 percent a year between 1988 and 1995. This is far lower than the rate of growth in per capita GDP (which was 8.1 percent a year for China as a whole) and almost certainly lower than the rate of growth of per capita urban GDP. This indicates that the share of households in GDP fell and the combined share of government and business rose.

Nevertheless, the growth in household income was quite high. A simulation exercise shows that this high growth of income would have reduced the broad poverty rate to under 1 percent of the urban population by 1995 had the distribution of urban income remained unchanged between 1988 and 1995. In other words, had there been no rise in inequality, such a rapid increase in average incomes would have sufficed virtually to eradicate urban poverty. The rise in inequality, however, offset the rise in per capita income and as a result the estimated effect on the incidence of poverty ranges from an insignificant improvement to a significant deterioration depending on the poverty indicator used and the cost of living index chosen to adjust the poverty income threshold.

The data in Table 5.2 indicate that, while the head count measure of urban poverty reported in the table is very low compared to other developing countries, the incidence of "broad poverty"—that is, poverty defined in terms of a relatively high poverty threshold—fell only 2.4 percent between 1988 and 1995, or from 8.2 to 8.0 percent of the urban population. Moreover the urban population itself grew rapidly. As a result, the total number of urban broad poor rose by 19.6 percent during the period, or from 23.5 million people in 1988 to 28.1 million people in 1995. Moreover, when we define poverty according to a somewhat lower poverty line (equal to 80 percent of the broad poverty line), the resulting head count for "deep poverty" actually increases substantially.

The other two poverty indexes, namely, the proportionate poverty gap (PPG) and the weighted poverty gap (WPG), are sensitive, respectively, to the average depth of poverty and the distribution of income among the poor. A rise in the PPG indicates an increase in the average shortfall of income of the poor below the poverty line. A rise in the WPG betokens growing inequality of distribution of incomes below the poverty line. Both measures deteriorated between 1988 and 1995 for both concepts of poverty.

The estimates of urban poverty in Table 5.2 are surprising, but the numerical indicators may actually be too comforting. There are reasons to believe that the consumer price index (CPI), which we used to estimate the growth in real income, understates the increase in the cost of living of the poor because its weights are based on the expenditure of an average consumer rather than a poor consumer. Average consumers spend a smaller proportion of their income on food grains than do the poor, and the price of food grains rose much more rapidly than average prices. If the price index used to calculate changes in real incomes of the poor were adjusted to take this bias into account, the head-count index even of broad poverty would show a significant increase in poverty between 1988 and 1995.[4] This is shown in Table 5.3, which adds a third, even lower definition of poverty that we call "extreme poverty" (threshold equal to 70 percent of the broad poverty threshold). Using a more realistic CPI, the broad poverty rate actually increases by 19 percent, rather than decreasing slightly, deep poverty grows much more sharply, and extreme poverty, although remaining a very small fraction of the population, increases most sharply of the three measures.[5]

The conclusion thus is inescapable: Economic reform in China has not succeeded in reducing urban poverty and by most measures urban poverty has increased. And, unlike in the case of rural poverty, the deeper urban poverty was the faster it grew.[6] Moreover, our sample does not include the "floating population" in urban areas, that is, people who have migrated to the cities but have not been given the status of legal urban resident nor the entitlements enjoyed by legal residents. Yet the available evidence suggests these migrants are poorer than the official urban population. The estimates of urban poverty, and perhaps inequality as well, would have been higher if they had been included. While this does not detract from China's achievement of a moderate reduction in rural poverty, it does challenge the claim that "a rising tide lifts all boats."

Table 5.2

Urban Poverty, 1988 and 1995: Change in Poverty Threshold Based on Official Consumer Price Index

	Head count (%)		Proportionate poverty gap		Weighted poverty gap	
	1988	1995	1988	1995	1988	1995
Broad poverty	8.2	8.0	1.4	2.0	0.4	0.8
Deep poverty	2.7	4.1	0.4	0.9	0.1	0.4

Note: The broad poverty line is based on the cost of 2,100 kilocalories per person per day with an adjustment for nonfood purchases, broadly consistent with the preference of low-income consumers. For 1995 this threshold is 2,291 yuan per person. The deep poverty threshold is defined as 80 percent of the broad poverty threshold. Details about the derivation of the poverty lines can be found in Khan and Riskin, 2001.

Table 5.3

Change in Urban Poverty Head-Count Index Using Alternative CPIs

Head-count index	Change with adjusted CPI (%)	Change with official CPI (%)
Broad poverty	+19.4	−0.2
Deep poverty	+86.4	+51.9
Extreme poverty	+145.5	+107.7

Disequalizing Policies

In 1988 the structure of wages was highly compressed (the concentration ratio for wage income was only 0.178), and this had a number of adverse incentive effects: It reduced the incentive to work hard within the firm, it provided weak signals, at best, to improve the allocation of labor among firms, and it reduced the incentive of workers to acquire skills and invest in their education. There was thus a strong case, as part of the process of reform and integration into the global economy, for increasing wage differentials. And this in fact is what happened, so that by 1995 the concentration ratio for wage income had increased to 0.247. Inequality in the distribution of wages accounted in that year for 45.6 percent of overall inequality.

Unfortunately the tax/subsidy system and other urban policies were not adjusted to compensate for increased wage inequality. Instead, public policy actually aggravated inequality by creating a highly disequalizing system of net subsidies, promoting a housing reform that resulted in an extremely uneven distribution of housing assets and housing services, and by failing to construct an adequate safety net before state enterprise reform began generating large numbers of layoffs of state sector workers at partial or no pay.[7]

Despite their possible adverse effects on efficiency, ration coupons in 1988 were the most equitably distributed of all urban subsidies and had an equalizing effect on urban income distribution. By 1995 the ration coupon system had been abolished and households were required to obtain their food supplies and other essentials on the free market. Housing subsidy in kind was the principal remaining element in a system of urban subsidies and, as discussed below, its distribution was far more unequal in 1995 than in 1988. The contribution of "net nonhousing subsidies" to total urban incomes fell from 20.94 percent to 1.25 percent between 1988 and 1995, and the residual subsidies were distributed less equally.

Reform of the housing system had similarly unfortunate consequences. In 1988 only 13.8 percent of the urban sample population lived in private housing; by 1995 the proportion living in their own homes had risen to 41.7 percent. The relative importance of housing subsidies in kind fell by nearly a half while the importance of the rental value of owned housing rose nearly three times (compare rows 6 and 7 in Table 5.1). Widespread privatization of the housing stock was in principle commendable, but it was done in such a way that it became highly disequalizing. The concentration ratio for housing subsidies increased by 65.9 percent (from 0.311 to 0.516) and the concentration ratio for the rental value of owned housing increased by 89.1 percent (from 0.338 to 0.639). In 1995, nearly 41 percent of the remaining housing subsidies were received by the richest 10 percent of the urban population and just over 60 percent of the rental value of owned housing accrued to the top 10 percent of the population. Housing policy—privatization and subsidies combined—accounted for 37 percent of overall inequality in the distribution of income in urban areas in 1995.

One of the reasons why poverty has persisted, in spite of rapid overall growth, is that the GDP elasticity of personal income was low, that is, the growth in personal income—the variable in terms of which poverty thresholds are measured—was much slower than the growth in GDP. This was due to macroeconomic policies that affected the distribution of incremental GDP among households, government, and "corporate" sectors and between consumption and accumulation. The dramatic fall in net subsidies and transfers from the government and collectives and the relentless drive for ever higher rates of accumulation, resulting in an increase in the domestic saving rate from an already high 37.5 percent of GDP in 1988 to a staggering 42 percent in 1995, are some of the manifestations of this process.

Rapid expansion of employment, arising from labor-intensive industrialization promoted by freer trade and greater integration into the global economy, might have offset at least in part greater inequality in the distribution of wage earnings. If this had occurred, the urban population would have been protected from rising poverty even if not from increased inequality. Unfortunately, industrialization during the period of globalization has so far been remarkably hostile to employment creation. Indeed, the output elasticity of employment has been extraordinarily low for urban industries as a whole, namely, 0.037. This has happened despite a very high output elasticity of employment in industries under private and other new forms of ownership. The problems have arisen from the significantly negative output elasticity of employment in the collective enterprises and the insignificant elasticity in the state enterprises.[8]

A principal reason why the collective and state enterprises performed so poorly in terms of employment creation is that, with the increase in market orientation at home and greater integration into the world economy, they were subjected to increased competition from domestic and foreign private enterprises. China's state and collective enterprises responded to increased competition by reducing the disguised unemployment they had inherited from the past as a consequence of the policy of guaranteed employment for all. The observed low output elasticity of employment in the period of reform and integration into the global economy conceals two divergent tendencies: (1) a high output elasticity of employment at constant intensity of work per worker, and (2) a rise in the intensity of work per worker due to a reduction of disguised unemployment. Once the transition is completed and the concealed unemployment in state and collective enterprises is eliminated, China's industries should be much more efficient and thereafter the observed output elasticity of employment should rise. However, there is also some disquieting evidence of adoption of more capital-intensive technologies by enterprises. Thus net value of fixed assets per worker in industry increased from 15,897 yuan in 1990 to 53,478 yuan in 1996; for state enterprises the increase was from 18,530 to 51,755 yuan.[9] A rapid increase in capital intensity fits very poorly with China's basic situation of labor surplus and growing unemployment. With both factors at work, the process of transition has been characterized by very slow growth of employment[10] and this has prevented the benefits of growth from being widely spread among the urban population. The consequence has been a rise in the incidence of poverty.

In summary, the increase in urban inequality between 1988 and 1995 was due to greater inequality in the distribution of most of the major components of income rather than to a change in the composition of income. Urban poverty failed to decline because the rise in personal income lagged far behind the rise in GDP, and the rise in average income that took place was offset by an extraordinary increase in inequality in the distribution of income. The extreme employment hostility of industrial growth made these difficulties even worse. Government policies as regards the social safety net, ration coupons, subsidies, and housing aggravated inequality and perpetuated poverty. Some increase in urban inequality probably was inevitable and even desirable in the context of market-oriented economic reforms, but regressive social policies made the burdens of transition greater than they need have been.

Notes

1. For details of the 1988 and 1995 surveys see Khan and Riskin, 1998.
2. Because of underreporting of this source of income, we put little credence in the estimates of its levels and distributions.

3. This is virtually the opposite of the case of rural income, for which all of the increase in inequality was due to changes in composition, and none to changes in distribution of individual income sources. See Khan and Riskin, 1998.

4. See Khan and Riskin, 2001, Chapter 4.

5. The incidence of extreme poverty, calculated using the adjusted CPI, was only 1.1 percent in 1988 and 2.7 percent in 1995. See Khan and Riskin, 2001.

6. For rural poverty the deeper kinds of poverty were reduced by greater percentages than the broader kinds. See Khan and Riskin, 2001, Chapter 4.

7. By the end of 1998 there were an estimated 9 million laid-off workers who had not been reemployed, and a total of 16 million unemployed of all kinds, amounting to about 8 percent of the labor force. See United Nations Development Programme, Chapter 4.

8. See Khan, *Poverty in China in the Period of Globalization: New Evidence on Trend and Pattern*, Issues in Development Discussion Paper 22, International Labour Office, Geneva, 1998.

9. Data provided by Hu Angang. See UNDP, 1999, Ch. 4.

10. Some of the growth of employment has been purely nominal, as laid-off workers are still considered to be employed. Of course, many urban jobs have gone to migrant workers, whose incomes have risen as a result. But migrant workers are not considered part of the urban population.

References

Azizur Rahman Khan, *Poverty in China in the Period of Globalization: New Evidence on Trend and Pattern*, Issues in Development Discussion Paper 22, International Labour Office, Geneva, 1998.

Azizur Rahman Khan and Carl Riskin, "Income and Inequality in China: Composition, Distribution and Growth of Household Income, 1988 to 1995," *China Quarterly,* June 1998.

————, *Inequality and Poverty in China in the Age of Globalization,* New York, Oxford University Press, 2001.

United Nations Development Programme, *The China Human Development Report*, New York, Oxford University Press, 1999.

6

A Spatial Analysis of Wages and Incomes in Urban China: Divergent Means, Convergent Inequality

John Knight, Li Shi, and Zhao Renwei

Introduction

In the mid-1980s economic reform began in earnest in urban China. This involved the gradual dismantling of central planning, the decentralization of decision making to enterprises, and the emergence of markets. Reform of the labor market was tardy, but both the decentralization and the introduction of market forces were likely to affect wage setting. The changes occurred at different rates across provinces and cities. A spatial analysis of urban wages and income per capita may therefore reveal interesting patterns.

Indeed, we show that this is the case. Between the survey years 1988 and 1995, intraprovince mean wages and income per capita diverged across provinces. Yet over the same period intraprovince wage- and income-inequality converged across provinces. We will analyze the extent of, and reasons for, the convergence of inequality. We will also examine the divergence of means and its causes. Our approach to understanding these processes is by means of various forms of decomposition analysis.

The first of our questions (What happens to the spatial inequality of income inequality?) has been posed rarely, if at all, but the second (What happens to the spatial inequality of mean incomes?) is now common. There is a lively and growing literature on economic convergence across countries (Barro and Sala-i-Martin, 1995, Chapter 12). The same authors (1995, Chapter 11) also reported a number of regional studies of convergence. They used measures of β-convergence (the relation between changes in the logarithm of income per capita and its initial value) and of σ- convergence (changes in the standard deviation of the logarithm of income per capita). They found evidence of β-convergence among U.S. states, Japanese prefectures, and European regions, both absolute and conditional convergence (standardizing for other variables). They also generally found σ-convergence.

A likely explanation for these results, along with technological diffusion, is that equilibrating flows of labor and capital tend to equalize incomes. Convergence should accordingly be weaker when the equation is standardized for net migration. However, the authors found, if anything, the opposite result, which they attributed to the endogeneity of migration. As with cross-country convergence, cross-region convergence of mean incomes is a common phenomenon that is not yet well understood.

Little research has as yet been published on trends in income inequality in urban China. Jian, Sachs, and Warner (1996) examined inequality among provinces over the period from 1978 to 1993, using data on provincial mean income per capita, based on the official national household survey. Their equations implied convergence during the period up to 1985, but the evidence for the period after 1985 was weak. In neither case was there evidence of conditional convergence or divergence, that is, the effect of initial income on its growth became insignificant when other explanatory variables were introduced into the equation.

The authors made no distinction between urban and rural areas, yet the administrative and economic divide between rural and urban China makes it important to analyze the two sectors separately. Such an analysis would be possible at the province level, using data from the urban sample of the official national household survey. However, as official data at the household level are not available, only our 1988 and 1995 surveys permit an analysis of the change in inequality within as well as among provinces.

Convergence in Inequality

This section is divided into three parts. First, we test for divergence or convergence in intraprovince inequality across provinces over the period from 1988 to 1995. Second, we examine the same relationship among cities. Third, we attempt to explain the convergence that we observe. Our method is to attempt various decompositions of the growth in inequality that occurred generally, but to varying degrees, over the seven years.

Convergence in Intraprovince Inequality among Provinces

Table 6.1 shows the Gini coefficient of earnings per worker and household income per capita in 1988 and 1995, and the change in the Gini coefficient, both the percentage change and the change in percentage points. In all provinces except Gansu there was a rise in inequality over the seven years. The increase in the Gini coefficient for the group of ten provinces common to the urban samples was by 7.8 percentage points in earnings and 5.1 percentage points in income. In each case the increase was greater for the four coastal provinces than for the six inland provinces (9.1 versus 4.8 percentage points for earnings, and 6.4 versus 2.3 percentage points for income). There was a good deal of variation among the provinces.

Table 6.1

The Level and Change in the Gini Coefficient of Earnings per Worker and of Income per Capita in Urban China, 1988–1995, by Province

Province	Earnings (%)				Income (%)			
	1988	1995	Change	Change, percentage points	1988	1995	Change	Change, percentage points
Beijing	20.4	26.1	27.9	5.7	17.0	21.5	26.5	4.5
Shanxi	24.9	29.7	19.3	4.8	23.0	26.6	15.7	3.6
Liaoning	17.4	28.8	65.5	11.4	15.7	23.4	49.1	7.7
Jiangsu	18.3	28.8	57.4	10.5	17.4	23.2	33.3	5.8
Anhui	24.3	27.8	14.4	3.5	21.5	22.1	2.8	0.6
Henan	22.4	30.1	34.4	7.7	21.6	28.4	31.5	6.8
Hubei	18.5	27.7	49.7	9.2	18.1	22.5	24.3	4.4
Guangdong	27.7	33.1	19.5	5.4	24.9	28.6	14.9	3.7
Yunnan	19.7	23.1	17.3	3.4	19.8	21.5	8.6	1.7
Gansu	27.6	27.1	-1.8	-0.5	26.8	22.5	-16.0	-4.3
Coastal	23.8	32.9	38.2	9.1	21.3	27.7	30.0	6.4
Interior	23.3	28.1	20.6	4.8	22.0	24.3	10.5	2.3
Total	24.1	31.9	32.4	7.8	23.2	28.3	22.0	5.1
Standard deviation	3.84	2.64	-31.3	-1.20	3.63	2.77	-23.7	-0.86

Note: The coastal region comprises Beijing, Liaoning, Jiangsu, and Guangdong; the interior region comprises Shanxi, Anhui, Henan, Hubei, Yunnan, and Gansu.

In order to discern patterns we estimated the following relationship:

$$G_1 - G_0 = a + bG_0 \tag{6.1}$$

where G = the Gini coefficient and the subscripts $0, 1$ = year 1988 and 1995 respectively. The coefficient b is a test of convergence ($b < 0$) or divergence ($b > 0$). The coefficient indicates whether the initial level of inequality hinders or assists its growth.

Table 6.2 tests across provinces for convergence or divergence in the intraprovince Gini coefficient (columns 1 and 3). We see that the coefficient on initial inequality is significantly negative. For both earnings per worker and income per capita, a reduction in the initial Gini coefficient by 10 percentage points raises its subsequent growth over seven years by 7 percentage points. When the proportionate growth in earnings or income is added as an explanatory variable, its coefficient is positive but small and not statistically significant (columns 2 and 4). When initial mean earnings or income is included, the coefficient is positive but not at all significant (equations not shown).

Convergence in Intracity Inequality among Cities

Because there are only ten provinces in the urban sample, our results might be due to the particular or idiosyncratic behavior of one or two provinces. The same analysis cannot be conducted on all thirty provinces because official intraprovince inequality measures are not available. However, information is available to estimate equation (6.1) for the sixty cities common to our two surveys.

Table 6.3 shows powerful and statistically significant evidence of convergence in inequality among cities. The coefficient b on G_0 is no less than -0.92 in the case of income and -0.79 in the case of earnings, that is, a 10 percent lower initial value of the Gini coefficient raises its increment by 8 percentage points or more. A pattern is therefore established: The convergence of inequality is a general phenomenon, applying not only among provinces but also, even more powerfully, among cities.

Explaining Convergence

In all but one province urban inequality rose between 1988 and 1995, but it rose more rapidly in those provinces that started with low inequality in 1988. The provinces were becoming more similar in their degree of urban inequality. How is this trend to be explained? One possibility is that the observed convergence is merely a statistical illusion: The regression of the change in a variable on its initial value is subject to errors-in-variables bias. Assume that measurement errors in the initial year and the final year are uncorrelated. If the initial value is underreported, the change is equivalently overreported. This reduces the estimated coefficient on the initial value, biasing it towards -1 and thus toward convergence. The extent of the

Table 6.2

The Interprovince Relationship Between Initial Gini Coefficient of Earnings and Income and its Growth, Urban China, 1988–1995

	Increase in Gini coefficient (percentage points)			
	Earnings		Income	
Equation:	1	2	3	4
Intercept	21.993***	19.190***	17.147	13.426*
Initial Gini coefficient	−0.715**	−0.669**	−0.666**	−0.582*
Proportionate growth in earnings/income		0.041		0.040
Adj. R^2	0.512	0.542	0.422	0.410
F-value	10.449**	6.332**	7.556**	4.123*
Mean value of dependent variable	6.110	6.110	3.450	3.450
Number of observations	10	10	10	10

Note: ***denotes statistical significance at the 1 percent, ** at the 5 percent, and * at the 10 percent level.

Table 6.3

The Growth of the Gini Coefficient of Income per Capita and Earnings per Worker, 1988–1995, as a Function of Their Initial Values, by City, Urban China

	Change in the Gini	
Equation:	Income	Earnings
Intercept	0.197***	0.202***
Initial value (G_0)	−0.922***	−0.793***
Adj. R^2	0.589	0.489
F-value	84.158***	56.443***
Mean of dependent variable ($G_1 - G_0$)	0.015	0.031
Number of observations	60	60

Note: *** indicates statistical significance at the 1 percent level.

bias increases with the proportion of the variance in the initial value that is attributable to measurement error. A common method of attempting to correct for such bias—instrumenting the initial value by means of the value of a contiguous year—is not open to us. Nor do we possess good proxies for the initial value (such as a coastal dummy) that are not correlated with the error term of the dependent variable. However, there are two pieces of evidence against the bias explanation.

First, we conducted a simple experiment to answer the question, What proportion of the variation in the initial value would have to be the result of measurement error for convergence to disappear? Accordingly, we set each initial province value at 20 percent, and then 50 percent, closer to the initial mean value. The coefficient on the initial Gini remained significantly negative in the former case, and had a negative value exceeding -0.3, albeit not significant, in the latter. Second, β-convergence is a necessary but not a sufficient condition for σ-convergence (Barro and Sala-i-Martin 1995, p. 385). The former tends to generate the latter, although this process can be offset by new disturbances that increase dispersion. We find that between 1988 and 1995 Φconvergence occurred in every case: Whether we consider earnings or income, the standard deviation of the Gini coefficient fell sharply among provinces (Table 6.1) and also among cities; and the coefficient of variation even more. This is a further indication that the β-convergence observed is not an illusion.

Our second approach is to conduct a decomposition analysis of the Gini coefficient in each province in 1988 and 1995 by component of earnings or of income, and then to decompose the rise in the Gini coefficient between 1988 and 1995 into the contributions made by the different components. We make use of the following property:

$$G = \sum \pi_i = \sum u_i C_i \qquad (6.2)$$

Where G = the Gini coefficient of income inequality

u_i = the ratio of the ith component of income to total income, that is, its share of the total

C_i = the concentration ratio of the ith component of income

π_i = the contribution of the ith component to the Gini coefficient.

The concentration curve $C_i(x)$ represents the share of component i received by the lowest x proportion of recipients of *total* income. The concentration ratio C_i is then derived from the concentration curve in exactly the same way as the Gini coefficient is derived from the Lorenz curve. The contribution made by each component of income to the Gini coefficient is given by

$$\pi_i = u_i C_i.$$

The basic information on earnings inequality is set out in Tables 6.4 to 6.9. Table 6.4 shows the percentage shares (u_i) of the different components of earnings. We see that the main component was basic wages (E_1), representing 54 percent in 1988 and 59 percent in 1995. Contrary to expectations, the share of bonuses (E_2) fell, from 19 percent in 1988 to 15 percent in 1995. The main distinction between the coastal and

Table 6.4

Shares of Earnings Components in Total Earnings, Urban China, 1988 and 1995 (%)

Province	E_1	E_2	E_3	E_4	E_5	Total
1988						
Beijing	52.2	17.2	17.8	0.3	12.5	100.0
Shanxi	59.7	17.2	15.4	0.7	7.1	100.0
Liaoning	55.0	18.2	17.3	0.2	9.4	100.0
Jiangsu	52.51	8.7	15.2	1.2	12.6	100.0
Anhui	54.0	20.2	14.7	1.2	9.9	100.0
Henan	63.8	14.2	12.5	0.5	9.0	100.0
Hubei	57.1	17.1	16.2	0.5	9.2	100.0
Guangdong	41.8	30.8	14.9	1.9	10.6	100.0
Yunnan	53.0	18.6	16.1	1.0	11.3	100.0
Gansu	59.1	9.6	17.9	1.5	11.8	100.0
Coastal	48.9	23.0	15.8	1.1	11.1	100.0
Interior	57.5	16.5	15.4	0.9	9.7	100.0
Total	53.7	19.4	15.5	1.0	10.3	100.0
1995						
Beijing	52.7	18.3	16.3	0.1	12.6	100.0
Shanxi	68.3	12.5	14.1	0.4	4.7	100.0
Liaoning	65.1	10.3	17.3	0.6	6.9	100.0
Jiangsu	60.5	16.0	16.7	0.3	6.6	100.0
Anhui	71.5	9.6	10.4	0.2	8.4	100.0
Henan	63.5	9.9	17.1	2.4	7.1	100.0
Hubei	63.2	12.2	16.1	0.7	7.9	100.0
Guangdong	43.6	28.5	16.5	1.7	9.8	100.0
Yunnan	59.8	10.1	24.2	1.1	5.0	100.0
Gansu	73.7	6.7	18.6	0.2	0.8	100.0
Coastal	52.1	19.4	16.6	0.8	11.1	100.0
Interior	65.0	10.6	17.1	0.9	6.5	100.0
Total	59.3	15.3	16.8	0.8	7.8	100.0

Notes: E_1 = basic wage of workers; E_2 = bonus of workers; E_3 = cash subsidy of workers; E_4 = earnings of private owners and self-employed; E_5 = other income. Coastal region includes Beijing, Liaoning, Jiangsu, and Guangdong; interior region includes Shanxi, Anhui, Henan, Hubei, Yunnan, and Gansu.

the interior provinces was the greater importance of bonuses and the lesser importance of basic wages in the former. Despite their relative decline, bonuses may well have been the driving force behind earnings in the period up to 1993 as the wage reform of 1994 consolidated part of the bonus into basic pay.

Table 6.5 shows concentration ratios for the different components of earnings. By comparing the concentration ratio (C_i) with the Gini coefficient, we can tell whether component i has an equalizing effect ($C_i < G$) or a disequalizing effect

Table 6.5

Shares of Income Components in Total Income, Urban China, 1988 and 1995 (%)

Province	E_1	E_2	E_3	E_4	E_5	Gini coefficient of earnings
1988						
Beijing	16.4	34.0	16.9	64.5	21.2	20.4
Shanxi	18.7	49.0	21.5	57.9	25.9	24.9
Liaoning	12.1	35.1	12.0	67.6	23.2	17.4
Jiangsu	14.8	32.4	11.9	73.0	15.3	18.3
Anhui	20.3	33.8	18.9	25.0	36.6	24.3
Henan	18.5	34.2	23.2	10.5	32.3	22.4
Hubei	12.8	34.1	15.8	63.2	28.3	18.5
Guangdong	18.3	40.3	19.4	63.6	33.8	27.7
Yunnan	15.6	27.1	17.3	3.6	32.0	19.7
Gansu	21.1	41.4	23.0	85.7	49.4	27.6
Coastal	15.5	42.3	17.7	73.8	25.6	23.8
Interior	17.8	36.5	21.4	40.6	35.5	23.3
Total	16.7	41.4	20.7	58.3	32.5	24.1
1995						
Beijing	25.9	31.1	21.2	7.8	25.4	26.1
Shanxi	25.6	47.5	34.7	−2.6	32.1	29.7
Liaoning	25.4	48.8	27.7	35.2	33.2	28.8
Jiangsu	19.7	53.1	34.3	1.9	41.5	28.8
Anhui	23.6	41.0	35.1	6.6	40.0	27.8
Henan	27.0	44.8	35.3	13.2	31.0	30.1
Hubei	23.6	39.3	32.2	34.0	32.5	27.7
Guangdong	18.7	46.0	39.1	35.7	48.9	33.1
Yunnan	18.3	37.0	24.2	39.0	43.4	23.1
Gansu	25.5	37.0	30.3	−25.6	25.1	27.1
Coastal	22.7	54.5	34.6	43.6	43.9	32.9
Interior	24.0	42.4	32.7	18.8	34.8	28.1
Total	24.3	53.5	34.3	29.8	42.6	31.9

Notes: E_1 = basic wage of workers; E_2 = bonus of workers; E_3 = cash subsidy of workers; E_4 = earnings of private owners and self-employed; E_5 = other income. Coastal region includes Beijing, Liaoning, Jiangsu, and Guangdong; interior region includes Shanxi, Anhui, Henan, Hubei, Yunnan, and Gansu.

($C_i > G$) on the Gini. For instance, we see that in Guangdong in 1995 the basic wage had an equalizing effect but all other components, especially the bonus, had a disequalizing effect. Indeed, the basic wage was equalizing and the bonus disequalizing in every province. Curiously, the cash subsidy (E_3) was equalizing in 1988 but had become disequalizing in all but two provinces in 1995.

Table 6.6

Contribution of Earnings Components to Total Earnings Inequality, Urban China, 1988 and 1995 (%)

Province	E_1	E_2	E_3	E_4	E_5	Total
1988						
Beijing	42.0	28.9	14.8	1.1	13.2	100.0
Shanxi	44.8	33.9	13.3	1.6	6.4	100.0
Liaoning	38.3	36.7	11.9	0.8	12.5	100.0
Jiangsu	42.2	32.4	9.9	4.8	10.5	100.0
Anhui	45.1	28.1	11.4	1.2	14.2	100.0
Henan	52.4	21.6	12.9	0.2	12.9	100.0
Hubei	39.3	31.3	13.8	1.7	13.9	100.0
Guangdong	27.6	44.8	10.4	4.4	12.8	100.0
Yunnan	42.0	25.4	14.1	0.2	18.3	100.0
Gansu	45.2	14.3	14.9	4.7	20.9	100.0
Coastal	31.9	40.9	11.8	3.4	12.0	100.0
Interior	43.8	25.8	14.1	1.6	14.7	100.0
Total	37.2	33.3	13.3	2.4	13.9	100.0
1995						
Beijing	52.3	21.9	13.3	0.0	12.3	100.0
Shanxi	58.7	19.9	16.3	0.0	5.1	100.0
Liaoning	57.3	17.4	16.6	0.7	8.0	100.0
Jiangsu	41.2	29.4	19.9	0.0	9.5	100.0
Anhui	60.6	14.2	13.1	0.0	12.1	100.0
Henan	56.9	14.7	20.1	1.1	7.3	100.0
Hubei	53.8	17.3	18.7	0.9	9.3	100.0
Guangdong	24.6	39.6	19.5	1.8	14.5	100.0
Yunnan	47.2	16.2	25.3	1.9	9.4	100.0
Gansu	67.0	9.2	18.2	−0.2	5.8	100.0
Coastal	36.5	32.5	17.8	1.1	12.2	100.0
Interior	55.5	16.0	19.9	0.6	8.0	100.0
Total	45.2	25.7	18.1	0.8	10.2	100.0

Notes: E_1 = basic wage of workers; E_2 = bonus of workers; E_3 = cash subsidy of workers; E_4 = earnings of private owners and self-employed; E_5 = other income. Coastal region includes Beijing, Liaoning, Jiangsu, and Guangdong; interior region includes Shanxi, Anhui, Henan, Hubei, Yunnan, and Gansu.

The proportionate contribution of each earnings component to total earnings inequality (π_i/G) is presented in Table 6.6. The contribution of the basic wage rises between 1988 and 1995, from 37 to 45 percent, and that of the bonus falls, from 33 to 26 percent. This switch occurs in both the coastal and the interior regions. The difference between them is that the basic wage makes a smaller contribution to inequality, and the bonus a greater contribution, in the coastal provinces.

The next step is to decompose the change in the Gini coefficient in each prov-

Table 6.7

Contribution of Earnings Components to Change in Earnings Inequality, Urban China, 1988 and 1995 (%)

Province	E_1	E_2	E_3	E_4	E_5	Change in Gini coefficient of earnings
Beijing	88.6	−2.7	7.8	−3.2	9.6	100.0
Shanxi	135.5	−53.4	33.9	−8.9	−7.1	100.0
Liaoning	86.8	−11.4	24.5	0.1	0.1	100.0
Jiangsu	39.7	23.3	37.5	−8.3	7.8	100.0
Anhui	176.9	−86.5	26.1	−8.6	−7.8	100.0
Henan	70.2	−5.5	41.2	3.5	−9.3	100.0
Hubei	83.8	−11.4	28.9	−0.9	−0.4	100.0
Guangdong	9.4	13.0	66.3	−11.2	22.5	100.0
Yunnan	78.9	−38.5	90.6	11.6	−42.6	100.0
Gansu	−741.2	199.4	−109.6	178.3	573.2	100.0
Coastal	48.9	9.7	33.9	−5.3	12.8	100.0
Interior	112.8	−32.1	48.3	−4.1	−24.9	100.0
Total	69.9	2.0	32.8	−4.4	−0.3	100.0

Notes: E_1 = basic wage of workers; E_2 = bonus of workers; E_3 = cash subsidy of workers; E_4 = earnings of private owners and self-employed; E_5 = other income. Coastal region includes Beijing, Liaoning, Jiangsu, and Guangdong; interior region includes Shanxi, Anhui, Henan, Hubei, Yunnan, and Gansu.

ince between 1988 and 1995 (Table 6.7). The contribution of each component is given by $\pi_{i1} - \pi_{i0}$, and the proportion due to each component by $(\pi_{i1} - \pi_{i0}) / (G_1 - G_0)$. For the sample as a whole, the major contribution is made by the basic wage (70 percent), followed by the cash subsidy (33 percent). However, the contribution of the basic wage is greater for the interior than for the coastal region (113 versus 49 percent) and that of the bonus correspondingly smaller.

We are now in a position to examine the proximate causes of the interprovince convergence of intraprovince inequality. We estimate variants of equation (6.1):

$$\pi_{i1} - \pi_{i0} = a + b\,G_0 \qquad (6.3)$$

$$\pi_{i1} - \pi_{i0} = c + d\,\pi_{i0} \qquad (6.4)$$

Equation (6.3) indicates whether, and to what extent, a particular component of earnings contributed to convergence in the Gini coefficient. Equation (6.4) indicates whether, and to what extent, the contribution of a particular component was itself subject to convergence. Table 6.8 shows that the coefficients of all compo-

Table 6.8

The Interprovince Relation Between the Contribution of a Component to the Change in Earnings Inequality and the Initial Contribution of the Component or the Initial Gini Coefficient

	The coefficient on the initial value of:	
	G_0	π_{i0}
Basic wage	−0.302	−0.008
Bonus	−0.101	0.101
Cash subsidy	−0.105	−1.233**
Income from self-employment	−0.074	−1.020**
Other earnings	−0.147	−1.028***

Note: ***denotes statistical significance at the 1 percent, and ** at the 5 percent level.

nents were negative in equation (6.3), but none was significantly so. The basic wage made the greatest contribution to the convergence in the Gini coefficient. However, we see in equation (6.4) that the minor components of earnings (the cash subsidy, earnings from self-employment, and "other earnings") were themselves subject to powerful convergence, whereas the basic wage was weakly convergent and the bonus weakly divergent. Convergence was thus common to all earnings components with the exception of bonuses. Even this result is not secure: Bonuses may have played a larger role than our results suggest, but this role could have been disguised insofar as the wage reform of 1994 produced a consolidation of part of the bonus into the basic wage.

Finally, we conduct a simulation analysis of the increase in the Gini coefficient in each province. What proportion of the increase is due to rising component concentration ratios and what proportion to the changing importance of the different components? The contribution of concentration ratios can be isolated by estimating:

$$G_1^* - G_0 = \sum u_{i0} C_{i1} - \sum u_{i0} C_{i0} \tag{6.5}$$

or, alternatively:

$$G_1 - G_0' = \sum u_{i1} C_{i1} - \sum u_{i1} C_{i0} \tag{6.6}$$

The contribution of component shares is given by:

$$G_1 - G_1^* = \sum u_{i1} C_{i1} - \sum u_{i0} C_{i1} \tag{6.7}$$

Or:

$$G_0' - G_0 = \sum u_{i1} C_{i0} - \sum u_{i0} C_{i0} \tag{6.8}$$

where G_i^*, G_i' represent alternative counterfactual estimates of the Gini coefficient.

Table 6.9

Simulation Analysis of the Contribution of Earnings Components to the Change in Earnings Inequality, Urban China, 1988–1995 (%)

| | Percentage of the change that is due to: | | | |
| | $G_1 - G_1^*$ | $G_1^* - G_0$ | $G_0' - G_0$ | $G_1 - G_0'$ |
Province	Shares	Concentration ratios	Shares	Concentration ratios
Beijing	2.9	97.1	1.7	98.3
Shanxi	−26.7	126.7	−37.9	137.9
Liaoning	−17.3	117.3	−16.3	116.3
Jiangsu	−17.7	117.7	−10.4	110.4
Anhui	−71.6	171.6	−49.1	149.1
Henan	−9.5	109.5	−11.5	111.5
Hubei	−9.6	109.6	−12.6	112.6
Guangdong	−10.4	110.4	−12.8	112.8
Yunnan	−77.8	177.8	−54.7	154.7
Gansu	−40.3	140.3	406.8	−306.8
Coastal	−23.2	123.2	−18.9	118.9
Interior	−26.5	126.5	−33.5	133.5
Total	−19.4	119.4	−18.3	118.3

Note: Coastal region includes Beijing, Liaoning, Jiangsu, and Guangdong; interior region includes Shanxi, Anhui, Hubei, Yunnan, and Gansu.

The results are presented in Table 6.9, showing the simulated change expressed as a percentage of the actual change. On both decompositions, the contribution of the rise in concentration ratios is overwhelmingly important and the contribution of changing shares (the growing importance of basic wages) is actually negative. The one exception, Gansu, is readily understandable because in this case we are explaining a slight fall in inequality.

Tables 6.10–6.15 present identical information for the decomposition of inequality of household income per capita. In Table 6.10 we see the dominance of wage income (Y_1), which contributed 80 percent of total income in 1988 and 77 percent in 1995. There was little variation among provinces or change over time, the main change being a rise in the importance of pensions (Y_2) and a fall in "other incomes" (Y_5). The concentration ratios indicate that wage income generally had an equalizing effect, whereas the earnings of private owners and the self-employed (Y_3) and property income (Y_4) were disequalizing (Table 6.11). Pensions were equalizing in the coastal region but disequalizing in the interior. These results carry through to the estimated component contributions to income inequality (Table 6.12). Wage income makes by far the greatest contribution in both years, but pensions, self-employment income, and property incomes become increasingly important—pensions more so in the interior than on the coast.

Table 6.10

Shares of Income Components in Total Income, Urban China, 1988 and 1995 (%)

Province	Y_1	Y_2	Y_3	Y_4	Y_5	Total
1988						
Beijing	72.2	14.6	0.3	0.5	12.3	100.0
Shanxi	85.3	7.3	0.7	0.4	6.4	100.0
Liaoning	81.2	7.4	0.2	0.7	10.6	100.0
Jiangsu	76.3	15.2	0.9	0.6	7.0	100.0
Anhui	82.7	8.4	1.0	0.1	7.5	100.0
Henan	82.3	11.1	0.4	0.7	5.5	100.0
Hubei	78.9	10.7	0.2	0.8	9.2	100.0
Guangdong	78.5	6.7	1.5	1.1	12.2	100.0
Yunnan	84.0	7.0	0.9	0.6	7.7	100.0
Gansu	80.9	7.1	1.1	0.7	10.2	100.0
Coastal	77.7	10.3	0.9	0.8	10.4	100.0
Interior	82.1	8.8	0.7	0.6	8.1	100.0
Total	80.0	9.4	0.8	0.7	9.1	100.0
1995						
Beijing	76.0	17.1	1.2	4.5	1.2	100.0
Shanxi	73.7	17.4	1.8	4.8	2.3	100.0
Liaoning	78.7	14.1	1.3	4.9	1.1	100.0
Jiangsu	68.6	24.1	1.2	4.6	1.5	100.0
Anhui	70.3	21.8	1.4	5.8	1.0	100.0
Henan	68.1	26.1	1.6	2.8	1.4	100.0
Hubei	75.7	16.9	1.3	4.1	2.1	100.0
Guangdong	80.1	10.6	2.7	5.6	1.0	100.0
Yunnan	79.1	11.8	1.6	5.8	1.6	100.0
Gansu	72.7	18.8	1.1	5.7	1.7	100.0
Coastal	78.0	14.8	1.6	4.4	1.2	100.0
Interior	76.9	15.6	1.5	4.3	1.7	100.0
Total	77.4	15.2	1.6	4.3	1.5	100.0

Notes: Y_1 = basic wage of workers; Y_2 = pensions and income of retired people; Y_3 = earnings of private owners and self-employed; Y_4 = household property income; Y_5 = other income. Coastal region includes Beijing, Liaoning, Jiangsu, and Guangdong; interior region includes Shanxi, Anhui, Henan, Hubei, Yunnan, and Gansu.

There is a sharp coastal-interior contrast in the contribution of different income components to the change in income inequality between 1988 and 1995 (Table 6.13). In the coastal region, wage income was the main reason for increased inequality, whereas it made no contribution at all in the interior region: there, inequality rose on account of pensions, self-employment income, and property income.

We see from Table 6.14 that wage income made much the largest contribution to the interprovince convergence in the Gini coefficient. The contribution of each component was itself strongly convergent except that of pensions. There is thus no single

Table 6.11

Concentration Ratios of Income Components, Urban China, 1988 and 1995 (%)

Province	Y_1	Y_2	Y_3	Y_4	Y_5	Gini coefficient of income
1988						
Beijing	16.8	11.4	53.4	39.9	23.0	17.0
Shanxi	22.0	31.4	24.6	50.7	26.1	23.0
Liaoning	14.7	21.1	76.8	34.6	17.4	15.7
Jiangsu	14.0	28.5	48.3	32.6	27.5	17.4
Anhui	21.6	21.6	−45.5	37.4	28.9	21.5
Henan	16.7	46.7	−2.0	47.1	35.7	21.6
Hubei	14.2	40.0	36.4	35.0	24.2	18.1
Guangdong	23.6	18.7	46.7	47.4	31.2	24.9
Yunnan	20.0	24.5	−7.0	26.4	16.2	19.8
Gansu	23.2	37.9	98.8	27.4	39.3	26.8|
Coastal	19.6	19.9	59.5	45.1	30.4	21.3
Interior	19.8	35.0	15.4	39.0	29.7	22.0
Total	20.7	31.1	38.5	44.3	33.4	23.2
1995						
Beijing	23.7	10.8	45.6	17.7	23.6	21.5
Shanxi	21.2	45.0	60.9	28.4	30.7	26.6
Liaoning	20.9	28.7	57.1	34.9	41.5	23.4
Jiangsu	20.9	24.6	42.9	40.0	40.4	23.2
Anhui	16.7	33.8	55.3	31.6	40.8	22.1
Henan	19.6	48.7	54.6	34.9	37.9	28.4
Hubei	19.9	27.7	36.9	36.9	34.3	22.5
Guangdong	27.5	23.5	62.9	36.0	32.0	28.6
Yunnan	17.3	40.3	24.9	38.5	26.7	21.5
Gansu	21.3	24.5	40.9	29.9	16.4	22.5
Coastal	27.1	23.2	59.7	38.3	35.7	27.7
Interior	20.6	36.5	46.2	35.1	31.6	24.3
Total	26.5	32.0	51.9	38.3	31.5	28.3

Notes: Y_1 = wage income of workers; Y_2 = pensions and income of retired people; Y_3 = earnings of private owners and self-employed; Y_4 = household property income; Y_5 = other income. Coastal region includes Beijing, Liaoning, Jiangsu, and Guangdong; interior region includes Shanxi, Anhui, Henan, Hubei, Yunnan, and Gansu.

component responsible for the convergence that we seek to explain. The only component that we can rule out is pensions, which appeared to have a divergent effect.

Finally, it is clear that the rise in income inequality in the coastal region owes nothing to the changing component shares of income (Table 6.15). This reflects the

Table 6.12

Contribution of Income Components to Total Income Inequality, 1988 and 1995 (%)

Province	Y_1	Y_2	Y_3	Y_4	Y_5	Total
1988						
Beijing	71.4	9.8	0.9	1.2	16.5	100.0
Shanxi	81.6	10.0	0.8	0.9	6.7	100.0
Liaoning	76.0	10.0	1.0	1.5	11.5	100.0
Jiangsu	60.8	24.6	2.5	1.1	11.0	100.0
Anhui	83.0	8.5	−2.1	0.2	10.1	100.0
Henan	62.5	23.6	0.0	1.4	12.5	100.0
Hubei	61.9	23.8	0.4	0.8	13.1	100.0
Guangdong	74.6	5.1	2.8	1.1	16.4	100.0
Yunnan	84.6	8.6	−0.3	0.6	8.9	100.0
Gansu	70.1	10.0	4.1	0.7	15.1	100.0
Coastal	71.6	9.6	2.5	1.7	14.8	100.0
Interior	73.8	14.0	0.5	1.0	10.8	100.0
Total	71.4	12.6	1.3	1.3	13.4	100.0
1995						
Beijing	83.8	8.6	2.6	3.7	1.3	100.0
Shanxi	58.7	29.4	4.1	5.1	2.7	100.0
Liaoning	70.2	17.3	3.2	7.3	2.0	100.0
Jiangsu	61.7	25.6	2.2	7.9	2.6	100.0
Anhui	53.1	33.2	3.5	8.3	1.9	100.0
Henan	47.0	44.7	3.1	3.3	1.9	100.0
Hubei	67.1	20.8	2.1	6.8	3.2	100.0
Guangdong	77.2	8.7	5.9	7.1	1.1	100.0
Yunnan	63.6	22.1	1.9	10.4	2.0	100.0
Gansu	68.8	20.5	2.0	7.6	1.2	100.0
Coastal	76.4	12.4	3.4	6.2	1.6	100.0
Interior	65.2	23.4	2.9	6.3	2.2	100.0
Total	72.5	17.2	2.9	5.8	1.6	100.0

Notes: Y_1 = wage income of workers; Y_2 = pensions and income of retired people; Y_3 = earnings of private owners and self-employed; Y_4 = household property income; Y_5 = other income. Coastal region includes Beijing, Liaoning, Jiangsu, and Guangdong; interior region includes Shanxi, Anhui, Henan, Hubei, Yunnan, and Gansu.

diminished importance of the disequalizing component "other income," which includes transfer income and income from second jobs. Component shares and concentration ratios make an equal contribution in the interior region, the former reflecting the disequalizing effect of the increasingly important component, pensions.

Our attempt to understand the proximate reasons for the interprovince convergence of inequality has thrown only a little light on the processes at work. In the

Table 6.13

Contribution of Income Components to the Change in Income Inequality, Urban China, 1988–1995 (%)

Province	Y_1	Y_2	Y_3	Y_4	Y_5	Change in Gini coefficient of income
Beijing	130.5	4.1	8.6	13.3	−56.5	100.0
Shanxi	−89.3	157.5	26.3	33.0	−27.4	100.0
Liaoning	58.9	32.4	7.7	19.2	−18.1	100.0
Jiangsu	64.6	28.2	1.4	29.1	−23.3	100.0
Anhui	−879.8	798.0	176.6	258.0	−252.8	100.0
Henan	−6.2	117.2	13.7	9.8	−34.5	100.0
Hubei	87.8	9.1	9.3	28.1	−34.3	100.0
Guangdong	93.5	33.1	26.6	39.9	−93.1	100.0
Yunnan	−189.9	183.3	28.1	128.5	−50.0	100.0
Gansu	77.8	−45.4	15.1	−35.8	88.3	100.0
Coastal	93.7	22.0	6.7	21.0	−43.4	100.0
Interior	−18.9	119.3	26.7	58.2	−85.3	100.0
Total	76.2	37.5	10.1	25.8	−49.6	100.0

Notes: Y_1 = wage income of workers; Y_2 = pensions and income of retired people; Y_3 = earnings of private owners and self-employed; Y_4 = household property income; Y_5 = other income. Coastal region includes Beijing, Liaoning, Jiangsu, and Guangdong; interior region includes Shanxi, Anhui, Henan, Hubei, Yunnan, and Gansu.

Table 6.14

The Interprovince Relation between the Contribution of a Component to the Change in Income Inequality and the Initial Contribution of the Component or the Initial Gini Coefficient

	The coefficient on the initial value of:	
	G_0	π_{i0}
Wage income	−0.681*	−0.917**
Pensions	0.187	0.427
Income from self-employment	−0.011	−0.857**
Property income	0.015	−1.117
Other income	−0.169*	−1.108***

Note: ***denotes statistical significance at the 1 percent, ** at the 5 percent, and * at the 10 percent level.

case of earnings per worker, it was the basic wage that made the greatest contribution to convergence, and in the case of income per capita, it was wage income. We can be confident only that bonuses, in the case of earnings, and pensions, in the case of income, were not part of the explanation.

Table 6.15

Simulation Analysis of the Contribution of Income Components to the Change in Income Inequality, Urban China, 1988–1995 (%)

	Percentage of the change that is due to:			
	$G_1-G_1{}^*$	$G_1{}^*-G_0$	$G_0{}'-G_0$	$G_1-G_0{}^*$
Province	Shares	Concentration ratios	Shares	Concentration ratios
Beijing	−7.3	107.3	9.9	90.1
Shanxi	78.1	21.9	58.3	41.7
Liaoning	−5.9	105.9	22.1	77.9
Jiangsu	1.5	98.5	24.7	75.3
Anhui	162.8	−62.8	41.3	58.7
Henan	54.6	45.4	52.1	47.9
Hubei	6.1	93.9	42.4	57.6
Guangdong	3.9	96.1	8.2	91.8
Yunnan	99.6	0.4	67.6	32.4
Gansu	−28.9	128.9	−13.3	113.3
Coastal	−5.8	105.8	3.1	96.9
Interior	48.2	51.8	46.4	53.6
Total	12.6	77.4	28.8	71.2

Notes: Coastal region includes Beijing, Liaoning, Jiangsu, and Guangdong; interior region includes Shanxi, Anhui, Henan, Hubei, Yunnan, and Gansu.

How then can we explain convergence, if it depended mainly on wage income and, within wage income, on the basic wage? It is possible that convergence was due to the uneven timing of reforms. Those provinces and cities that reformed early—during the period from 1985 to 1988—had higher inequality by 1988. In these cases inequality did not rise much more between 1988 and 1995. Those provinces and cities that commenced reforms later had lower inequality in 1988 but higher increases in the ensuing seven years.

To test this hypothesis, we need to measure the progress in reform that had been achieved by 1988. To a considerable extent, the proportion of earnings other than basic wages represents the degree of decentralized freedom to determine earnings that employers then possessed. We use this as our proxy for the extent of labor market reform in a province in 1988. Accordingly, Table 6.16 shows interprovince and intercity estimates of the equation:

$$G_0 = a + bW_0 \tag{6.9}$$

where W = basic wages as a percentage of earnings. The hypothesis is that $b < 0$. Indeed, we find that b is negative in three of the four cases but significantly so only in the equations for cities. Our evidence that the reforming provinces had higher

Table 6.16

The Interprovince and Intercity Relation Between the Gini Coefficient of Earnings and of Income, and the Proxy for the Extent of Reform, Urban China, 1988

	Earnings		Income	
	Provinces	Cities	Provinces	Cities
Intercept	26.704	27.663***	20.190	25.784***
Basic wage as a percentage of earnings	−0.084	−0.115*	0.007	−0.110*
Adj. R²	−0.106	0.029	−0.125	0.031
F–value	0.135	2.701*	0.001	2.898*
Mean of dependent variable	22.120	21.431	20.586	19.828
Number of observations	10	60	10	60

Note: ***denotes statistical significance at the 1 percent, and * at the 10 percent level.

Table 6.17

The Coefficient on the Initial Value of the Gini Coefficient of Earnings in the Interprovince Equations Predicting the Change in the Gini Coefficient, Urban China, 1988–1995

	Coefficient on the initial Gini
Production worker	−0.573***
Nonproduction worker	−0.713**
State sector	−0.576**
Nonstate sector	−0.853***

Note: ***denotes statistical significance at the 1 percent, and ** at the 5 percent level.

initial inequality is weak, but it remains our favored explanation for convergence.

A further approach was to examine the pattern of variation in convergence among various subgroups. A distinction was made between nonproduction and production workers ("staff" and "workers"), and between the state and nonstate sectors. We see from Table 6.17 that convergence is stronger for staff than for workers, and for the nonstate sector than the state sector. Provinces have come more rapidly into line in their extent of earnings inequality in the case of staff and of nonstate employees, both of whom are more likely to be subject to market forces.

Divergence in Means

We approach the analysis of the growth in intraprovince mean earnings and incomes in the same way as for intraprovince inequality. First, we test for conver-

Table 6.18

The Mean Values of Earnings per Worker and Income per Capita, Yuan per Annum, 1988 and 1995, at Constant (1988) Prices, Urban China, by Province, and Their Percentage Rates of Growth

Province	Earnings			Income		
	1988	1995	Percentage change	1988	1995	Percentage change
Beijing	2,022	3,722	84.1	1,612	2,933	81.9
Shanxi	1,632	2,088	27.9	1,093	1,538	40.7
Liaoning	1,835	2,449	33.5	1,402	1,872	33.5
Jiangsu	1,895	2,950	55.7	1,459	2,403	64.7
Anhui	1,725	2,160	25.2	1,249	1,764	41.2
Henan	1,531	2,044	33.5	1,144	1,604	40.2
Hubei	1,749	2,590	48.1	1,307	1,994	52.6
Guangdong	2,723	4,876	79.1	2,053	3,673	78.9
Yunnan	1,988	2,514	26.5	1,321	1,926	45.8
Gansu	1,898	1,972	3.9	1,327	1,467	10.6
Coastal	2,144	3,300	53.9	1,584	2,502	58.0
Interior	1,739	2,205	26.8	1,177	1,632	38.7
Total	1,900	2,646	39.3	1,336	1,995	49.3

Notes: The coastal region comprises Beijing, Liaoning, Jiangsu, and Guangdong; the interior region comprises Shanxi, Anhui, Henan, Hubei, Yunnan, and Gansu. The income concept used throughout excludes the housing subsidy and the imputed rent of privately owned housing. Because these are based on market rents, which tend to be high in prosperous provinces irrespective of the quality of housing, their inclusion would raise income misleadingly in those provinces.

gence or divergence in the means across provinces. Second, we extend the analysis to the sample of cities. Third, we explore the underlying reasons for the powerful divergence evident in our equations.

Divergence in Mean Income and Earnings among Provinces

Table 6.18 provides the basic data on mean real earnings from employment and mean household real income per capita for each of the ten provinces common to our urban samples of 1988 and 1995, and the corresponding percentage increases. It is notable that provinces diverged sharply over the seven years. For instance, earnings per worker rose by 84 percent in Beijing and 79 percent in Guangdong but only by 3 percent in Gansu and 27 percent in Yunnan. The percentage growth in earnings in the coastal provinces is double that of the interior provinces. Very similar results are obtained for income per capita.

Again, we test for convergence or divergence using the equation:

$$y_1 - y_0 = a + b y_0 \qquad (6.10)$$

where y = the natural logarithm of mean earnings or income. Table 6.19 (columns 1 and 5) shows equations for the growth of earnings and income respectively over the seven-year period. In both cases the coefficient on the base year value is significantly positive. In the case of earnings it implies that a 10 percent higher initial income involves growth that is faster by 6 percentage points; and in the case of income the growth is 5 percent faster. This constitutes strong evidence of interprovince divergence in earnings and income levels. Note the corresponding result in Table 6.18. Comparing the coastal and interior groups of provinces, we see that the coastal region had both higher initial mean values and faster growth in earnings per worker and income per capita than the interior region.

Table 6.19 also shows the equivalent equations using official data for all twenty-nine provinces (columns 2 and 6). Evidence of divergence is again found, although it is not quite so powerful, nor is it statistically significant in the case of earnings. We are observing a general phenomenon, which is not just the result of outliers in our ten-province sample.

The same equation estimated for the previous decade (1978–88), using official data for the twenty-nine provinces, is reported in columns 4 and 7 of Table 6.19. The results are quite different for this period: They indicate strong and statistically significant convergence of both earnings per worker and income per capita. Something happened to set different forces in motion during the later period. The most likely explanation is the urban economic reforms—involving the decentralization of control and the dismantling of planning—that commenced in the mid-1980s.

A further pointer to this explanation is provided by the addition of two proxies for labor market reform in the twenty-nine-province equation for 1988 to 1995 (column 3): The bonus as a percentage of total earnings, and employment other than by the state or urban collectives as a percentage of total employment. Both reflect the extent of managerial autonomy; both coefficients are positive and significant. Moreover, the initial earnings coefficient becomes slightly negative and not at all significant. It appears that the differential growth of bonus payments and of the private sector was responsible for the divergence of earnings among provinces.

Divergence in Mean Income and Earnings Among Cities

The equation was reestimated using the sample of sixty cities. In contrast to Table 6.19, Table 6.20 shows no sign of divergence in mean earnings or mean income among cities. The coefficient is slightly negative but not significantly different from zero. How is the difference in the results for cities and for provinces to be explained? One possibility is that labor is more mobile among the cities of a province than among cities of different provinces. Such mobility would tend to equalize incomes, this producing convergence among the cities of a province.

We test this hypothesis by estimating intraprovince equations for the seven provinces that contain at least six cities (Table 6.21, page 155). Given such small samples, it is hardly surprising that only two of the income coefficients are significantly differ-

Table 6.19

The Interprovince Relationship Between Initial Mean Earnings and Income per Capita and Their Growth, Urban China

Proportionate growth in:

	Earnings per worker				Income per capita		
	CASS	SSB			CASS	SSB	
	1988–95	1988–95	1988–95	1978–88	1988–95	1988–95	1978–88
Column:	1	2	3	4	5	6	7
Intercept	−4.184	−1.715	0.501	3.768***	−3.302*	−2.144***	2.843**
Initial income	0.600*	0.269	−0.059	−0.479	0.511**	0.366***	−0.351*
Percentage bonus			0.011**				
Percentage private employment			0.012*				
Adj. R^2	0.201	0.040	0.685	0.178	0.314	0.357	0.062
F-value	3.265*	2.175	18.803**	7.050**	5.125**	16.534***	2.858*
Mean of dependent variable	0.335	0.292	0.292	0.382	0.389	0.446	0.553
Number of observations	10	29	29	29	10	29	29

Sources: CASS: 1988 and 1995 household surveys, urban samples; SSB: official data on household incomes and earnings from employment.

Notes: *** denotes statistical significance at the 1 percent, ** at the 5 percent, and * at the 10 percent level. The 1995 data on earnings and incomes are deflated to 1988 figures using the urban consumer price index (which rose by 128 percent). Inflation was very similar across the ten provinces, the mean annual rate being 13.0 and the standard deviation 1.0 percent. Use of the province price indexes had a negligible effect on the divergence coefficient, raising it from 0.600* to 0.610* in equation 1 and lowering it from 0.511** to 0.475* in equation 5.

Table 6.20

The Growth of Income per Capita and Earnings per Worker, 1988–1995, as a Function of Their Initial Values, by City, Urban China

	Proportionate growth in:	
	Income	Earnings
Intercept	0.845	1.167
Initial value (y_0)	−0.068	−0.112
Adj. R^2	−0.014	−0.010
F-value	0.198	0.446
Mean of dependent variable $(y_1 - y_0)$	0.362	0.324
Number of observations	60	60

Note: None of the coefficients is significantly different from zero, even at the 10 percent level.

ent from zero. These are in the two provinces—Jiangsu and Guangdong—that have grown fastest and moved furthest toward a market economy. However, all seven coefficients are negative and four of them exceed −0.5. In these cases a 10 percent lower initial income raises the growth rate by over 5 percentage points. Very similar results are obtained for the earnings equations. Again, convergence is most powerful within Jiangsu and Guangdong.

Explaining Divergence

We investigate the reasons for the divergence in province mean earnings and incomes in three main ways. One is to decompose the mean increases into their component parts in order to discover which components of earnings or incomes contribute to the divergence. Second, we examine different subsamples in order to explore variation in the divergence. Third, we decompose the mean differences between four samples (coast, interior; 1988, 1995) in order to throw light on the reasons for these differences.

Table 6.22 shows the percentage growth in the components of earnings in each province between 1988 and 1995. The growth in basic wages (E_1) generally exceeded that in total earnings, as did the growth in the cash value of subsidies (E_3), whereas bonuses (E_2) grew less rapidly, and they actually fell in the interior region. Table 6.23 shows the contribution made by each component to the absolute increase in earnings, both in yuan and as a percentage. It is notable that Beijing and Guangdong had the largest increases not only in basic wages but also in bonuses and cash subsidies. The coastal region did better than the interior in all three components.

The decline in the share of wages paid in the form of bonuses may be misleading. Table 6.24 shows that bonuses were unimportant prior to the urban economic reforms that commenced in 1984. The proportion rose from 13 percent in 1983 to 19

Table 6.21

The Growth of Income per Capita and Earnings per Worker, 1988–1995, as a Function of their Initial Values, by Cities within Provinces, Urban China

	Shanxi	Jiangsu	Anhui	Henan	Hubei	Guangdong	Yunnan
				Growth of income per capita			
Intercept	1.252	15.181**	4.165	1.999	4.040	7.984*	1.594
Initial income	−0.146	−2.037**	−0.543	−0.248	−0.511	−0.992*	−0.173
Adj. R^2	−0.239	0.480	0.235	−0.140	0.105	0.278	−0.076
F-value	0.034	8.387**	2.540	0.140	1.702	3.698	0.508
Mean of dependent variable	0.250	0.443	0.326	0.286	0.421	0.520	0.359
Number of observations	6	9	6	8	7	8	8
				Growth of earnings per worker			
Intercept	0.665	17.251**	4.735	4.245	1.615	11.596	0.906
Initial income	−0.063	−2.236**	−0.60	−0.543	−0.167	−1.404**	0.152
Adj. R^2	−0.248	0.554	0.186	−0.075	0.182	0.613	0.006
F-value	0.006	10.954**	2.143	0.512	0.077	12.107**	1.041
Mean of dependent variable	0.206	0.421	0.230	0.290	0.369	0.539	0.424
Number of observations	6	9	6	6	7	8	8

Note: **denotes statistical significance at the 5 percent level, and * at the 10 percent level.

Table 6.22

Growth of Earnings Components, Urban China, by Province, 1988–1995 (%)

	E_1	E_2	E_3	E_4	E_5	Earnings
Beijing	85.5	95.9	68.6	−38.6	85.6	84.1
Shanxi	46.4	−7.0	71.1	−26.9	−15.3	28.0
Liaoning	58.0	−24.5	33.5	300.4	−2.0	33.5
Jiangsu	79.4	33.2	71.0	−61.1	−18.5	55.7
Anhui	65.8	−40.5	−11.4	79.1	6.3	25.2
Henan	32.9	−6.9	82.6	540.8	5.3	33.5
Hubei	63.9	5.7	47.2	107.3	27.2	48.1
Guangdong	86.8	65.7	98.3	60.2	65.6	79.1
Yunnan	42.7	−31.3	90.1	39.1	−44.1	26.5
Gansu	24.3	27.5	−5.4	−86.2	−46.3	3.9
Coastal	64.0	29.8	61.7	11.9	24.8	53.9
Interior	43.3	−18.5	40.8	26.8	−15.0	26.8
Total	53.8	9.8	50.9	11.4	5.5	39.3

Notes: E_1 = basic wage of workers; E_2 = bonus of workers; E_3 = cash subsidy of workers; E_4 = earnings of private owners and self–employed; E_5 = other income. Coastal region includes Beijing, Liaoning, Jiangsu, and Guangdong; interior region includes Shanxi, Anhui, Henan, Hubei, Yunnan, and Gansu.

percent in 1988; this trend was not confined to the state sector. The proportion rose further, to 22 percent, in 1993. However, in 1994 a dramatic increase in the basic wage occurred in the government sector, and this was generally followed in the enterprise sector. Employers responded to the wage reform by paying the basic increase partly from bonus funds. In 1994 the average wage rose by 8 percent in real terms, but this comprised a rise in "nonbonus income" (mainly the basic wage) by 18 percent and a fall in the bonus by 13 percent. The consolidation was not reversed in 1995: The share of the bonus was down to 16 percent. It is plausible, therefore, that the bonus, being the payment most subject to managerial and least subject to governmental control, was the dynamic element primarily responsible for the growth of earnings, and its spatial divergence, over much of our seven-year period.

We estimate the interprovince equations:

$$y_{i1} - y_{i0} = a + by_0 \qquad (6.11)$$

$$y_{i1} - y_{i0} = c + dy_{i0} \qquad (6.12)$$

where:

y_{ij} = log of earnings component i per worker in year j,

y_j = log of total earnings per worker in year j.

Table 6.23

Contribution of Earnings Components to the Change in Earnings, Urban China by Province, 1988–1995, in Yuan and as Percentage of Total

	E_1	E_2	E_3	E_4	E_5	Change in real earnings per worker
Beijing	906 (53.3)	333 (19.6)	247 (14.5)	−2 (−0.1)	216 (12.7)	1,700 (100.0)
Shanxi	454 (99.1)	−19 (−4.3)	43 (9.5)	−3 (−0.7)	−18 (−3.9)	457 (100.0)
Liaoning	583 (95.3)	−81 (−13.3)	106 (17.3)	11 (1.8)	−4 (−0.6)	614 (100.0)
Jiangsu	790 (74.9)	118 (11.1)	205 (19.4)	−14 (−1.3)	−44 (−4.2)	1,055 (100.0)
Anhui	612 (140.9)	−142 (−32.4)	−29 (−6.7)	−16 (−3.8)	11 (2.5)	435 (100.0)
Henan	321 (62.6)	−15 (−2.9)	158 (30.8)	41 (8.1)	7 (1.4)	513 (100.0)
Hubei	638 (75.9)	17 (2.0)	134 (15.9)	9 (1.1)	43 (5.2)	841 (100.0)
Guangdong	986 (45.9)	551 (25.6)	398 (18.5)	31 (1.5)	187 (8.8)	2153 (100.0)
Yunnan	446 (85.5)	−112 (−22.0)	287 (54.8)	8 (1.5)	−99 (−18.8)	526 (100.0)
Gansu	273 (368.2)	−50 (−67.7)	−18 (−24.7)	−25 (−33.1)	−106 (−140.1)	74 (100.0)
Coastal	739 (63.9)	147 (12.7)	209 (18.1)	3 (0.2)	59 (5.1)	1156 (100.0)
Interior	431 (93.0)	−53 (−11.4)	109 (23.4)	4 (0.9)	−25 (−5.4)	466 (100.0)
Total	548 (73.6)	36 (4.9)	149 (20.1)	2 (0.3)	11 (1.4)	746 (100.0)

Notes: E_1 = basic wage of workers; E_2 = bonus of workers; E_3 = cash subsidy of workers; E_4 = earnings of private owners and self-employed; E_5 = other income. Coastal region includes Beijing, Liaoning, Jiangsu, and Guangdong; interior region includes Shanxi, Anhui, Henan, Hubei, Yunnan, and Gansu.

Table 6.24

The Share of Bonuses in Total Wages, by Ownership, 1979–1995

	Percentage share			
	Overall	State-owned	Collective	Other
1979	7.5	7.9	6.0	—
1983	12.9	12.9	13.0	—
1988	19.2	19.5	18.0	20.0
1993	22.2	23.3	16.6	25.5
1994	17.9	17.9	15.3	24.2
1995	16.3	16.8	13.6	21.7

Source: PRC, MOL 1996, p. 41.

Table 6.25

The Contribution of Earnings Components to the Divergence of Earnings Across Provinces, Urban China, 1988–1995

	Coefficient on the explanatory variable	
Explanatory variable:	Initial earnings (y_0)	Initial component earnings (y_{i0})
Basic wage	0.481*	0.018
Bonus	1.296	0.466
Cash value of subsidy	0.747	0.218
Earnings from self-employment	−0.715	−0.788
Other earnings	0.825	0.215

Notes: *denotes statistical significance at the 10 percent level. The analysis relates to the ten provinces for which common urban samples are available in 1988 and 1995. The dependent variable is the proportionate growth of the earnings component ($y_{i1} - y_{i0}$).

Equation (6.11) indicates whether each component contributes to the divergence of earnings ($b > 0$), and equation (6.12) whether each component itself diverges over the period ($d > 0$).

Table 6.25 shows the contribution made by each component of earnings to the divergence in the growth of earnings across provinces. Only self-employment earnings have the wrong sign and the contributions of bonuses and subsidies are important. For instance, a 10 percent higher initial level of earnings raises the growth of bonuses by 13 percent, and that of subsidies by 7 percent. However, the importance of the basic wage in total earnings means that it contributes more in absolute terms to the divergence. We see from the second column that bonuses and subsidies, rather than basic wages, are themselves subject to the strongest divergence.

Tables 6.26 through 6.28 follow 6.23 through 6.25 but analyze the components

Table 6.26

Growth of Income Components, Urban China, by Province, 1988–1995 (%)

	Y_1	Y_2	Y_3	Y_4	Y_5	Income
Beijing	91.5	113.1	627.8	1,537.5	−82.2	82.0
Shanxi	21.6	235.4	261.8	1,588.6	−49.4	40.7
Liaoning	29.4	154.4	767.9	834.7	−86.1	33.5
Jiangsu	48.1	161.1	119.6	1,162.7	−64.7	64.7
Anhui	20.1	266.5	97.7	8,091.5	−81.2	41.2
Henan	16.0	229.7	460.8	460.8	−74.5	40.2
Hubei	46.4	141.0	891.7	681.9	−65.2	52.6
Guangdong	82.6	183.1	222.0	810.8	−85.3	78.9
Yunnan	37.3	145.8	159.2	1,309.4	−69.7	45.8
Gansu	−0.7	192.7	10.6	800.2	−81.6	10.6
Coastal	58.6	127.0	180.8	768.8	−81.8	58.0
Interior	29.9	145.8	197.1	893.7	−70.9	38.7
Total	44.5	141.4	198.7	817.3	−75.4	49.3

Notes: Y_1 = wage income of workers; Y_2 = pensions and income of retired people; Y_3 = earnings of private owners and self–employed; Y_4 = household property income; Y_5 = other income. Coastal region includes Beijing, Liaoning, Jiangsu, and Guangdong; interior region includes Shanxi, Anhui, Henan, Hubei, Yunnan, and Gansu.

of growth in income per capita. Apart from "other income" (Y_5), wage income (Y_1) tended to grow least rapidly (Table 6.26). Income involving capital—from self-employment (Y_3) and from property (Y_4)—grew most rapidly, both on the coast and in the interior. The increase in wage income is greatest in booming Beijing, Jiangsu, and Guangdong, both absolutely and as a percentage of the increase in total income, and lowest in less successful Henan, Shanxi, and Gansu, where the growth of pensions dominates (Table 6.27). Table 6.28 shows that the divergence of income per capita across provinces is overwhelmingly due to the behavior of wage income. Indeed, the other sources of income all have significantly negative coefficients in the second column, indicating that these components actually converged across provinces.

Our second approach is to examine the divergence of earnings in different subsectors (Table 6.29). Production and nonproduction workers are distinguished, as are the three ownership categories: nonstate enterprises, state enterprises, and government (almost all nonenterprise activities being in state hands). There is no difference at all in the degree of divergence as between staff and workers, and very little as between the three ownership categories (the range of coefficients being from 0.544 to 0.594). It appears that divergence among provinces occurred irrespective of occupation and of whether employers were subject to government control and of whether they were in a position to make profits and engage in rent sharing with their employees.

We decided to pursue the distinction between the coastal and the interior prov-

Table 6.27

Contribution of Income Components to the Change in Income, Urban China, by Province, 1988–1995, in Yuan and as Percentage of Total

	Y_1	Y_2	Y_3	Y_4	Y_5	Change in income
Beijing	1,064	266	30	124	−162	1,321
	(80.6)	(20.2)	(2.3)	(9.38)	(−12.4)	(100.0)
Shanxi	202	188	20	70	−35	445
	(45.2)	(42.2)	(4.5)	(15.6)	(−7.8)	(100.0)
Liaoning	334	160	22	82	−128	470
	(71.2)	(34.1)	(4.6)	(17.4)	(−7.2)	(100.0)
Jiangsu	535	357	16	102	−66	944
	(56.7)	(37.9)	(1.7)	(10.8)	(−7.0)	(100.0)
Anhui	204	277	12	101	−79	515
	(40.2)	(54.3)	(2.4)	(19.6)	(−14.8)	(100.0)
Henan	163	297	22	39	−61	460
	(32.8)	(63.4)	(4.6)	(8.0)	(−14.3)	(100.0)
Hubei	478	197	23	71	−78	692
	(69.6)	(28.7)	(3.4)	(10.4)	(−11.4)	(100.0)
Guangdong	1,331	252	68	183	−214	1,620
	(82.1)	(15.5)	(4.2)	(11.3)	(−13.2)	(100.0)
Yunnan	415	135	19	104	−68	605
	(68.4)	(22.30)	(3.1)	(17.2)	(−11.7)	(100.0)
Gansu	−7	182	2	74	−110	140
	(−5.0)	(129.7)	(1.1)	(53.1)	(−78.9)	(100.0)
Coastal	722	208	26	97	−135	918
	(78.5)	(22.6)	(2.8)	(10.5)	(−14.7)	(100.0)
Interior	291	151	16	64	−68	455
	(63.5)	(33.2)	(3.6)	(13.9)	(−14.9)	(100.0)
Total	475	178	21	76	−92	659
	(72.1)	(27.0)	(3.2)	(11.6)	(−13.9)	(100.0)

Notes: Y_1 = wage income of workers; Y_2 = pension and income of retired people; Y_3 = earnings of private owners and self–employed; Y_4 = household property income; Y_5 = other income. Coastal region includes Beijing, Liaoning, Jiangsu, and Guangdong; interior region includes Shanxi, Anhui, Henan, Hubei, Yunnan, and Gansu.

Table 6.28

The Contribution of Income Components to the Divergence of Income Across Provinces, Urban China, 1988–1995

	Coefficient on the explanatory variable	
Explanatory variable:	Initial income (y_0)	Initial component income (y_{i0})
Wage income	0.861***	0.878**
Pension	−0.451	−0.260*
Income from self-employment	0.115	−0.730***
Property income	−0.552	−0.844***
Other income	−1.412*	−0.830**

Notes: ***denotes statistical significance at the 1 percent, ** at the 5 percent level, and * at the 10 percent level. The analysis relates to the ten provinces for which common urban samples are available in 1988 and 1995. The dependent variable is the proportionate growth in the income component $(y_{i1} - y_{i0})$.

Table 6.29

The Coefficient on Initial Earnings in Equations Predicting the Growth of Earnings in Various Subsamples, Urban China, by Province, 1988–1995

Subsample	Coefficient on initial earnings
Production workers	0.581*
Nonproduction workers	0.581
Nonstate enterprises	0.594**
State enterprises	0.544
Nonenterprise sector (government)	0.566

Note: ** indicates statistical significance at the 5 percent, and * at the 10 percent level.

inces. In 1988 the ratio of coastal to interior mean earnings was 123 percent, and in 1995 it was 150 percent. The ratio of 1995 to 1988 mean earnings was 154 percent in the coastal provinces and 127 percent in the interior provinces. To what extent was the growing divergence between the two regions due to growing regional differences in the mean income-earning characteristics of workers and to what extent was it due to growing regional differences in the income-generation process itself?

We attempt to answer this question by conducting standard decomposition analyses of the difference in mean earnings both between the two regions and between the two years:

$$\bar{y} - \bar{y} = f_i(\bar{x}_i) - f_j(\bar{x}_j)$$

$$= f_i(\bar{x}_i) - f_i(\bar{x}_j) + f_i(\bar{x}_j) - f_j(\bar{x}_j)$$

$$= f_i(\bar{x}_i - \bar{x}_j) + f_i(\bar{x}_j) - f_j(\bar{x}_j) \qquad (6.13)$$

where $i, j = 1995, 1988$, or coast, interior; a bar over a variable indicates its mean value; and x is a vector of explanatory variables. The first term measures the component attributable to the difference in mean characteristics and the second term the component attributable to differences in earnings functions. The alternative decomposition is

$$y_i - y_i = f_j(\bar{x}_i - \bar{x}_j) + f_i(\bar{x}_i) - f_j(\bar{x}_i) \tag{6.14}$$

The competitive market prediction is that the income-generation mechanism should be the same everywhere. However, endowments of workers' characteristics could differ spatially, and it is this that would produce spatial differences in means (and in inequality) in a fully competitive economy. China does not have such an economy: We see in Table 6.30 that the earnings difference between the coast and the interior in both years was due entirely to differences in coefficients and not at all (the effect was negative) to differences in characteristics. Similarly, we see that changes in coefficients were overwhelmingly important to the increase in mean real earnings between 1988 and 1995 in both regions.

It is worth exploring further which explanatory variables contributed most to that part of the mean earnings gap that was attributable to the difference in coefficients (Table 6.31). In comparing the coastal and interior regions, we see that the intercept term was crucial in 1988, accounting for some 95 percent of the total. This represented the characteristics omitted from the earnings function analysis (male, aged 25–29, 0–3 years of education, Han, not a party member, production worker, in state sector manufacturing, self-employed), that is, what might be regarded as basic urban unskilled labor.

The mean real earnings difference between the regions attributable to coefficients rose from 450 to 1,140 yuan per annum over the seven years. In 1995 education accounted for no less than half of this difference, having had a slight negative effect in 1988. The intercept term accounted for the other half. In addition, ownership had a positive effect and age a negative effect. Age was less well rewarded at the coast than in the interior.

Of crucial importance were the differential returns to education. The premium on higher education relative to zero to three years of primary school was 92 percent at the coast and 49 percent in the interior. This helped to raise the relative mean earnings of coastal workers. It appears that pressure of demand for educated workers in the coastal provinces raised their pay and contributed to the divergence of earnings among provinces.

Conclusions

Using the urban samples of the CASS national household surveys of 1988 and 1995, we established two interesting results that deserve attention and explanation. First, there was a tendency for intraprovince inequality in both earnings per

Table 6.30

Decomposition Analysis of the Difference in Mean Earnings in Urban China: Coast-Interior, 1988–1995

	Percentage of the difference in mean earnings that is due to:	
	Coefficients	Mean values
1988–1995		
Coastal provinces		
Equation (6.13)	68.8	31.2
Equation (6.14)	90.0	10.0
Interior provinces		
Equation (6.13)	67.1	32.9
Equation (6.14)	81.1	17.9
Coast-interior		
1988		
Equation (6.13)	110.4	−10.4
Equation (6.14)	109.6	−9.6
1995		
Equation (6.13)	101.0	−1.0
Equation (6.14)	106.4	−6.4

Table 6.31

The Contribution of Each Worker Characteristic to the Regional Difference in Mean Earnings Attributable to Coefficients, Urban China, 1988 and 1995

	1988		1995	
Equation used:	(6.13)	(6.14)	(6.13)	(6.14)
Intercept	94.1	94.9	57.7	54.7
Sex	−0.9	−1.0	−1.2	−1.1
Age	13.8	13.1	−12.8	−13.3
Education	−13.9	−14.5	53.0	49.0
Party membership	−4.5	−4.0	4.3	3.8
Minority status	−1.9	−1.1	−3.0	−1.6
Ownership category	−19.9	−22.9	17.1	20.5
Occupation	5.1	4.6	−2.9	−2.9
Employment status	11.4	12.0	−17.2	15.0
Sector	16.7	18.9	5.0	5.9
Total	100.0	100.0	100.0	100.0

worker and household income per capita not only to rise in each province but also to converge across provinces. Second, there was a tendency for both province mean earnings per worker and household mean incomes per capita not only to rise in each province but also to diverge across provinces. The same tendencies were to be found at the regional (coastal-interior) and city levels. This chapter was concerned to establish these patterns and then to explain them. We did better in achieving our first objective than in achieving our second. We explored various avenues but could not produce conclusive explanations.

Our analysis to decompose inequality by source of income indicated that the basic wage was the most important reason for the general increase in earnings inequality. Moreover, the basic wage made the greatest contribution to the convergence of earnings inequality across provinces although other sources were themselves more powerfully convergent. The one exception was bonuses, which were divergent. With regard to inequality of income, wage income was the main reason for the increased inequality in the coastal region, but it made no contribution in the interior region, where pensions were crucial. Wage incomes made the greatest contribution to the convergence of inequality across provinces, but all components of income other than pensions were convergent.

The fact that convergence of earnings inequality appeared to be stronger for "staff" than for "workers" and for nonstate than for state employees suggests that market forces played a role in producing convergence. It is likely that the uneven timing of reforms also played a role: Those provinces and cities that reformed early had greater inequality in 1988 but a smaller increase in inequality thereafter. Our proxy measure of the extent of labor market reform in 1988 did indeed have a positive effect on inequality in that year.

Our analysis of the inequality of inequality appears to break new ground. Given competitive markets all round, the spatial convergence of income or earnings inequality would require that economies become more alike in their distribution of productive characteristics among households or workers. However, markets in China have by no means been competitive throughout. They became more competitive between 1988 and 1995, although the process was spatially uneven. We explained convergence in terms of the process and timing of market reforms.

The decomposition of the growth in mean earnings showed basic wages to be the main, and the most dynamic, component. Basic wages also made the largest contribution to divergence, although bonuses and subsidies were themselves subject to stronger divergence. The most dynamic component of income growth was income from capital, but wage income made the greatest contribution, and pensions were also important in the interior. The divergence of income per capita across provinces is due to the behavior of wage income, as all other components actually converged.

Divergence in earnings occurred irrespective of occupation or of type of employer. A decomposition analysis of the difference in mean earnings in coastal and interior provinces showed that it was due entirely to the difference in their income-generation processes. The widening of the difference over the seven years was partly due to the relative improvement in the pay of unskilled labor and partly to the sharper rise in the premium on education in the coastal provinces. This last finding suggests that market pressures for scarce labor were a driving force. Another indication that market forces were at work is the finding that mean earnings converged among the cities of a province but diverged among provinces, that is, mobility of labor limits divergence and assists convergence.

Bonuses are the component of wages over which enterprises probably have greatest autonomy. Their part in our story therefore deserves scrutiny. Being dependent on the profitability and negotiating power (over soft budgets) of enterprises, bonuses tend to segment the labor market by enterprise. Walder (1987) has argued that bonuses are fairly equally distributed within the enterprise, reflecting worker pressures and preferences. However, there may be as many work units as households in our urban sample. We found bonuses to be the most disequalizing component of earnings. Bonuses were more unequally distributed among workers, and also among provinces, in 1995 than in 1988, probably because of greater segmentation among enterprises. Bonuses do not help to explain the interprovince convergence of earnings inequality that we observed; indeed, their effect is divergent. Bonuses are also an important source of the interprovince divergence of mean earnings. The share of bonuses in earnings fell over the seven years. They may nevertheless have been the driving force behind the growth of earnings, a role that could have been concealed by the consolidating wage reform of 1994.

Convergence of mean incomes among economies is consistent with models of technological diffusion and with neoclassical growth models of closed economies. It is also consistent with increased factor mobility across economies. There is much evidence of conditional economic convergence around the world. However, we found economic divergence among the regions of urban China. The most plausible explanation is the relative lack of factor mobility and the weakness of market forces. The former permitted very different income-generation functions to exist, and the latter permitted wages in general, and bonuses in particular, to be influenced by rent-sharing behavior as well as by local supply-and-demand conditions.

If our interpretations of the results are correct, two policy conclusions follow. First, economic reform may have a once-for-all and finite effect on inequality. The growth of inequality is limited by the processes that produced cross-province convergence in inequality. Second, although divergence in mean earnings and incomes may continue across provinces, further reform of the labor market—assisting labor mobility, and giving more rein to market forces in the slower reforming provinces—can slow it down and may eventually reverse it.

Note

This chapter was written while Zhao Renwei and Li Shi were visiting Oxford from the Institute of Economics, Chinese Academy of Social Sciences, Beijing, Zhao Renwei as a Visiting Fellow of All Souls College. The support of the Economic and Social Research Council under grant R000236846 is gratefully acknowledged.

References

Barro, Robert J., and Xavier Sala-i-Martin (1995). *Economic Growth*, New York: McGraw-Hill.
Jian, Tianlun, Jeffrey Sachs, and Andrew Warner (1996). "Trends in Regional Inequality in

China," *China Economic Review*, 7, 1, Spring, 1–22.
People's Republic of China, Ministry of Labor (PRC, MOL) (1996). *China Labor Statistical Yearbook 1996*, Beijing.
Walder, Andrew (1987). "Wage Reform and the Web of Factory Interests," *China Quarterly*, 109, March, 22–41.

7

Urban Housing Welfare
and Income Distribution

Wang Lina

In recent years the continuing increase in income inequality among urban residents has aroused great concern. There are many factors contributing to the widening gap, including factors having to do with labor and other markets, problems left by history, contradictions of the dual economic system created during the transition,[1] and so forth. Among them, the delay of the housing reform is a factor that cannot be ignored.

Based on the data of the sample survey carried out by the international collaborative research team working with the Institute of Economics, CASS, and data from the State Statistical Bureau (SSB) and the Ministry of Construction, this chapter begins with a description of the formation of multiple housing prices in China's urban areas and examines the value differentials between public housing and commodity housing of various rents and sale prices, which have caused a decrease in housing welfare.[2] Then the chapter turns to the impact of housing welfare upon income distribution among urban residents in different occupations, positions, sectors of work unit ownership, and geographical locations. Finally, some policy recommendations are suggested for deepening the housing reform.

Formation of Multiple Housing Prices and Increase
of Housing Welfare

In a market economy housing is usually traded in two ways: through the rental of housing services or the sale of housing assets. Both rents and sales prices are market prices, and their difference lies in the fact that one is a realization of the exchange value of the housing asset in a lump-sum form, while the other is for the purchase of housing services on a monthly basis. Housing demand depends

Table 7.1

Urban Housing Investment, 1991–1995, 100 million yuan (%)

	1991	1992	1993	1994	1995
Total housing investment	523	750	1,750	2,487	2,993
By developers	180 (34)	331 (44)	839 (47)	1,089 (44)	1,757 (58)
By work units	343 (66)	419 (56)	911 (53)	1,399 (56)	1,236 (42)

Source: Ministry of Construction.
Note: Of the investment by work units, less than 5 percent was private.

primarily on people's income, while the forces of demand and supply connect rental levels and housing prices in a unified housing market.

China is in transition from a planned economy to a market economy. Although the reform in the past ten years has brought great changes to production, circulation, and consumption of housing, the traditional supply system still persists in which the work units are the main providers of workers' housing. The existence of a dual system of housing supply and distribution has led to the coexistence of multiple prices in housing markets, which in turn has had a negative impact upon income distribution.

Increase of Housing Subsidy Caused by Low Rents

China has a huge rental housing market. In most of the large and medium cities, 70 or 80 percent or more of dwellings are public rental units. Such a large rental market is the result of years of housing construction and in-kind distribution by the work units. Since 1980, when Deng Xiaoping first raised the idea of housing reform, and especially since the start of the nationwide housing reform in 1988, rent increases constituted the major part of the reform. However, after more than ten years of this, the results were far from satisfactory. Data from our survey show that the average rent was up from 0.13 yuan per square meter in 1978 to 0.71 yuan per square meter in 1995 in the sampled cities, an average annual increase of less than 0.05 yuan.[3] It really amounted to nothing, even with inflation remaining modest. It is inevitable that low rent has caused in-kind subsidies of the existing public housing stock to rise.

In addition to the old public housing stock in the rental market, a large number of new housing units are built annually. In recent years many new units were built by real estate developers and sold at market prices, while investment by work units in housing construction has kept declining. Since the umbilical cord between work units and workers has not been cut, the work units are still the main buyers in the housing market (Tables 7.1 and 7.2). They buy housing units at the market price and then allocate them to their employees at below market rent. Thus much of the newly built commodity housing stock has returned to the old welfare housing sys-

Table 7.2

Sales of New Housing Stock, 1991–1995, 10,000 Square Meters (%)

	1991	1992	1993	1994	1995
Sale of commodity housing	27.45	38.12	60.35	61.18	66.15
Purchased by individuals	9.27 (34)	14.56 (38)	29.43 (48.8)	33.45 (54.7)	35.12 (53.1)
Purchased by work units	18.19 (66)	23.56 (62)	30.92 (51.2)	27.74 (45.2)	31.03 (46.9)

Source: Ministry of Construction.

tem, as a result of which most urban residents with rental units provided by work units enjoy extremely low rent, far below market levels, in effect receiving substantial in-kind subsidies. Moreover, such housing subsidies are increasing with the improvement of people's housing conditions.

To measure the per capita value of the housing subsidy, we first calculate the price differential between the market rent of commodity housing and the controlled rent of public housing, and then multiply the differential by per capita housing space. Thus, the per capita housing subsidy is

$$\text{(housing space per head)} \times \text{(market rent }/m^2 - \text{controlled rent}/m^2). \tag{7.1}$$

Since there is still no fully competitive market rent determined solely by supply and demand in China, if only because of the price distortions caused by the dual housing system, we convert the average sale price per square meter of commodity housing in the sample cities into an approximate market rent, based on the principle that the sale price equals the present value of cash flow of rent payments. The calculation of monthly rent payments of commodity housing is just an application of the present value of an annuity, which can be determined as follows:

$$\text{Monthly rent payment} = \frac{\text{sale price/ square meter}}{\text{present value of an annuity of 1 yuan per month}} \tag{7.2}$$

The present value of an annuity of Y1 per month is $\dfrac{1-\dfrac{1}{(1+r)^n}}{r}$ (7.3)

where n = number of monthly rent payments

r = simple monthly interest rate (annual interest rate/12)

Here we assume $n = 600$, because the longevity of housing in China is around fifty years, and $r = 0.00667$ percent. The result of the calculation is shown in Table 7.3.

The comparison of controlled and market rents shows that in 1995 the average rent for public housing was 10 yuan lower than the average market rent, signifying that those occupying public housing received an annual subsidy of 120 yuan per square meter. If measured by an average per capita floor space of 10.80 square meter,[4] the annual subsidy per capita was around 1,296 yuan.[5] Although our estimate of the per capita annual subsidy is lower than SSB's estimate of 1,960 yuan,[6] it has shown that the housing subsidy is positively related to the area occupied and to the rent differentials. With the improvement of housing conditions, the increase in floor space per capita, and the growth of the rent gap, especially in large cities (e.g., Beijing and Guangzhou) the housing subsidy has grown for those still in public housing.

Table 7.3

Differentials Between Low Rents and Market Rents in 1995 (yuan /square meter)

Province	Controlled rents	Market rents	Rent differentials
Beijing	0.93	21.92	20.99
Shanxi	0.41	6.24	5.83
Liaoning	1.04	10.13	9.09
Jiangsu	0.59	8.47	7.88
Anhui	0.80	6.10	5.30
Henan	0.41	5.30	4.89
Hubei	0.29	14.86	14.57
Sichuan	1.34	7.13	5.79
Guangdong	0.43	21.05	20.62
Yunan	0.94	8.67	7.73
Gansu	0.44	7.94	7.50
Average	0.71	10.71	10.00

Notes: The data for controlled rent is from the sample provinces and cities. The market rent is calculated based on the average sale price of commodity housing in sample cities. The data for market prices on sale of commodity housing comes from the Ministry of Construction, as shown in Table 7.4 (p. 174). Note that this procedure obscures variations in price as among different neighborhoods in the same city and among different cities in the same province.

New Shadow Income from Multiple Sale Prices

The market for housing is at a nascent stage of establishment in urban China. Due to the coexistence of dual housing supply systems, the lack of proper legal regulation, and the absence of specialized real estate agents in property appraisal, consultation, and services, the prices of housing are widely different. At present there are at least two types of sales prices of housing, which are targeted to different income groups: (1) prices of commodity housing provided by real estate developers for high-income groups, and (2) prices of public housing provided by local governments and work units for low- and medium-income groups. Here we focus on the price differentials between the market price of commodity housing and the cost price used in the sale of public housing.

The sale of public housing on a large scale was advocated after the Third National Conference on Housing Reform in July 1994. According to the decision made by this conference, the sale of public housing at cost price is encouraged in order to stimulate housing commercialization. The cost price is based on the average cost of construction of public housing in various cities. More specifically it includes: (1) land acquisition and compensation for resettlement, (2) land development, survey, and design, (3) construction of housing, (4) infrastructure of the residential area (water pipelines, sewage, drainage, general heating, etc.), (5) maintenance and management, (6) loan interest payment, and (7) taxes.

To encourage the residents to purchase public housing, the government has provided some preferential policies, such as a low 1.5 percent depreciation rate for old housing stock, a working-age discount of 0.6–0.9 percent, and a 5 percent discount for purchase of currently occupied dwellings and for lump sum payment of the whole price. There is no doubt that such preferential treatment is a kind of compensation for workers' low wages in the past, which excluded the capital consumption cost of housing. And in view of the institutional change in the transition, such a policy will have a positive effect on the people's consumption behavior and stimulate their incentive to own their own home. But such an artificially low price and the resulting segmentation of the housing market also have distinct effects on the income distribution.

While the sale price of public housing is kept artificially low, the sale price of commodity housing has been rising rapidly. From 1988 to 1995 the average growth rate of commodity housing prices was 17 percent.[7] There are many underlying reasons for such a high inflation rate of commodity housing.

First, the in-kind distribution of housing by work units has distorted the mechanism for price formation. Although the supply of commodity housing by real estate developers had increased from 31 percent of the total housing supply in 1991 to 58 percent in 1995, a high percentage of such housing was bought by state-owned enterprises and institutions. With Beijing as an example, government work units were the main buyers and took 85 percent of the commodity housing in 1995 and 76 percent in 1996. Since the ordinary residents who are the final consumers have not entered the market themselves, the soft budget constraint of the work units creates a false demand, which drives the market price up far beyond the affordability of the final consumers.

Second, the inflow of huge amounts of foreign capital has added fuel to the overheating of the real estate market and pushed prices higher. In the years from 1991 to 1995, foreign investment in real estate took 2 percent, 4 percent, 6.2 percent, 9 percent, and 12 percent, respectively, of China's actual use of foreign capital.[8] The high profit-seeking behavior of foreign investors had induced domestic investors to pour more money into luxury hotels, office buildings, and apartments. In some large coastal cities, the rate of return on real estate investment was over 100 percent, much higher than in other sectors. In the second half of 1993 the government took decisive measures to ease the overheated real estate market. But the immediate effect of such blind investment was extremely high land prices and related high prices for housing.

Finally, the "rent seeking" behavior of government institutions and shortage of funds for urban infrastructure development also contribute to the rapid increase of land and housing prices. In China, urban land belongs to the state, but the present users and local governments have strong bargaining power in land transactions, which has led to rampant rent-seeking activities and corruption. Added to the irrational financing of infrastructure, a lot of illegal taxes, fees, and charges are added to the price of commodity housing. Some official surveys indicate that about 45 percent of the price of housing consisted of construction costs, 20 percent was land acquisition and development costs, 20 percent was basic infrastructure costs, and the remaining 15 percent was miscellaneous charges and fees. For instance, in Beijing seventy-six taxes and fees are approved by the municipal government. In fact, there are even more fees and charges. On occasion, a charge for an "unexpected cost" might take as much as 4 percent of the total sales price.

As a result of such high prices, much newly built commodity housing is overstocked, while large numbers of urban residents are still living in crowded conditions. The housing market has entered a vicious circle: The higher the price of commodity housing, the more difficult for residents to pay, the more they rely upon welfare housing, and the higher the price of commodity housing.

More fundamentally, urban residents do not have equal opportunity in a housing market with great price differentials, due to their different work units, the structure of ownership, and so forth. In general, most employees in the state-run work units have lived long in low-rent dwellings that they can buy at cost price with preferential treatment, while those outside the state sector have to buy commodity housing at high prices. Thus there is substantial discrimination in housing allocation.

The segmentation of the housing market forces different groups of people to accept different prices, which has given rise to a new "shadow income"—namely, the subsidies inherent in below-market prices. Especially in some large cities, the average sales prices of commodity housing are 4 to 22 times higher than the prices of public housing. The price differentials in our sample cities are shown in Table 7.4.

By the end of 1995, about 20 percent of public housing stock was sold in large and medium cities, while in some small cities and towns over 80 percent of public housing was sold. Although it is truly difficult to estimate the real differentials in sales prices, due to differences in quality, location, and types of construction styles between public and commodity housing, it is undeniable that much public housing, that is in fact newly built commodity housing bought by work units and resold to their workers, does not differ very much in quality from commodity housing.

Moreover, the buyers of public housing enjoy preferential treatment not available to nonstate sector workers. The latter pay not only higher prices for commodity housing but also more taxes, property insurance, and so forth. The deed tax alone costs the owner of commodity housing an extra 6 percent of the sale price. Thus, multiple sales prices and unequal treatment in the housing market has substantially affected the distribution of urban real income.

Effects of Housing Welfare on Urban Income Distribution

The above analysis of multiple prices in rental and sale markets for housing has shown that low rent has increased the shadow subsidy, as housing quality has improved and construction costs have risen. And the sale of public housing at low

Table 7.4

Price Differentials Between Sales of Commodity and Public Housing in 1995 (yuan/square meter)

Sample cities	Price of commodity housing	Price of public housing	Price ratio: commodity to public
Beijing	3226.52	403.68	7.99:1
Shanxi	919.06	238.56	3.85:1
Liaoning	1491.45	272.85	6.47:1
Jiangsu	1247.26	191.28	6.52:1
Anhui	897.80	105.83	8.48:1
Henan	780.02	166.80	4.68:1
Hubei	2187.50	98.53	22.10:1
Sichuan	1050.20	247.59	12.50:1
Guangdong	3100.00	87.04	12.07:1
Yunnan	1276.34	201.01	6.35:1
Gansu	1169.87	241.53	4.84:1
Average price	1576.91	204.97	7.69:1

Notes: The sale prices of public housing come from our 1995 sample survey. In the sale of public housing, a minimum price was set by local governments to prevent extremely low prices from obtaining because of working age discounts, low depreciation, etc. For instance, the cost price of public housing was 1165 yuan/square meter in Beijing in 1995, and the minimum price was set at 240 yuan/square meter. In practice, a large number of public housing units were sold at prices much lower than the cost.

The sale price for commodity housing comes from the Ministry of Construction, 1996.

prices has consolidated and locked in this shadow income. All this contributes to the explosion of what can be called "housing welfare." Moreover, this housing welfare has negative effects upon income distribution of urban residents. It makes the mean total income of urban residents classified by occupations, grades, ownership structure of work units, and geographical locations more unequal than simple wage income seems to be. Thus it affects the inequality of overall urban income distribution. This is demonstrated below in further detail.

Inequality of Income Among Employees Classified by Occupations

For years in China's urban areas, housing had long been regarded as social welfare provided by work units at low rent. But the distribution of such welfare lacked fair and feasible principles. The random allocation of housing funds by the government allowed some large state enterprises and institutions to enjoy more housing welfare than others.

Our survey shows that of all employees in urban areas, the responsible leaders in state-owned enterprises and government institutions have the highest per capita

Table 7.5

Inequality of per Capita Income of Employees by Occupation
(yuan per annum)

Occupation	Size of sample	Total income	Housing welfare	Money income
Private enterprise proprietors	30	6,756.02	1,510.72	5,245.30
Unit leaders of state enterprises and institutions	607	7,977.59	2,370.75	5,606.83
Department heads of state enterprises and institutions	1,178	7,478.09	2,107.56	5,370.52
Administrative staff	2,924	6,776.25	2,078.22	4,698.02
Technical workers	3,166	5,986.25	1,646.89	4,339.35
Nontechnical workers	2,597	5,842.33	1,776.83	4,065.50

income of 7,978 yuan, some 18 percent higher than the private proprietors' total income of 6,756 yuan (Table 7.5). The main factor contributing to this income differential is not monetary income but housing welfare. Comparing money income alone, the state enterprise unit leaders have only 362 yuan more than the private entrepreneurs, a difference of only 6.8 percent. But the former's housing welfare is 57 percent higher or 860 yuan more than that of the latter, and this difference contributes 70 percent of the total income differential between them.[9]

The department heads in state-owned enterprises and government institutions have the second highest income. In terms of wages, their wage income is only 125 yuan or 2.4 percent higher than the private proprietors. But the former enjoy housing welfare of 597 yuan, or 40 percent, more than the latter, which increases their total income advantage to 722.07 yuan.

Although administrative staff have a money income of 547 yuan or 11.6 percent less than private proprietors, they enjoy 568 yuan or 37.6 percent more of housing welfare, so that their total income turns out to be slightly (0.3 percent) higher than that of the private proprietors, rather than lower.

In addition, the money income of technical and nontechnical workers is 17 percent and 22 percent lower, respectively, than that of private proprietors. With housing welfare included, these gaps are much reduced: to only 11 percent and 14 percent, respectively.

Thus housing welfare exercises a substantial influence on urban income distribution by occupation. It widens the total income gap between state enterprise leaders and private proprietors, while narrowing the gap between the latter and technical and nontechnical workers.

Inequality of Income of Employees by Grades

Prior to the reform, housing delivery had long been characterized by administrative distribution according to rank and position. All staff members in government institutions and state-owned enterprises were graded based on their contribution, seniority, and position. As a rule, the higher one's official grade, the more housing space of good quality would be given. For instance, in 1981 public housing was classified into four categories for distribution to different groups of residents. In the first grade were dwellings of 42–45 square meters for ordinary workers; in the second grade were dwellings of 45–50 square meters for ordinary government officials; the third grade consisted of units of 60–70 square meters for allocation to engineers or those with equivalent professional titles and to officials at division chief level; fourth-grade housing was for associate professors, senior engineers or the equivalent, and officials at the level of bureau leader.[10] During the reform, since the dual housing system still exists, the in-kind distribution of housing has provided opportunities for some officials to occupy more housing for individual interests.

Our sample survey (Table 7.6) shows that the amount of housing welfare varies substantially by grade, which in turn affects inequality of per capita total income of urban residents.

First, among similar grades, the administrative officials have more housing welfare than professionals. For instance in our sample, the bureau directors have 1.44 times as much housing welfare as senior professionals; department directors' housing welfare exceeds that of middle-level professionals by 11 percent and division directors' exceeds primary-level professionals' by 5 percent.

Second, among all the administrative officials, the bureau directors' housing welfare is 1.46 times that of department directors and 1.67 times that of division directors. With housing welfare an important component of total income, the larger share of housing welfare means a reduced share and role of wages and salaries in total income. In our sample, bureau directors' housing welfare represents more than half of their money income.

As a result of the housing welfare difference, the advantage of bureau directors over department and division directors in per capita total income is 19 and 39 percent respectively, instead of the 9 and 28 percent that hold for money income alone. Obviously housing welfare has played an important role in increasing income inequality among employees of different grades.

Inequality of Income of Employees by Structure of Ownership

Since the economic reform, the multiple structure of enterprise ownership has broken the monopoly of the state. Of all employees in urban areas, workers in nonstate sectors have increased from 0.16 percent in 1978 to 25 percent in 1995. There were 20.45 million self-employed and workers in private firms, and 5.13 million employees in joint-venture enterprises by the end of 1995.[11]

With the introduction of multiple ownership, the pattern of "one country, two wage systems" has emerged, that is, there is a state-owned sector with low wages, low productivity, and surplus labor, and a nonstate sector with high wages, higher productivity, and fewer workers. The high wages in joint ventures and private firms

Table 7.6

Inequality of per Capita Income of Employees by Grades (yuan per annum)

Grades	Size of sample	Total income	Housing welfare	Money income	Share of housing welfare in total income (%)	Ratio, housing welfare to money income (%)
Senior professionals	491	9,022.48	2,363.93	6,658.55	26	36
Middle professionals	1976	7,562.29	2,114.29	5,447.99	28	39
Primary level professionals	1,645	6,784.45	1,937.44	4,847.00	29	40
Technicians	712	6,970.37	2,022.43	4,947.93	29	41
Bureau director	35	10,037.43	3,413.45	6,623.98	34	52
Department director	322	8,409.01	2,343.42	6,065.59	28	39
Division director	835	7,198.40	2,040.80	5,157.60	28	40

have aroused shock waves in Chinese society, causing many intellectuals and other venturesome individuals to "jump into the sea" of business. The large wage gap also aroused lots of resentment. But when the miscellaneous sources of nonwage income are included, especially housing welfare, the income gap between the state and nonstate sectors is not as large as many people have imagined.

Our survey data show clearly that employees in joint ventures have higher wages than those in the state sector (Table 7.7). The wages of joint-venture employees are 1.39 and 1.62 times higher, respectively, than those in the state-owned and collective enterprises. Because of the small sample size for private firm employees, we cannot say that their apparent 4 percent wage premium, compared with state-sector employees, is significant, but their 20 percent premium compared with the collective sector looks firmer.

Since many employees in joint ventures and private firms are young graduates from universities and colleges, they ought not to enjoy housing welfare. Nevertheless, our survey results indicate that many of them do—perhaps because they live with relatives employed in the state sector. As Tables 7.7 and 7.8 show, housing welfare does not substantially alter the average *relative* income differential between state-sector workers, on the one hand, and those in joint ventures or private firms, on the other: With regard to joint-venture workers, the difference in income is virtually identical whether it includes housing welfare (1.38:1 in favor of joint-venture workers) or not (1.39:1). Comparing state and private-sector workers, as well, housing welfare makes a minimal difference in the relative gap. However, in both cases, the *absolute* income gap is increased by housing welfare.

Housing welfare makes a slightly greater difference in the comparison between collective sector workers, on the one hand, and private or joint-venture workers, on the other. Because the relative advantage in housing welfare of the latter two sectors' workers is somewhat smaller than their advantage in wages, the overall income differential is slightly reduced by considering the housing factor. However, the relatively insignificant impact of housing welfare on the income differential between state and nonstate sector workers may have a simple explanation: If access to housing welfare by nonstate sector workers is due largely to their living with relatives who are state sector workers, then one would expect the amount of housing subsidy to be similar for both groups.

In recent years "one family, two systems" (family members work both in state and nonstate sectors) and "retaining one's position with salary suspended for a long period of leave" (*tingxi liuzhi*) have become popular phenomena in China's cities. The reasons behind this are simple: People are seeking higher pay in the nonstate sectors, but at the same time they do not want to give up the welfare of the state sector. The mixed pattern of employment enables family members to enjoy multiple sources of income, while commonly sharing their income and housing welfare. This makes estimating the mean per capita income of urban residents more complicated and confusing. Some nonstate workers enjoy more housing welfare through such a mixed pattern of employment among family members.

Table 7.7

Per Capita Money and Housing Welfare Income of Employees, by Structure of Ownership (yuan per annum)

Structure of ownership	Size of sample	Total income	Housing welfare	Wage income
State owned enterprise employees	12,019	6,716.57	1,909.34	4,807.23
Collective enterprise employees	2,382	5,947.31	1,807.59	4,139.73
Private firm employees	52	7,050.08	2,067.31	4,982.76
Joint venture employees	158	9,196.02	2,408.93	6,703.47

Notes: Employees in state owned enterprises includes employees in central, provincial, and municipal government owned enterprises and institutions.

Joint-venture employees include those working in joint Chinese and foreign-owned enterprises and in foreign enterprises.

Table 7.8

Comparison of Employees' Various Income Ratios, by Structure of Ownership

	Wage income ratio	Housing welfare	Total income ratio
Joint ventures: state owned firms	1.39:1	1.26:1	1.38:1
Private firms: state owned firms	1.04:1	1.07:1	1.05:1
Joint ventures: collective firms	1.61:1	1.33:1	1.55:1
Private firms: collective firms	1.20:1	1:14:1	1.18:1

This to some extent explains why workers in joint ventures enjoy more housing welfare in our survey.

Inequality of Income of Urban Residents by Geographical Locations.

Housing welfare also has obvious effects upon the income distribution among urban residents in different geographical locations. Our study shows (Table 7.9) that the urban residents in the eastern region of China had a wage income of 5,626.1 yuan, some 52 percent higher than the average wage income of 3,712.6 yuan in the central region and 41 percent higher than the 3,997.9 yuan in the west. Since the 2,413.2 yuan of housing welfare received by eastern residents is 76 percent higher than that received by western residents, the absolute total income inequality between the east and the west increases from the wage differential alone of 1,628 yuan to a total gap

Table 7.9

Inequality of per Capita Income of Employees by Geographical Locations
(yuan per annum)

Regions	Size of sample	Total income	Housing welfare	Wage income
East	7,865	8,039.23	2,413.15	5,626.07
Center	7,880	5,336.05	1,623.48	3,712.57
West	5,788	5,367.22	1,369.34	3,997.88
Ratio, East:Center		1.51:1	1.49:1	1.51:1
Ratio, East:West		1.50:1	1.76:1	1.41:1

of 2,672 yuan; and the relative differential grows from 1.4:1 to 1.5:1. Total income inequality between the eastern and central region grows in absolute terms as well, but remains unaffected in relative terms. This is because the difference in housing welfare is roughly proportional to the difference in wage income.

There are many factors contributing to the income inequality between urban residents of eastern and western China. Historically, most state investment was concentrated in the eastern region. In the Sixth Five-Year Plan (1981–1985), fixed asset investment by the state in eastern China made up 48 percent of the national total; this share rose to 52 percent in the Seventh Five-Year Plan, (1986–1990) and 55 percent in the Eighth Five-Year Plan (1991–1995).[12] With the share of investment in eastern China increasing, the share going to the center and west kept declining. Industrial development, infrastructural improvement, a relatively high quality of education and human capital, and a well-developed commodity market—all these are solid foundations for the differentially rapid development of the eastern economy.

In the economic reform and in opening to the world, the government had taken the strategy of "tilting toward the east and gradient development." Encouraged by preferential policy, four special economic zones were set up in 1980, and fourteen coastal cities opened to the outside world in 1984, followed by a great number of development zones in the Liaodong peninsula, the Jiaodong peninsula, the Yangtze River delta, the Pearl River delta area, and so forth.[13] This preferential treatment has stimulated the fast growth rate of the eastern economy beyond the effects of its preexisting locational advantages. It has in turn further contributed to the rapid increase in urban income in the east, while the west, with poor foundations, a shortage of funds and human resources, and facing policy discrimination, is left far behind.

From the above analysis it is clear that multiple rents and prices for housing have enabled some urban residents to obtain more housing welfare than others. This has certainly affected inequality of overall income among urban residents of different grades and in different geographical locations, as well as among urban employees of different occupations and in work units of different kinds of ownership. The comprehensive data suggest that these effects have contributed to increasing inequality of urban income. The World Bank estimates the Gini coefficient of urban income to have been only 0.16 in 1980.[14] Our own estimate of the Gini ratio for 1988 (calculated somewhat differently) was substantially higher, at 0.233.[15]

Table 7.10

Urban Income Inequality and Its Sources

Income and its components	Share of total income (%)		G or C_i	
	1988	1995	1988	1995
Cash income of working members (wages etc.)	44.42	52.53	0.178	0.226
Cash income of retired workers	6.83	10.41	0.335	0.311
Subsidies and income in kind:				
Housing subsidy	18.14	15.30	0.311	0.335
Other subsidy and income in kind	20.94	0.98	0.188	0.247
Rental value of owner-occupied housing	3.90	16.72	0.338	0.313
Income from private/individual enterprises	0.74	0.59	0.413	0.244
Income from property	0.49	1.09	0.437	0.473
Other	4.53	2.39	0.383	0.354
Total income	100.00	100.00	0.233	0.270

Editor's note: See Table 5.1 for definitions of concentration ratio (C_i) and Gini coefficient (G).

For 1995, we calculate it at 0.27. We believe this rising trend to be real and substantial. Table 7.10 contains the information on the urban Gini coefficient of the income distribution and the concentration ratios of the distribution of different components of income both in 1988[16] and 1995.

Due to extensive sale of public housing, the imputed value of rental services of owner-occupied housing had a remarkable increase from 3.90 percent of total income in 1988 to 16.72 percent in 1995, when it constituted the largest single source of income after cash (wage-type) income. Although housing subsidy as a share of income has declined from 18.14 percent in 1988 to 15.30 percent in 1995, it remains the third largest source of income of urban households.

In addition, the sum of the housing subsidy and imputed rental value of owner-occupied housing rose from 22 percent of total income in 1988 to 32 percent in 1995. To the extent that private housing was obtained at highly subsidized prices, the implication is that in China's market-oriented reform, housing welfare may actually have increased, only the method of distributing it having changed. With more public-housing stock sold and less rental stock of public housing left, housing welfare is now distributed more as a subsidized price of homeownership instead of a housing subsidy in kind as before. Moreover, both the housing subsidy and the imputed value of owner-occupied housing have significantly higher concentration ratios than the weighted average concentration ratios from all other sources. They thus have significantly disequalizing effects on urban income.

Housing is becoming an important symbol of people's wealth. Historical and current kinds of policy and price discrimination do have indisputable effects upon urban income distribution and, ultimately, on social stability.

Conclusions and Policy Recommendations

Housing subsidy and imputed rental value of owner-occupied housing are important elements affecting the inequality of urban income. In the transition, the dual housing supply system has enlarged price differentials in both rental and sale markets of housing. In the rental market, the small step increase in rents of public housing, from 0.13 yuan in 1978 to 0.71 yuan in 1995, contributes to an increase in the per capita housing subsidy received by those who still rent, given the disproportionate improvement in housing quality. The more housing is provided by work units through self-construction or purchase from real estate developers, the more housing subsidy is enjoyed by working members in the state sector. In the sales market for housing, while the speculative activities of foreign investors and domestic real estate developers and the rent-seeking activities of government officials and land users have pushed land and commodity housing prices sky high, the practice has been to encourage existing occupiers to purchase their homes by allowing them to pay cost prices well below the market price of equivalent commodity housing. Due to unequal access to housing units with different rents and sale prices, urban residents enjoy different amounts of housing welfare, which in turn differentially affects their total income.

To eliminate the arbitrary and inequitable effects of the current housing welfare system on income distribution, more efforts are needed in housing reform. First, the in-kind distribution of housing by work units should be stopped and financial institutions and capital for providing mortgage loans should be quickly expanded. With such a fundamental change in the housing supply system, final consumers will enter the housing market to rent or buy based on affordability and with the assistance of mortgage credit, while the government can concentrate its fiscal power on housing for the small group of low-income households who cannot afford to obtain housing through the market. With the withdrawal of work units from the purchase of commodity housing, hard budget constraints of final consumers will force developers to adjust their investment and housing prices to economically sustainable levels. Second, the wage reform should be deepened. The housing funds withheld from wages in the primary distribution of national income and controlled by work units should now be added into workers' wages. Full wage payment will improve the transparency in income distribution, and remove the inequality caused by implicit in-kind distribution of housing welfare. Finally, the government should strengthen the regulations on land transactions and establish stable financial resources for construction of infrastructure as well as mortgage lending, in order to get rid of miscellaneous charges and fees and keep housing prices affordable to urban households.

Notes

I would like to express my thanks to Professors Carl Riskin and Zhao Renwei, who gave me encouragement and help in finishing this chapter, and to Wei Zhong for assistance with the statistical calculations.

1. In the 1980s the government allowed state enterprises to sell surplus product on the free market, after meeting their quota obligations to the state at low state-set prices. Thus was created a dual economic system, with goods carrying two different prices, and the opportunity for well-positioned officials to profit by means of illegal arbitrage.

2. Here housing welfare is the sum of the value of the rent subsidy and the additional imputed rental value of owner-occupied housing created by the differentials of rent and sale prices between public housing and commodity housing.

3. The World Bank Report No. 12757-CHA, "China Enterprise Housing and Social Security Reform Project."

4. State Statistical Bureau, *Statistical Yearbook of China, 1996.*

5. Annual per capita housing subsidy equals: per capita floor space times average monthly rent differential per square meter times twelve months.

6. An SSB study, published in *China Securities Daily* (November 6, 1996), shows that the average welfare income of urban residents was 3,304 yuan in 1995, of which the housing subsidy was 1,960 yuan, pension fund 595 yuan, medicare 306 yuan, and the rest was for education, transportation, and other price subsidies.

7. Ministry of Construction, 1996.

8. Wang Lina, "Analysis on Flow of Funds in Real Estate Market."

9. The significance of this result is tempered by the small size of the sample of private owners, as well as by the likelihood that private income was substantially understated.

10. See Institute of Finance and Trade Economics, CASS, and Institute of Public Administration, *China's Urban Housing Reform*, p. 13.

11. State Statistical Bureau, *Statistical Yearbook of China.*

12. Yu Zhiyao, ed., *Studies on Income Distribution in Transitional China.*

13. The four special economic zones are Shenzhen, Zhuhai, Shantou, and Xiamen in southeast China, and the fourteen coastal cities are Dalian, Qinghuangdao, Tianjin, Yantai, Qingdao, Lianyungang, Nantong, Shanghai, Ningbo, Wenzhou, Fuzhou, Guangzhou, Zhanjiang, and Beihai, all on the east coast.

14. World Bank, *China: Socialist Economic Development*, The World Bank, Washington, DC, 1983, Vol. I, pp. 83–95.

15. Keith Griffin and Zhao Renwei, eds., *The Distribution of Income in China*, p. 45.

16. See Table 5.1 in Chapter 5.

References

Griffin, Keith, and Zhao Renwei, eds., *The Distribution of Income in China*, New York: St. Martin's Press, 1993. Chinese version, China Social Sciences Press, 1994.

Institute of Finance and Trade Economics, CASS, and Institute of Public Administration, *China's Urban Housing Reform*, Beijing, Economic Management Press, 1996.

Ministry of Construction, *Statistics on Chinese Real Estate Development, 1988 to 1995*, Beijing, 1996.

State Statistical Bureau, *Statistical Yearbook of China*, Beijing: China Statistical Publishing House, 1996.

Wang Lina, "Analysis of Flow of Funds in Real Estate Market," *Journal of Housing and Real Estate*, August 1996.

World Bank, *China: Socialist Economic Development.* Washington, DC: The World Bank,1983.

World Bank, Report No. 12757-CHA, "China Enterprise Housing and Social Security Reform Project," June 10,1994.

Yu Zhiyao, ed., *Studies on Income Distribution in Transitional China.* Beijing: Economic Science Press, November 1997.

8

Economic Transformation and the Gender Earnings Gap in Urban China

Björn Gustafsson and Li Shi

Introduction

How are women faring in the transformation from planned economies to market economies that began in the 1980s? Specifically, is the gender wage gap increasing or decreasing? A picture is now emerging, and it shows great diversity in findings from various countries. While available signs point to an increasing gender wage gap in Russia and Ukraine, it appears to be falling in Central and Eastern European countries moving toward a market economy (Brainerd, 1996a, b). This chapter attempts to add another example, as we focus on the size and development of the gender earnings gap in urban China from the second part of the 1980s to the middle of the 1990s. Although we study only the urban population of China, this alone is a labor force larger than that found in any other single country moving away from central planning.

While economic transformation in Central and Eastern Europe as well as in the former Soviet Union was accompanied by large decreases in output, the opposite has been the case in the People's Republic of China. Unlike the case with many other countries in transition, China's economic reform up to now has not meant large-scale privatization of state-owned enterprises. Instead reform has meant giving existing enterprises more freedom to maneuver, which includes greater autonomy in hiring and remunerating workers. Economic reform has also meant removing obstacles to growth for the nonstate sector in China. Much of the spectacular economic growth in China is due to the growth of this sector, composed predominantly of collective enterprises but also of private firms, joint ventures, and the self-employed.

The first task of the chapter is to describe the crude gender earnings gap and its changes. A second task is to analyze reasons for the crude earnings gap and its changes. For this purpose we run earnings functions for females and males in order to determine how much of the crude gender wage gap can be attributed to differences in variables and how much to differences in coefficients. While the latter is an (imperfect) measure of unequal treatment of women in the earnings determination process, the former covers unequal treatment in education and hiring as well as other factors that occur prior to the earnings determination process. Using the Oaxaca decomposition is nowadays a standard technique for analyzing differences in earnings between women and men. Its use is limited, however, as it compares the mean incomes of women and men. A fuller representation is provided in the newer approach of Jenkins (1994).

Obviously we are not the first to study gender aspects of earnings in China, though the existing literature is rather limited. One reason for the paucity of studies of this topic in China may be due to a general feeling among researchers that the gender earnings difference in China could not be a serious problem since the Chinese constitution guarantees women the right to equal pay for equal work. Moreover, there seems to have been serious efforts to implement this policy. Another factor inhibiting studies on gender aspects of earnings in China is the general problem of data availability.

Some studies using data for the 1980s report that, keeping characteristics constant, women earn less than men in urban China (Qian 1996). However, most of these studies do not focus on gender wage differences. One study that does is Meng and Miller (1995), who studied township, villages, and privately owned enterprises in four counties in *rural* China. The only study focusing on gender earnings differences in *urban* China known to us is Qian (1996). While her investigation is based on data from two provinces (Guangdong and Beijing) in 1993, our study covers ten provinces and it is based upon the two household income surveys that provide the empirical basis for this book (see the Introduction). The first survey was for 1988, which was a relatively early phase of the reform process, while the second measures circumstances seven years later, in 1995.[1] There seems to be no previous study of changes in the gender wage differential for urban China.

Changes Affecting Urban Workers[2]

Urban China was patterned after the Soviet economic system during the 1950s. State-owned enterprises (SOEs) came to be the dominating form of the production unit. Workers were administratively assigned to jobs, and wages were centrally regulated. After leaving school, almost all women entered the labor force, and the number of their working hours has been remarkably similar to that of men.

An important reason why women generally earn less than men is the interruption of their working career for childbirth. However, such interruptions have generally been rather short among mothers in urban parts of China. In addition, urban mothers typically do not have more than one child nowadays, and thus only one interruption for childbirth, a circumstance that sets them apart from mothers in many other countries.

While women in China are quite similar to men in working outside the home, they are also the main provider of housework. For example, a time-use study for 1990 shows urban males on weekdays spending half an hour longer on paid work than females. In contrast, women spent two hours longer on housework.[3] Having on average more household responsibilities than men, Chinese women would be expected on average to have less time and energy available to devote to a career, and this should show up in their earnings.

Many Chinese people believe women to be at a disadvantage in finding well-paid jobs.[4] Furthermore, such disadvantage may have increased during the transition process due to changes in work legislation. China has turned to "productive" legislation that focuses on the biological differences between women and men. These laws make an effort to accommodate women's reproductive needs in the workplace (Woo 1994) but, in so doing, have made women less attractive as workers.

The Chinese transition strategy has been a gradual one. It has relied on the creation of market competition through the entry of new domestic producers, while few state-owned establishments were privatized up to 1995. During the 1980s, the crucial role in the creation of competition was played by township and village enterprises (TVEs), which are collectively owned and located in rural China. However, in the 1990s, foreign-invested enterprises began to take the lead in domestic competition.

Table 8.1 shows the breakdown of industrial output by ownership composition in 1988 and each year from 1992 to 1995. As can be seen, the proportion of output coming from SOEs has decreased drastically, being only one-third of the total at the end of the period. Although of the same size at the end of the period, the collective sector is concentrated in rural China. Another expanding sector is that of individually owned enterprises. Foreign-owned enterprises and enterprises owned by overseas Chinese are also of importance. As of 1995, both produced somewhat more then 6 percent of the gross output value.

The Chinese reform process has had a clear regional dimension; for example, changes first took place in the southeast, which was the first to be opened to foreign investment. Economic growth has been much faster there, while interior regions have lagged behind. The development of Guangdong Province has been especially rapid and today its average household income is very high by Chinese standards. In the middle of the 1990s more than one-fourth of all foreign investment in China was going to Guangdong, a province with less than 6 percent of China's population.

Of course changes in ownership and geographical location are likely to have affected earnings of different workers differently. It is a general belief that earnings inequality in China has increased during the period of transformation. Expanding sectors attract new workers by paying more, and there are visible signs that the wages of workers in SOEs and other public organizations have lagged behind those of workers in foreign-invested enterprises.

Table 8.1

Gross Output Value of Industry by Ownership in China (billions of yuan)

	1988	1992	1993	1994	1995
Gross value	1,822.5	3,459.9	4,840.2	7,017.6	9,189.4
(%)	(100)	(100)	(100)	(100)	(100)
State-owned enterprises	1,035.1	1,782.4	2,272.5	2,620.1	3,122.0
	(56.8)	(51.5)	(47.0)	(37.3)	(34.0)
Collective-owned enterprises	658.8	1,213.5	1,646.4	2,747.2	3,362.3
of which:	(36.2)	(35.1)	(34.0)	(37.7)	(36.6)
Township enterprises	184.7	353.4	537.4	810.2	1,193.2
	(10.1)	(10.2)	(11.1)	(11.6)	(13.0)
Village enterprises	170.4	363.2	516.3	965.8	1,184.7
	(9.4)	(10.5)	(10.7)	(13.8)	(12.9)
Joint enterprises	43.9	87.0	132.2	261.1	213.4
	(2.4)	(2.5)	(2.7)	(3.7)	(2.3)
Individual-owned enterprises	79.1	200.6	386.1	708.2	1,182.1
	(4.3)	(5.8)	(8.0)	(10.1)	(12.9)
Other ownership	49.5	268.8	517.4	901.8	1,523.1
of which:	(2.7)	(7.8)	(10.7)	(12.9)	(16.6)
Shareholding			146.1		318.3
			(3.0)		(3.5)
Foreign-owned			185.3		540.8
			(3.8)		(5.9)
Overseas Chinese from			176.1		556.4
Hong Kong, Macao, Taiwan			(3.6)		(6.1)

Notes: Gross output values are in current prices; shares of components are calculated by the authors.

Sources: SSB, *China Statistical Yearbook 1996*, pp. 401, 406–407; SSB, *China Statistical Yearbook 1994*.

In addition to earnings differences caused by sector changes, the range of earnings within each sector has also widened. One would expect differences in earnings by skill level to have grown as productivity considerations have become more important in the wage-setting process. The growing freedom of decision making in SOEs should also cause earnings variation to increase. Several indicators point to the poor performance of industrial state enterprises relative to nonstate enterprises. The number of loss-making enterprises has grown steadily to be as high as 44 percent in 1995 (Naughton 1996, p. 289). Loss-making enterprises have more difficulty paying high wages than profit-making enterprises.

Although not at zero, rates of return to education in China have been low (Byron and Manaloto 1990, Li and Travers 1993). One would expect great pressure for more educated labor from the demand side during the process of transformation.

Countering this have been large increases in the supply of those with more education. What about rates of return to experience? After running earnings equations
for Russian samples collected at different times during the 1990s, Brainerd (1996a)
found a dramatic change, indicating that the human capital of older workers became obsolete during transformation while younger workers gained much ground.
However, it is far from clear if this has happened in China, as the Chinese process
of transformation has been much more gradual.

What have all the changes discussed above meant for the development of the
gender wage gap during transformation? In the old system, earnings were closely
linked to certain characteristics of the worker, without an explicit link to her or his
productivity. Our hypothesis is that during the transition, productivity has become
a more important determinant of individual earnings. In the case of women being
on average less productive than men, the gender wage gap would increase, an
increase that would not necessarily stand for increased wage discrimination.[5]

Methodological Considerations

In this section we analyse the gender earnings gap using the current standard decomposition attributed to Oaxaca (1973). It helps distinguish unequal treatment of women
before the earnings determining process (differences in variables) from unequal treatment in the earnings-determining process (differences in coefficients). In the literature the latter is most often referred to as "earnings discrimination" to distinguish it
from a wider concept of gender discrimination, including different treatment in education and occupational attainment. To the extent that women are overrepresented
among those of limited education, young adults (with short work experience), enterprises in low-paying sectors, enterprises having low-paying ownership, provinces
with low earnings, and so forth, this will show up as differences in variables.

In applying this framework, one faces a "fractal problem." For a given sample
one is likely to find that the more narrowly that occupational categories are defined, the smaller the part of the earnings gap that can be attributed to earnings
discrimination. Taken to extremes this can lead to the conclusion that there are no
two identical occupations and, as a consequence, all of the crude gender earnings
gap must be attributed to differences in variables. Thus, it is not possible to measure earnings discrimination at one time without referring to how broadly occupations are defined. When making comparisons over time, occupations (as well as
other variables) should be defined in the same way each year under observation.

Another well-known limitation when applying this decomposition approach is
the possibility of omitted variables bias. If variables omitted from the wage function are correlated with gender, it is not appropriate to interpret differences in
coefficients as an unbiased measure of discrimination. Consider the example of
increases in human capital by investment in on-the-job training, which typically is
not observed by the analyst but indicated by an experience or potential experience
variable. One year of potential experience for the average female might indicate

less on-the-job training and therefore less human capital than one year of potential experience for an average male. Therefore when estimating a regression model, a lower coefficient for the experience variable among females does not necessarily mean discrimination. Unfortunately, in this study (as in most other studies of the gender wage gap) we are not able to measure human capital acquisition by on-the-job training but have to rely on a variable indicating potential experience.

Data and Research Strategy

The data come from the Urban Household Income Surveys conducted in 1989 and 1996. As is pointed out elsewhere in this book, rural households living in an urban area without an urban household registration (*hukou*) were most likely not in the sample. It is not possible to make a well-based estimate of the size of this floating population.

The Urban Household Income Surveys covered ten provinces. Respondents were chosen from the parent SSB sample in order to represent conditions in various regions of China and of cities and towns of various size. The following ten provinces were surveyed: Anhui, Beijing, Gansu, Guangdong, Henan, Hubei, Jiangsu, Liaoning, Shanxi, and Yunnan.[6] There was very little nonresponse.

The two surveys used very similar, although not identical, instruments. The second survey includes some questions not asked earlier, and this permits a somewhat more detailed analysis for the most recent year. The two samples are large: there are 9,354 male and 8,533 female workers in the first sample, and 5,603 male workers and 5,011 female workers in the second.

Information on earnings is collected for the period of one normal month and is then converted to annual amounts by multiplying by twelve. Earnings are defined as the individual income received by active workers from their work unit or their own private business. Earnings consist of four major components: basic wage (or net revenue), bonus, subsidies, and other income.

Our analysis proceeds along the following four steps: First, we present descriptive statistics, allowing for comparisons over time. These include gender earning gaps according to several breakdowns such as age, education, ownership, occupation, and sector. This kind of information, to our knowledge, has not been published for China by the State Statistical Bureau. We also report on how earnings inequality has changed over time. Inspired by Blau and Kahn (1996) who analyzed cross-country differences in the gender wage gap, we investigate if the rank order of women in the distribution of males has changed or not.

The second step is to run earnings equations using logarithmic earnings as the left-side variable. A rather large number of explanatory variables are included, and estimation is made for males and females separately each year under observation.

The third step is to use the estimates from the regression models together with means for females and males to analyze the average earnings gap and its changes for the two years.

The average unadjusted logarithmic differential in gender earnings, defined as G, may be decomposed respectively into an "explained" part and a part that may be misleadingly called "unexplained," which stands for the same characteristics being rewarded differently.

$$\overline{\ln w}^m - \overline{\ln w}^f = (\overline{X}^m - \overline{X}^f)B^m + (B^m - B^f)\overline{X}^f \qquad \text{or}$$
$$\overline{\ln w}^m - \overline{\ln w}^f = (\overline{X}^m - \overline{X}^f)B^f + (B^m - B^f)\overline{X}^m \qquad (8.1)$$

Where m = male and f = female worker, the bar indicates mean values, X the vectors of characteristics, and the B the vectors of estimated coefficients.

Oaxaca's "discrimination" index, D^h, is the unexplained logarithmic gap expressed as an earnings differential. Depending on the weights used, it is given by

$$D^f = \left[\exp(\overline{X}^f (B^m - B^f)\right] - 1$$

$$D^m = \left[\exp(\overline{X}^m (B^m - B^f)\right] - 1 \qquad (8.2)$$

The fourth step is to make a fuller representation of earnings "discrimination" using the method of Jenkins (1994). This analysis also starts from estimated earnings functions. However, instead of analyzing earnings discrimination for a representative person, we look at the entire distribution of women and men. Thus it allows us to investigate if the "discrimination" experience is homogeneous in the sample studied. This analysis starts with the earnings gap defined as the absolute value of the difference between the predicted earnings of an individual when paid according to the men's and women's earnings schedules, respectively.

In a given sample, Jenkins's index can be written as

$$J_\alpha = \sum_{i \in F} \omega_i (1 - d_i^{-\alpha}) = 1 - \sum_{i \in F} \omega_i d_i^{-\alpha}, \qquad \alpha > 0 \qquad (8.3)$$

where

$$d_i = 1 + |\hat{r}_i - \hat{y}_i| / \overline{r}^f,$$

$$\varpi_i = (\overline{y}_i / n_f \overline{y}^f)$$

$\hat{y}_i$ is the predicted income of individual female workers with the rates of return to female attributes in the female wage equation, that is, $\hat{y}_i = \exp(X_i \hat{\beta}^f)$. $\hat{r}_i$ is predicted income of individual female workers with the rates of return to male attributes in the male wage equation, that is, $\hat{r}_i = \exp(X_i\hat{\beta}^m)$. $\bar{y}_i$ and $\bar{r}_i$ are mean values of $\hat{y}_i$ and $\hat{r}_i$ respectively. ϖ_i is wage share of a woman i. The index, $J_\alpha = 0$, when there is no discrmination against female workers, that is, $\hat{r}_i = \hat{y}_i$.

The parameter α reflects different assumptions about how earnings gaps should be aggregated. It can be interpreted as the degree of "discrimination" aversion, with a higher value for α corresponding to greater aversion (Jenkins 1994).

Jenkins's index is suitable for decomposition analysis, when the sample is partitioned into G mutually exclusive subgroups. Total earnings discrimination is the sum of the group's specific discrimination weighted by the size of the group. Decomposition along various breakdowns of the population allows us to paint a full picture of how differently women and men are remunerated. The decomposition formula is written as

$$J = \sum_{g=1}^{G} \theta_g J_g$$

where

$$\sum_{g=1}^{G} \theta_g = 1, \quad \theta_g > 0 \text{ for each } g = 1, \ldots, G.$$

(8.4)

A Statistical Picture of the Changed Urban Labor Force

Urban China underwent a number of important demographic changes between our two points of measurement. The size of the population increased rapidly mainly because of migration, although this has not been fully reflected in the official statistics. The average household size diminished and the population aged.

In Table 8.2 we use the two surveys to portray the urban labor force in 1988 and 1995 by gender, and here we comment on differences across gender and over time. Starting with the participation rates, we see slight decreases over time for both genders. This change is fairly general for all age and gender groups. The only exception pertains to the very low rate for women over their mandatory retirement age of 55; the participation rate for this group rose slightly, from 8 percent to 11 percent. The higher participation rates among older males is due mainly to their higher retirement age of 60. On the other hand, participation rates among the youngest adults is somewhat higher among females, which is consistent with females on average having a shorter education.

The aging of the labor force is clearly seen in Table 8.2. While slightly more than two out of five males in the labor force were below 35 years of age in 1988, this was true of one out of three in 1995. The proportion of women aged 36–45 increased from 33 percent to 42 percent. Because of earlier school-leaving age and earlier retirement, the female labor force is younger than the male labor force.

Any citizen of the People's Republic of China has been assigned one of fifty-six official nationalities. "Han" is the largest of the nationalities. China's national minorities are concentrated in rural areas. About 4 percent of the urban labor force

Table 8.2

Descriptive Statistics of Main Variables by Gender (%)

Variable	1988 Male	1988 Female	1995 Male	1995 Female
Participation rate				
Total	81.1	72.7	78.8	69.5
Aged 16–25	51.5	55.2	46.5	49.0
Aged 26–35	99.0	97.2	97.3	93.9
Aged 36–45	99.5	96.0	98.5	95.1
Aged 46–55	94.6	62.1	92.1	58.7
Aged 56–65	47.9	8.1	38.2	10.9
Composition of workers				
Age group				
16–25	15.3	17.8	10.4	12.2
26–35	25.8	32.6	23.3	27.9
36–45	28.9	32.5	36.4	42.4
46–55	23.4	16.2	22.6	15.5
56–65	6.6	1.0	7.3	2.0
Minority				
National minority	3.8	3.7	4.2	4.3
Nonnational minority	96.2	96.3	95.8	95.7
Party membership				
Member	34.2	11.7	33.3	15.0
Nonmember	65.8	88.3	66.7	85.0
Education				
4-year college	8.7	3.2	10.3	5.2
2-year college	8.2	4.9	18.1	12.6
Professional school	10.8	11.2	16.2	17.2
Upper middle school	24.1	25.4	22.7	26.1
Lower middle school	37.1	40.0	28.1	32.3
Primary school	9.0	11.8	4.3	6.0
Less than primary school	2.0	3.4	0.3	0.7
Ownership				
State-owned sector	43.4	33.8	30.1	22.5
Other public sector	40.3	36.9	53.7	52.0
Collective sector	14.3	26.6	11.1	19.3
Private or self-employed	1.1	1.4	1.7	1.9
Joint-venture or foreign firm	0.03	0.07	1.2	1.1
Other ownership	0.79	1.3	2.3	3.4
Occupation				
Owner of private firm	1.3	1.3	1.7	1.6
Professional or technician	15.6	15.8	21.2	22.2
Responsible officer or manager	7.5	1.5	5.5	1.5
Ordinary officer or manager	3.0	0.5	10.9	4.1
Office worker	25.5	20.9	18.7	21.7
Manual worker	46.6	59.3	42.0	49.1
Work unit profit status				
Enterprise making profits			41.8	40.1
Enterprise making loss			21.4	22.9
Institution			30.9	28.6
Other work unit			5.8	8.4

Table 8.2 *(continued)*

Employment				
Fully employed			88.1	85.4
Partly unemployed			5.9	7.2
Fully unemployed			6.0	7.4
Sector				
1	1.1	0.8	1.9	1.2
2	40.9	44.4	40.8	38.5
3	5.0	3.0	1.2	0.9
4	4.0	2.8	3.2	2.4
5	8.3	5.0	5.7	3.9
6	11.5	17.7	12.1	16.7
7	2.2	2.8	3.3	4.4
8	3.4	5.8	3.4	5.4
9	6.7	7.8	6.2	8.2
10	2.5	1.6	2.5	2.0
11	1.5	1.5	1.8	2.1
12	11.5	5.0	13.3	9.4
13	1.5	1.9	4.7	4.8
Status of job				
Permanent worker	98.6	98.0	94.0	91.3
Temporary or short-term	0.9	1.1	1.9	3.4
Contract worker	0.5	0.9	4.1	5.0
Province				
Beijing	5.1	4.5	7.3	7.0
Shanxi	11.2	10.4	9.6	9.3
Liaoning	10.0	10.7	10.6	10.3
Jiangsu	12.9	12.5	11.2	11.1
Anhui	9.9	9.9	6.8	7.2
Henan	11.7	11.9	8.5	8.1
Hubei	10.7	11.0	10.7	10.6
Guangdong	11.9	12.0	8.5	8.4
Sichuan	—	—	12.0	12.6
Yunnan	9.8	10.6	9.3	9.9
Gansu	6.9	6.6	5.6	5.6
Average years of working experience		—	20.9	17.8

Notes: Sector 1 = agriculture, forestry, animal husbandry, fishing, or water conservancy; Sector 2 = industry; Sector 3 = mining and geological survey, and prospecting; Sector 4 = construction; Sector 5 = transportation, communications, post and telecommunications; Sector 6 = commerce and trade, restaurants & catering, materials supply, marketing, and warehousing; Sector 7 = real estate, public utilities, personal and consulting services; Sector 8 = health, physical culture, and social welfare; Sector 9 = education, culture, arts, and broadcasting; Sector 10 = scientific research and technical services; Sector 11 = finance, insurance; Sector 12 = government and party organization, social organizations; Sector 13 = other.

belongs to a minority. While one out of three male workers is a member of the Communist Party, the proportion is much smaller among females. Turning to education, there were big increases between the two years studied. While in 1988, 17 percent of the male labor force had an education of at least two years of college, in 1995 the proportion had increased to 28 percent. However, in 1995 only

18 percent of the female labor force had at least two years of college, illustrating a clear gender difference, which is also reflected in the occupation distribution. Females are less frequently represented in the categories "professional or manager" and "responsible officer or manager" but more frequently in the category "manual worker."

Males are overrepresented in the state-owned sector, and females in the collective sector. There are some gender differences in the sector composition of the labor force: Females are overrepresented in "commerce and trade, restaurants, etcetera." and underrepresented in "government and party organizations and social organizations."

Table 8.3 shows that between 1988 and 1995 average male annual earnings increased by as much as 47 percent (in real terms) and inequality, as measured by the Gini coefficient, increased from 0.233 percent to 0.289. Turning to components of total earnings, we see that the average for basic wage and subsidies increased faster than total earnings. Subsidies actually more than doubled; they include housing subsidies, one-child allowance, price subsidies, regional subsidies, medical subsidies, and some others. The reforms of the early 1990s brought about a shift in compensation to workers from goods and services provided in kind, to subsidies. On the other hand, bonuses actually decreased. Furthermore, at each point in time the basic wage is the main component of total earnings, and it is more equally distributed than total earnings. Bonuses had the highest concentration coefficient.

In examining changes in earnings inequality over time, Table 8.3 shows that the increase can be traced to two sources: the basic wage and subsidies. The increase in the concentration coefficient is particularly large for subsidies. Thus, during the transition period, benefits from various subsidies have turned out to be much more concentrated among higher earners.

Table 8.4 reports mean earnings for men in 1988 and 1995 and the average gender earnings gap for different breakdowns of the population. We report a modest increase in the gender earnings gap since female earnings as a percent of male earnings fell from 84.4 to 82.5 percent. Although these numbers indicate a deteriorating relative position of urban Chinese women, by international standards the gender wage gap appears to be rather small. One point of reference is Sweden, where the female earnings ratio is known to be higher than in most other industrialized countries. For example, Gustafsson and Johansson (1997) report for full-time, full-year workers an average earnings ratio of females to males of 81.4 percent for 1983, declining to 77.8 in 1991.[7]

Next we look at earnings and the gender earnings gap for various breakdowns of the population, starting with age. While the gender earnings gap in urban China is small among the youngest adults, according to Table 8.4, it very clearly increases with age in both years. For example, in 1988 women aged 16–25 earned only 4 percent less than men of the same age, but the gap was 20 percent among those aged 46–54. The small fraction of women working after their general mandatory retirement age of 55 have earnings remarkably low in comparison to men of the same age, and this gap increased from over 40 percent in 1988 to an extraordinary 58 percent in 1995.

Table 8.3

Descriptive Statistics of Mean Earnings and Inequality by Gender

	1988		1995	
	Male	Female	Male	Female
Mean (yuan)				
Total earnings	2,064	1,727	3,030	2,507
Basic wages	1,088	904	1,775	1,440
Bonus	445	371	444	374
Subsidies	315	277	687	607
Other	216	175	124	86
Gini coefficient or concentration ratio				
Total earnings	0.233	0.237	0.289	0.311
Basic wages	0.158	0.155	0.219	0.225
Bonus	0.399	0.420	0.510	0.544
Subsidies	0.190	0.217	0.327	0.390
Other	0.332	0.308	0.288	0.163
Share of earnings components (%)				
Total earnings	100	100	100	100
Basic wages	52.7	52.4	58.6	57.4
Bonus	21.6	21.5	14.7	14.9
Subsidies	15.3	16.0	22.6	24.3
Other	10.4	10.1	4.1	3.4
Contribution to total inequality (%)				
Total earnings	100	100	100	100
Basic wages	35.7	34.2	44.4	41.6
Bonus	37.0	38.1	25.9	26.1
Subsidies	12.5	14.7	25.6	30.5
Other	14.8	13.2	4.1	1.8

Note: 1995 earnings and earning components are in 1988 prices.

There is also an interesting pattern in the education breakdown. The overall relation between the level of education and earnings is weak for 1988 but clearer for 1995. The change is probably at least partly due to urban workers being rewarded more according to their productivity, one of its determinants being human capital, and partly because the rapid growth of high-tech industries has resulted in a great demand for well-educated workers. The gender earnings gap is smallest among those with a longer education, and there is even a very small decrease in the gap between the two years of observation. On the other hand, the gender earnings gap is larger for those with less education. In addition, with the exception of the very lowest level of education the gender earnings gap has increased among those with less education.

Table 8.4 also gives breakdowns of the data by ownership, occupation, sector, status of job, and province. It is interesting to see that there is no example of

Table 8.4

Mean of Earnings of Men and Women by Population Group

	1988		1995	
Name of variables	Male	Female as percent of male	Male	Female as percent of male
Total	2,016	84	3,030	82
Age group				
16–25	1,229	96	2,231	91
26–35	1,882	91	3,002	88
36–45	2,170	87	3,582	86
46–55	2,416	80	3,920	79
56–65	2,382	59	3,902	42
Minority				
National minority	2,015	80	3,134	82
Nonnational minority	2,023	84	3,422	82
Party membership				
Member	2,326	93	3,902	91
Nonparty member	1,866	88	3,160	85
Education				
4-year college	2,477	87	4,156	89
2-year college	2,101	91	3,668	93
Professional school	2,125	91	3,439	92
Upper middle school	1,870	88	3,192	84
Lower middle school	1,943	85	3,188	78
Primary school	2,152	76	3,054	72
Less than primary school	1,920	71	2,359	79
Ownership				
State-owned sector	2,149	87	3,709	88
Other public sector	2,014	87	3,349	85
Collective sector	1,794	83	2,793	80
Private or self-employed	1,067	63	3,350	75
Joint venture or foreign firm	2,355	80	4,087	90
Other ownership	1,097	94	3,578	77
Occupation				
Owner of private firm	1,205	60	3,582	73
Professional or technician	2,278	87	3,763	90
Responsible officer or manager	2,354	87	4,132	97
Ordinary officer or manager	2,701	81	3,991	94
Office worker	2,106	88	3,334	88
Skilled worker	{1,828	87	3,159	80
Unskilled worker			2,700	84
Other	1,160	85	2,975	80

Table 8.4 *(continued)*

Work unit				
Enterprise making profit			3,568	81
Enterprise making loss			2,689	81
Institution			3,700	89
Other			3,341	78
Employment				
Fully employed			3,492	84
Partly unemployed			2,468	73
Fully unemployed			3,090	75
Sector				
1	2,022	85	3,633	77
2	1,951	85	3,184	82
3	2,021	72	3,456	83
4	2,005	87	3,579	75
5	2,206	81	3,786	77
6	2,053	83	3,184	79
7	1,842	76	3,752	73
8	2,146	87	3,750	91
9	2,153	87	3,828	85
10	2,280	86	3,948	83
11	1,991	84	3,879	92
12	2,067	91	3,528	92
13	1,470	78	3,429	80
Status of job				
Permanent worker	2,041	85	3,429	84
Temporary or short-term	294	67	2,807	71
Contract worker	1,267	86	3,229	75
Province				
Beijing	2,123	87	4,066	86
Shanxi	1,742	85	2,797	74
Liaoning	1,937	88	3,145	80
Jiangsu	1,998	86	3,601	83
Anhui	1,878	79	2,776	77
Henan	1,662	82	2,889	79
Hubei	1,829	89	3,095	88
Guangdong	2,842	85	6,175	85
Sichuan	—	—	3,151	85
Yunnan	2,141	82	3,119	87
Gansu	2,120	74	2,637	79

Notes: Sector 1 = agriculture, forestry, animal husbandry, fishing, or water conservancy; Sector 2 = industry; Sector 3 = mining and geological survey and prospecting; Sector 4 = construction; Sector 5 = transportation, communications, posts, and telecommunications; Sector 6 = commerce and trade, restaurants and catering, materials supply, marketing, and warehousing; Sector 7 = real estate, public utilities, personal and consulting services; Sector 8 = health, physical culture, and social welfare; Sector 9 = education, culture, arts, and broadcasting; Sector 10 = scientific research and technical services; Sector 11 = finance, insurance; Sector 12 = government and party organizations, social organizations; Sector 13 = other. Earnings in 1995 were deflated to 1988 provincial prices.

Table 8.5

Coefficients of Wage Functions of Male and Female Workers, 1988

	Male workers		Female workers	
	Coefficient	T-value	Coefficient	T-value
Intercept	7.206	127.671	6.851	119.558
Age group				
16–25	−0.414	−36.142	−0.330	−28.357
36–45	0.132	13.574	0.099	9.756
46–55	0.208	19.383	0.131	10.085
56–65	0.214	13.316	−0.017	−0.766
National minority	0.027	1.468	−0.005	−0.095
Party member	0.054	6.166	0.103	7.642
Education				
4-year college	0.089	5.785	0.111	4.525
2-year college	0.031	2.188	0.049	2.495
Professional school	0.018	1.413	0.044	2.969
Lower middle school	0.015	1.732	0.007	0.758
Primary school	−0.005	−0.357	−0.070	−4.965
Ownership				
State-owned sector	0.154	13.843	0.193	18.01
Other public sector	0.072	6.827	0.126	12.437
Private or self-employed	−0.354	−3.003	−0.217	−1.568
Joint venture or foreign				
firm	0.391	6.064	0.327	4.811
Other	−0.421	−5.3	−0.015	−0.322
Occupation				
Owner of private firm	0.206	3.043	0.502	7.011
Professional or				
technician	0.274	4.001	0.543	8.695
Responsible officer or				
manager	0.283	4.1	0.574	7.345
Ordinary officer or				
manager	0.355	5.686	0.559	5.118
Office worker	0.239	3.059	0.523	8.488
Skilled worker	0.198	1.887	0.467	7.22
Sector				
1	−0.013	−0.347	−0.023	−0.464
3	0.076	4.596	−0.085	−3.403
4	0.025	1.437	0.026	1.148
5	0.016	1.227	−0.001	0.055
6	−0.019	−1.44	−0.012	−0.74
7	−0.023	−0.867	−0.142	−5.442
8	−0.036	−1.686	−0.024	−1.029
9	−0.044	−2.646	−0.028	−1.346
10	−0.014	−0.545	−0.002	−0.002
11	−0.035	−1.167	−0.059	−1.673
12	−0.073	−5.395	−0.072	−3.161
13	−0.124	−2.813	−0.161	−3.409
Status of job				
Temporary or short-term	−0.253	−6.884	−0.527	−18.732
Contract worker	−0.337	−3.665	−0.390	−5.124

Table 8.5 (continued)

	Male workers		Female workers	
	Coefficient	T-value	Coefficient	T-value
Province				
Beijing	−0.010	−0.509	−0.030	−1.365
Shanxi	−0.237	−15.578	−0.275	−16.061
Liaoning	−0.075	−5.109	−0.055	−3.369
Anhui	−0.125	−8.364	−0.165	−9.791
Henan	−0.251	−17.561	−0.298	−18.603
Hubei	−0.161	−11.183	−0.130	−8.182
Guangdong	0.273	18.879	0.258	15.669
Yunnan	−0.016	−1.053	−0.037	−2.301
Gansu	−0.075	−4.438	−0.182	−9.466
Adj. R^2	0.447		0.394	
F-value	167.4		123.0	
Dep Mean	7.526		7.349	
Number	9,278		8,447	

female earnings being higher than or equal to male earnings. Differences in earning levels across provinces are rather large compared with differences in earnings along other dimensions.

What have changes in earnings inequality in urban China meant for the average gender earnings gap? Our calculations show that in 1988 the female median is located at the 38.3 percentile of the male earnings distribution. Seven years later the location is actually slightly higher, at the 39.7 percentile (in a now more unequal distribution). This indicates that the increase in the gender earnings gap in urban China is driven by increased earnings inequality, not by a deteriorating relative position of women in the earnings distribution.

Earnings Functions

Estimated earnings functions for males and females are reported in Table 8.5 for 1988 and in Table 8.6 for 1995. There are many results worth commenting on.

Earnings in urban China are very clearly related to age. In 1988 age effects increased in the male equation up to the age class 46–55, after which it leveled out. However, in 1995 the age effect for those over 55 was much smaller which might reflect that productivity considerations were more important than previously when determining earnings for older workers. Note also the large negative effect of being over 55 for female workers in 1995. Females working after the general retirement age are very low paid.

All estimated effects of minority status are small and have a low degree of statistical significance. On the other hand, being a Communist Party member has a positive effect, estimated with a high t-value. However, this effect, which might stand for a party member having more social capital than a nonparty member, is not particularly large, as the point estimates range from 5 to 10 percent.

Table 8.6

Coefficients of Wage Functions of Male and Female Workers, 1995

Variable	Specification I				Specification II			
	Male Workers		Female Workers		Male Workers		Female Workers	
	Coefficient	T-value	Coefficient	T-value	Coefficient	T-value	Coefficient	T-value
Intercep	7.332	134.34	7.190	130.49	7.710	152.29	7.722	164.63
Age Group								
16–25	−0.005	−0.13	−0.120	−2.92	−0.322	−13.31	−0.381	−14.32
35–45	0.010	0.42	−0.005	−0.21	0.197	10.23	0.173	8.29
46–55	0.021	0.63	−0.148	−4.33	0.235	10.80	0.026	0.82
56–65	−0.076	−1.54	−0.942	−13.91	−0.016	−0.44	−1.521	−13.03
Years working experience	0.036	8.13	0.042	8.65				
Years working experience	−0.001	−6.5	−0.001	−5.94				
Marital Status								
Unmarried	−0.220	16.30	−0.077	−1.99				
Other	−0.228	−2.80	0.029	0.46				
National minority	−0.016	−0.48	−0.050	−1.35	−0.029	−0.70	−0.073	−1.62
Communist Party member	0.058	3.55	0.063	2.79	0.091	4.57	0.098	3.66
Education								
4-year college	0.182	6.56	0.256	6.66	0.144	5.34	0.241	5.31
2-year college	0.067	3.03	0.120	4.37	0.058	2.09	0.128	4.06
Professional school	0.035	1.57	0.070	2.87	0.045	1.61	0.076	2.78
Lower middle school	−0.044	−2.31	−0.049	−2.43	−0.050	−2.34	−0.065	−2.31
Primary school	−0.129	−3.62	−0.211	−5.91	−0.210	−3.57	−0.267	−6.91
Less than primary school	−0.139	−1.06	−0.092	−1.01	−0.624	−4.02	−0.261	−2.35
Months of training	0.062	3.82	0.065	3.48				
Ownership								
State-owned sector	0.223	9.58	0.246	10.19	0.296	11.37	0.298	9.95
Other public sector	0.091	4.29	0.080	3.98	0.145	5.53	0.118	6.28
Private or self-employed	0.098	1.10	0.093	1.10	0.063	0.59	0.150	0.70

	Coef.	t	Coef.	t	Coef.	t	Coef.	t
Joint venture or foreign								
firm	0.329	5.08	0.364	5.04	0.377	5.26	0.453	5.08
Other	0.299	2.88	0.195	2.41	0.337	2.95	0.229	2.19
Occupation								
Owner of private firm	0.027	0.42	0.074	0.99	0.048	0.66	0.044	0.46
Professional or technician	0.093	3.56	0.188	6.94	0.089	2.11	0.150	8.58
Responsible officer or								
manager	0.128	3.48	0.114	1.79	0.139	4.63	0.076	0.93
Ordinary officer or								
manager	0.111	3.69	0.186	4.35	0.124	5.18	0.166	5.69
Office worker	0.031	1.23	0.102	4.27	0.044	1.08	0.049	1.33
Skilled worker	0.082	3.73	0.090	3.88	0.018	0.46	-0.065	-1.91
Other	-0.018	-0.42	0.071	2.15				
Sector								
1	0.013	0.27	-0.109	-1.62	0.051	0.86	0.001	0.01
3	-0.013	-0.22	-0.018	-0.23	-0.005	-0.30	-0.071	-0.61
4	0.061	1.63	0.013	0.28	0.049	1.02	-0.013	-0.20
5	0.067	2.29	0.039	1.01	0.108	2.96	0.083	1.73
6	-0.006	-0.27	-0.040	-1.76	-0.028	-1.00	-0.032	-0.76
7	0.056	1.48	-0.061	-1.62	0.038	0.81	-0.104	-2.28
8	0.060	1.49	0.047	1.22	0.067	1.43	0.065	1.55
9	0.060	1.79	0.048	1.37	0.083	2.24	0.059	1.57
10	0.052	1.13	-0.016	-0.27	0.082	1.51	0.032	0.62
11	0.229	4.46	0.253	4.71	0.104	1.66	0.269	4.98
12	0.023	0.80	0.026	0.76	0.025	0.89	-0.015	-0.42
13	-0.209	-2.79	-0.379	-4.47	-0.227	-2.55	-0.283	-4.28
Work unit								
Enterprise making profits	0.197	11.36	0.175	9.12				
Institution	0.147	5.94	0.155	5.58				
Other	0.095	1.99	0.141	3.49				
Employment								
Partly unemployed	-0.232	-7.95	-0.308	-10.34				
Fully unemployed	-0.404	-4.03	-0.963	-12.83				

(continued)

Table 8.6 (continued)

Variable	Specification I				Specification II			
	Male Workers		Female Workers		Male Workers		Female Workers	
	Coefficient	T-value	Coefficient	T-value	Coefficient	T-value	Coefficient	T-value
Status of job								
Temporary or short-term	−0.096	−1.89	−0.104	−2.39	−0.273	−3.42	−0.164	−4.45
Contract worker	−0.065	−0.92	−0.159	−2.39	−0.088	−0.96	−0.169	−3.16
Province								
Beijing	0.006	0.20	−0.049	−1.36	0.018	0.49	−0.066	−1.12
Shanxi	−0.291	−10.00	−0.441	−13.35	−0.327	−9.81	−0.478	−14.12
Liaoning	−0.163	−5.83	−0.263	−8.27	−0.182	−5.22	−0.270	−8.43
Anhui	−0.283	−8.98	−0.308	−8.91	−0.309	−8.85	−0.366	−9.40
Henan	−0.239	−8.02	−0.299	−8.82	−0.243	−7.51	−0.330	−9.39
Hubei	−0.215	−7.65	−0.197	−6.16	−0.236	−7.49	−0.214	−6.59
Guangdong	0.487	16.34	0.484	14.26	0.411	15.70	0.459	13.86
Sichuan	−0.165	−6.05	−0.192	−6.34				
Yunnan	−0.214	−7.18	−0.202	−6.09	−0.202	−6.45	−0.187	−5.87
Gansu	−0.326	−9.55	−0.399	−10.38	−0.340	−9.85	−0.415	−11.10
Adj. R^2	0.321		0.391		0.226		0.317	
Number	6,329		5,690		5,567		4,939	

Effects of education in our specification, which also includes variables measuring occupation, were small in 1988. However, over time they have increased dramatically. Thus while the 1988 results suggest that men with four years of college got earnings 9 percent higher than men with upper middle school education, the difference had increased to 15 percent in 1995. Effects of education are somewhat larger for female workers than for male workers.

Table 8.5 and Table 8.6 clearly show that ownership of the work unit affects earnings in urban China. It comes as no surprise that the highest paying ownerships are joint-venture or foreign-owned enterprises, followed by state-owned enterprises and, thereafter, other public but not collectively owned enterprises. Other effects of ownership are not as straightforward to interpret. Most effects of the economic sector are small. The main exception is finance and insurance, which show considerably higher earnings in 1995, while the corresponding size of the effect could not be established for 1988. This result is in line with what has been reported in the official statistics (SSB, 1995b, pp. 114–15). Finally we note the large effects of province in both years.[8]

Overall the results illustrate that what matters for how much a person earns in urban China is where he or she works, as indicated by location and by the ownership of the enterprise.

Whether or not one has long work experience as indicated by age is also of importance to earnings, as well as the person's education for 1995.

Decomposition of Average Gender Gaps

Using the estimated earnings functions reported in Tables 8.5 and 8.6, the average gender earnings gap in 1988 and 1995 is decomposed in Table 8.7. About half of the crude difference in average log-earnings can be explained by differences in average values for variables across genders. Evaluating the difference by parameters estimated for males, we find that the single most important variable for partly explaining the crude earnings gap in 1988 is age, to which 19 percent of the gap can be attributed. For the same year the second variable in importance is ownership, to which 10 percent of the observed earnings gap can be attributed. Other contributions come from party membership and occupation, each closing 7 percent of the crude earnings gap, while differences in education closes an even smaller proportion.

We now turn to changes between 1988 and 1995, as reported in Table 8.7. While the raw gender earnings gap is larger in 1995 than in 1988, almost no part of the increase can be attributed to differences in variables across genders.[9] The bottom part of Table 8.7 shows that, using the estimates of males, the explained proportion amounts to as little as one tenth of the increase in the earnings gap.[10] Table 8.7 also shows that the single most important source of the increase in the explained part is education. In the estimated equation for 1995, earnings effects of education are much larger than in the equation estimated for 1988, and on average men have longer educations than women. However, working in the opposite direc-

Table 8.7

Results of Decomposition of Gender Differences in China, 1988 and 1995

1988	$\beta_m X_m - X_f$	Percent of total	$\beta_m X_f - \beta_f X_f$	Percent of total
Intercept	0	0	0.3628	203.12
Age group	0.0340	19.02	0.0110	6.14
Minority status	0.00005	0.03	0.0011	0.59
Party membership	0.0124	6.92	−0.0057	−3.19
Education	0.0056	3.14	0.0059	3.33
Ownership	0.0184	10.32	−0.0354	−19.83
Occupation	0.0122	6.85	−0.1476	−82.64
Economic sector	−0.0003	−0.16	−0.1240	−69.41
Type of job	0.0039	2.17	0.0067	3.76
Region	−0.0014	−0.78	0.0190	10.62
Total	0.0849	47.51	0.937	52.49

1995	$\beta_m X_m - X_f$	Percent of total	$\beta_m X_f - \beta_f X_f$	Percent of total
Intercept	0	0	0.0462	19.86
Age group	0.0169	7.28	0.0645	27.73
Minority status	0.0001	0.02	0.0014	0.59
Party membership	0.0142	6.12	−0.0037	−1.60
Education	0.0172	7.40	0.0001	0.02
Ownership	0.0208	8.96	−0.0163	−7.03
Occupation	0.0114	4.92	−0.0199	−8.58
Economic sector	−0.0003	−0.14	−0.0087	3.76
Type of job	0.0026	1.12	0.0060	2.59
Region	0.0020	0.84	0.0601	25.86
Total	0.0855	36.80	0.1471	63.20

tion is age. The lower average age of the female worker had a smaller impact on the gender earnings gap in 1995 than in 1988. In 1995 the most important differences in variables across genders for closing the crude earnings gap were ownership (9 percent of the gap), education and age (both 7 percent of the crude gap), followed by party membership.

Decomposition Using the Distribution Approach

A number of interesting points stand out in Table 8.8, where we report numerical values for Jenkins's "discrimination" index.[11] Earnings "discrimination" has increased for most but not for all subgroups. Exceptions are people aged 36–45, the small group of people in private or other ownership, the heterogeneous occupation category "other," and in the provinces of Yunnan and Gansu. The largest increases in group-specific "discrimination" are reported for the youngest and those with primary education, which is consistent with the development of the crude gender gap as shown above.[12] The indexes for state-owned enterprises increased more

Table 8.8

Jenkins's Indexes of Discrimination in 1988 and 1995 in Urban China

	α = 0.5		α = 1		α = 2	
	1988	1995	1988	1995	1988	1995
Age						
16–25	0.02694	0.05672	0.05254	0.10867	0.10012	0.20014
26–35	0.03356	0.04229	0.06543	0.08199	0.12457	0.15441
36–45	0.04510	0.04354	0.08741	0.08435	0.16450	0.15861
46–55	0.06037	0.07969	0.11621	0.15200	0.21582	0.27752
56–65	0.12642	0.22311	0.23584	0.39328	0.41289	0.62450
Education						
High level	0.02936	0.04240	0.05722	0.08169	0.10883	0.15232
Middle level	0.04079	0.04718	0.07902	0.09093	0.14864	0.16945
Primary level	0.07845	0.17980	0.14974	0.33820	0.27376	0.60132
Missing	0.07255		0.13824		0.22199	
Ownership						
State-owned	0.04000	0.05053	0.07746	0.09712	0.14560	0.18010
Collective	0.05987	0.06065	0.11484	0.11600	0.21198	0.21305
Private	0.10157	0.06965	0.18852	0.13205	0.32784	0.23882
Other	0.12404	0.05357	0.22913	0.10303	0.39468	0.19123
Occupation						
Owner	0.09251	0.05301	0.17549	0.10139	0.31692	0.18638
Professional	0.03439	0.04062	0.06691	0.07849	0.12688	0.14704
Manager	0.04032	0.05003	0.07750	0.09598	0.14382	0.17748
Office worker	0.03849	0.04139	0.07452	0.07983	0.14001	0.14896
Skilled worker	0.05103	0.06432	0.09826	0.12324	0.18272	0.22708
Unskilled		0.07770		0.14781		0.26878
Other	0.14550	0.06890	0.26684	0.13134	0.45354	0.23986
Region						
Beijing	0.04010	0.05215	0.07771	0.10014	0.14631	0.18537
Shanxi	0.05303	0.07905	0.10210	0.15068	0.18981	0.27481
Liaoning	0.02877	0.06756	0.05628	0.12929	0.10781	0.23753
Jiangsu	0.03729	0.04405	0.07251	0.08511	0.13733	0.15941
Anhui	0.05669	0.04846	0.10720	0.09354	0.19914	0.17478
Henan	0.05271	0.05734	0.10153	0.10986	0.18889	0.20256
Hubei	0.02506	0.03679	0.04900	0.07137	0.09380	0.13462
Guangdong	0.04565	0.04792	0.08828	0.09248	0.16551	0.17275
Sichuan	—	0.04779	—	0.09219	—	0.17194
Yunnan	0.04459	0.03844	0.08636	0.07463	0.16229	0.14092
Gansu	0.08233	0.05732	0.15638	0.11014	0.28333	0.20396
Missing	0.04526		0.08765		0.16461	
Total	0.04518	0.05298	0.08720	0.10167	0.16287	0.18798

than for collective enterprises. We report very high numbers in both years for women aged 56–65. However, as women in those ages are over the general retirement age (this is not the general case for men), the results might also be labeled different treatment of retired workers.

Finally, we complement the description by looking at how total discriminaton is composed in 1988 and 1995, weighting the category specific indexes by number of people. Table 8.8, constructed by setting alpha equal to 1, shows contribution defined as the product of the within-group index and the predicted earnings share. All numbers are expressed as a percentage of the aggregated "discrimination" index for the particular year. Several comments can be made.

Although the highest category-specific "discrimination" indexes are reported in the ages when people enter and exit working life, "discrimination" at such ages contributes relatively little to total "discrimination" due to the relatively small proportion of the sample belonging to those categories. Most earnings "discrimination" in urban China can be attributed to people in the middle of their working life, as they make up the dominant bulk of Chinese workers. Thus, in both years about 40 percent of total earnings "discrimination" in urban China can be attributed to the relatively narrow age group of people aged 36–45.

Looking at results for the education breakdown, substantial changes between the years are evident. In 1995, 18 percent of total "discrimination" is attributed to those with a high education, while the corresponding figure was 6 percent in 1988. Mirroring this, the proportion of total "discrimination" attributed to the professional and manager occupations increased from 16 percent to 29 percent. At the other end of the spectrum, the contribution to total "discrimination" from those with only primary education decreased, although group-specific "discrimination" increased greatly. The dominant part of total earnings "discrimination" in urban China can be attributed to those with a middle level of education.

Finally, in looking at ownership, one sees that the proportion of total earnings "discrimination" attributed to state-owned and other collective enterprises actually has increased from two-thirds in 1988 to three-fourths in 1995.

Conclusions

Using large samples, we have investigated the gender earnings gap in urban China. We have taken advantage of samples covering many provinces and made comparisons between the years 1988 and 1995. During this period, China experienced rapid industrialization, urbanization, and transformation toward a market economy. A main result is that, compared with the situation in many other countries, the average gender earnings gap in urban China appears to be small. In 1988, average female earnings were 15.6 percent lower than average male earnings. The gender earnings gap is even smaller among the youngest wage earners and those with longer educations.

Another important result is that the gender earnings gap in urban China has increased somewhat, for in 1995 females earned on average 17.5 percent less than males. Parallel to this, earnings inequality has increased rapidly. Analyses of earnings components show that the increase in the total earnings distribution was driven by the development of the basic wage and of subsidies. The increased inequality in earnings is a sufficient explanation for the increase in the earnings gap for urban China.

Results from estimating earnings functions indicate that the size of earnings in urban China is highly dependent on geographic location and ownership of the enterprise. The best paid work is found in foreign-owned enterprises and in joint ventures, followed by the state sector. In addition, earnings are positively affected by age, the status of work experience, and also (especially in the 1990s) by education. The educational composition of the Chinese urban labor force has changed much from the end of the 1980s to the middle of the 1990s due more to the greater education of those people entering the labor force than those leaving due to retirement. This makes the strengthening of the relation between education and equivalent income observed during the period even more remarkable.

Decomposing the average crude earnings gap in urban China between women and men shows that in 1988 about half can be attributed to differences in average values for variables across gender. The decomposition analyses show that different forces have affected the explained part of the average gender wage gap. The shorter average education of Chinese women has tended to increase the gender earnings gap, but the fact that women workers on average are younger than male workers has worked in the other direction. Nevertheless, the results show that a substantial and increasing part of the average earnings gap cannot be explained by differences in variables between women and men. Actually, the overwhelming part of the increase in this gap is due to differences in coefficients between females and males. However, it is not self-evident whether this stands for increased earnings discrimination against women or for productivity considerations becoming more important and women on average being less productive than men.

In segments of urban China where market forces have gained in influence earnings differences between women and men have increased more rapidly than in other parts. Major examples of the former are young adults and persons with shorter educations. Analyses indicate that in such segments, wage differences between women and men having the same characteristics have increased particularly rapidly.

Notes

This work has been financially supported by the Swedish Council for Research in the Humanities and Social Sciences (HSFR) and the Swedish Council of Social Research (SFR). The Asian Development Bank and the Ford Foundation funded the two surveys we used. We thank Wu Hong for research assistance. An earlier version of the chapter was presented at the Workshop of Income Distribution in China, Beijing, August 1997, and we wish to thank its participants, particularly Simon Appleton, for useful comments. This applies also to Katarina Katz.

1. Knight and Song (1993) use the same data for 1988.

2. Recent useful introductions in English to the topic of China's economic transformation include articles in the December issue of *China Quarterly* (1995), Naughton (1996), World Bank (1996, 1997). See also Sachs and Woo (1997) for a discussion on the causes of Chinese economic growth.

3. SSB (1995a) reports the following point estimates referring to people of the urban population 15–64 years of age: Urban women (men) spend on paid work 7 hours and 7

minutes (7 hours and 30 minutes) and on housework 4 hours and 23 minutes (2 hours and 10 minutes). Rural women (men) are reported to spend on out-of-household work 5 hours and 46 minutes (7 hours and 13 minutes) and on housework 5 hours and 11 minutes (2 hours and 14 minutes).

4. White et al. (1996), p. 72 report results from an opinion survey made in two cities that points in this direction. Furthermore, a general perception was found that the government was not active in addressing this issue.

5. It seems as though the Chinese have differing opinions on the existence of earnings discrimination. White et al. (1996, pp. 71–72) report results from a survey of opinions made in two cities where the proportion of respondents agreeing that women receive lower pay than men was as large as the proportion who felt that there was no such discrimination.

6. In the second survey the province of Sichuan was added. However, for comparability reasons we have chosen to omit it from this study.

7. We have found a considerably higher gender wage gap for urban China than Qian (1996) who reported it to be 9 percent. Thus we do not share her conclusion that China has by far the smallest gender wage gap observed in the world (p. 114). One explanation for the differences between the studies is that the gender earnings gap is smaller in the two provinces in her study (which also are included in our study). We report in Table 8.4 for 1995 a gender earnings gap of 14 percent in Beijing and 15 percent in Guangdong, as compared with 18 percent for urban China as a whole. In addition there are differences in definitions between the studies. For example, our study encompasses earnings in general and includes the self-employed, while Qian's study focuses on wages, excluding the self-employed.

8. The issue of earnings convergence across provinces in urban China is investigated using the same samples by Knight, Li, and Zhao (2001).

9. In a sensitivity analysis we dropped variables indicating occupation and economic sector from the earnings functions but received similar results. The gender earnings gap due to differences in mean values accounts for 43.8 percent in 1988 while it dropped to 36.4 percent in 1995.

10. The explained part can in turn be decomposed into two terms: (a) "The variable effect," measuring how the difference in variables between men and women has changed (evaluated by coefficients of 1995); and (b) "The coefficient effect," showing how given characteristics are differently rewarded in 1995 compared with 1988 (evaluated by the difference in variables in 1988).

11. When constructing Table 8.8 we aggregated some cells into broader categories.

12. We do not have evidence as to why the increases are largest for those categories, so explanations have to be speculative. First, looking at young workers, one notices that they have been hired recently. It is most likely that any increased preference among employers to hire male workers is strongest for this category. Therefore, in order to get a job, young female workers have (probably) been increasingly willing to accept lower wages than males. Turning to the category of people with a short education, one can notice that much of the work done by such people is physically demanding. Women might be less productive performing many such tasks, and this might be an important reason why the "discrimination index" has increased for this category.

References

Blau, F., and Kahn, L. (1996) "Wage Structure and Gender Earnings Differentials: An International Comparison"; *Economica,* 63, Supplement, S 29–S 62.

Brainerd, E. (1996a) "Women in Transition: Changes in Gender Wage Differentials in Eastern Europe and the Former Soviet Union." Working Paper. Williamstown, MA: Department of Economics, Williams College.

Brainerd, E. (1996b) "Winners and Losers in Russia's Economic Transformation." Working Paper. Williamstown, MA: Department of Economics, Williams College.

Byron, R., and Manaloto, E. (1990) "Returns to Education in China," *Economic Development and Cultural Change*, 38, 783–796.

China Quarterly (1995) Special Issue: *China's Transitional Economy*, No. 144, December 1995.

Griffin, K., and Renwei, Z. (eds.) (1993) *The Distribution of Income in China*, London: Macmillan.

Gustafsson, B., and Johansson, M. (1997) "Earnings Inequality and the Gender Gap—An Accounting Exercise for Sweden, 1975–1991." Working Paper. Götbeborg, Sweden: University of Göteborg.

Jenkins, S. (1994) "Earnings Discrimination Measurements," *Journal of Econometrics*, 61, 81–102.

Knight, J., Li, S., and Zhao, R. (2001) "A Spatial Analysis of Wages and Incomes in Urban China: Divergent Means, Convergent Inequality." Chapter 4 of this book.

Knight, J., and Song, L. (1993) "Why Urban Wages Differ in China" in Griffin, K., and Zhao, R. (eds.) *The Distribution of Income in China*, Houndsmills, UK: Macmillan.

Li S., and Travers, L. (1993) "Estimates of Returns to Education in China" in Zhao, R., and Griffin, K. (eds.) *Research on Household Income Distribution in China*, Beijing: Publishing House of Chinese Social Science. (In Chinese.)

Meng, X., and Miller, P. (1995) "Occupational Segregation and Its Impact on Gender Wage Discrimination in China's Rural Industrial Sector," Oxford, UK: Oxford Economic Papers, 47, 136–155.

Naughton, B. (1996) "China's Emergence and Prospects as a Trading Nation," Brookings Papers on Economic Activity, no. 2, 273–344.

Oaxaca, R. (1973) "Male-Female Wage Differentials in Urban Labor Markets," *International Economic Review*, 14, 693–709.

Qian, J. (1996) Gender Wage Differentials in Urban China in the 1990s, Ph.D. dissertation. State University of New York at Binghamton.

Sachs, J., and Woo, W.T. (1997) "Understanding China's Economic Performance," National Bureau of Economic Research, Cambridge, MA: Working Papers Series, 5935.

State Statistical Bureau (1995a) *Women and Men in China—Facts and Data*, Beijing: China Statistical Publishing House. (In Chinese.)

State Statistic Bureau (1995b) *China Statistical Yearbook 1996*, Beijing: China Statistical Publishing House.

White, G., Howell, J., and Shang, X. (1996) *In Search of Civil Society. Market Reform and Social Change in Contemporary China*, Oxford, UK: Clarendon Press (IDS Development Studies Series).

Woo, M. (1994) "Chinese Women Workers: The Delicate Balance Between Protection and Equality," in Gilmartin, C., Hershatter, G., Rofel, L., and White, T. (eds.) *Engendering China: Women, Culture, and the State*, Cambridge: Harvard University Press. Harvard Contemporary China Series 10.

World Bank (1996) *The Chinese Economy: Fighting Inflation, Deepening Reforms*. Washington DC: World Bank.

World Bank (1997) *China 2020*. Washington DC: World Bank.

Part III

Rural China

9

Rural Interregional Inequality and Off-Farm Employment in China

Zhang Ping

Introduction

Since 1979, when an output-related contract system was introduced in rural China, the average household income per capita of rural regions, as well as income inequality among regions, have increased substantially. A growing imbalance has emerged in the regional pattern of economic development, and this has led to serious inequality in rural areas.

The problem has received much attention from both Chinese and foreign scholars, as well as from policymakers. Much research and analysis has focused on two issues. One is the trend with respect to interregional income inequality, with emphasis on the breakdown of inequality into between-region and within-region components. The other concerns the main reasons for the rise in rural inequality. Previous studies (e.g., Zhang Ping 1992, Zhu Ling 1992, Tsui Kai-yuen 1993, 1997, Rozelle 1994, Wei Houkai 1996, World Bank 1997, and Li Shi et al. 1998) have analyzed the sharpening inequality in per capita income of households in different rural areas, and basically come to a common conclusion, namely, that income from off-farm activities—especially from township enterprises—has become an increasing and dominant contributor to overall rural income inequality. The growing contribution of rural nonagricultural activities to overall rural income inequality can largely be explained by the increasingly uneven regional development of such activities.

Experience in other developing countries shows that off-farm activities, especially those of labor-intensive medium- and small-scale enterprises, often exert an equalizing influence on income distribution. The Taiwan example is typical. During the period from 1964 to 1980, when industrialization was proceeding rapidly, income inequality among Taiwan residents sharply fell. The fast-growing labor-intensive industrial enterprises on the island exerted a strong equalizing influence on income distribution (Fei et al. 1979, Zhu Yunpeng 1997). The question is, why has the same practice of developing off-farm and labor-intensive township enterprises in rural areas on the mainland not achieved the same favorable result? In fact, it has led to a widening rather than a narrowing income gap.

This chapter tries to extend previous work to explore the reasons for this paradoxical problem in rural China. It first analyzes the changing tendency of overall inequality and the inequality between region and within region by means of a breakdown of inequality by population subgroups. Second, it examines the influence of economic and geographical conditions on regional income, including total disposable income, income from farming, individual wages from TVEs, and so forth. Third, it analyzes the most important factors that determine income inequality between regions by means of decomposing inequality by factor components. Fourth, it focuses on the two basic elements affecting interregional income inequality during industrialization in rural areas: one is the earned wage from township enterprises, and the other is the opportunity for rural laborers to obtain industrial employment and thus earn an industrial wage. Nowadays, inequality of access to industrial employment is playing a more important role than industrial salary. Fifth, we discuss the convergence conditions on interregional income inequality. Finally, the article makes some policy suggestions based on the foregoing analysis.

Data on rural household per capita net income by province from the State Statistical Bureau are employed along with data from the 1988 and 1995 disposable income surveys. The discussion treats the province as the unit of analysis, and the terms "interregional" and "interprovincial" are used interchangeably. The author also follows the traditional division of China into eastern, central, and western parts.

The Changing Tendency of Interregional Income Inequality in Rural China

Changes in Regional Income Differentials at Different Stages in the Transition Period

The Household Responsibility System (individual family farming) was adopted in rural China in 1979 and had spread to virtually all farmers by 1984. Also, prices for farm produce were raised, which greatly increased incentives. Consequently agricultural output rose rapidly, along with farm income (Table 9.1). The per capita net income of rural households increased by 72 percent between 1980 and 1984, an annual average rise of 14 percent. But regional inequality in farmers' income did not change nearly as much as income itself during that time, the Gini coefficient rising only by about 7 percent altogether.

The main reason why the sharp increase in income did not bring about much change in regional income differentials is that farmers' income during this period

Table 9.1

Regional Income Inequality of Rural Residents (1980–1995)

Year	(1) Per capita real net income	(2) Gini coefficient of provincial average net per capita income	(3) Gini coefficient of all rural net income
1980	184.50	0.14	0.24
1981	210.83	0.13	0.24
1982	248.88	0.13	0.23
1983	280.11	0.14	0.25
1984	316.54	0.15	0.26
1985	348.96	0.15	0.26
1986	357.91	0.18	0.29
1987	371.94	0.18	0.29
1988	386.91	0.19	0.30
1989	381.83	0.19	0.30
1990	401.74	0.20	0.31
1991	424.58	0.20	0.31
1992	438.34	0.20	0.31
1993	452.37	0.22	0.32
1994	474.95	0.22	0.33
1995	501.53	0.23	0.34
Increase 1980–1995 (%)	170	68	42

Sources: Columns (1) and (2): State Statistical Bureau (1997); *China Statistical Yearbook.* Column (3): Tang Ping, "Income Distribution in China's Rural Areas," *Management World*, 1995, 2 (in Chinese).

came mainly from agriculture; and differences in farm output were caused chiefly by differences in natural resource endowments, which did not accumulate. Therefore, there was not much possibility for a big gap to develop in agricultural income. But since 1985 the development of rural industries has greatly changed the rural economic structure. The interregional income gap had become quite obvious by 1988: the interregional Gini coefficient was up by 27 percent over 1985, more than twice the increase in per capita net income (11 percent), and much higher also than the 14 percent rise in the Gini ratio for rural income as a whole. The off-farm activities in rural areas, especially industrial development, showed strong local characteristics that were quite significant in accelerating regional differences.

During the period from 1989 to 1991, macroeconomic policy adjustments by the state slowed the increase in farmers' income, while significant changes also occurred in the industrial structure. The pace of industrialization was slower than in 1988, and the comparative income gap rose only 0.01. Since 1992, China has accelerated its system reform program by moving strongly in the direction of a market economy. The national economy has grown rapidly, and rural industrial reform has accelerated, with the following features: (1) fast development of off-farm economic activities, (2) burgeoning rural labor migration, and (3) a resumption of rural income growth. During this period, the outstanding characteristics in rural development were further structural adjustment and an increasingly evident imbalance between different regions. The regional income gap widened from 0.20 in 1991 to 0.23 in 1995, an increase of 15 percent.

Viewed as a whole, income inequality among farmers widened by 42 percent during the period from 1979 to 1995, while the regional income gap widened by 68 percent. The interregional income gap has increased faster than overall income inequality in rural areas, and this is probably because off-farm development in rural China is regionally specific.

Aggregate Inequality and Its Breakdown into Intraprovince and Interprovince Components

This section makes use of the 1988 and 1995 survey data and the Theil index of inequality.[1] Here, we break total income inequality down into that within provinces and that among provincial averages, and analyze the contribution of each to overall inequality. We also make a comparison of the changes in inequality between the two years.

Aggregate inequality is given by the Theil index: $I_0 = (1/N)\Sigma_i \log(\mu/y_i)$

Aggregate inequality = intragroup inequality + intergroup inequality

$$I_0 = S_k V_k I_{0k} + S_k V_k \log(1/l_k)$$ (9.1)

where V_k = the population share of group k; m = the mean income of the total population; y_i = the income of unit i; I_{0k} is the inequality index of group k; λ_k = group k's mean income relative to the population mean.

Aggregate inequality is broken down into inequality within groups (provinces) and among groups. It can be seen clearly in Table 9.2 that: (1) overall inequality rose by 48 percent from 1988 to 1995; (2) within-province income inequality was dominant in the two years, contributing 78 percent of overall inequality in 1988 and 69 percent in 1995; (3) however, inequality among provinces increased much faster than inequality within provinces. The former rose by 111 percent and the latter by 31 percent. The contribution of inequality among provinces to overall inequality increased from 22 percent in 1988 to 31 percent in 1995. Thus, interprovincial income inequality played an increasingly important role vis-à-vis overall inequality.

The Influence of Regional Factors on Income

This section builds the income function of rural residents with 1995 data and analyzes the influence of regional factors on household income differences. The income function model is as follows:

Table 9.2

Theil Index of Inequality, 1988 and 1995

	Aggregate inequality	Inequality within a province	Inequality among provinces
1988	180.34	139.86	40.48
Contribution to inequality (%)	100	78	22
1995	267.34	183.75	85.58
Contribution to inequality (%)	100	69	31
Change in inequality index (%)	48	31	111

$$\ln(y) = a + b*r + c*ln(\text{labor}) + d*ln(p) + e*ln(land) + g*z_i \qquad (9.2)$$

where y is household disposable income,

    r is a dummy variable representing the characteristics of individual provinces,

    labor is number of working members in the household,

    p is productive fixed assets of the household,

    land is productive land of the household,

    z_i is a set of dummy variables, *i*, representing regional characteristics such as flat, hilly, or mountainous terrain, national minority area, poor county, and so forth.

With the income function, household income from agriculture and from industry (wages, etc.) in rural China can be calculated. When calculating industrial income, the function includes only regional features and household labor variables, because industrial income is individual income and it is not related to land or productive fixed assets of the household.

Three models are tried. Model I uses *total household disposable income* as the dependent variable, Model II, *household farm income,* and Model III, *household industrial* (or nonagricultural) *income*. The results are as follows (see Table 9.3): The parameter of the model variable is significant. The coefficient of the provincial dummy variable shows the logarithm of the income gap caused by residing in a particular province relative to the omitted province (Gansu), holding all other factors constant.

1. *Income distribution among the provinces.* The per capita income in Gansu Province is the lowest in the country, and Gansu is the omitted province. Model I shows that the coefficients for the provinces except Shaanxi are significant. The signs on all other province coefficients are positive, and the figures reveal that total disposable income of all other provinces is higher than that of Gansu. Converting the logarithms, we find that estimated household incomes in Beijing, Guangdong, Jiangsu, and Zhejiang are, respectively, 2.92, 2.51, 1.56, and 1.27 times that of Gansu, *ceteris paribus*. It can be inferred that location plays an important role in influencing the total disposable income.[2]

In Model II, with household farm income as the dependent variable, Beijing

Table 9.3

Income Functions of Rural Residents in 1995 (estimated coefficients)

Variable code	Name of variable	Household total disposable income MODEL I	Household agriculture income MODEL II	Household non-agriculture income MODEL III
P1	Beijing	1.37***	0.16	2.11***
P2	Hebei	0.29***	0.17***	0.71***
P3	Shanxi	0.12**	−0.06	0.29**
P4	Liaoning	0.25***	0.19***	0.62***
P5	Jilin	0.12**	0.19***	−0.12
P6	Jiangsu	0.94***	0.59***	1.42***
P7	Zhejiang	0.82***	0.46***	1.22***
P8	Anhui	0.41***	0.37***	−0.04
P9	Jiangxi	0.52***	0.56***	0.19
P10	Shandong	0.34***	0.32***	0.39***
P11	Henan	0.24***	0.29***	0.12
P12	Hubei	0.35***	0.50***	−0.53***
P13	Hunan	0.49***	0.57***	0.35***
P14	Guangdong	1.26***	0.95***	1.65***
P15	Sichuan	0.13***	0.26***	−0.12
P16	Guizhou	0.36***	0.48***	−0.13
P17	Yunnan	0.10**	0.19***	−0.27**
P18	Shaanxi	−0.01	−0.09*	−0.08
P19	Gansu	—	—	—
B401_1	Plains	0.23***	0.29***	0.02
B401_2	Hilly land	0.09***	0.10***	−0.03
	Mountains	—	—	—
B403_1	Old liberated areas	−0.15***	−0.06**	−0.23***
	Other areas	—	—	—
B404_1	Frontier areas	0.04	0.08	0.07
	Other areas	—	—	—
B405_1	Minority areas	−0.05	−0.02	−0.43***
	Other areas	—	—	—
B406_1	City suburbs	0.10***	−0.11***	0.16*
	Other areas	—	—	—
B407_1	Poor counties[a]	−0.22***	−0.15***	−0.39***
	Nonpoor counties[a]	—	—	—
B407_3	Don't know[a]	−0.34***	−0.17***	−0.81***
LLABOR	Household labor	0.23***	0.19***	0.27***
LLAND	Household arable land	0.06***	0.16***	
LP	Household production fixed assets	0.09***	0.12	
Adj. R²		0.37	0.26	0.23
F-value		139.94	85.00	66.55
Sample size		6,929	6,894	5,873

Notes: ***means significant at the 1 percent level, ** at the 5 percent level, and * at the 10 percent level.

[a]"Poor county" means a county officially designated as poor. "Nonpoor" means not so designated, rather than not poor. "Don't know" means respondent did not know whether his/her county had been so designated.

and Shanxi are not significant. Comparing the coefficients in Models I and II, it is clear that residing in a very high income province (e.g., Beijing, Guangdong, Jiangsu, Zhejiang) affects farm income much less than it does total income, while location in some middle-developed regions (Hunan, Hubei, Jilin) affects farm income more than total income. This suggests that the gap between middle-developed areas and underdeveloped Gansu Province lies mainly in farm income, while that between very developed regions and Gansu lies mainly in nonfarm income.

Model III, with nonfarm income (i.e., principally wage) as the dependent variable, makes even clearer the *relative* advantage of developed areas over underdeveloped ones in nonfarm income: the estimated nonfarm incomes of Beijing, Guangdong, Jiangsu, and Zhejiang, respectively, were 7.22, 4.19, 3.15, and 2.39 times that of Gansu, *ceteris paribus*. Indeed, the nonfarm incomes of "second tier" developed provinces, such as Liaoning, Hebei, Shandong, and Shanxi, more powerfully differentiate these regions from Gansu than either their farm or total incomes. Unlike for the very developed provinces, the coefficients for Jilin, Anhui, Jiangxi, Henan, Sichuan, Guizhou, and Shaanxi provinces are not significant for nonfarm income. It can be concluded that the income gap between the most developed areas, such as Beijing, Guangdong, Jiangsu, and Zhejiang, and other provinces comes mostly from industrial income.

2. *The geographical influence.* Topographical character greatly affects total income and farm income, as Table 9.3 shows clearly. The estimated total incomes of flat plains areas and hilly lands, respectively, are 23 percent and 9 percent higher than that of mountainous regions. The equivalent differences for farm income are higher indicating that geographical elements have a bigger effect on farm income. Farm income on the plains is 29 percent higher, and that of hilly land is 10 percent higher than that of mountainous regions. But for off-farm income, the coefficients of geographical factors are very small and not significant, indicating that the influence of these factors on off-farm income is negligible.

3. *The influence of economic regions.* Besides topographical differences, there are several other economic or policy-related criteria for distinguishing regions, including whether or not a region is an old liberated area, a frontier area, a home of minority nationalities, a designated poor area, or a suburb of a large or medium-sized city. The three coefficients for *old liberated area* are all negative and significant, indicating their income disadvantage relative to other areas. *The frontier area* designation is not significant in any of the models. Being a *minority area* is not significant in Models I and II but is significant in Model III, where its negative sign indicates lower nonfarm income. The *poor counties,* as one would expect, are disadvantaged with respect to all three measures of income, relative to nonpoor areas, *ceteris paribus;* the gap in farm income is 15 percent, while that in off-farm income is as high as 39 percent. Ironically, the category "don't know" (*bu qingchu*) carries an even greater income disadvantage than living in a poor county. Respondents who chose this category were not clear as to whether their county was an officially designated poor county or not. Such people probably did reside in poor

counties, but ones that most likely had not received the resources of China's poverty alleviation effort, which have been funneled almost exclusively into officially chosen poverty areas. This may explain why the income deficit for "don't know" is greater than that for "poor county." The *suburbs of big and medium-sized cities* get a negative in farm income, but a positive and a high of 16 percent in off-farm income. This reflects the fact that the development of these suburbs mainly depends not on farming, but on off-farm activities.

Location on the east coast, central China, or the western regions is often taken as a convenient indicator of the level of development, with the eastern coastal region being the most developed and the west the least. In Table 9.4, r1 and r2 represent provinces in eastern and central China respectively, while provinces in western China and their income figures are taken as the default value. It is easy to see that the locations of the three regions have great influence on their incomes. The geographical elements of eastern and central China have a positive effect on the total local income. With all other factors remaining the same, and converting the logarithms, the impact of an eastern and central region location on total income is 97 percent and 34 percent, respectively, compared to the western region. For farm income, the figures are respectively 50 percent and 31 percent, and for nonfarm income, 286 percent and 27 percent. The gap between the eastern and western regions mainly lies in off-farm income, while the gap between the central and western regions is fairly evenly divided between farm and nonfarm income. The advantage of the central region compared with the western region lies in land resources, and some industrialization in the former, while in addition to good land resources, the eastern region benefits from much greater industrialization of the countryside.

Decomposing Interregional Inequality by Source

The above information shows that the regional factor is obviously important in affecting household income. We now decompose rural interregional household incomes in both 1988 and 1995 by source in order to study the contributions of the various types of income to interregional aggregate inequality.

Based on income sources, to study the inequality of overall income, we use the formula $G = \Sigma u_i * c_i$, where G = the Gini ratio of disposable income, u_i = the share of the i-th source of income in total disposable income, c_i = the concentration ratio of the i-th source of household disposable income per capita. The concentration or pseudo-Gini coefficient c_i is similar to the Gini coefficient except that it measures the distribution of a given source of income over all income recipients, not only recipients of that particular source. Unlike for the Gini, the individual c_i's can have a negative value, which indicates larger shares of the income source going to lower income groups than to higher income groups. The percentage contribution to total inequality made by each income source is given by the formula $g_i = 100*(u_i*c_i)/G$. The g_i's sum up to 100 percent of the Gini ratio for total income.[3]

We calculated the interprovincial Gini coefficient based on rural average house-

Table 9.4

Income Functions of Three Regions in 1995

	Variable code	Household total income	Household farm income	Household off-farm income
Eastern region	r1	0.68***	0.41***	1.35***
Central region	r2	0.29***	0.27***	0.24***
Labor	labor	0.28***	0.24***	0.26***
Land	land	0.013*	0.11*	—
Means of production	lp	0.11***	0.14***	—
Constant term	constant	7.38***	6.80***	6.59***
Adjusted judgment coefficient	Adj. R²	0.22	0.17	0.15
F-value	F	393.9	280.58	354.67

Note: *** means significant at the 1 percent level, ** at the 5 percent level, and * at the 10 percent level. Table items are estimated coefficients of regressions of the logarithm of income on the independent variables.

hold disposable income per capita in nineteen provinces, and decomposed inequality by income sources. Table 9.5 shows that the interprovincial Gini ratio increased by about 44 percent from 0.18 to 0.26 between 1988 and 1995. The most rapidly growing source of income inequality is individual wages, whose contributed share of total inequality rose from 35 percent in 1988 to 55 percent in 1995, an increase of about 57 percent. The contribution to inequality of income from household production activities dropped from 49 percent in 1988 to 31 percent in 1995, indicating a basic change in the traditional production pattern of rural households.

Table 9.5 also contains information concerning the change of shares and of concentration ratios for various sources of income. A concentration ratio lower (higher) than the Gini coefficient means that the corresponding source of income has an equalizing (disequalizing) effect on the overall distribution income. In 1995 the most unequally distributed income source was wages, followed by property income, rental value of owned housing, and income from household nonagricultural business. Increase in the share of any of these items, *ceteris paribus,* will enlarge the inequality of total income.

Let us study this further. The formula for the Gini coefficient consists of two parts: one is each income source's share of disposable income, the other is the concentration coefficients for each income source. Suppose the 1988 concentration coefficients were unchanged. By multiplying them by the 1995 income shares, we can derive the inequality change coming from change in income structure alone: $(1995U_i)^* (1988C_i) = 0.226$. That is, if only the structure of income had changed, the Gini coefficient would have increased from 0.18 in 1988 to 0.23, a large proportion of the actual increase to 0.26. On the other hand, if we keep the 1988 income shares unchanged and only change the concentration coefficients to their

Table 9.5

Inequality of Provincial Average Incomes in 1988 and 1995

	1988				1995			
	(1)	(2)	(3)	(4)	(1)	(2)	(3)	(4)
Individual wages	103.06	0.13	0.45	0.35	603.11	0.28	0.50	0.55
Income from household production activities	579.86	0.73	0.12	0.49	1,290.4	0.61	0.13	0.31
Income from agriculture	—	—	—	—	1,047.9	0.49	0.09	0.17
Income from household operations, nonagricultural	—	—	—	—	243.66	0.11	0.31	0.14
Self-consumption	312.46	0.41	0.16	0.19	—	—	—	—
Property income	1.31	0.00	0.26	0.00	12.25	0.01	0.42	0.01
House rents	76.40	0.10	0.21	0.12	190.97	0.09	0.34	0.12
Transfer payment income	−14.20	−0.02	0.08	−0.01	−61.11	−0.03	0.04	−0.01
Other income	48.81	0.06	0.19	0.07	93.65	0.04	0.13	0.02
Total disposable income	795.25	1.00	0.18	1.00	2129	1.00	0.26	1.00

Notes: Columns: (1) Average income from source; (2) Share of source in total income; (3) Concentration ratio of income source, or, for total income, the Gini coefficient; (4) Proportion of total inequality contributed by the income source. Separate data on net income from farm and nonfarm activities were not collected in 1988. Self-consumption in 1988 is in terms of gross value; its distribution was not calculated in 1995. See Khan and Riskin, 1998.

1995 values, we obtain $(1988U_i)*(1995C_i) = 0.199$, a quite small change in overall inequality. Clearly structural change—the increase in share of more unequally distributed income sources in total income—was a much more important reason for increasing interprovincial inequality than was the increase in inequality of individual income sources.[4] Off-farm income, particularly income from individual wages, is the most important contributor to interprovincial income inequality, responsible for more than half of total inequality in 1995, and its share of average provincial rural income rose sharply, from 13 percent in 1988 to 28 percent in 1995.

According to international experience, the development of medium and small enterprises, particularly labor-intensive firms, are important ways of narrowing the income gap, as happened notably in Taiwan. However, the appearance of a contrary trend on the mainland should be noted. Its most likely cause is the extremely uneven geographical disposition of rural industry, which has arisen mostly in the more developed eastern coastal regions and in the Yangzi valley, and thus helped mainly rural residents who were already well off relative to their interior compatriots. The much greater size of the mainland, relative to Taiwan, makes it more difficult for rural industry to diffuse and reach all segments of the population. The next section explores this issue further.

Inequality of Wages and Employment Opportunities among Regional TVEs

There are two possible reasons why rural industrial income causes differences in household per capita income. One is regional differences in wage levels in rural industries; the other, regional differences in the level of rural industrial development, which means regional differences in opportunities for farmers to gain industrial wage employment.

The traditional analysis of income inequality assumes homogeneity of labor, then compares incomes among households. However, given the structure of China's traditional rural sector, labor is heterogeneous, and there is inequality in employment opportunities, so that some people with access to industry can get wages from TVEs, but most farmers do not have the chance to work in TVEs and are limited to getting income from farming. We thus have the following formula:

$Aryw = Awage*\text{IN/N}$

Aryw means household wage income per capita, *Awage* means average wage of wage-earning family members, *IN* is the number of household wage earners, *N* is the number of household members. *IN/N* can be taken as a measure of industrial employment opportunity. Alternatively, this can be represented by the ratio of wage earners to *working* members of the household.

The formula above can account for differences in household income per capita by the statistical technique, ANOVA (Fields 1980). These differences can be explained by two factors: one is the differential in average wages of industrial employees, and the other involves differing employment opportunities for rural workers in the industrial sector.

From the wage perspective, increasing market competition caused by the spread of capital and technology-intensive industries means that further development of enterprises requires high quality workers, including well-educated staff with good work experience. As there is a shortage of such people in the rural areas, those who do possess the necessary skills have seen their wages increase rapidly. Thus, where this type of industry exists, wage levels will tend to rise relatively fast. However, if an area is dominated by labor-intensive enterprises that only need simple skills, with a ready availability of labor, then wage levels will be relatively low and have little upward trend. The difference between these two situations is thus associated with differences in wage level between township enterprises in different regions.

Income inequality among regions is also based on differences in opportunity to participate in the industrial process. In developed regions the high level of township industry development offers many employment opportunities, so that household income from industrial sources is much higher than that from farming. However, in underdeveloped regions such employment opportunities are more limited, so that farmers experience difficulty in obtaining any income from industrial work.

As development proceeds, households will have more and more equal access to industrial employment. The industries of more backward regions will grow up faster as development begins to take hold, so that employment opportunities will expand and backward regions will gradually gain equality in this regard. When relatively equal access to industrial employment has been achieved, income inequalities will mainly come from wage differentials. (In a competitive market environment, these too should eventually trend downward, *ceteris paribus.*) Of course, equalization of employment opportunities assumes convergence of speed of the various regions' industrial development. Increased regional wage inequality, on the other hand, is based on a differentiation of rural industrial structure, in the short and medium term, into those that require high-quality labor and those that do not. Regionally unequal income expansion is thus based on regionally unbalanced development, a condition that will not be eliminated in a short time.

Again taking Taiwan as an example, the rapid development of its industry and its limited land area meant that its industrial expansion could attract sufficient rural workers in about four years. Employment opportunities for rural laborers are fairly equal, and workers in labor-intensive enterprises receive relatively equal wages. Therefore, industrialization in general proceeded in a relatively egalitarian way.

In trying to study the pattern in China, however, one is faced with a lack of complete data. Here, I only present data for provincial wage and employment levels (see Table 9.6). My study of the 1995 data involves the following: (1) According to occupation, and subtracting individuals without fixed income, we extract skilled and unskilled workers from the rural labor force and show average individual wages (including bonuses and subsidies) of this group from rural industries. The interprovincial Gini coefficient is 0.14, indicating that wage inequalities are very small within the industrial sector. (2) Deleting from the sample "agricultural workers," "unemployed and those without work," those under 16 and over 60, disabled and chronically ill people, the unemployed, and enrolled students, we define the residue sample as the employed nonagricultural labor force. We then take the proportion of workers, skilled plus ordinary, and that of nonagricultural workers in the total labor force to produce interprovincial Gini coefficients of 0.628 and 0.47, respectively, both of which are much larger than the Gini ratio of interprovincial average household incomes, and represent big interprovincial differences in employment opportunities in industry or other off-farm activities.

For the distribution of wages of ordinary and skilled workers among provinces, the Gini coefficient is 0.14, well below the inequality in regional household per capita income, demonstrating that if farmers can find employment in rural enter-

Table 9.6

1995 Employment and Wages in Rural Nonagricultural Work

	Monthly average wages of ordinary and skilled labor	Ordinary and skilled workers	Nonagri-cultural labor force	Number in labor force	Proportion of unskilled and skilled workers in labor force	Proportion of nonagri-cultural workers in labor force
Beijing	470.00	36	159	237	0.152	0.671
Hebei	297.43	30	133	1,184	0.025	0.112
Shanxi	358.75	8	78	647	0.012	0.121
Liaoning	335.14	22	80	712	0.031	0.112
Jilin	364.50	4	22	707	0.006	0.031
Jiangsu	413.84	218	353	1,349	0.162	0.262
Zhejiang	503.37	164	242	1,035	0.158	0.234
Anhui	268.67	24	120	1,207	0.020	0.099
Jiangxi	449.00	4	95	1,060	0.004	0.090
Shandong	347.14	111	215	1,877	0.059	0.115
Henan	317.12	68	131	1,838	0.037	0.071
Hubei	217.00	7	41	1,085	0.006	0.047
Hunan	227.86	7	57	1,213	0.006	0.047
Guangdong	549.33	90	239	1,383	0.065	0.173
Sichuan	390.52	23	143	2,190	0.011	0.037
Guizhou	250.00	1	31	841	0.001	0.037
Yunnan	300.00	1	16	930	0.001	0.017
Shaanxi	313.82	11	61	730	0.015	0.084
Gansu	370.00	2	34	872	0.002	0.039
Gini coefficient	0.14				0.628	0.47

prises and obtain relatively fixed wage incomes, regional income inequality will be reduced. Currently, the reason for the increasing income inequality is the unbalanced development of regional industry. Workers in developed regions have good opportunities for participating in off-farm work, while in the underdeveloped regions they have fewer such opportunities.

Tendency of Future Regional Inequality

The differences in wages and off-farm employment opportunities cause the inequalities in rural household wage income. In view of the continuing development of nonagricultural activities and rural industry, the less developed regions are likely to speed up their development, and the gap in employment opportunities will eventually decline. At the same time, wage inequalities will become the new focus of regional differences. If a region is dominated by labor-intensive enterprises, there will be general wage equality; if such enterprises convert to a technology-intensive orientation due to market competition, however, the wage gap will widen.

Table 9.7

China's Regional Rural Industrial Employment and Wages

	1988		1995	
	Rural industrial employment rate (%)	Average monthly wage of township enterprise workers	Rural industrial employment rate (%)	Average monthly wage of township enterprise workers
Beijing	28.91	125.11	27.83	326.75
Tianjin	31.34	100.77	27.83	326.75
Hebei	10.45	94.03	12.63	100.25
Shanxi	11.25	92.53	13.00	91.05
Inner Mongolia	3.06	83.76	3.02	71.43
Liaoning	12.56	102.49	9.74	155.84
Jilin	4.79	95.86	3.76	76.40
Heilongjiang	5.29	107.37	5.81	86.32
Shanghai	49.08	123.14	46.01	384.20
Jiangsu	20.51	91.10	19.18	240.44
Zhejiang	20.59	102.95	21.33	204.22
Anhui	5.39	70.32	6.69	152.24
Fujian	6.84	102.78	9.13	160.65
Jiangxi	7.52	78.43	6.37	87.10
Shandong	9.71	86.15	10.02	137.46
Henan	5.48	69.43	7.03	117.43
Hubei	7.37	75.85	7.23	114.65
Hunan	5.56	81.53	6.16	103.33
Guangdong	10.64	146.87	13.99	229.61
Guangxi	2.36	70.76	3.05	153.17
Hainan	2.78	73.70	2.96	79.16
Sichuan	4.81	67.17	4.71	90.60
Guizhou	3.01	87.64	3.03	54.45
Yunnan	2.27	70.58	2.59	84.74
Shaanxi	5.09	68.14	5.03	64.59
Gansu	3.48	109.67	3.98	69.34
Qinghai	2.82	71.34	3.67	125.45
Ningxia	2.49	79.22	2.77	151.52
Xinjiang	2.38	92.79	2.50	138.33
Gini coefficient between provinces	0.48	0.12	0.46	0.28

Source: State Statistical Bureau 1996.

The proportion of China's rural off-farm labor in 1995 was 28 percent, compared with 22 percent in 1988; the proportion of employment in rural industry was 8.82 percent in 1995, compared with 8.52 percent in 1988 (State Statistical Bureau 1996). While rural off-farm activities and industry have been developing slowly, the development of regional inequalities has taken quite a long time to appear (Table 9.7).

We present the differences in wage levels and employment opportunities in the township enterprises from data provided by the State Statistical Bureau. From the table we can see that: (1) the gap in employment opportunities has declined somewhat, with a general slowing of TVE employment growth; and (2) wage inequalities have expanded rapidly, with a doubling of the Gini coefficient. This is a matter of concern as it may enlarge the income gap among regions.

The present regional inequalities belong to the question of the development process. Only through regional economic development can such gaps be reduced.

Conclusions

1. China is one of the most unequal countries in Asia, with a 0.416 Gini within rural areas (Khan and Riskin 1998, World Bank 1997). The increasing contribution of the rural nonagricultural sector to overall rural income inequality can largely be explained by uneven regional development of rural nonagricultural activities.

2. Income from nonagricultural activities has become a dominant contributor to interregional income inequality. This is closely related to the emergence of rural off-farm work opportunities, particularly the unbalanced development of township industries. Thus the regional inequality of employment opportunities in off-farm industry far exceeds interregional wage inequality.

3. Because rural off-farm employment is the key to regional income inequality, especially unbalanced industrial development, the further development of township industry and other off-farm activities in less-developed regions is the key issue to be tackled. Only when the industrial level is more balanced in disposition can nonagricultural employment opportunities achieve relative equality and regional differences be narrowed. We must also pay attention to wage inequality in China's rural industry, which is not good for balanced regional development, and may be related to the overdevelopment of capital and technology-oriented township enterprises.

Notes

1. The Theil index, while an arbitrary formula for measuring inequality and without a simple intuitive interpretation, has the advantage of being directly disaggregable into component parts, making it possible to analyze the contributions of each component to overall inequality. See Sen, 1973, pp. 35–36.

2. In this statement and others like it, the reader should remember that only some possible influences on income other than regional location are represented in the models. Others, such as education level, are not represented, and might well be contributing to the regional coefficients.

3. See Khan et al. 1993 for a detailed explanation of concentration curves and their relation to the Gini coefficient.

4. Compare Khan and Riskin, 1998. They make a similar analysis for rural household per capita disposable income (rather than for provincial average household income, as is done here), with broadly similar results.

References

Fei, John C.H., G. Ranis, and S.W.Y. Kuo (1979), *Growth with Equity: The Taiwan Case.* Oxford and New York: Oxford University Press.

Fields, Gary W. (1980), *Poverty, Inequality and Development.* Cambridge and New York: Cambridge University Press.

Khan, A.R., K. Griffin, C. Riskin, and R. Zhao (1993), "Household Income and Its Distribution in China," in K. Griffin and R. Zhao, eds., *The Distribution of Income in China.* London: Macmillan.

Khan, Azizur Rahman, and Carl Riskin (1998), "Income and Inequality in China: Composition, Distribution and Growth of Household Income, 1988 to 1995," *The China Quarterly,* 154, June.

Li Shi, Zhao Renwei, and Zhang Ping (1998), "China Economic Transition and the Change in Income Distribution," *Jingji Yanjiu* (Economic Research), No. 3.

Rozelle, Scott (1994), "Rural Industrialization and Increasing Inequality: Emerging Patterns in China's Reforming Economy," *Journal of Comparative Economics,* 19.

Sen, Amartya, *On Economic Inequality* (1973), New York, W.W. Norton.

State Statistical Bureau (1996), *Statistical Yearbook of China, 1996.* Beijing, China Statistical Press.

Tang Ping (1995), "Income Distribution in China's Rural Areas," *Management World,* 2 (in Chinese).

Tsui Kai-yuen (1993), "Decomposition of China's Regional Inequalities," *Journal of Comparative Economics,* 17.

Tsui Kai-yuen (1997), "Factor Decomposition of Chinese Rural Income Inequality: New Methodology, Empirical Findings and Policy Implications," (unpublished paper).

Wei Houkai (1996), "Income Difference in China's Rural Areas," *Jingji Yanjiu* (Economic Research), No. 8.

World Bank (1997), "Sharing Rising Income: Disparities in China," Washington, DC.

Zhang Ping (1992), "China Rural Household Income Difference," *Jingji Yanjiu* (Economic Research), No. 2.

Zhang Ping (1997), "Income Distribution During the Transition in China," Working paper No.138, World Institute for Development Economics Research (Helsinki).

Zhu Ling (1992), "The Difference in Income in China's Rural Off-Farm Households," *Jingji Yanjiu* (Economic Research), No. 3.

Zhu Yunpeng (1997), "Employment Expansion and Payment," unpublished paper, Economics Department of Taiwan University, Taipei.

10

Food Security of Low Income Groups in Rural China

Zhu Ling

"Food security" means that people are able to get the nutrients adequate to maintaining a healthy life and normal activity at all times. It implies that a country or region not only has sufficient food supplies and stable market conditions, but also that all people have access to sufficient food (FAO 1996a). The rural economic reforms starting at the end of the 1970s enabled China to eliminate shortages in food supply. It can be anticipated that, under circumstances of continuing technological progress and economic globalization, China should be able to attain food adequacy for the next century through developing domestic agriculture and through international trade (Liang Ying 1996). This study assumes an adequate food supply at the macro level, and focuses on the food consumption and nutrition status of households and individuals

At the household level income is a significant constraint to accessibility of food. In low-income countries, inequality of nutrition among different population groups usually reflects inequality of income: food consumption of the rich is in excess or even wasteful, while the poor often lack adequate food and suffer from malnutrition (Habicht 1994). This phenomenon more or less still exists in present-day China. Apparently the logical solution is income intervention and food intervention to enable the poor to have access to adequate food. During the period of transition from the planned to the market economy, the instruments of income intervention have not yet been effectively put in practice, while those of food intervention are mainly adapted to disaster prevention and relief. Moreover, the two have not yet been well coordinated with each other in all sectors of socioeconomic development. Only the rural poverty alleviation program includes, at the same time, the two functions of income intervention and food intervention.

The first priority in implementation of the poverty alleviation scheme is to solve the food shortage problem for the rural poor in order to rescue them from hunger (State Council 1994). Here, the emphasis is put on securing a minimum subsistence diet for the poor, especially, an adequate calorie intake. Beyond that, nutrition intervention has not yet been given priority. In fact, the poverty threshold in rural China was formulated on the basis of identifying the food poverty line (minimum energy intake). For the purpose of examining the impact of poverty reduction programs on improvement of the food security of the poor, and studying the possibilities of improving income and food policy, this chapter will use the information derived from the national nutrition surveys and from the rural household sample survey for 1995. We briefly review the changes in income distribution and nutrition status of the rural population since the 1980s, analyze the nutrition status of low-income groups and the income status of energy-deficient groups, observe the responses of these groups to food shortage, point out some outstanding problems in current income policy and food policy, and present tentative countermeasures.

Changes in Income and Nutrition Status of the Chinese Population

In the past three decades the world food supply increased remarkably, and its total reached a level sufficient to meet the food requirement of the entire population. Nevertheless, an estimated one-fifth of the people in developing countries still live under the threat of hunger. This situation has produced a common understanding in the international community: while food production and availability have an impact on people's diet and nutrition, the root causes of present-day hunger and malnutrition are poverty, social inequality, and inadequate education (Lupien 1996). Among these factors, the effects of poverty are especially striking. For those who are malnourished due to low income, an increase in their income would inevitably lead to improvements in their diet and nutrition.

Theoretically speaking, the quantity of food and nutrients that are sufficient to meet the needs of human beings for maintaining a healthy life are treated as a limit to the demand for food and nutrition. When that limit is reached, and provided that people are educated about diet and nutrition, then overall intake would generally not increase despite further rises in income, although quality and variety might continue to increase. Therefore, household income and food consumption may tend to be positively correlated only below this limit. However, differentiation of income within the same low-income group will lead to a correlative differentiation in diet and nutrition. This can be seen from the types of changes in households' income and nutrition status since the economic reforms of China.

Prior to the economic reforms, personal income was generally low, but it was relatively equally distributed within the urban and rural sectors, respectively. At that time, income inequality mainly manifested itself in the urban-rural gap. Enjoying the advantage of subsidies to basic consumer goods and services, urban residents could avoid hunger despite low wages. The rural majority of the Chinese population did not enjoy such welfare. It has been estimated that the rural population who suffered from a shortage of food in the mid-1970s amounted to between 350 million and 400 million people, accounting for about two-thirds of the entire rural population (Zhou Binbin 1991).

The market-oriented reforms have brought improvements in economic efficiency to the whole country and a general increase in people's income. The average annual per capita income available for urban households increased from 316 yuan in 1978 to 3,898 yuan in 1995; the average annual net income per capita of rural households rose from 134 yuan to 1,578 yuan. Deflated by the consumer price index, the average per capita income of urban and rural inhabitants rose 187.2 percent and 275.4 percent respectively (State Statistical Bureau 1996). During the same period, remarkable changes in income distribution occurred, as follows.

First, income inequality has increased. The income gap between the urban and rural sectors, as well as within each of the two sectors, has become larger. The Gini coefficient of the rural income distribution rose from 0.21 to 0.34 and that of the urban income distribution rose from 0.16 to 0.28. The ratio of urban to rural real income per capita expanded from 2.36:1 to 2.79:1 (Zhao Renwei and Li Shi 1997). As for interprovincial personal income gaps, the ratio of per capita urban income of the highest income province to that of the lowest grew from 1.81:1 in 1981 to 2.34:1 in 1995; the same ratio for rural provincial income grew from 2.8:1 in 1981 to 4.82:1 in 1995 (Zhang Ping 1997).

Second, rural poverty is declining while urban poverty is rising (the poorest are still concentrated in the countryside, however). Rural poverty has gradually declined together with economic growth and implementation of poverty reduction programs. The number of rural poor fell from 250 million in 1978 to 65 million in 1995, the head-count index dropping from 30.7 percent to 7.1 percent (Institute of Rural Development 1996). In contrast to the rural poverty trend, that of urban poverty has been upward in the 1990s, largely because of the effects of the adjustment of the economic structure and the transition from concealed to open unemployment. In 1995 the urban poor amounted to 12.42 million and the poverty incidence was reported to be 4.4 percent (Li Shi 1996). China thus has manifold poverty problems. The rural poor make up the great majority of China's poor, and rural poverty is far more serious than urban (the poverty threshold for urban people was 1,547 yuan in terms of annual per capita income available for living, while that for rural people was 530 yuan in 1995).

The changes in income level and distribution are also more or less reflected in the changes in the diet and nutrition status of Chinese. This can be shown using the sample data of the national nutrition surveys. Since the founding of the People's Republic of China, the Ministry of Health has organized three nationwide nutrition surveys—in 1959, 1982, and 1992 (Ge Keyou, ed. 1996)—which have yielded the most detailed and reliable information about diet and nutrition of the Chinese people so far available. The published survey results for 1982 and 1992 allow for viewing the development of nutrition status during the period of economic reform.[1]

Table 10.1

Food Consumption Pattern by Income Levels
(grams per reference person per day: nationwide)

	1992				1982
	Low income	Mid-income	High income	Means	Means
Rice	230.4	231.9	220.2	227.5	208.0
Wheat flour	191.8	183.2	159.8	178.3	198.0
Coarse grain	53.2	28.8	17.6	33.2	92.0
Tubers	115.9	87.4	56.7	86.7	163.0
Dry beans	4.0	3.3	2.6	3.3	9.6
Legume products	5.3	7.5	11.0	8.0	5.3
Vegetables	299.7	313.2	324.5	312.4	298.0
Pickled vegetables	11.0	9.8	8.6	9.8	13.7
Fresh fruit	26.1	42.2	80.7	49.7	28.0
Pork	18.9	33.7	59.7	37.4	42.3
Other meats	9.4	17.7	35.4	20.9	—*
Milk	5.6	10.4	26.8	14.2	9.0
Egg	7.6	13.9	26.9	16.1	9.7
Fish, shrimp	16.0	25.1	42.3	27.7	11.8
Vegetable oil	16.0	21.6	29.5	22.4	12.0
Animal fat	6.7	7.5	6.3	6.8	6.0
Sugar, starch	2.8	4.6	6.5	4.6	8.7
Other	5.9	10.4	17.5	11.3	9.3

Source: Ge Keyou et al. (1995).

Notes: The sample households are arranged in a rank by per capita income (from low to high) and divided in tripartite groups. The average per capita income of each group is 337 yuan, 888 yuan and 2,428 yuan respectively. * = No data are available.

These results show that the nutrition status of Chinese improved broadly during the period from 1982 to 1992. This is demonstrated most clearly by the tendency toward diversification of food consumption. Within that decade, cereal and tuber intake per reference person per day fell by 59 and 76 grams, while intake of milk, eggs, aquatic products, and vegetable oil increased by 5, 6, 16, and 10 grams, respectively. Meat, vegetables, and fruit consumption increased considerably, while consumption of pickled vegetables decreased significantly (Table 10.1). The shares of animal food, fat and sugar, and other food that contributed to total energy intake, rose 1.4, 3.9, and 3.2 percent, respectively; accordingly, energy from cereal and tubers dropped (Table 10.2).

The Chinese Nutrition Association recommended in 1988 that daily energy intake per person should reach a level of 2,400 kilocalories, of which energy from fat should account for 20–25 percent. Protein intake should amount to 70–80 grams, making up 11–14 percent of total energy. The proper share of carbohydrates should be about 60–70 percent (Institute of Nutrition 1991).

During the period from 1982 to 1992, the average dietary pattern of the Chi-

Table 10.2

Dietary Pattern of Chinese (%)

	1992			
	Urban	Rural	Urban + rural	1982
Energy source:				
Cereals	57.4 (66.7–50.6)	71.7 (76.4–65.8)	66.8 (75.6–56.6)	71.2
Beans	2.1 (1.6–2.4)	1.7 (1.6–1.8)	1.8 (1.5–2.2)	2.9
Tubers	1.7 (2.4–1.1)	3.9 (5.2–2.6)	3.1 (4.8–1.6)	6.2
Animal food	15.2 (8.7–20.1)	6.2 (3.4–9.8)	9.3 (3.8–16.1)	7.9
Fat and sugar	14.3 (12.6–15.5)	10.2 (8.2–12.4)	11.6 (8.8–14.3)	7.7
Others	9.4 (8.0–10.3)	6.4 (5.3–7.6)	7.4 (5.5–9.4)	4.2
Source of nutrients:				
Protein	12.7 (11.5–3.7)	11.3 (10.9–11.8)	11.8 (10.9–12.9)	10.8
Fat	28.4 (22.7–32.8)	18.6 (14.8–23.1)	22.0 (15.6–29.0)	18.4
Source of protein:				
Cereals	48.8 (63.0–38.6)	68.3 (75.0–59.7)	61.6 (74.2–64.5)	66.6
Beans	5.8 (4.7–6.2)	4.8 (4.4–5.3)	5.1 (4.3–5.9)	10.7
Animal food	31.5 (18.4–41.4)	12.4 (6.6–20.0)	18.9 (7.5–33.2)	11.4
Others	14.0 (13.9–13.8)	14.6 (14.1–15.0)	14.1 (14.1–14.4)	12.8
Source of fat:				
Animal food	38.7 (33.3–42.7)	36.4 (32.9–39.6)	37.2 (33.9–24.6)	40.3
Vegetable food	61.3 (66.7–57.3)	63.6 (67.1–60.4)	62.8 (66.6–58.8)	59.6

Source: Ge keyou et al. (1995).
Note: The urban and rural sample households are arranged respectively in a rank by per capita income (from low to high) and divided in tripartite groups of each rank. The average per capita income of the three urban income groups is 736 yuan, 1,579 yuan, and 3,024 yuan and that of the rural groups are 228 yuan, 637 yuan, and 1,870 yuan, respectively. Data from the low to high income groups are in the parentheses.

nese population gradually approached these recommended dietary allowances (see Table 10.2). Though the energy intake per reference person per day was slightly less than 2,400 kilocalories, it was considered to be sufficient to meet energy requirements for improvements in children's physical development and increases in the adult body mass index (Ge Keyou et al. 1995).

The nutritionists also noticed that the nutrition status of different income groups improved to varied extents. The intake of a number of nutrients, such as fat, protein, niacin, vitamin E, calcium, zinc, selenium, et cetera, increased as income rose. The nutrient intake of the low-income group was mostly below the level of the Recommended Dietary Allowances. The energy intake of the high-income group was distinctly larger than that of the other groups. In 1992 daily energy intake of urban residents amounted to 2,395 kilocalories per reference person, which was 101 kilocalories higher than that of the rural population. The energy intakes of the three rural income groups, in ascending order from lower to higher incomes, were 2,293, 2,274, and 2,315 kilocalories, respectively (Ge Keyou, ed. 1996).

Diet survey results mainly show nutrient intake in the short run, while measures of children's physical development allow us to ascertain their nutritional status in the long run. The heights and weights of Chinese preschool children show that the differences in nutritional status widened between urban and rural populations and between people of different regions. During the years 1982 to 1992, the heights and weights of urban children, both boys and girls, registered much bigger increases than those of rural children. Taking boys age 6 as an example, urban children grew 4.6 centimeters in height, while rural children grew 4.0 centimeters; the former gained 2.4 kilos in weight, whereas the latter gained only 1.2 kilos (Ge Keyou, ed. 1996). It is estimated that for rural children the incidence of low weight for age and low height for age accounted for 17.8 percent and 39.1 percent, respectively, of all rural children, which were 3–4 times the rates for urban children. These chronically malnourished children were largely distributed in the poor areas of southwest and northwest China (Chinese Academy of Preventive Medicine and the State Statistical Bureau 1997).

The above facts show that trends in diet and nutritional status of the Chinese people were consistent with the income trend. Although income is not the only factor influencing diet and nutrition—nutritional education, dietary habits, ecological environment, safety of drinking water, health care and sanitation, agricultural production, market conditions, food prices, even the demand for nonfood consumption, all are factors that should not be neglected—deficient nutrition is mainly to be found among low-income groups, especially rural low-income groups. This undoubtedly shows the decisive impact of income on diet and nutrition status of low-income groups at the household level. Furthermore, poverty and disease are often both causes and results of each other, which gives rise to the phrase "poverty plus disease" (*pin bing jiao jia*) to describe the predicament of low-income groups. Therefore, it is important to study the income status of nutritionally deficient groups and the nutritional status of low income groups, in order to help vulnerable groups obtain food security with effective income transfer and food interventions.

Diet and Nutrition of the Rural Poor

Through descriptive statistics, this section will identify the energy-inadequate groups and present the diet and nutrition status of the rural poor. For this purpose we turn to the 1995 rural household income and expenditure survey. This survey did not include a nutrition component, but it did record items and annual quantities of food consumption of sample households. With regard to information about diet and nutrition, the data are not as accurate as that of the national nutrition survey, but they can provide socioeconomic information that the national nutrition survey could not, such as the food and nonfood consumption expenditures of individual households, responses of energy-inadequate households to food insufficiency, public intervention regarding food shortage problems, and so forth.

Here, per capita net income of every sample household in 1995 was calculated

Table 10.3

Classification of the Sample Individuals by Income and Energy Intake

| Energy intake (kcal./ref. person/day) | Per capita net household income | | | |
	< 530 yuan	530–699 yuan	700 yuan and above	Row total
Less than 2,100	545	456	4,823	5,824
	(21.61)	(18.01)	(16.70)	(17.16)
2,100 to 2,399	308	299	2,960	3,567
	(12.21)	(11.81)	(10.25)	(10.51)
2,400 and above	1,699	1,777	21,105	24,551
	(66.18)	(70.18)	(73.06)	(72.33)
Column total	2,522	2,532	28,888	33,942
	(7.43)	(7.46)	(85.11)	(100.00)

Source: Households income and expenditure survey organized by the Institute of Economics, Chinese Academy of Social Sciences, in 1995. The following tables and diagrams are derived from the same source except those referred to the other sources.

Note: The figure in the first row of each cell refers to the number of individuals, while that in the second row (in brackets) is the percentage of the respective group in the column total.

using the income definition given by the State Statistical Bureau. Then 530 yuan and 700 yuan were taken as cutoff points to divide the sample individuals into three groups (Table 10.3). These two cutoff points correspond, respectively, to the officially declared rural poverty line and the estimated food and clothing sufficiency threshold for rural people in 1995. The sufficiency threshold is in fact an objective set by the central government for its poverty reduction schemes. In addition, using the method recommended by the Institute of Nutrition, Chinese Academy of Preventive Medicine, energy intake per reference person per day of each sample household was estimated. Energy intakes of 2,100 and 2,400 kilocalories. were adopted as the lower and upper limits to classify the income groups further. By such cross-classification, nine income-nutrition groups (simplified as I-N groups and differentiated from each other by number, see Table 10.4) are obtained. Energy intake is selected as one of the criteria for classification because security of adequate energy intake for the rural poor was put forward as one of the basic goals of the poverty reduction programs designed by the Chinese government. The basis for estimating the rural poverty line was 2,100 kilocalories of daily energy intake, and those whose energy intake falls below this line are deemed to be an energy-insufficient group, while 2,400 kilocalories is the recommended energy allowance that has been widely accepted in China.[2]

The energy-inadequate group (group N1) accounted for 17.16 percent of the total sample, and most of them were nonpoor; for instance, 83 percent of this group had incomes of 700 yuan and above (group I3/N1). Second, about two-thirds of the poor

Table 10.4

Shares of Food in Total Consumption Expenditures of Sample Rural Households by Level of Income and Energy Intake, 1995

		Group I1 (<530 yuan)	Group I2 (530 to 699 yuan)	Group I3 (700 yuan and above)
Group N1 (<2,100 kcal.)	Food/total consumption (%)	68.45	68.79	62.53
	Observations	545	456	4,823
	Standard deviation	0.134	0.141	0.173
Group N2 (2,100 to 2,399 kcal.)	Food/total consumption (%)	76.86	73.21	65.17
	Observations	308	299	2,960
	Standard deviation	0.131	0.141	0.164
Group N3 (2,400 kcal. and above)	Food/total consumption (%)	76.90	78.65	69.12
	Observations	1,669	1,777	21,105
	Standard deviation	0.145	0.134	0.170

(group I1/N3) consumed enough energy to meet the Recommended Dietary Allowances. Third, although the poor (of group N1) only accounted for 7.43 percent of the total sample, energy-inadequate people made up more than one-fifth of it.

How should the above phenomena be explained? The resource constraints on households' food consumption should be taken into account. The absence of adequate energy among the poor is easily enough explained by low income. But if the nonpoor are also energy deficient, this is probably related to their preference for nonfood consumption. Let us examine the allocations of total consumption expenditures by the sample households.

First, within the same income group, the higher people's energy intake is, the larger is their share of food expenditures to total consumption.

Second, among the poor, only those allocating over 70 percent of total expenditures to food consumption were in the energy-adequate groups. Their purchases of other basic consumer goods and services, such as clothes, housing, fuel, power, education, and health care, would then have had to be severely restricted. Apparently, those households at the levels of per capita income between 530 and 700 yuan should also be deemed as poor. Their average net income per capita of 700 yuan was merely 35.6 percent of the average (1,961 yuan) for the total sample.

Third, per capita income of the group with higher incomes but energy insufficiency (I3-N1) was computed at 1,701 yuan, lower than the average level of the total sample. This group can then be deemed as the mid-low income group, but its share of nonfood consumption is the highest among all income/nutrition groups. The guess can thus be hazarded that the group I3/N1 fell below the minimum energy allowance because many of its members cut food consumption in order to meet other demands. This phenomenon has not been so rare in Chinese society, as suggested by the traditional saying, "dressing and eating frugally" (*jie yi suo shi*). The author's field observations in poor counties of Shanxi province in 1997 can be used to further illustrate this phenomenon. Many low-income and poor families there lived merely on corn and pickled vegetables, saving and borrowing money to build new houses, purchase furniture and color TV sets, prepare banquets for weddings, and so forth. At the least, they would spend 20,000 yuan on a marriage, equivalent to 20–40 times the per capita annual income of their families. Such a consumption pattern comes from either the demonstration effect of the higher income groups or the influence of the tendency in present Chinese society to pursue luxury consumption. If the low-income groups did not follow such a trend, their young men would be unable to marry (Zhu Ling 1997).

Further, if we compare households' production resources in groups N1 (energy intake below the minimum level) and N3 (energy intake meets the recommended allowance), we notice that there was little difference between the two groups in total number of family workers, educational background, or the number of persons employed in nonagricultural work. However, household size and the number of sick workers in group N1 were both higher than in group N3. And differences between the two were also found for land resources. The per capita area of arable land per household of group N1 was 0.3 *mu* less than that of the group N3 (15 *mu* = 1 hectare). This gap can be considered remarkable in rural China, where the per capita area of arable land amounts to only about 1 *mu*. Moreover, on average only 32.2 percent of total land area of group N1 was irrigated, compared to 40 percent for group N3. The irrigation index reflects the potential productivity of land. Thus, in both quantity and quality of land resources, group N3 has a substantial advantage. Differences among the sample households in diet and nutrition can be partly explained by their differences in land holdings. The rural low-income group, in particular the poor population, mainly engage in farming. Land is not only an important determinant of their income level, but it also directly affects their food supply and thus their dietary patterns.

It can be easily noticed by comparing dietary patterns of various sample groups that the main source of energy consumption of the rural people is foodgrain. In the same income groups, the higher the energy intake that people have, the larger the share of grain in their diet. Within the same nutrition group, the higher the income, the greater the proportion of animal food, fat and sugar, and other food in the diet. Protein intake shows a similar pattern. The impact of income on diet and nutrition of the rural population seems to be manifested primarily through diversification of food sources, reflecting differences of quality rather than quantity of food consumption. Only a diversified diet can meet the physiological need for manifold nutrients, especially various micronutrients.

At present the diet of the rural population to a large extent still depends on family farming. With regard to all major food items consumed by rural households, the self-produced part forms a large proportion. For instance, self-produced grain accounts for 77–84 percent of total foodgrain consumption; for meat consumption, the ratio is 38–60 percent; eggs, 63–72 percent; vegetable oil, 40–61 percent; and vegetables, 77–86 percent. This should at least remind policymakers that one of the most feasible measures for improving the diet and nutrition status of the rural population, particularly that of poor people, is to promote a diversified family agriculture.

The above discussion can be summed up in the following four points: first, virtually all energy-inadequate people belong to the mid-low income and poor groups, which indicates that income is still an influential constraint on the food consumption of these population groups. Second, the majority of poor people already obtain adequate energy intake; however, this is achieved at the cost of reducing their other basic consumption. Third, the higher the income of rural people, the more diversified their diet. Moreover, the food they consume comes mainly from their own family agriculture. Fourth, since nutrition-deficient people include both the poor and the nonpoor, different policy instruments should be adopted to different population groups when public intervention is undertaken.

Income Intervention and Food Intervention

This section will present the responses of the rural households to food shortage, briefly introduce the Chinese government's policies for income and food intervention in the rural sector, point out the main problems with current policies, and try to identify the best orientation for further policy improvements.

Table 10.5 is designed to demonstrate the effects of food relief, food gifts, and borrowing on energy intake of the sample population. On the assumption that the sample households did not receive relief grain, the table indicates that the number of people in the group I2–N2 increases slightly, while the number of those in the group I2–N3 remains almost unchanged. This implies that very few people got relief food in the sample. Relief intervention caused only four people to move up to the level of the recommended allowance. Relief grain neither reached the poorest, nor was it given to the people who were the most energy inadequate.

In contrast to relief, the borrowing of grain and foodgrain gifts presented between farmers played a more significant role in combating food shortage among the poorest (group I1) and the poor (group I2). Without such measures the energy-inadequate people in group I1/N1 would have grown by 0.75 percentage points, and those in group I1/N2 would have grown by 0.43 points; even the energy-deficient people among the nonpoor (group I3) would have increased by 0.17 percentage points. These results suggest that mutual assistance among farmers is a useful organizational form for realizing risk sharing and food security at the household level. Private income transfers as well as lending and borrowing in kind, cash gifts, and loans had a similar function. According to survey data about financial activities of the three nutrition groups, loans taken for the sake of solving house-

Table 10.5

Responses of the Sample Households to Food Shortages (%)

		Group I1	Group I2	Group I3	Row total
Group N1 (<2,100 kcal.)	Actual situation	21.61	18.01	16.70	17.16
	If households had not received relief grain	21.61	17.94	16.70	17.15
	If hh had not received grain gifts from relatives	21.85	18.01	16.72	17.20
	If hh had not borrowed grain	22.36	18.21	16.84	17.36
	Without all of above three actions	22.36	18.14	16.87	17.37
Group N2 (2,100–2,399 kcal.)	Actual situation	12.21	11.81	10.25	10.51
	If households had not received relief grain	12.21	11.98	10.25	10.52
	If hh had not received grain gifts from relatives	11.97	12.01	10.25	10.51
	If hh had not borrowed grain	11.78	11.81	10.21	10.45
	Without all of above three actions	11.78	12.17	10.22	10.48
Group N3 (>=2,400 kcal.)	Actual situation	66.18	70.18	73.06	72.33
	If households had not received relief grain	66.18	70.08	73.06	72.32
	If hh had not received grain gifts from relatives	66.18	69.98	73.03	72.29
	If hh had not borrowed grain	65.86	69.98	72.94	72.20
	Without all of above three actions	65.86	69.68	72.91	72.15
Column total		7.43	7.46	85.11	100.00

Note: The classification of sample individuals is the same as that in Table 10.3. In each cell, the figure in the first row refers to the share of that income/energy intake group in the entire income group (see Table 10.3); those in the 2nd to 5th rows refer to the percentages under each assumed situation; the differences between these and the percentages under the actual situation show the effects of relief, gifts, and borrowed grain on the energy intake of the sample population. Moreover, the column totals, i.e., the number of people in each income group and the entire population are not changed (Table 10.3).

holds' living difficulties in groups N1 and N2 were evidently larger in average size than those in group N3. This could well be—at least in part—a response of energy-inadequate people to food crisis or income crisis.

Since the effects of public intervention are observed to have been quite weak, it is necessary to trace the causes of this weakness and identify the deficiencies in the food-assistance policies. Based on the principles formed by the Food and Agriculture Organization (FAO) of the United Nations, the targets of food assistance can be expressed as follows: first, appropriate, adequate, and timely relief should be given to people, especially women and children, who have encountered food crisis because of emergency conditions. Second, public action should be undertaken to intervene in chronic hunger, that is, relief should be given to those who at certain stages of the life cycle or in certain periods of the year have insufficient access to food for their subsistence. Third, food aid should be used as a means to promote human development, because only by way of improving nutrition can those suffering from hunger benefit from health care, education, training, and other income-generation projects (FAO 1996b). China's existing public food-assistance program includes all three of these aspects of hunger, but it does not always cover the target groups identified in the above principles.

During the period of the planned economy, an effective relief system for mitigating food crises and natural disasters was already established. In addition, the government used the method of "reselling grain"—that is, taking foodgrain procured by the state at low prices and selling it back to grain-deficient farmers—to balance regional food distribution and provide food subsidies to the grain-deficient groups. However, the most distinctive kind of food intervention at that time lay in the urban food-supply system. A rationing system was established for urban citizens. Only registered urban residents were entitled to purchase food at subsidized consumer prices using coupons (coupons for grain, vegetable oil, meat, eggs, milk, bean curd, etc.). This system was considered a response to shortages in the total food supply, but it also originated from the underlying strategy of urban-biased industrialization. The system subsidized the urban population, whose living standard was always higher than that of the rural majority, and consequently led to the worsening of urban-rural income inequality.

In the process of market-oriented reform, some instruments of food intervention have been retained, such as disaster relief, while others are weakened or even abolished, such as the food coupon system for urban inhabitants. Given that the ban on the free marketing of farm products was gradually lifted, most subsidies to urban consumers have become a component of wages and salaries. Meanwhile, the system of reselling grain to rural grain-deficit households has weakened: although the state agencies continue to provide food to grain-deficient farmers, price subsidies are no longer offered. Such deals actually have become part of the operation of the grain market, which now plays an increasingly important role in the process of grain distribution. Even in the remote and high mountains, there are small traders who bring foodgrain into the villages to sell to farmers either for cash payment or through barter trade. For instance, in the Taihang mountains in the spring of 1997, the exchange rates of important foodgrain items were: 0.5 kilograms of wheat flour to 1.2 kilograms of corn; and 0.5 kilograms of rice to 1.5 kilograms of corn. Such transactions not only make up the food deficit for some farmers, but they are also helpful in diversifying the farmers' diet. Of course, all of these changes were made possible by the agricultural production reforms undertaken at the end of the 1970s: Land-use rights were equally distributed among the households within almost every village community. This not only stimulated farmers to produce more and provide the nation with adequate food supply, but it also enabled every farm household to possess the basic resources for achieving food security. This can be considered a special characteristic of the food policy reforms and also an important measure to reduce rural income inequality in China.

The introduction of the market reform substantially improved efficiency of food production and distribution, but market forces are not appropriate to tackle the hunger caused by disasters and poverty, since the low purchasing power of the poor often impedes them from obtaining adequate food. Currently the main problem that China encounters is lack of a rural social security system, and the operation of the existing disaster mitigation and social relief system is far from sufficient to meet the needs of the vulnerable groups during the economic transition period. In 1995, 31.5 million people in rural poor households—less than half of the total poor population—received relief funds. In the same year, only about one-tenth of "five guarantee" households[3] received periodic and fixed amounts of government relief funds, while the rest were entirely dependent on subsidies provided by their village communities. Furthermore, the amount of relief funds is very meager and the coverage is very narrow. Relief funds provided to the urban poor totaled 562.1 million yuan in 1995, less than 16 yuan per recipient for the whole year (State Statistical Bureau 1996). Food assistance has mainly been used for mitigating disasters; however, usually less than one-third of areas actually affected by disasters are covered by relief intervention (Zheng Gongcheng 1994). Moreover, the target groups for such intervention are usually those most damaged by the disaster rather than the poorest. All of this helps to explain why neither the poorest nor the most energy-inadequate people received relief grain, as shown in Table 10.5.

As for the food shortage problems of the chronic poor in rural China, the government has tried to tackle it mainly by implementing regional poverty reduction programs since the mid-1980s (Zhu Ling and Jiang Zhongyi 1996). As was mentioned earlier, the rural poverty alleviation scheme has actually become the policy instrument that closely combines income intervention with food intervention. It has several facets:

- Public works programs to improve the rural infrastructure and ecological environment and to invest in farmland capital construction in order to raise agricultural productivity. Projects include, for example, construction of roads, bridges, small-sized water conservancy projects, facilities for improved drinking water, land terracing, expansion of irrigated area, grass and tree planting, and forestry development.
- Agricultural extension work to promote appropriate crop varieties and technologies in order to raise grain-crop yields.
- Credit programs to encourage farmers to develop animal production and sidelines and to stimulate the development of nonagricultural sectors so as to expand employment opportunities.

The chief objectives of the poverty reduction program can be summed up as (1) ensuring greater and more stable access to food for the rural poor by promoting development of family agriculture, and (2) promoting nonagricultural income-generating activities for the poor through rural industrialization and labor migration. These direct and indirect food intervention measures have played a significant role in improving the diet and nutrition of the population in poor areas, as shown by information provided by the nutrition surveillance system of the Chinese Academy of Preventive Medicine. The per capita energy intake of the affected population increased from 1,819–2,129 kilocalories per day in 1990 to 2,089–2,513 kilocalories in 1992 (Chen Chunming 1996).

Our rural household income data corroborate the information of the nutrition surveillance system. According to the household records, sample individuals in poor counties accounted for 24 percent of the total sample. About 17 percent of this population had inadequate energy intake, but they made up a quarter of all the energy-deficient people in the total sample. This shows that the majority of the population in the poor counties have been released from the threat of food shortage due to economic growth and the implementation of poverty reduction schemes for more than a decade. According to statistics, prior to the large-scale poverty alleviation actions, at least two-thirds of the population of poor counties were short of food. Second, these numbers also reveal that a considerable number of the energy-deficient people live in nonpoor counties. An evident weakness of the existing poverty alleviation approach lies in its failure to cover the poor living in nonpoor areas.

Moreover, nutrition intervention has not yet been a major component in decision makers' approaches to poverty reduction. People wrongly believe that rationalization of nutrition only becomes an issue after income has been substantially raised. The saying "first eat one's fill, then think about eating better" (*xian yao chibao, hou yao chihao*) actually expresses such views. Nevertheless, it has been very common that, due to a lack of knowledge about health and nutrition, problems of nutritional imbalance and micronutrient deficiency have afflicted the poor even while their energy intake has been rising. The incidence of malnourished poor children is much higher than that of energy inadequacy. On account of this, the Chinese Academy of Preventive Medicine has undertaken an experiment in nutrition intervention in 101 poor counties since the end of the 1980s. The results show that it is possible significantly to improve the nutritional status of the poor, even without an increase in their incomes, simply through providing nutritional information, advising poor farmers to plant vegetables and raise chickens in their courtyards, encouraging them to expand soybean production and persuading them to add more soybean food to their household diet (Chen Chunming 1996).

The following conclusions can be drawn from the above policy discussion:

1. The fundamental measure that would enable low-income people to achieve food security is the establishment of a social security system appropriate to the market economy. Before such a system is fully in place, the highest priority is to strengthen relief functions and improve instruments of relief intervention.

2. The rural poverty reduction scheme should be extended to nonpoor areas, so

that its function of food and income intervention can reach more needy people. The transition from the planned to the market economy is a long-term process, and poverty alleviation programs also need to be undertaken for the long run. Moreover, the policy instruments should be more diversified in order to help the poor in different circumstances with appropriately relevant measures. As to food intervention, agricultural development programs set up for the energy-deficient poor should be continuously supported. Nutrition education needs to be carried out for this group, while measures leading to nutrition rationalization should be undertaken mainly for low-income groups already relatively secure from hunger. The introduction of nutrition intervention in poverty alleviation programs would not only more effectively improve the welfare of the poor but it can also promote nutrition rationalization among the nonpoor.

3. Mutual assistance among farmers is essential for them to overcome food and income crises at the household level, and it is also an effective supplement to public intervention. Some informal credit institutions and food bank and lending organizations have already been formed during the economic transition, but they lack legal status and are not able to engage in credit business like formal institutions. The size of their funds usually is quite small so that the ability of these organizations to provide disaster resistance and poverty reduction is very limited. Moreover, many of them have faced problems of inadequate operational funds and bad management. As a result, a number of these organizations are not sustainable (Zhu, Jiang, and von Braun 1997). Therefore, the state should support mutual assistance among farmers through legislation to encourage farmers to establish food banks or self-help credit organizations, and to permit informal institutions to link themselves with formal grain agencies or credit institutions. Such modest changes would promote the construction of an institutional infrastructure for better food and income intervention.

Notes

The author is extremely indebted to Li Shi for his valuable suggestions and computation assistance. Thanks are also expressed to Aziz Khan and Keith Griffin for their constructive comments.

1. The nutrition surveys conducted in 1982 and 1992 covered all the provinces and regions except Taiwan, and stratified multistage cluster random sampling was adopted in both cases. In 1982, the survey included 8,600 households and 546 collective units (collective catering units for schools, factories, and government institutions). The survey included three components: a dietary survey, an anthropometric assessment, and biochemical tests. The sample population amounted to 240,000, 50,000, and 17,000 people respectively for the three survey components. In 1992 the survey did not include collective units. There were 25,033 sample households, consisting of 8,474 urban households and 16,559 rural households, which accounted for 33.9 percent and 66.1 percent of the total sample households respectively. The survey covered a total of 100,201 people at different ages, among whom the urban population accounted for 30.8 percent and the rural for 69.2 percent. In this survey, besides the contents of the 1982 survey, income indicators had been added to the questionnaires. Consequently, the published data included dietary and nutrition information by income groups.

2. The average proportion of food consumption to total consumption expenditures for

rural households in our sample is well above the 58.6 percent reported by the State Statistical Bureau for its parent rural sample in 1995. We have no explanation for this difference.

3. This refers to childless old people, orphans, and handicapped people unable to work and without financial resources. They are taken care of by the collectives and guaranteed food, clothing, housing, medical care, and funeral expenses (or schooling for orphans).

References

Chen Chunming (1996), "Nutrition Problems of the Poor," *Tribune of Economic Development*, No. 7, Beijing.

Chinese Academy of Preventive Medicine and State Statistical Bureau (1997), *Report on Food and Nutrition Surveillance of 1995; Report on Diet and Nutrition Status of the Chinese Population and on Policy Options*, Beijing.

FAO (1996a), Technical Background Documents, Volume 1, World Food Summit, Rome.

FAO (1996b), Technical Background Documents, Volume 3, World Food Summit, Rome.

Ge Keyou (ed.) (1996), *The Dietary and Nutritional Status of Chinese Population in the 1990s* (1992 National Nutrition Survey), People's Health Publishing House, Beijing.

Ge Keyou et al. (1995), "The dietary and nutritional status of Chinese population in the 1990s," *Acta Nutrimenta Sinica*, Vol. 17, No. 2, pp. 125, 127.

Habicht, T.P. (1994) "Information Needs from Food and Nutrition Surveillance in China," in Chen and Shao (eds.) *Food, Nutrition and Health Status of Chinese in Seven Provinces in 1990*. Beijing: China Statistical Publishing House.

Institute of Nutrition, Chinese Academy of Preventive Medical Science (1991), *The Table of Food Components*. Beijing: People's Health Publishing House.

Institute of Rural Development, Chinese Academy of Social Sciences, and General Team of the State Statistical Bureau for the Rural Socio-economic Survey (1996) *'95 Rural Socioeconomic Development Report of China*. Beijing: Social Science Press of China.

Li Shi (1996), *Changes in Poverty Reduction in China*, Beijing.

Liang Ying (ed.) (1996), *Can Chinese Feed Themselves?* Beijing: Economic Science Publishing House.

Lupien, J.R. (1996), A Global View of Food Supply, Access to Food and Nutrition Adequacy, in *Biomedical and Environmental Sciences*, Vol. 9, Nos. 2–3, published under the auspices of the Chinese Academy of Preventive Medicine, Beijing.

State Council (1994), *National Planning on Poverty Alleviation for the Years of 1994– 2000*. Beijing.

State Statistical Bureau (1996), *China Statistical Yearbook*, pp. 279, 305, 725. Beijing: China Statistical Publishing House.

Xian Zude and Sheng Laiyun (1996), *The Measurement and Decomposition of Rural Poverty of China*, Beijing.

Zhang Ping (1997), *Income Distribution in China During the Transition Period*, Beijing.

Zhao Renwei and Li Shi (1997), "Aggravation of Income Inequalities and Its Causes," *Economic Research*, No. 9.

Zheng Gongcheng (1994), *On Disasters Mitigation and Insurance*. Changsha: Hunan Publishing House.

Zhou Binbin (1991), Poverty Problems During the Period of the People's Communes," *Economic Development Forum*, No. 3.

Zhu Ling (1997), "The Vestiges of History," *Women's Daily of China*, July 4.

Zhu Ling and Jiang Zhongyi (1996), *Public Works and Poverty Alleviation in Rural China*, New York: Nova Science Publishers.

Zhu Ling, Jiang Zhongyi, and Joachim von Braun (1997), *Credit System for the Rural Poor in China*. New York: Nova Science Publishers.

11

Reexamining the Distribution of Wealth in Rural China

Mark Brenner

Introduction

Since the time of the classical political economists, the role of wealth and its distribution has figured centrally in understanding the dynamics of economic development. Prominent issues such as the distribution of income and the incidence and severity of poverty have been linked to wealth distribution,[1] as have such considerations as the long-term rate of growth and the dynamic efficiency of the economy. Indeed even neoclassical economists, long advocates of the separability of equity and efficiency concerns, have recently demonstrated a renewed attention to the distribution of wealth and its role in the development process.[2] Yet analyses of the distribution of wealth in developing countries are exceedingly rare. Moreover, where carried out, they seldom offer a comprehensive treatment of all productive assets, and often suffer from substantial shortcomings in their definitions or data, or both.[3]

The 1988 survey has provided one of the rare exceptions to this general case, offering us rich insights into the wealth holdings of rural China, with few of the limitations that plague other such studies in developing countries.[4] These results have been particularly timely, as concern for wealth distribution in the Chinese countryside—as such—has been a relatively new phenomenon, accompanying the dramatic institutional changes of the postreform period. Yet it is likely that the conclusions drawn from this earlier work, as well as those for the many other topics analyzed with the 1988 survey, have not been immune to the dramatic changes that continue to mark rural China. Moreover, given the sharp rise in rural income inequality discussed in Khan and Riskin (1998) together with the aforementioned links posited between income and wealth distribution, it is natural to wonder if the source of rising income inequality can be found in a parallel shift in the distribution of productive assets.

Definitions, Data, and Measurement

In the following analysis we will use the 1988 and 1995 surveys to create estimates for household wealth (net worth). As in prior work, wealth will be comprised of four principal components: land, fixed productive assets, financial assets, and housing, all expressed in value terms. Land values are not directly reported, and despite the many other changes that have swept rural China, a rental market for land seems stubbornly slow to emerge.[5] Thus we will impute the value of land as in 1988, based on the gross value of its agricultural output.[6] Unlike the 1988 survey, current housing value is not reported, and is calculated by applying the provincial average of the estimated market value per square meter of rural housing to the size of the house in square meters. This estimate is net of housing-related debt, thereby capturing the owner's equity. Fixed productive assets are valued at their current market price, and financial assets are considered in gross terms. Nonhousing debt has been subtracted from the total to obtain an estimate of net worth.

Three additional technical issues merit discussion. First, for the purposes of strict comparability the nine provinces that were excluded from the 1995 rural survey have also been excluded from the 1988 survey, and the levels and distribution of wealth for that year recalculated based on this reduced sample. This necessarily implies differences with the results reported in McKinley (1993a). It results in the calculation of household averages and coefficients of variation using 7,998 households in 1995 and 8,363 households in 1988. However, to take account of household size in the distribution of assets, the calculation of Gini coefficients and concentration ratios (discussed below) are performed on a per capita basis, with 34,739 individuals in 1995 and 41,089 in 1988.

Second, as in earlier chapters, we will be using the Gini coefficient as the primary measure of inequality. This choice is based on its wide usage in other work, facilitating comparison, as well as the fact that the Gini coefficient satisfies several desirable theoretical properties while at the same time being subject to fewer drawbacks than many other competing measures.[7] However, to compensate for one of the Gini coefficient's drawbacks—the insensitivity of the measure to redistribution to or from the tails as opposed to the center of the distribution—we have included another common measure of dispersion, the coefficient of variation. This measure is particularly sensitive to shifts in the tails of the distribution, so it serves as a suitable complement to the Gini coefficient. In addition, to compensate for another shortcoming of the Gini, namely its nondecomposability, we make much use of the concentration ratio, discussed in Khan and Riskin (1998). As noted there, although the concentration ratio does not provide a direct alternative to decomposition of the Gini, it does allow us to determine both the equalizing or disequalizing nature of various components of household net worth as well as their contribution to overall inequality.

Finally, Kakwani (1990) has provided a method for performing statistical inference using several popular measures of inequality, where these measures are estimated from survey samples. We have taken advantage of these methods to statistically test the differences between the Gini coefficients and concentration ratios estimated for 1995 and 1988, with the reported test statistics appearing in parentheses below their respective inequality measures. This statistic follows an asymptotically normal distribution, so for our purposes any value above 1.96 can be considered significant at the 5 percent level.[8]

The Composition and Distribution of Wealth: 1988 to 1995

Table 11.1 contains the basic results for level, composition, and real growth rate of household assets.[9] The means for 1995 have been expressed in real terms, with 1988 as the base year, using the rural consumer price index of 220.09 as a deflator.[10] Land, as in 1988, still comprises the bulk of household net worth in 1995, although its percentage of the total has fallen from 59.9 to 50.3. This decline as a percentage of total wealth is largely explained by the fact that land has demonstrated the slowest real rate of growth, increasing annually at only 1.79 percent. Housing remains the second most important element in household wealth, where it rose slightly as a percentage of the total, from 30.9 in 1988 to 33.4 in 1995. Housing equity displayed one of the higher real rates of growth, increasing annually by 5.54 percent.

One of the most remarkable changes in wealth holdings since 1988 is the newfound prominence of financial assets in overall net worth. Not only have financial assets replaced fixed productive assets as the third most important component in overall wealth, rising in importance from 2.8 to 10.9 percent of the total, but they also have displayed the most substantial growth rate, by far, of all the components of net worth, increasing annually by 26.98 percent. Although now in fourth position, fixed productive assets have declined only marginally in importance, falling from 7.2 to 6.3 percent of total wealth, while demonstrating a restrained 2.3 percent rate of growth. Finally, nonhousing debt has changed little, remaining less than 1 percent of total net worth. The overall result of the combination of these various components is a 4.37 percent annual growth rate of total net worth between 1988 and 1995, slightly lower than the overall growth rate of per capita income, 4.71 percent, seen in Khan and Riskin (1998).

Turning to the distribution of assets, Table 11.2 displays the various measures of inequality calculated for household wealth and its components. Considering first the overall distribution of wealth, it is evident that it has worsened somewhat since 1988. The coefficient of variation increased from 0.64 to 0.86 over the seven-year period. Similarly, the Gini coefficient increased from 0.300 to 0.351, with the change registering strong statistical significance. Both these observations must be

Table 11.1

Mean, Composition, and Growth Rate of Household Assets, 1988 and 1995

Asset	Mean value (yuan)		Percent of total		Real growth rate (per annum)
	1988	1995	1988	1995	1988 to 1995
Total wealth	14,676	19,803	100	100	4.37
Land value	8,791	9,953	59.9	50.3	1.79
Housing	4,532	6,609	30.9	33.4	5.54
Fixed productive assets	1,058	1,241	7.20	6.30	2.30
Gross financial assets	406	2,158	2.80	10.9	26.98
Nonhousing debt	−111	−158	0.75	0.80	5.26

Note: Growth rates are expressed as a percentage.

qualified by first noting that wealth in 1995, as in 1988, remains more equally distributed than income, where the Gini coefficient for per capita income was 0.317 in 1988 and 0.416 in 1995.[11] Second, the increase seen in the Gini coefficient of per capita wealth distribution is nowhere near as dramatic as that observed for per capita income, a 17 versus 31 percent increase, respectively. Finally, even with this increase in inequality registered between 1988 and 1995, wealth distribution in the Chinese countryside is still likely one of the most equal in all of the developing world, with both the coefficient of variation and the Gini coefficient registering low values relatively speaking.[12]

Turning to the various components of wealth, several interesting findings emerge. First, and perhaps most surprising, is the fact that land in physical units appears to have become much more equally distributed since 1988, with the Gini coefficient falling statistically significantly from 0.499 to 0.431. This is mirrored in an even more dramatic decrease in the coefficient of variation, which fell from 3.48 to 0.92 over the same period. Similarly, if we attempt to adjust for land quality, taking as a rough adjustment one *mu* of irrigated land equal to two *mu* of unirrigated land, the same trend is present. In these "irrigation adjusted" units, the Gini coefficient for land distribution falls from 0.465 to 0.414, while the coefficient of variation falls from 2.96 to 0.83.[13]

Considering land in value terms, here we see a continuation of the pattern seen in 1988, where in value terms land is much more equally distributed than when considered in either physical units or "irrigation adjusted" units. However, unlike the other two measures of land discussed above, land in value terms has become more unequally distributed in 1995, with its Gini coefficient rising significantly from 0.323 to 0.393 and it coefficient of variation moving from 0.72 to 1.17. When considering land's effect on overall inequality in 1995, however, it can be seen from the concentration ratio of 0.317 that land in value terms continues to exert an equalizing effect on overall wealth distribution in 1995. Indeed, as can be seen from the last two columns of Table 11.2, despite the increase in inequality of land value, its overall contribution to inequality *declined* from 53.48 percent in 1988 to 45.38 percent in 1995.[14] All of these results are interesting in their own right and taken together merit further discussion. Thus we will return later to the issue of land distribution and its role in overall wealth distribution.

As equally striking as the changes seen in land distribution is the continuity witnessed in the second most important element of household wealth, the equity value of owner-occupied housing. Both our measures of inequality fall only slightly between the two years, from 1.04 to 1.02 in the case of the coefficient of variation and from 0.465 to 0.461 in the case of the Gini coefficient. Moreover, in the case of the Gini coefficient, this decline is not statistically significant. Taking account of the effect of housing on the overall distribution, the concentration ratios for both years indicate that housing stock has a disequalizing effect on overall wealth distribution, as their values are above those for the Gini coefficient for total wealth. Indeed housing contributes roughly 35 percent to overall inequality in both years. One question that immediately arises from these results, however, is whether they are an artifact of the two different methods used for measuring housing equity. There appears to be evidence to support this case. When the 1995 method of estimating housing value is applied to the 1988 data and the distribution of this new estimate is measured, it registers a much more equal distribution than that reported in Table 11.2, with a Gini coefficient of 0.356 compared with 0.465 and a coefficient of variation of 0.82 versus 1.04.[15] Thus it is undoubtedly true that our estimates for 1995 understate the inequality actually present in the distribution of housing stock valued at current market prices, although we have no direct way to estimate to what extent.[16]

Considering next the third most important asset in overall wealth holdings, gross financial assets, here too major shifts have been recorded since 1995. As noted earlier, this element of overall wealth has displayed the most dramatic overall growth rate, albeit starting from a relatively low base. Moreover, it has seen a large decline in its inequality, evidenced by the statistically significant fall in the Gini coefficient, from 0.869 to 0.627, and the fall of the coefficient of variation from 3.34 to 1.9. Judging from these figures, both phenomena are likely part of a process of financial deepening in the Chinese countryside. Indeed, whereas in 1988 only 50 percent of all households reported holding any financial assets, in 1995 virtually all households report holding them.[17] This helps explain both their rapid growth in real terms, as well as their still unequal overall distribution. While the concentration ratio for financial assets has declined somewhat from 1988 to 1995, it still is significantly higher than the Gini coefficient for total wealth, indicating the continued disequalizing nature of financial assets in rural China. Moreover, despite this declining concentration ratio, the contribution of financial assets to overall inequality *increased* from 4.66 to 13.82 percent between 1988 and 1995, due to

Table 11.2

Distribution of Household Assets, 1988 and 1995

Asset	Coefficient of variation		Gini coefficient		Concentration ratio		Contribution to inequality (%)	
	1988	1995	1988	1995	1988	1995	1988	1995
Total wealth	0.64	0.86	0.300 (11.853)	0.351 (11.853)	0.300	0.351	100	100
Land value	0.72	1.17	0.323 (11.640)	0.393 (7.961)	0.268	0.317	53.48	45.38
Land (*mu*)	3.48	0.92	0.499 (3.857)	0.431	—	—	—	—
Irrigation—adjusted land (*mu*)	2.96	0.83	0.465 (3.472)	0.414	—	—	—	—
Housing	1.04	1.02	0.465 (0.735)	0.461 (4.184)	0.347	0.371	35.77	35.28
Fixed productive assets	1.84	1.95	0.560 (4.869)	0.622 (4.843)	0.257	0.316	6.19	5.65
Gross financial assets	3.34	1.90	0.869 (12.993)	0.627 (3.378)	0.504	0.445	4.66	13.82
Nonhousing debt	8.63	7.13	0.935 (0.133)	0.944 (0.081)	0.032	0.037	0.08	0.08

Note: One *mu* of land is equal to approximately one-sixth of an acre or approximately one-fifteenth of a hectare.

the growth in these assets as a proportion of all wealth. Given these substantial changes, both in overall distribution and contribution to total wealth holdings, we will return to the issue of financial assets later.

Rounding out our estimates of wealth distribution are the current value of fixed productive assets and nonhousing debt. With regard to the former, here, as with several other elements of wealth, we have witnessed a significant rise in the inequality of the holding of fixed productive assets. The Gini coefficient has risen from 0.560 to 0.622, while the coefficient of variation has risen from 1.84 to 1.95. As in 1988, however, fixed productive assets in 1995 still exert an equalizing influence on total wealth distribution, as seen in the concentration ratios for both years. Indeed, as with land in value terms, despite rising inequality in the distribution of fixed productive assets, their contribution to overall wealth inequality declined, albeit only marginally (from 6.19 percent in 1988 to 5.65 percent 1995). Due to the continued role of fixed productive assets in offsetting total wealth inequality in 1995, we will later take up a closer examination of this component of total wealth holdings. Finally, nonhousing debt remains the most unequally distributed element of total wealth in 1995, with a virtually unchanged Gini coefficient of 0.944. However, because of its minute contribution to total wealth, its concentration ratios were not statistically different from zero, and its contribution to overall inequality remained less than one-tenth of 1 percent.

Institutional Context and Analysis of Major Findings

In this section we turn from the reporting of our major findings to a preliminary attempt to situate them both institutionally and within the context of our overall survey. We will confine our treatment to three components of wealth—land, financial assets, and fixed productive assets, although when necessary, their interrelations or their interactions with other components of wealth will be discussed.

Land

As noted in the previous section, land continues to be the largest single component of household wealth in 1995. Yet its distribution in physical terms has become dramatically more equal. Almost paradoxically, however, in value terms land has become significantly more unequally distributed. What are the origins of this double movement, and do the 1988 and 1995 surveys offer any clues as to their sources? As will be seen, our surveys do not yield definitive answers, but nonetheless suggest several likely explanations.

Prior to delving into the changes witnessed regarding land distribution, a comment is merited on the robustness of these inequality movements, particularly with regard to the measurement of land holdings. As is noted in several places in this volume, the 1995 survey provided us an opportunity to improve upon several aspects of the 1988 effort. One particular area where additional information was collected in 1995, as opposed to 1988, was with regard to land holdings. In 1988 respondents were asked four questions regarding their land holdings. In 1995 the number of questions was expanded to nine,[18] including more detailed information on the sources and uses of land. This, in turn, permitted us to construct a more precise definition of the economically productive agricultural land controlled by the household for 1995.[19] The inequality measures in Table 11.2 use this more restricted definition of land for 1995. Yet there is reason to believe that the 1988 land variable is a broader measure of land holdings than that specified for 1995. Moreover, when we take the summary measure of land controlled by the household found in our 1995 survey (i.e., the one that more likely corresponds to the measure for 1988), the reported decline in inequality of land holdings is even more dramatic. In such a case the Gini coefficient falls from 0.499 in 1988 to 0.378 in 1995. Thus our 1995 survey offers reason to believe that, if anything, the decline in inequality in land holdings seen in Table 11.2 is a conservative estimate.[20]

Turning to the sources of this increase in the equality of land holdings, three possible explanations emerge as likely. First, as has been documented by an increasing number of scholars, many villages have engaged in a pattern of systematic land reallocation since the onset of decollectivization. This reallocation also appears to take place in a context overwhelmingly dominated by egalitarian considerations.[21] For example Kung (1995), in his survey of four counties in rural Sichuan and Hunan, finds that 90 percent of his 400 sample households have experienced land readjustments—with 52 percent having experienced five or more since decollectivization. Moreover, 85 percent of these reallocations were made on a per capita basis, usually to account for changes in household size due to births, deaths, or marriages.[22] Thus, given the apparently widespread practice of reallocation, coupled with its overwhelmingly egalitarian nature, it is possible that the dramatic decline in land inequality seen in our surveys is due to these village-level adjustments that continue to take place across rural China. This explanation is all the more likely given the fact that such reallocations appear to have started only shortly before our 1988 survey.[23]

The second possible explanation for increasingly equal land distribution involves demographic changes present in the Chinese countryside. As shown by McKinley and Griffin (1993) large landholdings in China are not necessarily associated with large incomes, in fact the reverse. Small landholders were wealthier on average than large ones in 1988, with the ratio of average per capita income between the top and bottom quintile of landholding households at 0.74.[24] Moreover, as has been well established, population growth is higher in those relatively poorer areas of rural China, thus by implication those areas with the largest landholdings. This could imply that demographic pressure in those areas where land is relatively abundant is acting to reduce, relatively, per capita landholdings. However, this does not appear to be the case, as illustrated by the fact that the ratio of average household size between the top and bottom quintile of landholders has fallen from 1.47 in 1988 to 1.32 in 1995, exactly opposite that implied by the demographic shift explanation.[25]

More support can be found, however, for the third likely explanation, that off-farm migration has served to reduce land inequality. This explanation follows from the fact that many of the more land-constrained regions are also those more advantageously situated vis-à-vis urban markets or high-growth coastal regions, part of the explanation for the inverse relationship between landholdings and per capita income. However, this proximity also appears to have facilitated migration as well as the marketing of agricultural surplus, thereby lowering household size and easing the pressure on land. Indeed, evidence from the 1995 survey indicates not only that migration has increased between the two years but that its pattern is consistent with such an explanation of increased equality of landholdings. For example, consider that both in 1988 and in 1995 a larger fraction of the households in the bottom quintile of the landholdings distribution received remittances from household members who had migrated out of the household than did those in the top quintile. In 1988, 7.7 percent of the households in the bottom quintile and 4.7 percent in the top received remittances, with the numbers increasing to 19.3 and 9.7 percent, respectively, for 1995. More important, as can be seen immediately from these numbers, the gap between the bottom and the top quintiles of landholdings in terms of access to migration *increased* in relative terms, with the ratio of the top to bottom equal to 0.61 in 1988 and 0.50 in 1995.[26] Thus, in conclusion, we find support for the arguments that village-level land readjustment, and rural out-migration have both served to make the distribution of land in physical units substantially more equal in 1995 than in 1988.

We now turn to the fact that the distribution of land in value terms has moved in the opposite direction. What is more, the increase in inequality in land value is greater in percentage terms than is the decrease in inequality in physical units, 21.7 and 13.6 percent, respectively. To locate the source of this second movement, it is absolutely necessary to explain the shifting patterns in agricultural returns, which are, after all, the basis of the land-value calculations. This, in turn, necessitates an engagement with the complex political economy of cropping in post-Mao China. Although a full investigation of these issues is beyond the scope of this work, there are nonetheless certain aspects that emerge as potential explanations.[27]

One logical starting point is with the movements in agricultural prices in the various regions of China. As has been noted in prior work on Chinese agriculture, there does exist considerable variation in prices across regions in rural China.[28] Moreover, given that the gross value of agricultural output (the basis for our estimate of land value) is in nominal terms, it is possible that these uneven price increases have served to create a regional divergence in returns to agriculture that would disappear if they were valued in real terms or compared in physical units. This however, seems not to be the case, as provinces that have experienced the fastest price inflation are also the ones that have the lowest average land values. Indeed, if we calculate the correlation coefficient between the average land value for 1995 and the percentage growth of prices between 1988 and 1995 for the nineteen provinces in our survey, we obtain a value of -0.56, statistically significant at the 5 percent level.[29]

Such an explanation, of course, does not take into account movements in *relative* prices (regionally or nationally), which may have had an important impact on movements in the value of total agricultural output and thus on land distribution. Indeed, relative price movements are the likely source of the major shift in cropping patterns witnessed between the two years.[30] From this, it is possible to conclude that due to agroclimatic constraints, coupled with the unevenness of internal trading possibilities, many regions may have been limited in the degree to which they could respond to these relative price movements. This may have, in turn, contributed to the rising inequality in land value. Yet, if this were so, it seems unlikely that the pattern would be that which we witness, where grain nearly doubles in importance in the gross value of agricultural output. This follows from the fact that, despite the rise in grain prices between 1988 and 1995, it is still a relatively unprofitable crop and wholly unattractive relative to off-farm employment. In addition, we do not find patterns in land value consistent with trends in grain production, where output growth has been highest in the north, northeast, and northwest of the country, and slowest in the south, southeast, and southwest. Indeed, we see no apparent pattern between average land values and growth in grain output at all, as high grain-growth regions possess both some of the highest average land value provinces (Jilin and Liaoning) and some of the lowest (Beijing, Shanxi, and Gansu).[31]

This might indicate a related phenomenon at work, where rather than capitalize on relative price movements, certain areas have been able to take advantage of access to markets that others, due to inadequate infrastructure or networks, could not access. Indeed, much has been made in the popular press of the ability of suburban farming villages to capture lucrative vegetable and produce markets that more remote areas cannot yet tap, substantially enriching themselves and their villages in the process. However, this explanation, too, finds little support in our data. When we calculate correlation coefficients between the per capita value of landholdings and a binary variable registering whether the household resides in a suburb of a middle or large city, we find that the correlation is slightly negative in 1988, with a Pearson's correlation coefficient of -0.05, significant at the 1 percent level, and not significantly different from zero in 1995.

Instead, we find more empirical support for a related explanation of rising land inequality, namely the widening gap between production for market and for self-consumption. As has been noted above, agricultural procurement prices, particularly for grain, increased dramatically between 1988 and 1995, as the overall agricultural procurement price index rose 116 percent between the two years (SSB, 1996). This, in turn, led to a somewhat expected response on the part of rural households in terms of increased commercial agricultural activity, reflected in rising general rates of commercialization of output. But, as has been all too rarely noted, rural households continued to rely heavily on self-provisioning, with more than 45 percent of the gross value of agricultural output being self-consumed in both years. Moreover, given relatively weak incentives to produce for the market in 1988 and much stronger ones in 1995, we have reason to suspect that it is this price response that has led to the increased dispersion of the rather compressed distribution of agricultural output value (and hence land value) from 1988 to 1995. Indeed, we find evidence to that effect, calculating the Spearman rank correlation coefficient between per capita land value and the commercialization rate of agricultural output, which rises from 0.42 in 1988 to 0.62 in 1995, both significant at the 1 percent level.

This dispersion of agricultural output value between the two years due to market responsiveness is likely to be further complicated by the last possible explanation that we take up, namely the ever-evolving relationship between agricultural and nonagricultural employment, and its effects on agricultural output. As has been frequently documented, both within this volume and elsewhere, returns to nonfarm employment continue to outpace the growth of those for agricultural activity.[32] As a result a greater and greater percentage of the rural labor force is shifting away from agriculture. This is producing an interesting phenomenon, where many rural households continue to hold their land allotments and farm, but they do so with part-time household labor.[33] It is possible that this reduction of household labor inputs is also contributing to increasingly dispersed returns to agriculture. Such an explanation would be consistent with the compressed distribution of agricultural output value in 1988, where as noted above, market incentives were weak and most household production was for self-consumption, and it would have also constrained certain households' abilities to respond to more favorable market conditions in 1995, widening the dispersion of agricultural returns. Here, too, we find empirical support in our data sets. For example, consider the fact that in 1988 each decile of landholdings in value terms reported between 43 and 50 percent of the households having access to nonfarm employment, either locally or through rural out-migration. By 1995 that range had widened, with between 44 and 65 percent of the households reporting access to off-farm employment opportunities. Most important, in both years the decile with the lowest average land value reported the highest average access to nonfarm employment, and the decile with the highest average land value reported the lowest. Furthermore, in 1995 the lowest average land value decile witnessed a 30 percent increase in access to off-farm employment from 1988, whereas the highest average land value decile experienced a slight decline of 6 percent. While this does not definitively establish that low-value landholders are indeed farming with part-time labor, thereby indirectly increasing measured inequality in land value, it is consistent with such a proposition. Moreover, given recent case study evidence, it is becoming an increasingly more reasonable conclusion to draw.[34]

Financial Assets

Next we consider the changes witnessed in gross financial assets. These assets have increased dramatically, both in absolute terms and as a percentage of total wealth holdings. We will describe the pattern of financial holdings in the Chinese countryside, discuss the emergence of new financial instruments and their effect on financial holdings, and outline the characteristics of financial deepening that is taking place. In each case we will briefly discuss the implications of these developments for overall wealth holdings.

In Table 11.3 we present the various components of gross financial assets as a percentage of their total value, for both years, along with their concentration ratios. Given the dramatic changes between the two years, and to highlight the major difference in definitions between the two years, we have listed 1988 and 1995 separately. In 1995, in addition to information concerning savings deposits and bond holdings, households were asked to enumerate their cash in hand, their production funds for family production, and the value of money they had lent out. We have no comparable information for 1988, and thus have no way of determining the extent of such holdings for that year. Given the importance of these cash balances in the overall total for 1995, however, we have much reason to believe that our 1988 estimate is understated vis-à-vis this more complete definition of financial wealth.[35] Nevertheless, it must be noted that even if these components are excluded from the 1995 calculation, financial holdings enjoyed a real growth rate of 11 percent per annum, thus retaining their status as the fastest growing component of household wealth by a substantial margin. Moreover, this rapid rate of growth sheds light on an issue that has puzzled other analysts, namely how China has been able to combine a rapid expansion in the supply of money with only a moderate degree of inflation. Indeed, it is likely due to the fact that the propensity to save, in the form of cash, savings deposits, and other financial assets, is remarkably high and growing.

Turning to the results for 1995, as noted above, cash in hand is the most important single component of financial assets, comprising nearly one-half of all holdings. Moreover, with a concentration ratio of 0.341, it has a slightly equalizing effect on overall wealth distribution. Next in importance is fixed term savings accounts, comprising 28.2 percent of the total, followed by current account deposits with 9.4 percent. Thus both of these two forms of savings have a disequalizing effect on total wealth holdings, with concentration ratios of 0.560 and 0.551, respectively.

But production funds for family production, which comprise roughly 8 percent of total financial assets, have the lowest concentration ratio of any component of financial holdings, 0.336, and thus serve to equalize wealth distribution, albeit only slightly. Money lent out comprises the next most important element of financial assets, representing approximately 3 percent of the total. In contrast with the other cash-based assets, namely production funds and cash in hand, lent funds have a disequalizing effect on total wealth holdings. Taken together, however, these cash-based assets serve to equalize wealth holdings, indicating that the concentration ratio for financial assets as a whole may be overstated in 1988, due to their absence. Stocks, bonds, and other investments in enterprise represent less than 2 percent of total financial asset holdings combined. All three have a disequalizing effect on wealth distribution, but in the case of bond holding, this effect is slight.

Table 11.3

Financial Asset Holdings

Asset	Percentage of total	Concentration ratio
1995		
Cash in hand	45.6	0.341
Fixed term savings accounts	28.2	0.560
Current account deposits	9.4	0.551
Production funds for family production	8.1	0.336
Money lent out	2.9	0.455
Bonds	0.45	0.371
Investment in other enterprises	0.41	0.551
Stocks	0.34	0.515
1988		
Total savings deposits	90.4	0.504
Total time deposits	44.1	0.496
Current savings deposits	35.1	0.513
Government treasury bills	2.4	0.275
Bonds	0.35	0.419

Note: As in Table 11.2, the concentration ratios are calculated from a ranking based on per capita net worth. Percentages do not total 100 due to the presence of unclassified household financial assets counted in the total, but not appearing in a subcategory.

Several patterns emerge from this summary description. First, cash in hand is the most prevalent form of financial assets held, with virtually every household in our survey reporting it. This surely reflects, in part, an optimal liquidity position for rural households, but it also may reflect the continued underdevelopment of the rural financial system.[36] Indeed, only 43 percent of the surveyed households report having savings deposits in 1995, and only 47 percent report any borrowing or savings activity with a formal financial institution. Moreover, when viewed as a separate group, the non-saving households, with incomes less than 50 percent of those of savers, hold roughly the same proportion of household income as cash in hand (27 percent), and have an average cash holding 70 percent of that held by saving households. Although far from definitive, this may be taken as evidence that it is not transactions costs that keep households from storing financial wealth in formal savings institutions, but rather the uneven development of the Chinese rural financial system. We will return to this point when we consider the question of financial deepening below, as well as in our discussion of fixed productive assets below.

A second pattern that emerges from the above table is that, despite the fact that much has been made inside and outside China of the development of equity markets since 1990, stocks and investments in other enterprises do not figure in the financial holdings of most rural Chinese. Indeed, taken together, less than 1 percent of the surveyed households report holding either. However, of those households that do hold stocks, one particularly interesting development has occurred.

These financial instruments have surpassed both cash in hand and savings deposits as the most important financial asset for these households, equaling nearly 26 percent of total household income in value terms.[37] This may be indicative of the high returns these equities have displayed since their emergence at the beginning of the decade, or it may reflect their more liquid nature. In either case, it is unlikely that in the near future the average rural household will shift its pattern of financial holdings toward that of stock-holding households, although the implications for those that do are surely interesting.

A third pattern to emerge from the above table is one of the most puzzling developments in our 1995 survey—the virtual disappearance of government-issued bond holding. Although quantitatively unimportant in 1988, accounting for less than 3 percent of the total value of financial holdings, these government bonds were nonetheless held by approximately a quarter of rural households. This is largely explained by the involuntary nature of these bond issues, where local governments were coerced into buying national bonds, and individuals were even given these securities in the place of wages in the workplace. It is possible that their disappearance is due to the legalization of the secondary market for national bonds in the late 1980s. This can be seen in the fact that prior to legalization, bonds were trading on the secondary market at roughly 50 percent of their face value. By 1990 bonds were trading at slightly above their face value on the secondary market.[38] This may imply, given the involuntary nature in which they were acquired coupled with legalization of the secondary market, that bondholders took advantage of these markets to dispose of these government bonds. In contrast to the disappearance of government bonds, miscellaneous other bonds show signs of expansion. Although negligibly more important in financial holdings in 1995 than in 1988, these bonds are held by twice as many households, 3.5 percent in 1995 versus 1.4 in 1988.[39] Both developments are interesting from the point of view of total wealth holdings as well, because government bonds in 1988 actually played an equalizing role in overall wealth distribution, and miscellaneous bond holdings in 1995 were only slightly disequalizing. Overall, if bond holdings were strengthened as a store of wealth this could have an equalizing effect on total wealth, whereas increasing the holding of almost every other modern financial instrument would appear to serve a disequalizing role.

Finally, a point needs to be made concerning the question of financial deepening in rural China touched on in several places above. As indicated, financial asset holding has indeed increased between 1988 and 1995.[40] Over this period, for example, households reporting savings deposits increased by 29 percent. However, as noted before it is still the case that less than 50 percent of all surveyed households report contact with modern financial institutions. This, together with the cash-holding behavior described previously, indicates that although financial markets are continuing to emerge in rural China, their penetration is uneven, and their development far from complete. This has interesting implications for the disequalizing nature of several of these modern financial instruments, seemingly implied by their high concentration ratios seen in Table 11.3. Indeed, it is distinctly possible that several modern financial instruments such as savings deposits and bonds may become an equalizing force in overall wealth holdings as these markets continue to develop, much as cash in hand serves an equalizing role at present. Such a conclusion is reinforced by our following finding that certain fixed productive assets may at present be serving as a store of value for rural households in the presence of fragmented financial markets. Thus, if these markets do penetrate sufficiently, and if households begin to substitute out of cash holdings or other more traditional stores of value, it would be incorrect to conclude that all modern financial assets will serve a disequalizing role in the overall wealth distribution. This is especially true because the income elasticity of demand for financial assets appears to be high for low-income households and to decline as incomes rise.

Fixed Productive Assets

Finally we turn to the movements of fixed productive assets witnessed between 1988 and 1995. They are of particular interest because fixed productive assets, despite the significant increase in their inequality over the period, continue to offset other forms of wealth holdings and thus serve to *reduce* overall inequality. Moreover, understanding this aspect of household accumulation may offer insights into a problem that has been widely discussed both in the popular press in China as well as in the academic literature, namely the decline in fixed investment—especially in agriculture.[41] We will attempt to draw out some of these considerations below, after first describing the changes witnessed in fixed productive asset holding, and exploring the contours of their offsetting feature mentioned above.

Table 11.4 contains a disaggregated view of the changes in fixed productive assets between the two years. We first analyze the various fixed productive assets as a percentage of their total value to get a sense of the relative importance of each component. This is an important key to understanding the relative strength of each component's equalizing or disequalizing effect, both for overall fixed productive asset value and for household net worth. Here it is useful to follow McKinley (1993a) and divide fixed productive assets into two broad groupings: traditional assets and modern capital inputs. In so doing we see that traditional assets—which are comprised of livestock, buildings, tools, and the residual category "other fixed productive assets"—have fallen in their relative importance, from 76.2 percent of the total value in 1988 to 61.9 in 1995. Livestock and tools saw particularly large decreases, together comprising almost the entire decline. This relative decline of traditional fixed productive assets is crucial to understanding the movements in the distribution of total fixed productive assets. Indeed, had these traditional assets maintained their importance in the composition of overall fixed productive assets then the Gini coefficient would have risen only to 0.584, much lower than the 0.622 actually observed. However, as this exercise indicates indirectly, the inequality of these traditional assets themselves has also worsened. Indeed, only tools are more equally distributed in 1995 than in 1988.[42]

Table 11.4

Fixed Productive Assets: A Closer Look

Asset	Percentage of total		Concentration ratio	
	1988	1995	1988	1995
Fixed productive assets	100.0	100.0	0.257	0.316
			(4.843)	
Livestock	34.0	25.7	0.092	0.131
			(4.265)	
Buildings	22.2	25.3	0.299	0.281
			(1.103)	
Transport equipment	14.9	18.3	0.492	0.517
			(0.435)	
Tools	13.3	5.3	0.285	0.127
			(7.475)	
Agricultural machinery	6.5	14.4	0.415	0.431
			(0.607)	
Industrial machinery	2.3	4.9	0.334	0.573
			(3.038)	
Construction machinery	0.1	0.5	0.234	0.582
			(2.185)	
Other productive assets	6.7	5.6	0.174	0.261
			(2.164)	

Note: The "Percentage of total" columns are calculated with reference to "Fixed productive assets," whereas the "Concentration ratio" columns are calculated with regard to total "net worth." Test statistics are in parentheses.

Turning to the effect of the various fixed assets on the distribution of total wealth, another useful aspect of the division between traditional and modern fixed productive assets becomes readily apparent. Indeed, as the concentration ratios for the four traditional assets demonstrate, these elements are the source, *within* total fixed productive assets, of the equalizing effect on overall wealth distribution, as their concentration ratios are all lower than 0.351, the Gini coefficient for net worth. Yet the increased inequality of these traditional assets is also witnessed in the concentration ratios seen in Table 11.4, as only tools sees a statistically significant fall in its concentration ratio, whereas livestock and other productive assets witness statistically significant increases. In sum, modern capital inputs continue to play a disequalizing role both for fixed productive assets and for overall net worth. Moreover, given their rising importance in the composition of total fixed productive assets, it is likely that these modern capital inputs may eventually serve to make fixed productive assets as a whole a disequalizing component of net worth, although at present this is still not the case.

From the above discussion it is apparent that although traditional assets themselves have witnessed a rise in inequality, they continue to be the source for the equalizing nature of fixed productive assets. Yet when this fact is considered in conjunction with the relatively unequal distribution of each traditional asset individually (all four have Gini coefficients well above that for net worth and total fixed productive assets), it must be the case that these traditional fixed productive assets offset the disequalizing effects of other components of net worth. A natural question then is which elements of wealth holdings do these traditional assets offset? Table 11.5 offers a bit of insight into this question, depicting the asset holdings of each decile of the 1995 survey. In particular, what emerges from the table is the fact that traditional fixed productive assets serve to offset, relatively, *all* other types of household wealth holding, but particularly financial asset holdings and housing stock. This can be seen, for example, in the fact that the bottom 50 percent of all wealth holders control 35.1 percent of the traditional fixed productive assets, whereas they control only 27 percent of total wealth, 28.2 percent of total land value, 26.6 percent of the housing stock, and 22.6 percent of the financial assets.

This pattern may reflect the fact that, given continued imperfections in rural financial markets discussed above and the high fixed cost of housing investment, households are using traditional fixed productive assets as alternative stores of wealth.[43] Such a proposition would accord with several features of the transition in the Chinese countryside. For example, it has been frequently noted that rural China, like many other rural developing areas, faces a thin and particularly fragmented financial market (Feder et al., 1993). It has been argued that in such a context, fixed asset accumulation may substitute for the store of wealth function of financial assets as well as serve as a buffer stock in the face of income variability (Deaton 1990).

Fixed assets, in such a context, would also possess several distinct advantages as compared with other traditional stores of wealth, such as jewelry.[44] First, as is evident, these assets are productive over their lifetime, and thus offer more certain economic returns than other traditional assets. Second, it is often the case that markets for traditional assets such as livestock are well developed, making their divestiture through "distress" sales less likely. Finally, in the case of livestock, as against land or buildings, their mobility allows farmers to guard against spatially covariate shocks such as drought or flood.

Turning to the data, we find evidence for the hypothesis that fixed assets may serve as an alternative store of wealth in three ways. First, holding livestock and buildings (by far the most important of the traditional assets) is much more closely associated with holding cash in hand than with savings account deposits, an indication that holders of these traditional assets may face poorly functioning financial markets.[45] Second, the current prices of livestock and buildings witnessed an

Table 11.5

1995 Asset Holdings by Decile, as a Percentage of Total

Decile	1st	2nd	3rd	4th	5th	6th	7th	8th	9th	10th
Total wealth	2.7	4.5	5.6	6.6	7.6	8.8	10.1	12.0	15.1	27.0
Land value	2.3	4.7	5.9	7.1	8.2	9.3	10.6	12.5	15.0	24.2
Housing	3.2	4.4	5.6	6.1	7.3	8.3	9.7	11.3	15.1	29.1
Financial assets	2.7	3.6	4.5	5.6	6.2	7.9	9.0	11.1	15.0	34.4
Fixed productive assets	3.4	4.4	5.4	6.7	7.5	7.9	10.7	12.8	15.8	25.4
(Traditional)	4.9	5.9	7.1	8.1	9.1	8.9	11.2	11.8	14.6	18.4
(Modern)	1.2	1.9	2.7	4.5	5.2	6.2	9.9	14.6	17.1	36.7
Nonhousing debt	5.7	8.4	7.2	7.5	12.1	6.6	14.2	8.5	10.0	19.6

Note: The 1st decile represents the bottom 10 percent of wealth holders, while the 10th represents the top 10 percent.

average appreciation of 20 percent over their purchase prices, whereas all forms of modern capital inputs experienced moderate depreciation, evidence consistent with their function as a store of wealth.[46] Third, the value of livestock and buildings has a mild negative association with housing value, indicating that the two are possible substitutes for storing wealth, especially when the value of wealth to be stored is of a particularly modest level.[47] Thus, if fixed productive assets are indeed serving as a store of wealth for households without sufficient resources to invest in housing or access to a well-functioning financial market, the deepening of rural financial markets between 1988 and 1995 may help explain their relative decline in importance. Moreover, such a phenomenon would still be consistent with the observation of other scholars that housing investment has outpaced other fixed investment (especially in agriculture), also seen in our data by the real growth rates of 5.54 and 2.30, respectively.

Taken as a whole, this analysis of fixed productive assets serves to confirm both the fears of Chinese officials and predictions of Western researchers that present incentives are insufficient to promote fixed investment in agriculture. This is especially true since it appears that much of the accumulation that has taken place has been serving as a store of wealth rather than a productive capital investment per se. Moreover, opportunities for investment in nonagricultural activity or housing, coupled with better functioning financial markets, have served to divert resources away from such fixed investments where they are being made.[48] This may also help explain the emerging role of the local state in securing fixed investment or working to ameliorate poor agricultural incentives through input or credit provision.[49]

The Relationship between Wealth and Income

In the preceding two sections we have detailed the composition, distribution, and changes observed in wealth holdings as well as provided a more elaborate treatment of the major results and their institutional context. Yet, as noted in the introduction, there are many reasons to believe that changes in the composition and distribution of wealth will have substantial effects on the composition and distribution of income. Moreover, given the rapid rise in income inequality detailed in Khan and Riskin (1998), it is worthwhile to explore in greater detail the links between household wealth and income.

In particular, we are interested in discerning whether this increased income inequality can be traced to particular changes in the distribution of wealth. It must be reiterated that we are treating wealth here in the neoclassical sense, as a stock of productive (income generating) assets. However, income flows can differ not just from different distributions of these productive assets, but also because of different rates of return to these assets. This is especially problematic if markets are fragmented or malfunction, in which case identically "valued" assets may in fact have different productivities and thus yield different returns. Furthermore, they can also differ because of access to returns from nonprivately owned assets—such

Table 11.6

Income Concentration Ratio by Asset

Asset	Income concentration ratio 1988	Income concentration ratio 1995	Test statistic
Total income	0.317	0.416	18.728
Total wealth	0.211	0.268	13.199
Land value	0.184	0.215	5.230
Land in *mu*	0.021	0.001	2.004
Land in irrigation-adjusted *mu*	0.063	0.051	1.342
Housing	0.263	0.321	10.486
Housing debt	0.387	0.429	0.908
Fixed productive assets	0.113	0.177	6.100
Livestock	−0.044	−0.068	2.829
Buildings	0.199	0.168	2.174
Transport equipment	0.302	0.432	2.830
Tools	0.121	0.062	3.427
Agricultural machinery	0.143	0.202	2.489
Industrial machinery	0.244	0.508	3.449
Construction machinery	0.110	0.596	2.926
Other fixed productive assets	0.108	0.251	3.771
Financial assets	0.425	0.390	2.064
(1995 subcomponents)			
Cash in hand	—	0.300	—
Fixed term savings accounts	—	0.505	—
Current account deposits	—	0.529	—
Production funds for family production	—	0.268	—
Money lent out	—	0.398	—
Bonds	—	0.436	—
Investment in other enterprises	—	0.390	—
Stocks	—	0.648	—
(1988 subcomponents)			
Total savings deposits	0.439	—	—
Total time deposits	0.490	—	—
Current savings deposits	0.397	—	—
Government treasury bills	0.239	—	—
Bonds	0.416	—	—
Nonhousing debt	0.088	0.124	0.911

as a collectively owned enterprise—or inalienable noncapital assets such as simple labor power. Unfortunately, we do not have complete information regarding many of these other factors that influence income distribution. However, where possible we will attempt to provide evidence indicative of the pattern of their influence.

Turning first to the question of the influence of wealth holdings on income distribution, one way of approaching the issue is to consider the various components of wealth held according to a ranking based on per capita income rather than per capita wealth. Such an income-based concentration ratio may reveal patterns in the interrelationship between the holding of various productive assets and the distribution of income. Table 11.6 displays these income concentration ratios for all assets, for both years. Perhaps the most striking pattern to emerge is that in both years virtually all aspects of household wealth are more equally distributed than income, when the distribution of each is calculated based on its per capita income rank. There is also a substantial degree of continuity between 1988 and 1995 in this finding. In fact, of the five principal subcomponents, only financial assets in 1988 displayed an income concentration ratio higher than the Gini coefficient for per capita income in that year. By 1995, with the addition of cash-based holdings to its definition, even this component became more equally distributed than income, based on a per capita income rank.

Yet that is not to say that there were not interesting developments, either within or between the two years, that merit comment. For example, one remarkable aspect is that when ranked by per capita income, the distribution of land in physical units is exceedingly equal, with an income concentration ratio near zero. In fact, in 1995 the income concentration ratio was not statistically significantly different from zero, indicating that each decile of the population ranked by per capita income held approximately 10 percent of the total land. Another interesting finding is that financial assets seem to be the only component of wealth to display a pattern of distribution more consistent with that seen in other countries. That is to say that modern (noncash-based) financial instruments in both years were more unequally distributed than income when households were ranked according to per capita income, a characteristic often found in both developed and developing countries (where the flow of receipts from asset holdings are less unequally distributed than the assets themselves).[50]

Finally, it is also worth noting that in both years fixed productive assets have an income concentration ratio lower than total wealth and the other three major components. In fact, livestock, the most important subcomponent of total fixed productive assets, has a *negative* income concentration ratio, indicating that, for example, the lower deciles of the population ranked by per capita income hold *more* livestock than do the upper deciles. One substantial change within the subcomponents of fixed productive assets, however, is that by 1995 all of the modern capital inputs, with the exception of agricultural machinery, had income concentration ratios higher than the Gini coefficient for per capita income, a reversal of the 1988 pattern. This could reflect the development of the market for capital inputs between the two years, where these assets are now starting to generate scarcity rents. It is also possible, however, that it reflects the continuing general divergence between farm and off-farm incomes where the ownership of nonfarm capital inputs here serves as a surrogate for off-farm employment.[51]

This last point returns us to the question of the link between the distribution of productive assets and the distribution of income. Specifically, do any of the aforementioned developments offer any indication as to whether the dramatic rise in income inequality is due to a worsening in the distribution of wealth, or rather to other nonwealth factors, such as access to nonfarm employment? Before turning to the evidence, let us first say a word about differential rates of return for identically "valued" assets. As noted earlier, this outcome is possible when markets are incomplete or fragmented, and could produce results similar to those observed between 1988 and 1995, where the richest segment of the population controls increasingly more income than it does wealth.[52] Yet, we find that this divergence of wealth and income is most pronounced in many of the areas where markets are the most developed. For example, in rural Beijing the ratio of the percentage of total wealth to percentage of total income controlled by the top 20 percent of households, ranked by per capita income, fell from 0.914 in 1988 to 0.778 in 1995. For Guangdong, this shift was less dramatic, from 0.842 to 0.776. However, compare these two with the less developed province Gansu, where the ratio fell from 0.893 to 0.872, or with Guizhou, where it fell from 0.866 to 0.826. Thus, while not definitive evidence on these matters, we have reason to doubt that the dramatic rise in income inequality witnessed between 1988 and 1995 originates in wealth holdings, where similar movements in the wealth distribution are not seen due to market imperfections.

Moreover, certain facts are indicative that indeed access to nonfarm employment, either locally or via migration, has been the source of the dramatic worsening in income inequality. For example, consider the ratio of average income for those households without access to nonfarm employment to those with it. In 1988 this ratio was 0.695 for income, while the same ratio for net worth was 0.886. By 1995, that ratio had fallen to 0.559 for income while it had *risen* to 0.902 for net worth. This is consistent with evidence found in other places in this volume concerning the sharpening divergence between farm and nonfarm income. Moreover, it also suggests that access to nonfarm employment, while dramatically affecting income, has had little impact on wealth. Similar conclusions follow from the correlation between the percentage of the total household labor force in nonagricultural employment and total household income versus total net worth. In 1988 the correlation was 0.26 for total income, while it was 0.08 for net worth, both statistically significant at the 1 percent level. By 1995 those figures had risen to 0.36 and 0.11, respectively, again with both significant at the 1 percent level. Finally, consider the correlation between total net worth and total household income and compare it with the correlation between net worth and household income *net of wage income*. In 1988 these correlation coefficients were, respectively, 0.61 and 0.64, both highly significant. By 1995, the overall correlation between net worth and total income had fallen to 0.51, while the correlation between net worth and total income net of wage income had risen to 0.68, again both significant at more than the 1 percent level. This indicates that, if anything, wealth is becoming more important in the determination of income not related to wages, especially given the decline of various forms of state subsidies and administrative allocations and the simultaneous emergence of various markets for financial and productive capital. But as wages become a larger and larger part of total rural income (as seen in Khan and Riskin [1998] their percentage rose from 8.73 to 22.38), wealth is becoming less important as a determinant in overall rural income, and by implication rural income inequality.[53] Thus, in summary, we find that while wealth continues to influence the level and distribution of income, other nonwealth factors such as access to non-farm employment are likely to have played a more decisive role in generating the rapid rise in income inequality witnessed between 1988 and 1995. However, with the deepening of both financial and physical capital markets, the holders of these assets may begin to collect scarcity rents, which could have an important influence on income distribution in the future. Indeed, the shifts in the relationship between wealth and income indicate that this process is already under way.[54]

Conclusion

This chapter has outlined the broad contours of the distribution of wealth in 1995 and its changes since 1988. What we find is that wealth distribution has worsened somewhat between the two years, but continues to be remarkably equal in comparison to both rural income distribution in China and wealth distribution in other countries. Of the four components of wealth, land value continues to be the most important, contributing over 50 percent to the total value of wealth holdings, and it continues to exert an equalizing effect on overall wealth distribution. Housing remains the second most important component in total wealth, and retains its slightly disequalizing effect. One of the most important shifts in the composition of wealth concerns financial holdings, which rose dramatically between 1988 and 1995. Indeed, by 1995 financial assets had become the third most important component of wealth, and while they continue to exert a disequalizing effect, it is slighter than in 1988. Fixed productive assets are now the fourth most important component of wealth holdings, and continue to exert an equalizing effect on the overall distribution of net worth.

Probing deeper into the changes within each component of wealth, several even more interesting findings emerge. First, we find that land holdings have displayed a "double movement," whereby in physical units land distribution has substantially improved between the two years—owing mainly to the elimination of extremely large landholdings—while in value terms land distribution has substantially worsened. While land redivision at the local level, coupled with out-migration in land-scarce areas, may be an explanation for the decreased inequality in physical land holdings, the origins of the simultaneous increase in inequality in land value are less clear. We find some evidence, however, that the latter resulted from the growing wedge between agricultural production for self-consumption versus for the market, as well as the increase in part-time farming in certain rural areas, coupled with restored incentives to specialized agricultural households. Second, we see that the addition of cash-based financial assets to the definition of total financial holdings is the source of much of their newfound equalizing effect. This is especially true given the disappearance of government bond holding, which, although quantitatively unimportant in 1988, was nonetheless the sole equalizing element of financial holdings in that year. Third, we find that, as in 1988, the source of the equalizing effect of fixed productive assets derives from the holding of more traditional fixed assets, such as livestock, hand tools, and buildings, whereas the possession of modern capital inputs such as transport or construction equipment has a disequalizing effect. Moreover, we find evidence that these traditional assets serve in particular to offset holding financial or housing assets, which may reflect their dual role both as a substitute store of value given imperfect financial markets and high fixed costs for housing investment, and as a purely productive asset.

Finally, turning to the question of the relationship between income and wealth, we witness the upper income groups controlling a larger and larger share of total income relative to the share of total wealth under their control. While such a phenomenon is consistent with fragmented markets, and as mentioned above we find evidence of their existence, it appears that this is not the source of the divergence between wealth holdings and income receipts. Indeed, it seems more likely that the source of the growing divergence between wealth and income distribution is to be found in access to nonfarm employment for household members, either through off-farm migration or local nonagricultural employment. Thus the situation in rural China, where rural wage laborers are some of the wealthiest residents of the Chinese countryside, is unlike almost any other country in the developing world. Although access to nonfarm employment seems, at present, to dominate the relationship between wealth and income, we do see evidence that the development of financial and productive capital markets may serve to create conditions in rural China more like those found in other countries, where asset distribution is more, not less, unequal than income distribution.

Notes

1. This link between wealth distribution and the distribution of income is derived from the neoclassical notion of income, at its most general level, as a flow of returns to a given stock of some productive factor, perhaps best seen in the work of Sir John Hicks (1939). Viewed in this manner, the distribution of wealth, that is, the economy-wide stock of physical, natural, and human capital, will have important implications for the distribution of the returns to those productive factors. Thus, given the stock of productive assets, the equalizing effect on income likely from their more equitable distribution would, *ceteris paribus,* reduce the incidence and (likely) the severity of poverty. Indeed, it is this link that lies at the heart of another, normative motivation for the study of the distribution of wealth, namely its central role in many conceptions of distributive justice (see Roemer 1996 for an overview).

It must be noted, however, that distribution of wealth cannot be viewed as the sole determinant of income distribution, or the incidence of poverty, as one important factor for income generation, namely simple labor power, is not included in such a conception of wealth. Indeed, as both the 1988 and 1995 surveys demonstrate, the ability to sell one's labor power, especially in off-farm employment, is a powerful determinant of income inequality in rural China, a point to which we will return later.

2. For a review of recent contributions to this debate, see Griffin and Ickowitz (2000). In a related vein, Hoff (1996) surveys the empirical and theoretical consequences of asymmetric information for the relationship between wealth distribution and economic growth and efficiency.

3. McKinley (1993a) treats several of these limitations in the developing country context. For a more general consideration of wealth analysis, see Wolff (1990).

4. See, for example, McKinley (1996, 1993a, 1993b) and McKinley and Griffin (1993). As is noted in McKinley (1993a), the primary disadvantage to these works is that land is not reported in value terms and thus must be imputed indirectly. This shortcoming remains true of the present work, as discussed below.

5. In the 1995 survey only 3.59 percent of all households report either leasing in or leasing out land (down from 4.88 in 1988). However, it is likely that there is an incentive for rural residents to inaccurately report land leasing practices, both of the informal and more substantive variety. Land redistribution at the village level has been common since the initial reforms of the early 1980s, and the leasing of land has been used as one criterion by which reallocation has been decided. Indeed, this is a plausible explanation of the decrease in land leasing reported since 1988. For a discussion of the issue of land redistribution see Kung (1995) or Judd (1992). A more detailed discussion of these issues in the context of this chapter will be taken up below.

6. Specifically, we assume that 25 percent of the gross value of agricultural output can be attributed to the factor land, and we capitalize the value of future agricultural output assuming an 8 percent rate of return. This reflects our adherence to the neoclassical notion of wealth as the present value of the future stream of income derived from ownership of a productive asset, with usufruct rights considered here as de facto land ownership.

7. Thus the Gini coefficient satisfies the properties of (1) symmetry, (2) scale independence, and (3) the Pigou-Dalton transfer principle, with its largest drawback being the fact that it is not decomposable, for example to within- and between-group inequality. For a more detailed treatment of these theoretical properties and their implications, see Blackwood and Lynch (1994).

8. It also merits note that the formula for one component of the test statistic used by Kakwani (1990) contained a somewhat serious error. This was discovered by the author and subsequently verified by one of the editors of the volume in which his article appears. The calculations presented here reflect use of the corrected test statistic, the derivation of which is available from the author upon request.

9. As in Khan and Riskin (1998) we estimate annual growth rates based on point estimates in the two years of our survey. Thus, no inference should be drawn about the movements in wealth in the intervening years.

10. As noted in Khan and Riskin (1998), the use of the consumer price index, a Paasche index, is likely to understate the actual rise in prices experienced in rural China.

11. The Gini coefficient for rural per capita income in 1988 is calculated based on the reduced sample used throughout this chapter. Thus it differs from that reported in Griffin and Zhao (1993).

12. Unfortunately, as noted in the introduction, few if any estimates of wealth distribution in developing countries exist. However, Wolff (1996, p. 446) lists Gini coefficients for net worth in several industrialized countries during the mid-1980s, all of which are substantially higher than our findings for rural China: the United States (1988) 0.761, Germany (1988) 0.694, Canada (1984) 0.690, and Japan (1984) 0.520. All estimates are from household surveys, while the Japanese and Canadian definitions differ slightly from that used here. In the Japanese case all consumer durables are included in net worth, while in the Canadian case the value of vehicles are included, but all other consumer durables are excluded.

13. With all four of these values falling below their "unadjusted" counterparts, the argument that adjustments need to be made when considering land of differing qualities is strongly reinforced, particularly in a country as vast and geo-climatically diverse as mainland China.

14. This figure is arrived at by multiplying the concentration ratio for land value by the percentage of total wealth that land value comprises, and dividing that product by the Gini

coefficient for total wealth. See Khan and Riskin (1998) for more details on this indirect decomposition procedure.

15. Similarly, the Gini coefficient for total wealth distribution using this valuation method declines from 0.300 to 0.275, and the contribution of housing to overall inequality declines from 35.77 to 29.1 percent. In contrast, the mean value of housing stock actually increases using this valuation method, from 4,532 to 4,819 yuan.

16. One indirect method of assessing the degree of bias involves the comparison of the original housing value between the two years. Based on such a method, the Gini coefficient for housing value rose from 0.473 in 1988 to 0.565 in 1995. These dramatic differences with the Gini coefficients presented in Table 11.2 are largely due to the fact that our chosen method for estimating housing value in 1995 is unable to adequately discern intraprovincial inequality, particularly between suburban and more peripheral areas of a given province.

17. It must be noted here that with the inclusion of additional questions in 1995 concerning cash on hand, financial holdings for production, and money lent out, the comparisons between the two years will artificially inflate the prevalence of financial asset holdings in 1995 as compared with 1988. However, as we will discuss in further detail below, we do find evidence for some financial market deepening, although not to the extent reflected in these percentages.

18. In 1988 respondents were asked to list the total area of cultivated land used by the household, the amount that was irrigated, and the amounts either leased in or leased out. In 1995 additional information was included on nonirrigated agricultural land, land left fallow, land used for homesteading, and the amount of land either contracted out from the collective or assigned for meeting foodgrain needs (*kouliang tian*).

19. Whereas in 1988 we took the total amount of cultivated land used by the household as the relevant variable, in 1995 we defined land holdings as the combination of irrigated land, nonirrigated land, land left fallow, and land leased out to others, netting out any land leased in from others. This reflects a shift from a summary to a disaggregated measure of land between the two years.

20. One other point merits note here. The sharp decline in inequality between the two years can be attributed almost entirely to the decline in land holdings in the upper tail of the distribution. In 1988 the maximum land holding for the entire survey was 970 *mu* (approximately 162 acres, or 65 hectares), whereas in 1995 the maximum value reported was 64 *mu* (11 acres, or 4 hectares). Moreover, 57 households in 1988 report landholdings greater than this 1995 maximum. When these households are excluded from the distributional calculation for 1988, the Gini coefficient falls to 0.366, making the 1988 distribution statistically significantly *more equal* than that for 1995. It must be added immediately that we find no reason, either a priori or within the data, to exclude these 57 households from the 1988 analysis, and thus for our purposes they are retained. Moreover, the period between 1988 and 1995 has seen a continuation of fiscal decentralization, which has forced local governments to increasingly rely on fees, taxes, and levies to sustain local budgets. Given that these fees are frequently applied on a per *mu* basis, coupled with the increasingly unprofitable nature of agriculture generally, we have reason to believe there were indeed economic forces at work that served to reduce landholdings between the two years. See, for example, the discussion in Croll and Huang (1997) for more on this.

However, it still must be acknowledged that it is possible that either the 1988 survey contains an outlying number of large landholding households or, conversely, that the 1995 survey has somehow undersampled large landholders. Unfortunately, there exist relatively few alternative sources documenting land holdings in China to which we can refer for guidance. Moreover, of those that do exist, the variability in their reported measures is greater than that reported between our two surveys. Compare, for example, average land holdings reported in Kung (1995, p. 84) (9.2 *mu* in 1984 and 10.7 *mu* in 1988) and those reported in Dong (1996, p. 916) (8.4 *mu* in 1984, 7.1 *mu* in 1986, and 6.3 *mu* in 1990), with the averages from our two surveys. In 1988 landholdings averaged 10.2 *mu,* whereas in 1995 they fell to 6.3 mu for our more precise definition and 7.5 mu for our aggregate measure.

21. As with many aspects of rural China, there is extreme heterogeneity in land alloca- tion patterns, but egalitarian allocations, which predominated during decollectivization, still continue today in many parts of the countryside. These egalitarian allocations are usu- ally made to households on a per capita basis, or in more limited cases, a per worker basis. See, for example, the discussion in Kung (1995), Kung (1994), and Putterman (1985).

22. Similar results have been found in more extensive surveys, such as that conducted in 280 villages by the Research Development Center of the State Council (see He, 1995). Moreover, these readjustments on egalitarian criteria continue to elicit considerable support from rural households. For example, Dong (1996, p. 917) cites three separate surveys in which rural house- holds expressed approval for these reallocation systems at rates of 80 percent or higher.

23. For example, Kung (1995, n. 23) notes that in one surveyed village land readjust- ment did not begin until 1986. Indeed, this may explain why the upper tail of our 1988 distribution contained so many more large holders than did that for 1995, assuming those landholdings larger than 4 hectares were probable targets for reallocation within their re- spective villages, and that with the passage of time mismatches between household land- holdings and labor resources became increasingly likely.

24. Per capita household income and landholdings also displayed a more systematic negative relationship in 1988, with a Spearman correlation coefficient of –0.149, signifi- cant at the 1 percent level.

25. This relative decline in the gap between the size of large and small landholding households took place in the presence of an *absolute* decline of household size for both groups from 1988 to 1995. In 1988 the average household size for landholders in the top 20 percent was 5.82, while for the bottom 20 percent it was 3.96. In 1995 the figures were 4.89 and 3.69, respectively. The negative relationship between per capita income and landhold- ing remains for 1995, however, with a Spearman correlation coefficient of –0.117, signifi- cant at the 1 percent level. Note that for these comparisons between 1988 and 1995 land- holdings we have employed the broader, aggregate measure of land. The results for the more precise, disaggregated measure are similar.

26. In the 1995 survey there were several additional questions concerning migration as compared with 1988. For our purposes we counted any household that reported receiving remittances, either to the household as a whole or to individuals within it, as having access to migratory employment opportunities for its members. It must be noted that in 1988 no question regarding the receipt of remittances by individuals within the household existed. When we restrict ourselves in 1995 to only those *households* that report positive remittance income, the increase from 1988 to 1995 is nowhere near as dramatic, with 8.79 percent of the 1995 bottom quintile of landholders and 4.75 percent of the top reporting remittance income. While it is possible that our 1988 survey underreports remittance income, due to the absence of questions concerning *individual* receipt of remittance income, we have no way of determining this. More important, it does not affect our conclusions with regard to the widening relative gap between the top and bottom quintiles of landholders, in terms of their access to off-farm migration.

27. For a more complete discussion of the complexities of agricultural production in rural China than is possible here, see Sicular (1993, 1995), Kung (1992), or Blecher and Wang (1994).

28. This follows, if from nothing else, from the extreme variation in procurement prac- tices regionally. See Cheng (1997) for a discussion of the variation in grain marketing systems and the subsequent price differentials these induce.

29. This result is for the Pearson correlation coefficient, where price growth is based on the regional movements in the rural retail price index taken from the State Statistical Bureau (various years).

30. For rural Chinese households in 1988, grain accounted for 27 percent of the gross value of agricultural output, economic crops 21 percent, and animal husbandry 38 percent, on average. By 1995 those percentages had shifted to 50 percent, 16 percent, and 22 percent, respectively. While it is true that these percentages tell us little about the changes in cropping patterns or land use between the two years, due to the absence of data on physical quantities and the sharp changes in prices (especially the evolution of government procurement prices for grain), they still are dramatic. Moreover, they accord with the generally unfavorable position of grain production in the late 1980s vis-à-vis the mid-1990s.

31. For more on regional trends in grain production, see Yang (1996).

32. We also will return to this issue later in this chapter, as it appears to play an important role in the relationship between wealth and income.

33. See, for example, Croll and Huang (1997) and Wu and Meng (1997).

34. Another interesting aspect of the role of part-time farming in raising land value inequality is its potential role in equalizing land distribution in physical terms. Indeed, if farming is becoming an increasingly part-time occupation for most household labor, it is possible that this is reinforcing the role of land distribution as a means of ensuring food security and basic welfare, discussed at length by Burgess (1997). If so, it is not surprising that village-level allocations are becoming increasingly more equal over time, nor that such egalitarian distributions enjoy overwhelming support from the rural population, as discussed by Dong (1996).

35. This suspicion is reinforced by the work of Wang (1995), who reports the average value of financial assets in rural China as 747 yuan for 1986. This figure is inclusive of cash in hand and is nearly 84 percent higher than our estimate for financial assets in 1988. On the other hand, Aaberge and Yu (1998), reporting on savings behavior in urban Sichuan and Liaoning, note that 1988 was an inflationary year, and that urban households were seen taking money out of savings deposits and cash balances and storing their wealth in other forms, such as consumer durables. Again, we have no way to investigate whether this was also the pattern in rural China, but it is a possibility, in which case cash balances may not be understated to the extent described above and in the text.

36. See, for example, the discussion in Feder et al. (1992, 1993) for more on the fragmentation of rural financial markets.

37. Cash in hand and savings deposits are equal to 18.5 and 10.7 percent of total household income, respectively, for households reporting stock holdings.

38. See Bei et al. (1992, p. 169) for further discussion of these issues.

39. Moreover, when cash-based financial assets are subtracted from total financial holdings then miscellaneous bonds account for approximately 1 percent of the total. Although not stunning, this is still a trebling of its 1988 level.

40. Again, it must be stressed that this increase is independent of the inclusion of cash in hand to the 1995 definition of financial assets.

41. See, for example the discussion of Fan (1997) for a general overview. For a more detailed discussion of one area of agricultural fixed investment, that of irrigation, see Vermeer (1997).

42. The Gini coefficients for traditional fixed productive assets were as follows: Livestock, 0.633 and 0.749; Tools, 0.766 and 0.736; Structures, 0.736 and 0.764; and Other fixed productive assets, 0.859 and 0.913; all for 1988 and 1995, respectively.

43. Indeed, the average purchase price of housing was 8 times the average purchase price of livestock, the largest traditional asset in value terms. For further discussion of credit market imperfections and their relationship with residential construction, see Feder et al. (1992, 1993).

44. See, for example, the recent discussions of livestock as a store of wealth in the context of Africa (Fafchamps et al. 1998) and India (Rosenzweig and Wolpin 1993).

45. The Spearman correlation coefficient between the current value of livestock and buildings and the value of cash in hand was 0.166, significant at the 1 percent level, while the correlation between these traditional assets and savings deposits was not statistically different from zero.

46. The one exception to this was agricultural machinery, which witnessed a 3 percent appreciation between its current and purchase price.

47. The Spearman correlation coefficient between housing value and livestock and buildings was −0.033, significant at the 1 percent level.

48. One factor that tempers these conclusions somewhat is that the prevalence of ownership of agricultural machinery in 1995 has increased significantly since 1988. The percentage of households who reported holding agricultural machinery was 28 percent in 1995, up from 12 percent in 1988. However, it must also be noted that at the same time the value of these holdings for these households increased by less than 1 percent per annum.

49. See, for example, the discussion in Croll (1994, Chapter 4) or Oi (1995). Dong (1996, p. 916) offers evidence to complement the detailed discussion in Croll (1994), noting one recent nationwide survey that found that 43 percent of fixed productive assets were still held by the village. He takes this as evidence of the market failures to which we alluded earlier.

50. See Wolff (1996) for more on this point.

51. This is all the more likely given the low income concentration ratio for agricultural machinery, 0.143 in 1988 and 0.202 in 1995.

52. In 1988 the ratio of the percentage of wealth to percentage of income controlled by the top 20 percent of households ranked by per capita income was 0.796. By 1995 that figure had fallen to 0.742. Thus, by 1995 the richest 20 percent of the rural population were controlling less of the total stock of productive assets—vis-à-vis the amount of total income they controlled—than they were in 1988. As noted, this could be due to the fact that assets held by the rich are actually more productive than those held by the poor, hence they generate higher incomes. However, because of malfunctioning markets their "value" does not totally reflect these differentials in productivity.

53. It is also worth bearing in mind that, as shown in Khan and Riskin (1998), wage income accounted for nearly 40 percent of overall rural inequality, up from 18.3 percent in 1988. Thus, *ceteris paribus,* we would expect this to mitigate to some extent the influence of wealth distribution on income distribution.

54. This is seen by the fact that in 1988 the income concentration ratios for all modern capital inputs were below the Gini coefficient for income, whereas by 1995 all except agricultural machinery had risen above it. For modern financial instruments, the income concentration ratios were above the Gini coefficient for income in both years.

References

Aaberge, Rolf, and Yu Zhu (1998), "The Pattern of Household Savings During a Hyperinflation: The Case of Urban China in the Late 1980s," Discussion Paper # 217, Statistics Norway, Research Department.

Bei, Duoguang, Arden Koontz, and Xiangqian Lewis (1992), "The Emerging Securities Market in the PRC," *China Economic Review* Vol. 3, No. 2, pp. 149–72.

Blackwood, D.L., and R.G. Lynch (1994), "The Measurement of Inequality and Poverty: A Policy Maker's Guide to the Literature," *World Development* Vol. 22, No. 4, pp. 567–78.

Blecher, Marc, and Shaoguang Wang (1994), "The Political Economy of Cropping in Maoist and Dengist China: Hebei Province and Shulu County, 1949–90," *The China Quarterly* No. 137, March, pp. 63–98.

Burgess, Robin (1997), "Land, Welfare and Efficiency in Rural China," London School of Economics, mimeo.

Cheng, Yuk-shing (1997), "China's Grain Marketing System Reform in 1993–94: Empirical Evidence from a Rural Household Survey," *China Economic Review* Vol. 7, No. 2, pp. 135–53.

Croll, Elizabeth (1994), *From Heaven to Earth*. New York: Routledge.

Croll, Elizabeth, and Huang Ping (1997), "Migration For and Against Agriculture in Eight Chinese Villages," *The China Quarterly* No. 149, March, pp. 128–46.

Deaton, Angus (1990), "Saving in Developing Countries: Theory and Review," *World Bank Economic Review*, Suppl., pp. 61–96.

Dong, Xiao-Yuan (1996), "Two-Tier Land Tenure System and Sustained Economic Growth in Post-1978 Rural China," *World Development* Vol. 24, No. 5, pp. 915–28.

Fafchamps, Marcel, Christopher Udry, and Katherine Czukas (1998), "Drought and Saving in West Africa: Are Livestock a Buffer Stock?" *Journal of Development Economics* Vol. 55, pp. 273–305.

Fan, Shenggen (1997), "Public Investment in Rural China: Historical Trends and Policy Issues," in *Agricultural Policies in China*. Paris: Organization for Economic Cooperation and Development.

Feder, Gershon, Lawrence J. Lau, Justin Y. Lin, and Xiaopeng Luo (1992), "The Determinants of Farm Investment and Residential Construction in Post-Reform China," *Economic Development and Cultural Change* Vol. 41, No. 1, pp. 1–26.

———— (1993), "The Nascent Rural Credit Market in China," in Karla Hoff, Avishay Braverman, and Joseph Stiglitz, eds., *The Economics of Rural Organization*. New York: Oxford University Press, pp. 109–30.

Griffin, Keith, and Amy Ickowitz (2000) "The Distribution of Wealth and the Pace of Development," in Keith Griffin, *Studies in Development Strategy and Systemic Transformation*. London: Macmillan.

Griffin, Keith, and Zhao Renwei, eds. (1993), *The Distribution of Income in China*. London: Macmillan.

He, Daofeng (1995), "Changes in the Rural Land Tenure System at the Village Level," in *Transition of China's Rural Land System*, University of Wisconsin Land Tenure Center, LTC Paper 151, pp. 69–95.

Hicks, John R. (1939), *Value and Capital, 2nd ed.* Oxford: Clarendon Press (reprinted 1953).

Hoff, Karla (December 1996), "Market Failures and the Distribution of Wealth: A Perspective from the Economics of Information," *Politics and Society* Vol. 24, No. 4, pp. 411–32.

Judd, Ellen (1992), Land Divided, Land United," *The China Quarterly* No. 130, June, pp. 338–56.

Kakwani, Nanak, (1990), "Large Sample Distribution of Several Inequality Measures: With Application to Côte d'Ivoire," in R.A.L. Carter, J. Dutta, and A. Ullah, eds., *Contributions to Econometric Theory and Application: Essays in Honour of A.L. Nagar*. New York: Springer, pp. 50–81.

Khan, A.R., and Carl Riskin (1998), "Income Inequality in China: Composition, Distribution and Growth of Household Income, 1988 to 1995," *The China Quarterly* No. 154, June.

Kung, James Kaisung (1992), "Food and Agriculture in Post-Reform China: The Marketed Surplus Problem Revisited," *Modern China* Vol. 18, No 2, pp. 138–70.

———— (1994), "Egalitarianism, Subsistence Provision, and Work Incentives in China's Agricultural Collectives," *World Development* Vol. 22, No. 2, pp. 175–88.

———— (1995), "Equal Entitlement versus Tenure Security under a Regime of Collective Property Rights: Peasants' Preference for Institutions in Post-reform Chinese Agriculture," *Journal of Comparative Economics* Vol. 21, pp. 82–111.

McKinley, Terry R. (1993a), "The Distribution of Wealth in Rural China," in Keith Griffin, and Zhao Renwei, eds., *The Distribution of Income in China*. London: Macmillan, pp. 116–34.

————(1993b), "Agrarian Transformation and the Distribution of Fixed Productive Assets in China," *Development and Change* Vol. 24, pp. 487–510.
————(1996), *The Distribution of Wealth in Rural China*. New York: M.E. Sharpe.
McKinley, Terry R., and Keith Griffin (1993), "The Distribution of Land in Rural China" *Journal of Peasant Studies* Vol. 21, No. 1, pp. 71–84.
Oi, Jean C. (1995), "The Role of the State in China's Transitional Economy," *The China Quarterly* No. 144, December, pp. 1132–49.
Putterman, Louis (1985), "The Restoration of the Peasant Household as Farm Production Unit in China: Some Incentive-Theoretic Analysis," in Elizabeth Perry, and Christine Wong, eds., *The Political Economy of Reform in Post-Mao China*. Cambridge, MA: Harvard University Press, pp. 63–82.
Roemer, John E. (1996), *Theories of Distributive Justice*. Cambridge, MA: Harvard University Press.
Rosenzweig, Mark R., and Kenneth I. Wolpin (1993), "Credit Market Constraints, Consumption Smoothing, and the Accumulation of Durable Production Assets in Low-Income Countries: Investments in Bullocks in India," *Journal of Political Economy* Vol. 101, No. 2, pp. 223–44.
Sicular, Terry (1993), "China's Agricultural Policy During the Reform Period," in Joint Economic Committee of the U.S. Congress, *China's Economic Dilemmas in the 1990s: The Problems of Reforms, Modernization and Interdependence*. New York: M.E. Sharpe, pp. 340–64.
Sicular, Terry (1995), "Redefining State, Plan and Market: China's Reforms in Agricultural Commerce," *The China Quarterly* December, 1995, pp. 1020–46.
State Statistical Bureau (various years), *China Statistical Yearbook*. Beijing: China Statistical Publishing House.
Vermeer, Eduard B. (1997), "Decollectivisation and Functional Change in Irrigation Management in China," in *Agricultural Policies in China*. Paris: Organization for Economic Cooperation and Development.
Wang, Yan (1995), "Permanent Income and Wealth Accumulation: A Cross-Sectional Study of Chinese Urban and Rural Households," *Economic Development and Cultural Change* Vol. 43, No. 3, pp. 523–50.
Wolff, Edward N. (1990), "Methodological Issues in the Estimation of the Size Distribution of Household Wealth," *Journal of Econometrics* Vol. 43, pp. 179–95.
————(1996), "International Comparisons of Wealth Inequality," *Review of Income and Wealth* Series 42, No. 4, pp. 433–51.
Wu, Harry X., and Xin Meng (1997), "Do Chinese Farmers Reinvest in Grain Production," *China Economic Review* Vol. 7, No. 2, pp. 123–34.
Yang, Hong (1996), "Trends in China's Regional Grain Production and Their Implications," Chinese Economic Research Center Working Paper 96/10. Adelaide, Australia: University of Adelaide.

12

Gender Effects on Household Resource Allocation in Rural China

Lina Song

The Issues

While the distribution of income among social groups attracts serious concern in China, resource allocation among members of households seems overlooked. Research on household issues has been dominated by the "unitary" model of household decision making, which treats all household members as if they behaved as one. Understanding how rights, responsibilities, and resources are allocated among household members can help policymakers to monitor how inequality among household members is changing.

How China's aggregate economic growth affects income distribution is a leading issue for the country, but how growth affects intrahousehold resource allocation is seldom addressed. An increase in household income will not necessarily be equally distributed among all household members. For instance, children or aged members may not be decision makers within the household, being instead dependent on others. Growth in household income may not benefit such dependents much if their needs are given low weight by household decision makers. In the case of rural China, girls' education can be badly affected by the need to increase household labor. Aged members of households may be relatively deprived when they lose their capacity to work. However, the structure of power within the household may vary, for example, in terms of gender. Women may be expected to have a greater influence on household decision making if their own income or education is high relative to that of men.

Econometric studies from other countries have tended to show that if men have more power in decisions over household expenditure, more goods would be purchased for adults or men than for children and general family use. In the Côte d'Ivoire, men appear to spend a greater proportion of the income they earn on goods such as alcohol and cigarettes; by contrast, women are more likely to purchase goods for children and for general household consumption (Hoddinott and Haddad 1995). The identity of the individual receiving nonwage income affects the pattern of household expenditure in Brazil (Thomas 1990). Phipps and Burton (1993) find that Canadian men and women in full-time employment have differential spending patterns. Bourguignon et al. (1993) obtained similar findings for French households. As yet, there have been no comparable studies for China. How do consumption patterns of Chinese households vary as the bargaining power of women increases relative to men?

It is commonly assumed that a country like China, with its official support for equality between the sexes, would not exhibit substantial job discrimination and wage discrimination against women. Researchers have indeed found that urban women in China have a high rate of job participation relative to other countries. Possession of education may protect Chinese women against discrimination or give them access to jobs with less discrimination. However, a gender differential has been found in urban wages even after controlling for gender differences in education, age, and several other observables. Such wage discrimination appears to affect the younger age cohorts less than the older ones (Knight and Song 1993). Further, men have received more years of education than women both in urban and rural China (Knight and Li 1993). In the rural areas, women are less active in seeking off-farm jobs; while men work in the urban sector, women are more likely to stay in the villages, maintaining the farm and looking after families (Song 1999).

The Setting

Until recently most economic research at the household level has been motivated by "unitary" household models. That is to say, the household has been modeled as maximizing a single objective function. Contrary to what is sometimes claimed, this approach can be used to analyze intrahousehold allocation. Intrahousehold inequality may be ascribed to compensating or reinforcing responses to differences in individual members' productivity. Rosenzweig and Schultz (1982) explained why "excess" female mortality in India was associated with low female labor market participation in terms of the reinforcement of productivity differences. Alternatively, intrahousehold inequalities may reflect differences in the relative weights given to individuals' interests in the household objective function. For example, Behrman (1988) found a "pro-son bias" in lean seasons in three Indian villages. However, the unitary model provides a somewhat restricted perspective. In particular, it gives no role to inequalities in intrahousehold bargaining power in explaining intrahousehold inequalities in resource allocation. There is a given household objective function, and it is impervious to factors that might be expected to alter the bargaining power of household members. For example, Folbre (1984) argued that an alternative explanation of Rosenzweig and Schultz's (1982) results was that higher female labor market participation raised the bargaining power of women and hence led to better treatment of girls. As Folbre argues:

> The suggestion that women and female children voluntarily relinquish leisure, education and food would be somewhat more persuasive if they were in a position to demand their fair share. It is the juxtaposition of women's lack of economic power with the unequal allocation of household resources that lends the bargaining power approach much of its persuasive appeal.

This richer view of intrahousehold allocation has been formalized in the class of "collective" household models. These recognize that household decisions are the result of interaction among members with sometimes divergent preferences. Collective models may be further distinguished, following the terminology of game theory, into cooperative and noncooperative variants. Under the former, binding agreements may be entered into and outcomes may be determined by bargaining processes. Under the latter, no binding agreements are possible and household members do the best they can given the actions of others.

In cooperative models, bargaining power depends in part on an individual's "fallback" position, that is, on what their welfare would be were cooperation to fail. There are various interpretations of what such fallback positions would be in practice. They are commonly taken to be separation and the dissolution of the household. However, this may be rather extreme: For more mundane disagreements, the household may persist but perhaps act noncooperatively.

It is natural to assume a cooperative or unitary model in studying the behavior of rural Chinese households. Chinese society in general has been characterized by close family ties. This is particularly true of rural China, where all members of an extended household are supposed to share income and consumption (Ling 1989; Fei, 1986). In terms of resource allocation, those who need more are supposed to consume more. Those who can earn more in the labor market are given the chance to earn. These patterns of behavior reflected a family hierarchy, where normally a leading role was given to the most senior male of the household (Fei 1985). However, in recent years there has been a gradual fall in the number of extended families in both urban and rural China and a corresponding rise in the number of nuclear families.[1] The typical rural family is no longer multigenerational but is a nuclear household with simply two generations—parents and children (73 percent of the 1995 CASS rural sample). This change has given married couples more control over family activities and may have given wives more influence. At the very least, issues of bargaining arise less between generations (between grandparents and parents) and more within a generation (husband and wife). This simplifies our research.

In this chapter we study rural household expenditure patterns, paying special attention to gender issues. We examine the determinants of resource allocation within the household, focusing on the impact of the relative bargaining power of spouses on different demographic groups defined by age and sex. How do gender differences in bargaining power affect the distribution of welfare within the household? The consequences for household outlays on education and medical care for girls are given special attention.

Hypotheses, Models, and Methods

We mainly focus on three hypotheses: (H1) that increasing the relative bargaining power of women alters household expenditure patterns; (H2) that households allocate fewer resources to daughters than to sons; and (H3) that increasing the relative bargaining power of women may increase their daughters' well-being within the family.

The first hypothesis concerns whether rural households in China exhibit consumption behavior consistent with "unitary" or "collective" models. The second hypothesis concerns sex bias in the allocation of consumption. Although it is arguable that the two hypotheses are linked, this is not necessarily so. The first hypothesis is true under collective, but not unitary, household models; the second may be true under both. Therefore we propose the third hypothesis to see the links between mothers' bargaining power and their daughters' well-being—whether there is any change in spending on girls with the change of wives' bargaining power. Appleton et al. (1998) have explored this hypothesis for Uganda using similar methods to this chapter, but found no evidence to support it.

In our empirical work, we focus on a wife's education relative to her husband's as our main measure of bargaining power—calculating the percentage of the wife's education in years to the sum of the years both husband and wife received.[2] If the fallback position is marital dissolution, then education is a likely determinant. More educated individuals may be better able to obtain paid employment or a new spouse. In noncooperative outcomes, education may also be important. Ulph (1988) presents a noncooperative model in which two household members each separately earn income and make household purchases from their individual earnings. The Nash equilibrium has the property that expenditure patterns vary with the share of household income attributable to each member. Since education is likely to influence income shares, it should also be a determinant of expenditure patterns in noncooperative models such as Ulph's.[3] By contrast, it is not clear why a wife's education relative to her husband's would have any effect in a unitary household model. However, we cannot claim that the variable provides a decisive test of the unitary model. The ratio may matter even in a unitary model to the extent that female education has different market and nonmarket productivity effects from male education.

In addition to relative education, we use a number of other indicators of bargaining power based on the characteristics of the household head. Perhaps the most direct is the sex of the household head. This reflects the administrative convention that registered husbands are automatically defined as being the household heads. Women will only be defined as household heads if they have no husbands or if their husbands have permanent migrant employment (i.e., they are registered elsewhere). One might expect women to have more influence over household expenditures if they have been registered as household heads. Even if women household heads have husbands, the fact that the husbands are registered elsewhere presumably reduces their day-to-day influence over household expenditures. We also include variables for the sector in which the heads are employed and for whether they are Communist Party members. In both cases, we allow these variables to have different impacts on male and female household heads.

We test our first hypothesis by including proxies for bargaining power as explanatory variables in household expenditure functions. In particular, we estimate an augmented Working-Lesser expenditure function, where the share, W_j, of total household expenditure on goods of type j is given by

$$W_j = a_j + b_{1j}\ln(Y/N) + b_{2j}\ln N + b_{3j}S_i + b_{4j}R_i + c^1_j Z + \sum_{k=1}^{K-1} Q_{kj}N_k/N + e_j \qquad (12.1)$$

where:
Y = household income (predicted)
N = household size
N_k = number of household members in demographic group K
S = 1 if household head is a man, 0 otherwise
R = ratio of wife's years of education to that of both husband and wife
Z = vector of other control variables
e = error term
and a, b, c, and Θ are parameters

The dependent variables are the value of purchases of the jth good as a share of total household purchases.[4] Eleven types of goods were reported by this household survey: food; cigarettes/alcohol; clothing; transport; daily used goods; durable goods; medical care; housing (repairs only); education; financial support to nonresident parents; and other nonspecified items. We separate spending on education into that on children's schooling and that on adults' training. Unfortunately, most of the expenditure categories used by the survey cannot be defined as exclusively adults' or children's goods, nor men's goods or women's goods. However, information from the survey shows that only a small percentage of adult women smoked (9 percent of women household heads compared with 80 percent of male household heads). Hence, cigarette and alcohol spending are treated as male adult goods. Full-time education before university should be treated as children's consumption.

The budget-share models control for household size and demographic composition. The N_k/N variables also provide an indirect test of our second hypothesis. The surveys do not directly record the resources individuals received from their household. However, some inferences are possible based on the effect of household demographic composition on the pattern of household expenditures. For example, if a higher proportion of boys in a household is associated with more educational spending than an equivalent higher proportion of girls, then this suggests that less is spent on girls' education. Moreover, Deaton (1987) has argued that expenditures on adult goods may be a way of gauging discrimination in favor of sons. In particular, if an extra boy is associated with a larger fall in expenditure on adult goods than an extra girl, then it could be inferred that the household was making larger sacrifices for boys than for girls.

To test the third hypothesis, we divide the whole sample into four quarters, sorted by women's bargaining power—the ratio of the wife's education in years to that of both husband and wife. The budget models will be estimated separately for each quarter to see if boy-girl discrimination varies with women's bargaining power.

Among the set of independent variables, we have controlled for some characteristics of the household head, and their interaction terms* with gender. The political and occupational status of the household head may affect decisions about household spending. Consequently, we include dummy variables for Communist Party membership and for occupation. The occupations are classified as farm worker, manual nonfarm worker, skilled nonfarm worker, professional, cadre, individual trader, and other nonspecified category. We allow for the fact that more educated households may have different spending patterns than less educated households, by controlling for the education, E_i, of the household head. We have also tried the total educational years of the husband and wife in the models instead of E_i. However, it has less statistically significant effects than the educational level of household heads, and the two sets of variables are highly correlated.

Other variables controlled for in the expenditure functions are household income per capita (to control for the effect of income) and household location. Total household income per capita is endogenous to expenditure shares, and consequently we use its predicted value (Table 12.1).[5] Dummy variables for household generation type are also controlled in the models: nuclear households might have a different consumption pattern compared with households with grandparents or grandchildren, or with those with only one generation in the household. Location variables included in the models were provincial dummy variables and whether the household lived in an officially designated poor county.

The Results

Descriptive Statistics

Table 12.2 reports the mean shares of expenditure on the different categories of goods and services identified in the data. The biggest proportion of household cash spending is on food (38 percent), followed by clothing (13 percent).[6] Spending on education (mostly for schooling) is the third biggest consumption item (9.9 percent), but spending on cigarettes and alcohol is almost as large (9.2 percent). Expenditure on health care averages 5 percent.

Editor's note: An "interaction term" measures how a dummy variable (such as gender) affects the impact of other variables (such as occupation) on the dependent variable (such as expenditure on education).

Table 12.1

Least Squares Regression Model to Predict Household Annual Income

Independent variable	Dependent variable: household annual income per capita in actual terms	
	Coefficient	T-ratio
Intercept	6,171.4877	44.2 ***
Number of household members	−318.3909	14.0 ***
Farming land (in *mu*)	17.8182	3.3 **
Households located in plains areas	—	—
Households located in mountainous areas	−870.5935	10.5 ***
Households located in hilly areas	−361.7688	5.1 ***
Province		
Beijing	321.3933	1.2
Hebei	−2,587.8579	16.5 ***
Shanxi	−3,057.3012	16.4 ***
Liaoning	−2,486.2777	13.5 ***
Jilin	−2,394.5021	12.5 ***
Jiangsu	—	—
Zhejiang	−985.9064	5.9 ***
Anhui	−2,620.5612	16.2 ***
Jiangxi	−2,432.5391	13.7 ***
Shandong	−1,845.8708	12.8 ***
Henan	−2,773.7275	19.2 ***
Hubei	−2,529.2943	15.2 ***
Hunan	−2693.6845	16.7 ***
Guangdong	269.2576	1.7
Sichuan	−2,918.2638	19.2 ***
Guizhou	−2,261.9363	11.5 ***
Yunnan	−2,627.4369	14.1 ***
Shaanxi	−2,974.0192	16.3 ***
Gansu	−2,959.7061	15.3 ***
Adj. R^2	0.1857	
F–value	83.891	
Dependent mean	2,467.18	
Number of observations	7,998	

Source: 1995 Rural Household Survey.
Notes: The omitted dummies in this model are households located in the plains areas and Jiangsu province. ***Denotes the significance level at 1 percent and below and ** at 2 percent.

In this sample 96 percent of the households are headed by men (Table 12.3). Compared with their female counterparts, male household heads are younger; more likely to be married than widowed or single; more often Communist Party members; better educated; and less likely to be full-time house workers. However, female-headed households have higher household income per capita together with higher values of bank savings and houses. Eighty percent of all male household heads smoke compared to only 9 percent of female household heads.

Table 12.2

Dependent Variables Used in the Analysis

	Mean	Standard deviation
Total household cash expenditure (in yuan)	3,622.34	5,059.72
Percent spent on:		
Food	37.78	17.09
Cigarettes and alcohol	9.15	7.27
Clothing	13.15	9.47
Transportation	3.25	7.25
Daily goods	6.29	5.60
Durable goods	2.53	6.97
Medical costs	5.01	8.52
Education	9.87	13.19
of which for schooling only	9.44	12.82
Housing (repairs)	2.12	7.40
Payments to parents	0.39	3.07
Other (nonspecified)	10.79	11.45
Number of observations	7,997	

Source: 1995 Rural Household Survey.

Women have less education than men in this sample (Table 12.4). On average, the ratio of wives' education in years to the total of husbands' and wives' is 36 to 100. There are 48 percent of households with wives' educational levels equal to their husbands'; 41 percent have husbands' educational levels higher than their wives'; only 6 percent of the wives' educational levels are higher than their husbands.[7]

The household structure by gender and age is also reported in Table 12.4. Household members aged 0–6 years are preschoolers; those 7–12 are of primary school age; those 13–15 are of middle school age while those 16–18 are of high school age. We term those aged 56 to 65 as likely to be a semiretired group. We refer to those aged over 66 as the aged group.

The Role of Gender in Bargaining Power

Table 12.5 (pages 288–290) reports the expenditure functions for seven categories of goods and services: food purchases (excluding self-consumption), cigarettes and alcohol, school education (excluding adults' job-training costs), clothing, medical costs, durable goods, and daily-use goods.[8]

We do not reject our first hypothesis. Wives' bargaining power, measured in terms of education relative to their husbands,' has a significant effect on household expenditure patterns, *ceteris paribus*. This is contrary to what would be predicted by unitary household models but consistent with collective models. Specifically, as wives' education rises relative to their husbands,' so do expenditures on children's education, clothing, and durable goods. The opposite effects are apparent with purchases

Table 12.3

Main Characteristics of Households by Gender

Variable	Male	Female
Household heads		
Average age (in years)	43.93	46.54
Marital status (%)		
Married	97.1	81.2
Widow(er)	1.6	16.0
Not married	1.3	2.8
Communist Party membership	14.7	11.8
Production status (%)		
Agricultural work	79.4	70.8
Off-farm work	14.8	11.5
House work	1.3	12.7
Other	4.5	5.0
Educational level		
High school and above	14.5	12.4
Middle school	42.1	33.1
6 years primary school	32.0	25.6
3 years primary school	5.7	8.4
No education	5.4	20.5
Smokes	79.8	9.4
Household		
One-generation households	4.0	6.3
Two-generation households	73.3	67.1
Three-generation households	22.1	24.7
Other household type	0.6	1.8
Mean household assets (current price in yuan)	703.63	466.74
Mean household savings (in yuan)	4,698.72	5,942.21
Mean value of house owned (original price in yuan)	9,532.05	12,213.42
Mean debts (in yuan)	605.31	673.50
Household income per capita	2,431.99	3,280.75
Number of observations	7,666	332
Percent of households	95.9	4.1

Source: 1995 Rural Household Survey.

of food, cigarettes and alcohol, medical costs, and daily goods. The coefficient on the variable for the ratio of wives' education to their husbands' can be interpreted as the change in the relevant budget share arising from a 100 percent percent change in the ratio. Thus, if wives' education increased from zero to 100 percent of husbands' education, spending on children's clothing would rise by 1.1 points. Given that the mean budget share is 9.9 percentage points, this translates into a proportionate rise in

Table 12.4

Independent Variables Used in the Analysis

Variable	% (Mean)	STD
Male household head	95.85	19.94
Wives' education years over the sum of education years of both husbands and wives	36.04	20.79
Educational level of household heads		
High school and above	14.65	35.37
Middle school	41.75	49.31
4–6 years primary school	31.77	46.56
1–3 years primary school	5.85	23.47
No education	5.96	23.68
Communist Party member	14.57	35.28
Male Communist Party member	14.08	34.78
Household heads mainly worked as		
Farm worker	85.85	34.85
Manual worker	2.93	16.88
Skilled worker	0.08	2.73
Professional	0.31	5.58
Cadre	0.75	8.62
Individual trader	1.67	12.83
Other nonspecified	8.3	27.72
Male household heads mainly worked as		
Farm worker	72.94	44.42
Manual worker	7.14	25.74
Skilled worker	1.58	12.45
Professional	1.54	12.30
Cadre	5.69	23.16
Individual trader	5.94	23.64
Log (no. of household members)	1.4236	0.3067
Log (household income per capita) (predicted)	7.6830	0.5879
Demographic groups of household members:		
Male aged 0–6	3.69	9.09
Male aged 7–12	6.38	12.21
Male aged 13–15	3.31	8.59
Male aged 16–18	3.23	8.57
Male aged 19–55	29.93	15.07
Male aged 56–65	3.52	10.34
Male aged 66–	1.78	6.56
Female aged 0–6	3.00	8.37
Female aged 7–12	5.38	11.08
Female aged 13–15	2.71	7.60
Female aged 16–18	2.98	7.97
Female aged 19–55	29.05	13.56
Female aged 56–65	2.74	8.96
Female aged 66–	2.30	7.22
One-generation households	4.05	19.71
Two-generation households	73.04	44.37
Three-generation households	22.26	41.60

(continued)

Table 12.4 *(continued)*

Variable	% (Mean)	STD
Demographic groups of household members *(cont'd)*:		
Other types of households	0.65	8.04
Households in poor county	22.63	41.85
Province		
Beijing	1.25	11.11
Hebei	6.2	24.16
Shanxi	3.75	19.00
Liaoning	3.75	19.00
Jilin	3.75	19.00
Jiangsu	6.24	24.19
Zhejiang	5.00	21.79
Anhui	5.63	23.05
Jiangxi	4.38	20.46
Shandong	8.75	28.26
Henan	8.75	28.26
Hubei	5.03	21.85
Hunan	6.25	24.21
Guangdong	6.25	24.21
Sichuan	9.98	29.97
Guizhou	3.75	19.00
Yunnan	3.75	19.00
Shaanxi	3.75	19.00
Gansu	3.75	19.00

Source: 1995 Rural Household Survey.

spending on children's education of over 10 percent. For clothing, the corresponding figure is also large. Increasing wives' education from zero to 100 percent would raise the clothing budget share by 1.7 points. For durable goods, the effect is 0.4 percent. The negative effects are also sizable: 1.7 percent for food purchases; 1 percent for cigarettes/ alcohol; and 1.1 percent for medical costs.

The effects of our other proxy for women's bargaining power—whether they are the head—are consistent with the ratio of wives' education to husbands' education in all but two cases (food purchases and durable goods). In particular, households headed by women spend more on education and clothing; less on alcohol and tobacco.

Our results seem consistent with the hypothesis of "maternal altruism": that women prefer to spend more on children's goods and less on adult goods. However, our measures of children's goods (schooling) and adult goods (cigarettes/alcohol) are rather specific. Although undoubtedly a children's good, schooling is also an investment in human capital. Parental education may complement learning acquired from school. Indeed, it is conceivable that mother's education is more of a complement with child schooling than father's education. This provides one possible explanation for our finding within a "unitary household" framework. In China, women smoke much less than men, indicating that cigarettes at least are more men's goods than women's goods. Alcohol may also be more of a man's good, although perhaps to a lesser degree. Nonetheless, this does not invalidate referring to the alcohol/cigarettes expenditure function as a test of the unitary model. Even if alcohol/cigarettes are exclusively consumed by men, after controlling for the proportion of men in the household, proxies of female bargaining power should have no effect.

One surprising finding worthy of comment is that wives' education relative to husbands—and having a woman household head—lowers expenditure on medical care. Were the wives' educational ratio to rise from zero to 100 percent, spending on medical costs would fall by 1 percentage point (a proportionate increase of approximately one-fifth). This might reflect women giving a lower priority to health care. Alternatively, wives' education may improve the health of household members, making health care less required.

Boy-Girl Discrimination

Inferences about intrahousehold resource allocation can be made by examining the coefficients of household age and gender groups. This shows how household expenditure on particular types of goods and services vary with the age and gender composition of the household.

We argued a priori that cigarette and alcohol are mainly men's goods. This is reflected in the results. All the included age-sex groups have negative coefficients compared with the default group of men aged 19–55. Applying Deaton's (1987) test, there is some evidence of discrimination in favor of the youngest boys and against the youngest girls. In particular, the coefficient on boys aged 0–6 is –3.4 percent (significant at 1 percent) compared with only –2.1 percent (significant at 10 percent) for girls aged 0–6. This difference is statistically significant at the 2 percent level and suggests that men sacrifice more for very young boys than for very young girls; indeed the effect of the latter is statistically less significant. However, the reverse is true of children aged 13–15: more sacrifices seem to be made for middle school girls than middle school boys.

Perhaps the most disturbing finding is that boys aged 6 years or below have a coefficient on medical cost more than double that for girls of the same age. However, note that the coefficients calculated in the model are relative to the effect of the male group aged 19–55: they are not the actual medical spending on the groups. However, the coefficients do suggest that over 50 percent more is spent on the health care of a young boy than on that of a young girl.[9] This is a sizable effect but may have two interpretations. It may imply discrimination against young girls: households may treat their boys' health problems more seriously than their girls.' Alternatively, it may merely be that there is a higher incidence of child illness amongst young boys than young girls. It is well known that boys are biologically more susceptible to illness at a young age than girls. However, it is unlikely that the differential is sufficient to warrant a 50 percent differential in health spending per child. Indeed, the gender difference in children aged 0–6 indicates that boys do not suffer from higher infant mortality and instead there is evidence of excess female infant mortality.

Table 12.5

Two Stage Least Squares Budget Share Regressions

	Model 1	Model 2	Model 3	Model 4	Model 5	Model 6	Model 7
	Food	Cigarettes, alcohol	Education	Clothing	Durables	Medical costs	Daily goods
Intercept	0.4088(5.6)***	0.1676(5.2)***	0.1378(2.9)**	0.1571(3.9)***	0.0195(0.6)	0.0317(0.8)	0.1056(4.1)***
Male household head	−0.0253(2.2)**	0.0225(4.6)***	−0.0075(1.0)	−0.0089(1.4)	0.0038(0.7)	0.0079(1.3)	0.0041(1.1)
% of women's education years to men's education	−0.0169(1.7)*	−0.0101(2.4)**	0.0108(1.7)*	0.0171(3.1)***	0.0043(1.0)*	−0.0110(2.2)**	−0.0010(0.3)
Educational level of household heads:							
High school and above	—	—	—	—	—	—	—
Middle school	−0.0228(2.9)***	−0.0105(3.1)***	0.0182(3.6)***	0.0028(0.6)	0.0050(1.4)	−0.0061(1.5)	−0.0018(0.7)
6 years primary school	−0.0141(2.1)**	−0.0065(2.3)**	0.0130(3.1)***	0.0046(1.3)	0.0024(0.8)	−0.0057(1.7)*	−0.0011(0.5)
3 years and below	−0.0050(0.8)	−0.0077(2.8)***	0.0102(2.5)***	−0.0009(0.2)	0.0006(0.2)	−0.0019(0.5)	−0.0024(1.0)
Communist Party member	−0.0206(0.7)	0.0221(1.8)**	−0.0083(0.4)	0.0273(1.8)*	−0.0230(1.8)*	−0.0020(0.1)	−0.0040(0.4)
Non-CP member	—	—	—	—	—	—	—
Male CP member	0.0182(0.6)	−0.0150(1.2)	0.0057(0.3)	−0.0333(2.1)**	0.0257(2.1)**	−0.0018(0.1)	0.0024(0.3)
Female non-CP member	—	—	—	—	—	—	—
Household heads mainly worked as:							
Farm worker	—	—	—	—	—	—	—
Manual worker	0.0189(0.5)	−0.0188(1.2)	−0.0104(0.4)	−0.0313(1.6)	0.0207(1.4)	0.0196(1.1)	0.0028(0.2)
Skilled worker	0.0337(0.6)	−0.0198(0.7)	−0.0084(0.2)	−0.0167(0.5)	−0.0021(0.1)	0.0026(0.1)	−0.0058(0.2)
Professional	−0.0355(0.7)	−0.0307(1.3)	−0.0463(1.3)	0.0423(1.4)	0.0061(0.3)	−0.0022(0.1)	0.0404(2.1)**
Cadre	−0.1207(2.2)*	−0.0075(0.3)	0.0201(0.6)	−0.0166(0.6)	−0.0150(0.6)	−0.0061(0.2)	−0.0240(1.2)
Individual trader	−0.0611(0.4)	−0.0356(0.5)	−0.0748(0.7)	−0.0011(0.0)	0.1379(2.0)**	−0.0390(0.5)	0.0307(0.5)
Other nonspecified	−0.0504(1.5)	−0.0051(0.3)	0.0214(0.9)	0.0151(0.8)	−0.0165(1.1)	−0.0092(0.5)	−0.0173(1.4)
Male household heads mainly worked as:							
Farm worker	—	—	—	—	—	—	—
Manual worker	−0.0242(0.6)	0.0198(1.3)	−0.0174(0.8)	0.0238(1.2)	−0.0024(0.2)	−0.0132(0.7)	−0.0036(0.2)

Skilled worker	−0.0578(0.8)	−0.0007(0.0)	−0.0279(0.6)	0.0235(0.6)	0.0562(1.9)	0.0072(0.2)	0.0174(0.7)
Professional	0.0090(0.1)	0.0352(1.3)	0.0370(0.9)	−0.0518(1.5)	0.0092(3.4)	0.0020(0.1)	−0.0574(2.7)***
Cadre	0.1270(1.8)*	0.0275(0.9)	−0.0189(0.4)	0.0270(0.7)	−0.0039(1.3)	0.0164(0.4)	0.0077(0.3)
Individual trader	0.0946(0.6)	0.0156(0.2)	0.0577(0.5)	0.0024(0.0)	−0.1229(1.8)*	0.0198(0.2)	−0.0275(0.5)
Other non-specified	0.0467(1.3)	0.0123(0.8)	−0.286(1.3)	−0.0105(0.5)	0.0570(1.7)*	0.0037(0.2)	0.0202(1.7)*
Log (no. of household members)	−0.0210(2.0)**	−0.0151(3.3)***	−0.0181(2.6)***	−0.0145(2.5)**	0.0013(0.3)	—	−0.0080(2.2)**
Log (household income per capita, predicted)	0.0050(0.6)	−0.0028(0.9)	−0.0163(3.4)***	−0.0022(0.5)	0.0021(0.6)	−0.0016(0.4)	−0.0048(1.9)*
Demographic groups of household members							
Male aged 0–6	0.0886(3.7)***	−0.0335(3.2)***	−0.0167(1.1)	0.0198(1.5)	−0.0223(2.2)**	0.0692(5.5)***	−0.0130(1.6)
Male aged 7–12	−0.0400(2.1)**	−0.0395(4.7)***	0.148(12.1)***	0.0284(2.7)***	−0.0193(2.3)***	0.0223(2.2)**	−0.0151(2.3)**
Male aged 13–15	−0.0882(3.7)***	−0.0430(4.2)***	0.258(16.7)***	0.0228(1.7)*	−0.0234(2.3)***	0.0061(0.4)	−0.0158(1.9)**
Male aged 16–18	−0.1681(7.0)***	−0.0652(6.2)***	0.238(15.3)***	0.0567(4.3)***	−0.0218(2.1)***	0.0010(0.1)	−0.0148(1.8)*
Male aged 19–55	—	—	—	—	—	—	—
Male aged 56–65	0.0933(4.1)***	−0.0234(2.4)**	−0.0070(0.4)	−0.0467(3.7)***	−0.0328(3.3)***	0.0472(3.9)***	−0.0001(0.0)
Male aged 66–	0.1505(4.7)***	−0.0207(1.5)	0.0038(0.2)	−0.5190(3.0)***	0.0314(2.2)***	0.0358(2.1)**	0.0018(0.2)
Female aged 0–6	0.0996(3.8)***	−0.0206(1.9)*	−0.0058(0.3)	0.0143(1.0)	−0.0261(2.4)***	0.0340(2.5)***	−0.0161(1.8)*
Female aged 7–12	−0.0245(1.2)	−0.0449(5.1)***	0.169(12.7)***	0.0206(1.8)*	−0.0300(3.1)***	0.0201(1.8)*	−0.0245(3.5)***
Female aged 13–15	−0.1306(4.9)***	−0.0821(7.1)***	0.269(15.7)***	0.0408(2.8)***	−0.0123(1.1)	0.0136(0.9)	−0.0098(1.0)
Female aged 16–18	−0.1002(3.8)***	−0.0683(5.9)***	0.210(12.4)***	0.0312(2.1)**	−0.0369(3.2)***	0.0076(0.5)	−0.0060(0.6)
Female aged 19–55	−0.0001(0.0)	−0.0311(3.6)**	0.0084(0.7)	0.0164(1.5)	0.0018(0.2)	0.0429(4.0)***	0.0137(1.9)*
Female aged 56–65	0.0702(2.5)***	−0.0310(2.5)***	−0.0063(0.3)	−0.0041(0.3)	−0.0009(0.8)	0.0468(3.1)***	0.0049(0.5)
Female aged 66–	0.0879(2.8)***	−0.0457(3.4)***	−0.0270(1.4)	−0.0303(1.8)*	−0.0011(0.8)	0.0494(3.0)***	0.0017(0.2)
One-generation households	0.0167(1.4)	−0.0059(1.1)	−0.0032(0.4)	−0.0300(4.6)***	0.0042(1.6)*	0.0031(0.9)	0.0004(0.2)
Two-generation households	—	—	—	—	—	—	—
Three-generation households	−0.0106(1.7)*	0.0012(0.5)	−0.0059(1.5)	0.0062(1.9)*	0.0017(0.2)	−0.0118(1.0)	−0.0053(0.7)
Other types of households	0.0123(0.6)	−0.0104(1.0)	−0.0207(1.3)	0.0043(0.3)	−0.0053(2.5)***	0.0056(2.2)**	−0.0017(1.0)
Households in a poor county	−0.0115(2.4)**	0.0152(7.2)***	−0.0091(2.9)***	0.0028(1.0)	—	—	—

(continued)

Table 12.5 (continued)

	Model 1	Model 2	Model 3	Model 4	Model 5	Model 6	Model 7
	Food	Cigarettes, alcohol	Education	Clothing	Durables	Medical costs	Daily goods
Households in a rich county	—	—	—	—	—	—	—
Province							
Beijing	0.0315(1.8)*	−0.0343(4.3)***	0.0077(0.7)	0.0050(0.5)	0.0187(2.4)**	0.0170(1.8)*	−0.0168(2.7)***
Hebei	0.0286(2.3)**	−0.0190(3.8)***	−0.0475(6.4)***	0.0253(4.0)***	−0.0120(2.4)**	0.0104(1.7)*	−0.0006(0.2)
Shanxi	0.0150(1.1)	−0.0285(4.5)***	−0.0357(3.9)***	0.0535(6.8)***	−0.0172(2.7)***	0.0098(1.3)	0.0054(1.1)
Liaoning	0.0505(3.9)***	−0.0409(7.1)***	−0.0275(2.2)**	0.0107(1.5)	−0.0191(3.4)***	0.0049(0.7)	−0.0094(2.2)**
Jilin	0.0514(4.0)***	−0.0356(6.4)***	−0.0344(4.2)***	0.0148(2.1)**	−0.0243(4.4)***	0.0253(3.8)***	0.0111(2.5)**
Jiangsu							
Zhejiang	0.0286(2.6)***	−0.0096(2.0)**	−0.0158(2.2)**	−0.0330(5.4)***	−0.0111(2.3)**	0.0207(3.6)***	0.0009(2.1)*
Anhui	0.0096(0.7)	−0.0026(1.1)	−0.0268(3.4)***	−0.0012(0.2)	−0.0111(2.1)**	−0.0019(0.3)	0.0121(2.8)***
Jiangxi	0.0262(2.1)**	−0.0404(7.2)***	−0.0341(4.1)***	−0.0193(2.8)***	−0.0136(2.5)**	0.0172(2.5)***	0.0205(4.7)***
Shandong	0.0451(4.5)***	−0.0189(4.3)***	−0.0088(1.3)	0.0100(1.8)*	−0.0107(2.5)**	−0.0047(0.9)	−0.0004(0.1)
Henan	−0.0387(3.4)***	−0.0246(4.9)***	−0.0193(2.6)***	0.0643(10.2)***	−0.0137(2.7)***	−0.0247(4.0)***	0.0039(0.9)
Hubei	−0.0842(6.8)***	−0.0110(2.0)**	0.0486(6.1)***	−0.0106(1.6)	−0.0147(2.7)***	−0.0176(2.7)***	0.0084(2.0)***
Hunan	0.0191(1.5)	−0.0386(6.9)***	0.0070(0.8)	−0.0368(5.3)***	−0.0171(3.1)***	−0.0044(0.6)	0.0160(3.6)***
Guangdong	0.1192(12)***	−0.0552(12)***	0.0488(7.3)***	−0.0710(12.6)***	−0.0120(2.7)***	−0.0084(1.5)	0.0033(0.9)
Sichuan	−0.0202(1.6)	−0.0117(2.1)**	−0.0139(1.7)*	−0.0118(1.7)*	−0.0155(2.9)***	−0.0128(1.9)**	0.0034(0.7)
Guizhou	−0.0282(2.0)*	−0.0211(3.4)***	−0.0483(5.2)***	0.0158(2.0)**	−0.0181(3.0)***	−0.0202(2.7)***	0.0349(7.1)***
Yunnan	0.0684(4.9)***	−0.0078(1.3)	−0.0146(1.6)*	−0.0154(2.0)**	−0.0141(2.4)***	−0.0116(1.6)	0.0129(2.7)***
Shaanxi	−0.0638(4.5)***	−0.0240(3.9)***	−0.0112(1.1)	0.0386(5.0)***	−0.0095(1.6)	−0.0424(5.7)***	0.0176(3.6)***
Gansu	−0.0436(2.8)***	−0.0289(4.2)***	−0.0010(0.1)	0.0214(2.5)**	−0.0127(1.9)*	−0.0404(4.9)***	0.0018(0.3)
F-value	22.798	14.035	42.756	26.346	4.240	5.693	6.300
Adj. R²	0.1327	0.0838	0.2267	0.1511	0.0222	0.0319	0.0359
Sample size	7,977	7,977	7,977	7,977	7,977	7,977	7,977

Source: 1995 Rural Household Survey.

Notes: The omitted dummies in these models are female household head, non–Communist Party member, household head working in the farming sector, educational level at 3 years or lower of household heads, household working in the farming sector, male aged from 19–55, households of two generations, households located in a rich county and Jiangsu province. *** denotes the significance level at 1 percent and below, ** at 5 percent and * at 10 percent.

Only 3 percent of household members are girls aged 6 or under, whereas 3.69 percent are boys of the same age. This contrasts with figures from Côte d'Ivoire, where the proportions of young girls and boys aged under 6 are almost exactly equal (9.0 percent and 9.2 percent of all household members respectively). These sex ratios suggest that, as Sen (1990) alleged, China may suffer from excess female mortality or "missing women." Official statistics also show high male-female sex ratios, rising in the 1980s. In 1998, the sex ratio of children aged 0–6 was 106.10 (CASS 1991). The sex ratio of children aged 0–6 increased to 110.50 in 1990 (SSB 1991). By 1993, the ratio was even higher: 114.16 (SSB 1994). Our figure for 1995 is much higher than this, at 1.23.

Traditionally boys are more welcome to rural households in China, whereas infant girls can sometimes be found abandoned in orphanages and there have been suggestions that they were sometimes victims of infanticide.[10] This may reflect some old Chinese traditions of inheritance and succession to property. According to the old civil law before the 1930s, daughters and widows could not inherit household assets. If the deceased (male) had no sons, his household assets could only be inherited by his brother's sons if there were any. If the deceased had no brothers, any other male relative should inherit his assets but not his own daughters or widow. These pro-son traditions were greatly weakened during the middle part of the twentieth century. A new Civil Law introduced by the Nationalist Government in the 1930s had changed the old law, so that daughters as well as widows could inherit household assets (Fei 1986). However, Fei had observed a failure in observing the new civil law in real life. He found that villagers still applied what the older tradition required. In the 1950s, the Communist government gave official support to equality between the sexes. Substantial job discrimination and wage discrimination against women are officially outlawed. Researchers have indeed found that urban women have a high rate of job participation in China relative to other countries. Possession of education protects Chinese women against discrimination, or gives them access with less discrimination. Neither the 1953 census nor that of 1964 showed an excess of boys over girls.

Things appear to have begun to change in the late 1970s. The 1982 census showed more boys than girls, with a sex ratio of 107 (for more detailed analysis of this phenomenon, see Hull 1990; Davin 1990; Johansson and Nygren 1991; Zeng et al. 1993; Johnson 1996). Three possible causes have been put forward for the rise in the male-female sex ratio: underreporting of girls (for example, if more are in orphanages); infanticide; and pre-natal sex selection. Although the three explanations differ in degree of malignity, they all imply a pro-son preference. Two factors may explain why this preference appeared to intensify after the late 1970s. The first is on the demand side, with the introduction of the one-child policy in 1979. It seems that if Chinese couples can only have one child, they will favor a boy. If couples were free to have more children, some might prefer a balance between sons and daughters, weakening any sex bias. However, the relaxation of the one-child policy to allow rural households to have another child if the first one is a girl does not appear to have halted the rise in the male-female ratio. The second change is on the supply side, with increasing availability since 1980 of services that can identify the sex of a fetus. However, we cannot dismiss the possibility that the unbalanced sex ratios could be due, at least in part, to some cruelty happening to girls before or after birth. Consistent with this, our findings give rise to some concern about discrimination against very young girls in terms of health care.

Our results can be compared with those of Burgess and Wang (1995), using a rural household survey of three Chinese provinces. For Sichuan province they found a large disparity between the coefficients of boys and girls aged 0–4 years in their model of the share of health spending in the household budget: The coefficient for the boys is 3.14 and the coefficient for the girls is only 1.30. However, the gaps in the other two provinces were not substantial.

Any discrimination against girls in terms of health care does not appear to be extended to schooling. Household spending on schooling varies similarly with proportions of boys and girls, suggesting no discrimination in outlays on schooling. Even at the high school age, where the presence of boys is associated with greater school spending than the presence of girls, the effects are quantitatively small.

Does Mothers' Bargaining Power Affect Boy-Girl Discrimination?

In planning this research we considered three indicators of women's bargaining power: the ratio of wife's education relative to her husband's; wife's working time relative to her husband's; and the proportion of wife's cash income to the total earned by both the husband and wife. Ultimately, we decided to use the indicator of wife's bargaining power proxied by education. This variable proved to be more statistically significant in the regressions but was also highly correlated with women's share of the cash income. We divide the whole sample into quarters by ordering wives' share in education to their husbands.' The first quartered sample represents the households with wives having the lowest bargaining power; and the fourth, the highest. Table 12.6 provides the mean characteristics by the quartered samples. This shows that women's share of cash income is higher in quarters with higher bargaining power (in terms of education). However, women's share of the working time does not vary by quarters in this way. Women in quarters 1 and 3 have lower percentages of working time compared with their counterparts in quarters 2 and 4. Therefore we control women's share of working time as an additional independent variable. Aside from this, we have employed the same regression models used in Table 12.5 but only estimated them by the quartered sample for three models: cigarettes and alcohol, medical costs, and school fees. We find that mother's higher bargaining power affects boy-girl discrimination in terms of cigarette spending, school fees, and medical expenditure but usually in the opposite direction to that expected: girls appear to do worse relative to boys in households where women have higher bargaining power.

Table 12.6

Mean Characteristics by Quartered Sample in Terms of Wives' Bargaining Power

Variable	Quarter 1	Quarter 2	Quarter 3	Quarter 4
Gender indicators between husbands and wives:				
Male household head (%)	0.9905	0.9870	0.9640	0.8923
Female household head (%)	0.0095	0.0130	0.0360	0.1076
Percent of wives' education (in years) to the sum of both husbands and wives	0.0727	0.3119	0.4849	0.5726
Percent of wives' working time (in days) to the total of both husbands and wives	0.3522	0.4480	0.3465	0.5557
Cash income earned by husbands (in yuan)	663.9725	850.0365	932.0790	636.1994
Cash income earned by wives (in yuan)	87.5865	140.1900	206.9935	166.7671
Percent of wives' cash income over their husbands'	7.6606	20.0329	39.0341	67.4826
Households:				
Actual income per capita	2,298.9	2,553.7	2,763.0	2,253.1
Percent of household heads' educational level above high school to the quartered sample	0.13	0.14	0.24	0.07

Source: 1995 Rural Household Survey.

Superficially, the sex ratio is an example of such unexpected findings: there are fewer girls relative to boys in households where female bargaining power is high. Table 12.7 shows that the lowest quarter (women with lowest bargaining power) has the highest sex ratio among the four quartered samples—93.3 girls for 100 boys, compared with 87.1, 87.4, and 88.6 for quarters 2, 3, and 4 respectively. However, on closer examination it seems unlikely that this implies higher excess female mortality in households with high female bargaining power. But when breaking down the sex ratios by age group, households with the lowest women's bargaining power (quarter 1) have much lower sex ratios of children aged 0–6: 78.7 compared with 92.0 of the households in quarter 4, in which women have the highest bargaining power. In fact, the ratios of quarter 1 exceed those of quarter 4 after children of age 7. By the age of the high school level, the gap of sex ratios between quarters 1 and 4 is much enlarged.[11] The sex ratios of children at age 16–18 should be less affected by the one-child family policy, which was issued in 1979: By 1995, the survey year, most children aged 16 should have been already born.

More compelling evidence on the unexpected effects of female bargaining

Table 12.7

Comparison of the Quartered Samples: Actual Number of Children from Age 0–18 by Sex and Age and Sex Ratios

	Aged 0–6			Aged 7–12			Aged 13–15			Aged 16–18			Total Ratio
	Boys	Girls	Ratio	Boys	Girls	Ratio	Boys	Girls	Ratio	Boys	Girls	Ratio	
Quarter 1	287	226	78.7	463	429	92.7	302	292	96.7	304	319	104.9	93.3
Quarter 2	362	259	71.5	542	513	94.7	326	246	75.5	316	328	103.8	87.1
Quarter 3	354	296	83.6	629	538	85.5	259	220	84.9	242	243	100.4	87.4
Quarter 4	350	322	92.0	627	510	81.3	279	266	95.3	279	262	93.9	88.6
Total	1,353	1,103	81.5	2,261	1,990	88.0	1,166	1,024	87.8	1,141	1,152	101.0	89.0

Source: 1995 Rural Household Survey.

Note: Ratios are the number of girls per 100 boys.

power on boy-girl discrimination is provided by data on medical expenditure, spending on alcohol and cigarettes, and education (results not reported in tables, but available upon request). Households with higher women's bargaining power do not exhibit less boy-girl discrimination in their household medical spending than other households. As a matter of fact, households in the fourth quartered sample (with highest bargaining power of women) yield a coefficient on young boys (aged 0–6) 3 times higher than the girls at the same age (0.081 compared with 0.025).

Similarly, in the top two quarters in terms of women's bargaining power, spending on cigarettes and alcohol fall less with the presence of girls than with boys. The opposite is true for the half of the sample with the lowest female bargaining power (Table 12.8).

However, households with women of higher bargaining power tend to spend more money on their daughters' education up to middle-school level than their sons—this is the same result we obtained from the analysis of the whole sample (see Table 12.5). But mothers' high bargaining power does not raise the coefficient on the daughters at high school level. In fact, it raises only the coefficient on the variable for the proportion of boys of high school age. Among the quarter with the highest women's bargaining power, the coefficient on high school–aged boys is twice that of girls (0.34 compared with 0.15). Among the lowest quarter, the gap is far more modest (0.23 compared with 0.19) (Table 12.9). These variations in the relative effects of high school age girls and boys reflect variations in enrollment rates (Table 12.10). Enrollment ratios for boys of high school age rise slightly with female bargaining power. However, for girls, high school enrollment rates are lowest for households with either the highest or lowest female bargaining power. There appears to be no gender discrimination in terms of educational spending per student. This can be seen by splitting the demographic variables for children into those for children in school and children out of school. The sensitivity of educational expenditure to children in school provides an indirect measure of educational spending per student. After carrying out this decomposition, we see that educational spending responds equally to the presence of male or female students for all age groups. This is invariant to female bargaining power, being true for each of the four quarters of the sample (Table 12.11).

Conclusions

Our findings have confirmed that the consumption behavior of Chinese rural households is more consistent with a collective model than with a unitary model. Men and women appear to have different preferences in consumption. Women's high bargaining power strengthens their influence on household consumption decisions: the share of spending on children's education and clothing rises with women's bargaining power. Conversely, the budget share of alcohol and cigarettes—and that of medical spending—falls as women's bargaining power increases.

We also find suggestions of some discrimination against very young daughters

Table 12.8

Does Mothers' High Bargaining Power Make Their Daughters Suffer Less in Terms of Cigarette Spending? (second stage regression models by mothers' bargaining power)

Gender-age group	Dependent variable: ratio of spending on cigarettes and alcohol to total household spending			
	Quarter 1	Quarter 2	Quarter 3	Quarter 4
Male				
0–6	−0.0331	−0.0124	−0.0320*	−0.0521***
7–12	−0.0352**	−0.0338**	−0.0297**	−0.0527***
13–15	−0.0679***	−0.0173	−0.0413**	−0.0352*
16–18	−0.0553***	−0.0735***	−0.0693***	−0.0589***
19–55	0	0	0	0
56–65	−0.0238	0.0157	−0.0482**	−0.0234
66 and over	−0.0389	−0.0133	−0.0032	−0.0142
Female				
0–6	−0.0458*	−0.0400*	0.0031	−0.0195
7–12	−0.0413**	−0.0365**	−0.0517***	−0.0510***
13–15	−0.0874***	−0.0728***	−0.0618***	−0.0942***
16–18	−0.0555***	−0.0873***	−0.0754***	−0.0514**
19–55	−0.0115	−0.0513***	−0.0046	−0.0455***
56–65	−0.0097	−0.1263***	−0.0008	−0.0275
66 and over	−0.0535***	−0.1013***	−0.0012	−0.0369
Adj. R²	0.0764	0.0741	0.0874	0.0882
F–values	4.845	4.719	5.452	5.490
Dependent means	0.0987	0.0923	0.0877	0.0871
Number of observations	1,999	1,999	1,999	1,997

Source: 1995 Rural Household Survey.

Notes: For brevity, we only report the coefficients on variables for proportions of certain age-sex groups. Other independent variables included in these models but not reported in the table are those referred to in Table 12.5. ***Denotes statistical significance at 1 percent, ** at 5 percent and * at 10 percent.

(aged 0 to 6 years old) in favor of sons. The evidence is of three kinds. First, very young daughters lead to less of a reduction in the share of spending on cigarettes and alcohol than very young sons. Following Deaton (1987), this may reflect adults making fewer material sacrifices for very young daughters than for very young sons. Second, we find that the presence of very young girls in the household is associated with much smaller increases in the share of spending on health care than is the presence of young boys. One rough estimate is that 50 percent more is spent on the health care of young boys than young girls. While it is true that young boys are biologically more vulnerable than young girls, it is unlikely that this can fully account for a discrepancy on this scale. Finally, we find that the sex ratio among very young children is very uneven, with 123 boys for every 100 young girls. While not as bad as some sex ratios reported in the past in rural China, the

Table 12.9

Does Mothers' High Bargaining Power Increase Household Spending on Their Daughters' Education? (second stage regression models by mothers' bargaining power, with selected coefficients on school-aged children by age and sex)

Gender-age group	Dependent variable: ratio of household spending on school fees to the total household cash spending			
	Quarter 1	Quarter 2	Quarter 3	Quarter 4
Boys				
7–12	0.1902***	0.2054***	0.1869***	0.1977***
13–15	0.3445***	0.2957***	0.3059***	0.3060***
16–18	0.2332***	0.2641***	0.2641***	0.3438***
Girls				
7–12	0.2051***	0.1658***	0.2373***	0.2142***
13–15	0.2921***	0.2935***	0.3050***	0.4087***
16–18	0.1928***	0.2766***	0.3547***	0.1491***
Adj. R^2	0.2634	0.2001	0.2206	0.2271
F-values	17.627	12.628	14.159	14.647
Dependent means	0.08438	0.09636	0.09517	0.10172
Number of observations	1,999	1,999	1,999	1,997

Source: 1995 Rural Household Survey.
Notes: For brevity, we only report the coefficients on variables for proportions of school-aged groups. Other independent variables included in these models but not reported in the table are those referred to in Table 12.5. ***Denotes statistical significance at 1 percent.

figure compares poorly with the virtually even sex ratio in many other developing countries, such as Côte d'Ivoire. Taken together, these pieces provide some evidence in support of Sen's (1990) allegation of serious pro-son bias in China.

We find no evidence in favor of our third hypothesis, that higher mothers' bargaining power reduces boy-girl discrimination. If anything, the reverse is true. Sex ratios are less favorable to girls in households with high female bargaining power, although this does not necessarily imply greater excess female mortality. However, households with high female bargaining power appear to spend much more (relative to other households) on medical care for young boys compared to young girls. Similarly, as female bargaining power increases, the negative impact of young boys relative to young girls on spending on cigarettes and alcohol becomes stronger. This is consistent with adults (presumably, mainly men) in households making fewer material sacrifices for their young daughters than for their young sons as female bargaining power rises. Finally, girls of high school age are associated with smaller increases in educational spending relative to boys in households with high female bargaining power. This reflects lower enrollment ratios for girls in such households. In summary, while there is evidence that women's bargaining power affects household allocation and that there is some boy-girl discrimination, there is no evidence that women's bargaining power reduces boy-girl discrimination.

Table 12.10

Number of Children by Age and Sex and School Enrollment Ratios of the Quartered Samples

	Total		Quarter 1		Quarter 2		Quarter 3		Quarter 4	
	Number	Ratio	Number	Ratio	Number	Ratio	Number	Ratio	Number	Ratio
Boys aged 7–12 in school	2,059		413		493		569		584	
Boys aged 7–12 not in school	202	0.91	50	0.89	49	0.91	60	0.91	43	0.93
Girls aged 7–12 in school	1,791		375		449		508		459	
Girls aged 7–12 not in school	199	0.90	54	0.87	64	0.88	30	0.94	51	0.90
Boys aged 13–15 in school	1,046		264		291		241		250	
Boys aged 13–15 not in school	120	0.90	38	0.87	35	0.89	18	0.93	29	0.90
Girls aged 13–15 in school	866		238		202		201		225	
Girls aged 13–15 not in school	158	0.85	54	0.82	44	0.82	19	0.91	41	0.85
Boys aged 16–18 in school	538		135		156		118		129	
Boys aged 16–18 not in school	603	0.47	169	0.44	160	0.49	124	0.49	150	0.46
Girls aged 16–18 in school	496		122		160		111		103	
Girls aged 16–18 not in school	656	0.43	197	0.38	168	0.48	132	0.45	159	0.39
Total	8,734		2,109		2,271		2,131		2,223	

Source: 1995 Rural Household Survey.
Note: Ratios are calculated as the following: children in school/(children in school + children not in school).

Table 12.11

Second Stage Regression Models by Mothers' Bargaining Power: With Selected Coefficients on School-Aged Children Both in School and Not in School, by Age and Sex

	Total	Quarter 1	Quarter 2	Quarter 3	Quarter 4
		Dependent variable: ratio of household spending on school fees to the total household cash spending			
Boys aged 7–12 in school	0.1238***	0.1673***	0.1447**	0.0536	0.1347*
Boys aged 7–12 not in school	0.1917***	0.2111***	0.1861***	0.1375***	0.2375***
Boys aged 13–15 in school	0.3313***	0.3875***	0.2970***	0.2836***	0.3415***
Boys aged 13–15 not in school	0.1579***	0.1883***	0.0464	0.0704	0.2683***
Boys aged 16–18 in school	0.5093***	0.5075***	0.5270***	0.4177***	0.5573***
Boys aged 16–18 not in school	0.0662***	0.0436	0.0037	0.0015	0.1958***
Girls aged 7–12 in school	0.2113***	0.2097***	0.1665***	0.1874***	0.2546***
Girls aged 7–12 not in school	0.1145***	0.1774***	0.1068*	0.0682	0.0774
Girls aged 13–15 in school	0.3598***	0.3308***	0.3165***	0.3042***	0.4493***
Girls aged 13–15 not in school	0.1198***	0.1321*	0.0725	0.2433***	0.0721
Girls aged 16–18 in school	0.5249***	0.5091***	0.5097***	0.5164***	0.5372***
Girls aged 16–18 not in school	0.0132	0.0137	−0.0015	−0.0354	0.0351
Adj. R²	0.2821	0.3305	0.2638	0.2400	0.2822
F-values	65.120	21.140	15.620	13.883	17.018
Dependent means	0.0944	0.0852	0.0954	0.0902	0.1069

Source: 1995 Rural Household Survey.

Notes: For brevity, we report only the coefficients on variables for proportions of school-aged groups. Other independent variables included in these models but not reported in the table are those referred to in Table 12.5. ***Denotes statistical significance at 1 percent, ** at 5 percent, and * at 10 percent.

Notes

The author is grateful to John Knight, Carl Riskin, Li Shi, and Keith Griffin for discussions on the paper. The author is particularly grateful to Simon Appleton for his valuable advice on the research methods. ESRC grant No. R00023 4332 is acknowledged. All errors remaining are the author's.

1. Two pieces of evidence from our surveys suggest a modest reduction from 1988 to 1995. The first is on the proportion of two and three generation households. In 1988, 2.5 percent of the sampled rural households were in the subcategory of one generation, 71.4 percent were nuclear households, 25.7 percent were multi-generation households, and 0.4 percent were other types of households. In 1995, the comparable figures were: 4.1 percent one-generation households, 73.0 percent nuclear households, 22.2 percent multi-generation households, and 0.7 other types. The second piece of evidence is the increase in the number of one-generation households with aged heads. In 1988, only 15 percent of the one-generation households were headed by people aged over 55 years; this increased to 53 percent by 1995, suggesting that by 1995 more elderly people in the rural areas lived without children than in 1988.

2. If a male household head has no spouse, the bargaining power should be set equivalent to zero; but for a female household head who has no spouse, her bargaining power is set the highest, 100 percent in this case.

3. Hoddinott and Haddad (1995) used Ulph's model to motivate their empirical work relating expenditure patterns to income shares. Women's share of household income did appear to affect expenditure patterns and was in turn determined by women's education relative to men's.

4. Household self-consumption—the consumption of farm products produced by the household—is not included in the analysis. Most self-consumed goods are simple foods (like grain) a household produced on its own farm to meet basic needs and so arguably reflect bargaining power less than cash expenditures.

5. The identifying instruments were geographic dummies: whether the household was in plains, mountainous, or hilly areas. These instruments were all highly significant in the model (see Table 12.1).

6. Unfortunately, one cannot split spending on clothing into spending on children and spending on adults.

7. In the sample, 5 percent of the household heads do not have spouses—they are either widows, widowers, or single. For the purpose of this study, we set the ratio of their education to their (nonexistent) husbands to 100 percent for women heads; for male heads, the variable was set to 0.

8. Spending on house repairs, transportation, and payments to aged parents who do not stay within the household are not reported in the same table, but the results are discussed in the chapter. Other nonspecific spending is not discussed due to problems of interpretation given its ambiguous definition.

9. A rough if rather contrived estimate is to compare the predicted share of spending on health care of a household comprised entirely of young boys (with otherwise mean characteristics) with the share from an identical household comprised entirely of young girls. The former is predicted to spend 9.5 percent on health care; the latter only 6.1 percent.

10. This was suggested by Fei Xiaotong in his anthropological study of 1935, after finding a very uneven sex ratio between very young boys and girls aged 0–5 (118 boys versus 87 girls, yielding a ratio of 1.36) in Kai Xuan Gong village, Jiangsu province.

11. So is the sex ratios of children of ages 7–12 between the two quarters.

References

Appleton, S., Chessa, I., and Hoddinott, J. (1998). "Looking for Gender Differences in Gender Bias in Uganda," (mimeo).

Behrman, Jere (1988). "Intrahousehold Allocation of Nutrients in Rural India: Are Boys Favored? Do Parents Exhibit Inequality Aversion?" *Oxford Economic Papers* 40(1), 32–54.

Bourguignon, F., Browning, M., Chiappori, P.A., and Lechene, V. (1993). "Intrahousehold Allocation of Consumption: A Model and Some Evidence from French Data," *Annales d'Economie et de Statistics* 29, 137–56.

Burgess, Robin, and Wang, P.P. (1995). "Chinese Rural Household Expenditure Analysis," *London School of Economics, Suntory-Toyota International Centre for Economics and Related Disciplines*, working paper EF No. 13.

Chinese Academy of Social Sciences (CASS), Population Research Institute (1991). *Almanac of China's Population, 1990*, Beijing, Economic Management Publication House.

Coale, Ansley J. (1991). "Excess Female Mortality and the Balance of the Sexes in the Population: An Estimate of the Number of 'Missing Females,'" *Population and Development Review* 17, No. 3, 517–23.

Davin, Delia (1990). "'Never Mind If It's a Girl, You Can Have Another Try': The Modification of the One-Child Family Policy and Its Implications for Gender Relations in Rural Areas," in Delmen, Ostergaard, and Christiansen (eds.). *Remaking Peasant China*, Denmark: Aarhus University Press, 81–91.

Deaton, A. (1987). "The Allocation of Goods Within the Household: Adults, Children, and Gender," *World Bank Living Standards Measurement Study Working Paper*, No. 39.

Deaton, A., and Case, A. (1988). "Analysis of Household Expenditures," *LSMS Working Paper No. 28*, World Bank, Washington, DC.

Fei, Xiaotong (1985) *Rural China* (Xiangtu Zhongguo), Sanlian Publishing House (in Chinese).

——— (1986). *Jiang Village Economy, Peasant Life in China*, (Jiangcun Jingji). The English version was first published by Routledge, 1939. The book was translated from its English version, entitled *Peasant Life in China*, into Chinese and published by Jiangsu Renmin Publication House, 1986.

Folbre, Nancy (1984). "Market opportunities, genetic endowments and intra-family resource distribution: Comment," *American Economic Review* 74, 518–20.

Griffin, Keith, and Zhao Renwei (1993), *The Distribution of Income in China,* New York: St. Martin's Press.

Guyer, J. and Peters, P. (1987). "Introduction," *Development and Change* 18, 197–214.

Haddad, Lawrence, and Hoddinott, John (1994). "Women's Income and Boy-Girl Anthropometric Status in the Côte d'Ivoire," *World Development* 22, 543–53.

Haddad, Lawrence, Hoddinott, J., and Alderman, H. (eds., 1997). *Intrahousehold Resource Allocation in Developing Countries: Model, Methods, and Policy*. Baltimore and London: The Johns Hopkins University Press, published for the International Food Policy Research Institute.

Hoddinott, John, and Lawrence Haddad (1995). "Does Female Income Share Influence Household Expenditures? Evidence from Côte d'Ivoire," *Oxford Bulletin of Economics and Statistics* 57, No. 1, 77–96.

Hull, Terence H. (1990). "Recent Trends in Sex Ratios at Birth in China," *Population and Development Review* 16, No. 1, 63–83.

Johansson, S., and Nygren, O. (1991). "The Missing Girls in China: A New Demographic Account," *Population and Development Review* 17, No. 1, 35–51.

Johnson, K. (1996). "The Politics of the Revival of Infant Abandonment in China, with Special Reference to Hunan," *Population and Development Review* 22, No. 1, 77–98.

Knight, John, and Li Shi (1993). "The Determinants of Educational Attainment," in Griffin and Zhao (eds.) *The Distribution of Income in China*. New York: St. Martin's Press.

Knight, John, and Song, Lina (1993). "Why Urban Wages differ in China," in Griffin and Zhao (eds.) *The Distribution of Income in China*. New York: St. Martin's Press.

Ling, Yaohua (1989). *The Golden Wing: A Sociological Study of Chinese Familism* (Jinyi). The book was first published by Routledge and Kegan Paul, 1947. It was translated and republished by Sanlian Publishing House (in Chinese).

Lundberg, S., and Pollak, R. (1993). " Separate Spheres, Bargaining and the Marriage Market," *Journal of Political Economy*, 101, 988–1010.

Phipps, S., and Burton, P. (1993). "What's Mine Is Yours? The Influence of Male and Female Incomes on Patterns of Household Expenditure," mimeo, Halifax: Dalhousie University.

Rosenzweig, M., and T.P. Schultz (1982). "Market Opportunities, Genetic Endowments and Intra-Family Resource Distribution: Child Survival in Rural India," *American Economic Review*, 72(4):803–15.

Secondi, Giorgio (1996). *The Economic Behavior of the Family in Contemporary China: Private Transfers, Intrafamily Resources Allocation, and Preference for Sons*. Ph.D. Thesis, Ann Arbor: University of Michigan.

Sen, A.K. (1990). "More Than 100 Million Women Are Missing," *New York Review of Books* 37, No. 2, December 20, 61–66.

Song, Lina (1999). "The Role of Women in Labor Migration," in Loraine West et al. (eds.) *Women of China: Economic and Social Transformation*. London: Macmillan.

SSB (1991). *10 Percent Sampling Tabulation on the 1990 Population Census of the People's Republic of China*. Beijing: SSB Publishers.

——— (1994). *China Population Statistics Yearbook*. Beijing: SSB Publishers.

Thomas, D. (1990). "Intra-household Resource Allocation: An Influential Approach," *Journal of Human Resource* 25, 636–64.

Ulph, D. (1988). "A General Non-Cooperative Nash Model of Household Consumption Behavior," mimeo. Bristol, UK: University of Bristol.

Zheng, Yi, Tu Ping, Gu Baochang, Xu Yi, Li Bohua, and Li Yongping (1993). "Causes and Implications of the Recent Increase in the Reported Sex Ratio at Birth in China." *Population and Development Review* 19, No. 2, 283–303.

13

Labor Migration and Income Distribution in Rural China

Li Shi

Introduction

Rural labor migration and income distribution are two issues urgently in need of appropriate policies in China. The two issues are mutually interactive and determinative, each playing reciprocally the roles of cause and effect. This chapter attempts an empirical analysis of the interactive relations between the two, with the emphasis on the effects of rural-urban labor migration on income distribution in rural China.

The first issue discussed is to what extent rural workers away from their home villages contribute to the growth of their household income. To anticipate, we find that out-migrant workers have not only a direct effect on the growth of their household income but an indirect effect, as well, in that their out-migration raises the labor productivity of members remaining in their households.

The impact of rural migration on income inequality in rural areas is rather complicated. To a large extent it depends upon whether most of the out-migrant workers are from low-income or high-income families. The data from the 1995 survey of household income indicate that most of the migrants were from households with medium incomes. This is not unexpected, since medium income household members are more likely to have both the incentive to seek improvement and the means to finance travel and job search.

However, it makes it more difficult to infer the effect of migration on income distribution in a simple way. Therefore, we investigate two aspects of the problem:

first, by estimating the effects of the remittances sent back by the out-migrants; and second, by comparing the contribution to overall income inequality in rural China of the out-migrants' forgone income (opportunity cost) with that of their actual income. We estimate separately the effects of rural labor migration on overall inequality in rural areas as a whole, on the rural income differentials between different provinces, and on the rural differentials within these provinces.

The Rural-Urban Divide in the Labor Market and the Size of Rural Migration

The Rural-Urban Divide and Control of Labor Mobility

During the twenty years from the implementation of the household registration system in 1958 to the start of the reform in 1978, mobility of the labor force and population in China had been reduced to the lowest level in history.[1] The migration of people, within rural areas, within urban areas, and between city and countryside, was all institutionally controlled.

Although two decades have elapsed since the start of the economic reform in 1978, China has not yet come to terms with one of the biggest institutional defects in the socioeconomic system—the rural-urban divide. Ever since the implementation of the household registration system in 1958, rural and urban people have been institutionally separated into two independent and unequal communities with different economic systems.

The first stroke of the rural economic reform that started at the end of the 1970s was to break the institutional deadlock brought about partly by restrictions imposed on labor force mobility. The "household responsibility system" implemented in the villages and the dissolution of the People's Commune System granted farmers more freedom in managing production and in their personal lives and also eased restrictions on villagers' mobility. The effect of the reform in boosting farm production and in the vigorous development of township and village enterprises (TVEs) alleviated tremendously the shortage of consumer goods in urban areas, thus providing material conditions for the implementation of urban economic reforms.

However, the urban economic reform at that time focused on reforming commodity prices, while reform of the price of labor—wage setting—was neglected. Neither the rationalization of wages through the establishment of competitive and mobile labor markets, nor the establishment of a unified national labor market so as to utilize the entire urban and rural labor force more efficiently, was considered. In addition, the remaining labor control system in urban China, the institutional obstacles hindering labor from moving from rural to urban areas, and the distortions in labor prices produced thereby, had all to a large extent misled urban industry into adopting an excessively capital-intensive strategy of development.

Moreover, the reform of urban enterprises at that time emphasized improvements in internal management and in work incentives through such approaches as "decentralization of decision-making rights from the state to the enterprises" and "giving more material incentives to workers." There was a tendency toward an accelerated increase in wages, which further widened the gap between the labor incomes of urban and rural workers. Even more important is the fact that an ever-growing proportion of national income had been going back to urban areas through state investment in fixed capital, infrastructure construction, and public utility investments, all of which further widened the gap in the overall development level between rural and urban China to a degree well beyond the income gap alone. Thus, while urban residents are well along in the process of modernization, much of the rural population is still far from entering this process. Such a pattern runs the danger of becoming cumulative and self-reinforcing.

During the early years of reform, the lag in development of an urban labor market did not have much of a negative effect on the processes of the reform, while the fast-growing TVEs absorbed part of the surplus labor from the agricultural production, thus easing the pressure of rural labor on the land. However, in the second half of the 1980s, rural enterprises changed their development strategy from a labor-intensive to a capital-intensive approach, thus weakening their capacity to absorb surplus labor. On the other hand, due to population growth and the intensification of farming, the absolute size of the rural labor force and the amount of rural surplus labor were still on the increase. So the migration of part of this surplus labor to urban areas became inevitable.

Although migrant rural workers were not allowed to freely enter the labor market in urban China, they were eagerly demanded by various urban sectors. First and foremost, it was the rapidly growing nonstate sectors that demanded large numbers of migrant workers. Second, the migrants themselves created a number of informal urban sectors which they peopled, thus creating their own demand. Third, there were urban job vacancies for dirty, humble, heavy, and unprofitable work that full-status urban workers were reluctant to do, and the only alternative was to employ migrant labor. Fourth, financially hard-pressed state enterprises found it cheaper to employ migrants, especially for short-term jobs. For all these reasons, since the late 1980s rural residents started to pour into urban areas to accept or hunt for new and higher paying job opportunities.

The Size and Pattern of Labor Migration in Recent Years

The size of rural labor migration has not been very clear up to now. One reason lies in conceptual confusion. For example, one of the terms frequently used in the Chinese research literature and the media is the "floating population in cities" and another one is the "floating labor force in the countryside." At times these two different concepts have been lumped together as one. But actually they are different because the latter (in the countryside) includes those having migrated into the cities and those having migrated to other rural areas or small towns. Further, the concept of "floating population in cities" represents a much wider concept. It covers not only the floating rural labor force but also part of the rural floating population that is not in the labor force, as well as the floating population coming from other cities and towns, including those both within and outside of the labor force. A survey of the floating population in 1988 (Li and Hu 1991) showed that there were altogether 7.18 million members in the eleven biggest cities, such as Beijing and Shanghai, among which about 4.26 million were from rural areas, constituting 59.3 percent of the total. Again, among the total floating population, 48.3 percent were employable, and part of these had come from other cities and towns. The floating rural workers made up only about 45 percent of the total floating population in cities. Unfortunately, even knowing the above data, it is still difficult to estimate the size of the entire migrant rural labor force in urban China.

Since the 1980s there have been a number of different estimates of the size of the rural floating labor force and the number of rural migrants in urban areas. The estimates of the former during the late 1980s and early 1990s range from 40 million to 80 million people—a puzzlingly large difference, indeed. Further, faced with so many different estimates, it is difficult to know the proportions of the rural floating labor force flowing into urban areas and to other rural regions. A 1994 survey of rural labor migration carried out by the Ministry of Labor in eight provinces of rural China indicated that about 20 percent of the total rural labor force were working away from their home villages, among which 40 percent were working within their home counties (Chai et al. 1996). Calculating on this basis, and keeping in mind that the eight provinces surveyed had higher than average proportions of out-migrants, the total number of rural migrants working away from their home villages in the entire country may have numbered roughly 45 to 50 million. In addition, the 1995 survey of household income that is the occasion for this book indicated that rural workers working away from their home villages constituted 9.9 percent of the total labor force, which puts the total number for the whole country in that year at about 45 million. However, although these two surveys allow us to estimate the overall size of the rural floating labor force, it is still difficult to get at the number of migrant workers moving into the cities.

The 1995 national 1 percent sample population survey published by SSB helps us further. According to the statistical calculations in this survey, the total number of migrants away from their registered places of residence for more than half a year stood at about 49.7 million in 1995, among which about 48.4 million had been living in their current places of residence for more than half a year. Due to the fact that the division of residential places and registered places was made according to towns, townships, and districts (Office of the National Population Sample Survey, 1997, p. 643), part of the floating population moved within their counties or cities while others were making intercounty and intercity moves. The latter part of the floating population constituted 58.5 percent of the total, reaching 29 million people. It can be said that they were fundamentally job-oriented. We define this part of the long-term floating population, which constituted 2.4 percent of the total Chinese population in 1995, as the "immigrant workers" (see Table 13.1). Among "immigrant workers," 19.8 million flowed from rural areas, which accounts for about 68 percent of the total. These long-term rural immigrant workers constituted 2.04 percent of the total rural population in 1995 (see Table 13.2).

Making use of the data of the 1995 national 1 percent population sample survey, we deduce that the immigrant population in cities came to about 19.4 million, accounting for 66.6 percent of the total immigrant population in China. That is to say, about 33.4 percent of the total flowed to rural areas or to small towns. An examination of the composition of the immigrant population in urban areas (see Table 13.1), shows that 74.9 percent of the total had come from other localities within the same province while 25 percent were from other provinces. Among those coming from the same province, 56.3 percent were from other cities and 43.7 percent were from the countryside; while among the immigrant population from other provinces, 39 percent were from urban areas and 61 percent were from rural areas. Thus we deduce that about 9.6 million long-term rural inhabitants were living as migrants in the cities in 1995, making up approximately 50 percent of the total (long-term) immigrant population in cities.[2]

Based on the same survey, we also calculated the number of immigrants in different provinces, and the number of immigrants in cities, the detailed results of which can be seen in Table 13.1. The interprovincial differences in number of immigrants is obvious, with higher numbers in the relatively developed regions. Thus the number was 4.2 million people in Guangdong Province, or 14.4 percent of the national total, while the nine most advanced provinces of Beijing, Shanghai, Tianjin, Liaoning, Jiangsu, Zhejiang, Shandong, Fujian, and Guangdong together accounted for 14.7 million immigrants, or 50.6 percent of the national total. The proportion of long-term immigrants in the economically backward northwestern provinces was much lower. For example, the total number in the three provinces of Ningxia, Qinghai, and Gansu was less than 700,000, representing only 28 percent of the number in Jiangsu Province alone. With respect to absorption of immigrant rural laborers, the difference between the provinces was even more striking. The more the economically developed the province, the more immigrants it absorbed. Immigrant rural labor in the cities of Guangdong reached 1.82 million, or 19 percent of the national total, while that in Jiangsu's cities came to 858,000, representing 9 percent of the national total.

Effects of Labor Migration on Income Growth and Distribution in Rural China

Table 13.3 presents information about the size of rural labor migration from our 1995 household income survey, including the proportion of migrant workers and of households with migrant workers in each province. Table 13.4 shows the personal characteristics of the migrant workers, in comparison with nonmigrants.

The existing literature has universally regarded rural China as a labor surplus economy. Theoretically, in such an economy labor out-migration should benefit income growth. However, due to various obstacles to the free movement of productive resources, especially labor, the theoretically expected effect on income growth may not show up clearly in the real economy. We now turn to this issue, using the data from the sample surveys.

Table 13.1

Long-Term Migrants in Cities by Province, 1995

Province	Immigrants			Urban immigrants from (percent)		Urban immigrants in (4) who come from		Urban immigrants in (5) who come from	
	(1) Total (10,000)	(2) In cities (10,000)	(3) Ratio of (2)/(1) (percent)	(4) Within province	(5) Outside province	(6) Rural areas	(7) Urban areas	(8) Rural areas	(9) Urban areas
Beijing	138.6	121.4	87.6	57.6	42.4	7.9	92.1	62.1	37.9
Tianjin	54.2	51.1	94.3	65.4	34.6	8.0	92.0	61.4	38.6
Hebei	101.4	71.7	70.7	73.2	26.8	50.6	49.4	54.5	45.5
Shanxi	52.2	30.0	57.5	71.8	28.2	58.9	41.1	70.4	29.6
Inner Mongolia	91.4	43.9	48.0	78.0	22.0	51.5	48.5	69.2	30.8
Liaoning	138.8	112.9	81.3	78.3	21.7	32.1	67.9	73.8	26.2
Jilin	60.3	45.5	75.5	84.3	15.7	26.1	73.9	47.9	52.1
Heilongjiang	146.8	102.2	69.6	83.4	16.6	36.4	63.6	74.7	25.3
Shanghai	122.8	105.4	85.8	50.7	49.3	3.9	96.1	65.0	35.0
Jiangsu	248.7	164.3	66.1	82.8	17.2	50.2	49.8	62.1	37.9
Zhejiang	109.2	48.6	44.5	83.3	16.7	44.4	55.6	71.3	28.7
Anhui	63.0	44.9	71.3	89.9	10.1	49.5	50.5	44.4	55.6
Fujian	91.2	42.8	46.9	86.4	13.6	57.2	42.8	64.5	35.5
Jiangxi	55.1	29.1	52.8	92.6	7.4	49.2	50.8	57.7	42.3
Shandong	147.7	110.0	74.4	85.1	14.9	60.8	39.2	49.1	50.9
Henan	82.5	55.5	67.3	88.6	11.4	45.1	54.9	37.9	62.1
Hubei	105.8	77.7	73.4	84.6	15.4	49.1	50.9	68.0	32.0

Hunan	101.6	76.0	74.8	90.0	10.0	59.4	40.6	54.6	45.4
Guangdong	419.2	291.5	69.5	60.8	39.2	49.9	50.1	80.3	19.9
Guangxi	62.1	41.3	66.5	92.7	7.3	60.2	39.8	50.1	49.9
Hainan	22.4	14.1	63.0	69.7	30.3	42.3	57.7	30.1	69.9
Sichuan	153.3	85.8	56.0	94.1	5.9	57.4	42.6	45.5	54.5
Guizhou	54.5	32.3	59.3	72.2	27.8	51.0	49.0	67.5	32.5
Yunnan	92.5	39.2	42.4	81.6	18.4	42.4	57.6	77.3	22.7
Tibet	5.4	3.0	54.7	37.6	62.4	62.9	37.1	66.2	33.8
Shaanxi	49.0	34.5	70.4	71.9	28.1	52.5	47.5	75.2	24.8
Gansu	38.8	22.8	58.8	73.8	26.2	58.7	41.3	74.4	25.6
Qinghai	21.5	7.8	36.3	79.9	20.1	23.4	76.6	23.9	76.1
Ningxia	9.5	5.7	60.0	47.2	52.8	42.6	57.4	78.9	21.1
Xinjiang	68.5	25.9	37.8	41.8	58.2	27.9	72.1	71.7	28.3
National	2,908	1,936.8	63.9	74.9	25.0	43.7	56.3	61.0	39.0

Source: Office of the National Population Sample Survey, 1997; State Statistical Bureau, 1996.
Note: Immigrants are defined as residents who left their *hukou* places for more than half a year.

Table 13.2

Number and Proportion of Immigrants and Out-migrants in Provinces, 1995

	(1)	(2)	(3)	(4)	(5)	(6)	(7)	(8)
Province	Population (millions)	Immigrants (millions)	Out-migrants (millions)	Rural out-migrants (millions)	Ratio of immigrants to population = (2)/(1) (percent)	Ratio of out-migrants to population = (3)/(1) (percent)	Proportion of rural out-migrants to rural population (percent)	Net immigrant population (millions)
Beijing	12.51	1.39	0.78	0.09	11.1	6.2	1.98	0.61
Tianjin	9.42	0.54	0.37	0.04	5.7	3.9	1.09	0.17
Hebei	64.37	1.01	1.09	0.78	1.6	1.7	1.46	−0.08
Shanxi	30.77	0.52	0.44	0.29	1.7	1.4	1.24	0.08
Inner Mongolia	22.84	0.91	0.76	0.57	4.0	3.3	3.68	0.15
Liaoning	40.92	1.39	1.14	0.53	3.4	2.8	2.35	0.25
Jilin	25.92	0.60	0.74	0.40	2.3	2.9	2.70	−0.14
Heilongjiang	37.01	1.47	1.66	0.88	4.0	4.5	4.31	−0.19
Shanghai	14.15	1.23	0.62	0.07	8.7	4.4	1.79	0.61
Jiangsu	70.66	2.49	2.17	1.46	3.5	3.1	2.75	0.32
Zhejiang	43.19	1.09	1.37	0.87	2.5	3.1	2.42	−0.27
Anhui	60.13	0.63	1.29	1.00	1.0	2.1	2.01	−0.66
Fujian	32.37	0.91	0.81	0.58	2.9	2.5	2.25	0.10
Jiangxi	40.63	0.55	0.90	0.72	1.4	2.2	2.23	−0.35
Shandong	87.05	1.48	1.49	1.19	1.7	1.7	1.82	−0.01
Henan	91.00	0.83	1.34	1.08	0.9	1.5	2.60	−0.51

311

Hubei	57.72	1.06	1.10	0.71	1.8	1.9	1.67	−0.04
Hunan	63.92	1.02	1.55	1.24	1.6	2.4	2.38	−0.53
Guangdong	68.68	4.19	2.39	1.26	6.1	3.5	2.64	1.80
Guangxi	45.43	0.62	1.07	1.03	1.4	2.4	2.75	−0.45
Hainan	7.24	0.22	0.19	0.11	3.0	2.6	2.04	0.03
Sichuan	113.25	1.53	2.83	2.53	1.4	2.5	2.72	−1.30
Guizhou	35.08	0.55	0.65	0.58	1.6	1.9	1.96	−0.10
Yunnan	39.90	0.93	0.82	0.59	2.3	2.1	1.70	0.11
Tibet	2.40	0.05	0.03	0.03	2.1	1.3	1.30	0.02
Shaanxi	35.13	0.49	0.52	0.47	1.4	1.5	1.69	−0.02
Gansu	24.38	0.39	0.47	0.43	1.6	1.9	2.13	−0.07
Qinghai	4.81	0.22	0.20	0.08	4.6	4.2	2.33	0.02
Ningxia	5.12	0.10	0.09	0.08	1.9	1.8	2.06	0.01
Xinjiang	16.61	0.69	0.25	0.15	4.2	1.5	1.41	0.44
National	1,211.21	29.10	29.13	19.86	2.4	2.4	2.31	0

Sources: (1) *China Statistical Yearbook,* 1996; (2) Data of *National 1 Percent Population Sample Survey* 1995, China Statistical Press, 1997; (3) *China Regional Economy: 17 Years of Reform and Open-Up,* China Statistical Press, 1996.

Notes: (1) The national population figure is not equal to the sum of the provincial figures as the former includes people who served in the army and the latter does not. (2) Immigrants are defined as residents who left their *hukou* places for more than half a year. (3) The number of out-migrants was calculated by the author from data of the *National 1 Percent Population Sample Survey* 1995.

Table 13.3

Distribution of Migrant Workers by Province, 1995

	Workers (percent of column total)			Households (percent of column total)		
				Households with	Households without	
Province	Migrant workers	Non-migrants	All workers	migrant workers	migrant workers	All households
Beijing	0.09	1.36	1.25	0.11	1.57	1.25
Hebei	3.97	6.68	6.51	4.70	6.66	6.23
Shanxi	3.79	3.79	3.81	3.95	3.69	3.75
Liaoning	1.53	3.30	3.15	1.43	4.40	3.73
Jilin	2.84	3.43	3.41	3.21	3.90	3.75
Jiangsu	5.37	6.53	6.43	5.33	6.51	6.25
Zhejiang	3.79	5.16	4.98	3.09	5.53	5.00
Anhui	7.62	5.17	5.43	8.31	4.88	5.63
Jiangxi	9.47	4.10	4.47	8.54	3.22	4.38
Shandong	7.94	9.12	8.99	7.62	9.07	8.75
Henan	6.40	9.37	9.13	6.53	9.37	8.75
Hubei	2.12	5.07	4.82	2.06	5.86	5.03
Hunan	7.30	4.95	5.19	7.79	5.82	6.25
Guangdong	10.69	5.63	5.92	9.00	5.48	6.25
Sichuan	14.16	9.20	9.61	13.98	8.86	9.98
Guizhou	4.55	3.87	3.96	4.99	3.40	3.75
Yunnan	1.76	4.77	4.53	1.95	4.25	3.75
Shaanxi	3.97	3.73	3.77	4.24	3.61	3.75
Gansu	2.66	4.78	4.64	3.15	3.92	3.75
National	100	100	100	100	100	100

Source: 1995 Rural Household Income Survey.
Notes: Migrant workers are those who worked outside their villages or left them to look for work for more than one month in 1995. Households with migrant workers are those having at least one migrant worker.

Income of Households with and without Out-migrants

The total rural labor force can be divided into two categories: migrants and nonmigrants, and all rural households can correspondingly be divided into households with out-migrant workers (hereafter MH) and those without out-migrant workers (NMH). On the basis of these classifications, we calculate first of all the per capita income of households with and without out-migrant workers and the income per worker for each province and the entire sample. These calculations are presented in Table 13.5.

Table 13.5 shows that, for China as a whole, the per capita income of MH was slightly (about 1.5 percent) lower than that of NMH, while income per worker of the former was 16 percent below that of the latter. However, the situation was different in different provinces. Among the nineteen sampled provinces, there were

Table 13.4

Statistical Description of Rural Migrant and Nonmigrant Workers, 1995

	Migrant workers (percent)	Nonmigrant workers (percent)	Total (percent)
Gender			
Male	72.1	49.2	51.3
Female	27.9	50.8	48.7
Age group			
18 or below	10.0	7.1	8.3
19–25	46.3	18.0	20.5
26–30	13.6	10.4	10.7
31–35	9.1	10.6	10.2
36–40	7.5	11.7	11.3
41 or over	13.6	42.0	38.9
Marital status			
Married	47.5	77.7	73.8
Single	51.5	20.0	23.7
Other	1.0	2.3	2.5
Education			
College	0.2	0.6	0.6
Professional	1.7	1.2	1.3
Upper middle	11.4	8.3	8.5
Lower middle	55.9	39.2	40.5
Primary	30.5	50.3	48.6
Household size			
2 and below	1.62	3.0	2.87
3	12.72	15.4	15.38
4	28.27	33.2	32.95
5	25.29	25.6	25.53
6	14.83	13.2	13.25
7 and above	17.27	9.7	9.98
Minority	5.30	7.5	7.1
Han	93.05	91.1	91.1

Sources: 1995 Rural Household Income Survey.

Notes: Migrant workers are those who worked outside their villages or left them to look for work for more than one month in 1995. Households with migrant workers were those having at least one migrant worker.

six in which per capita income of MH was below that of NMH, most of the six being relatively developed provinces, such as Guangdong and Zhejiang. The last two columns in Table 13.5 give a very rough indication of the wage gap between out-migrant and nonmigrant workers in 1995.[3] In thirteen of the nineteen sampled provinces per worker income of MH was below that of NMH, and in six it was higher. These six provinces were Gansu, Shaanxi, Sichuan, Henan, Liaoning, and Shanxi. All six are relatively backward in economic development, and the wages earned by their out-migrant workers was higher than the income of the workers

Table 13.5

Income of Households with and without Migrant Workers

Province	Sample size Households (1) With	(2) Without	Income per capita Households (1) With	(2) Without	Income per worker Households (1) With	(2) Without
Total	1,641	6,332	2,074	2,104	3,243	3,777
Beijing	2	98	2,627	4,824	4,127	7,974
Hebei	78	416	1,404	1,816	2,781	3,915
Shanxi	51	248	1,443	1,216	3,187	2,695
Liaoning	22	277	2,251	1,977	4,034	3,369
Jilin	55	244	2,366	1,963	3,795	3,797
Jiangsu	90	409	3,718	3,628	5,386	5,473
Zhejiang	50	348	2,396	3,795	3,372	6,045
Anhui	139	310	1,537	1,759	2,464	3,290
Jiangxi	147	202	1,800	1,617	2,844	3,149
Shandong	126	570	2,906	2,560	4,098	4,151
Henan	102	597	2,170	1,603	3,619	2,925
Hubei	36	365	1,787	1,727	2,666	2,986
Hunan	129	370	1,499	1,435	2,450	2,971
Guangdong	143	354	3,671	4,306	5,709	8,564
Sichuan	238	560	1,759	1,408	2,444	2,264
Guizhou	80	219	1,367	1,233	1,995	2,423
Yunnan	31	268	1,189	1,391	1,698	2,481
Shaanxi	67	233	1,612	1,291	3,067	2,965
Gansu	55	244	1,090	1,047	1,985	1,957

Source: 1995 Household Income Survey.
Notes: Migrant workers are those who worked outside their villages or left them to look for work for more than one month in 1995. Households with migrant workers were those having at least one migrant worker.

engaged in local farming activities. Moreover, in some provinces such as Jilin, Jiangsu, and Shandong, the income per worker differential between MH and NMH was not very large, suggesting that some out-migrants had failed to find jobs, or had originally earned such low incomes that only through migration could they bring earnings up to the provincial average.[4] Even in more developed provinces, some workers left their home villages to find more lucrative opportunities. Most provinces are large, populous, and divided into geographically and economically diverse regions. Even advanced Guangdong has a poor, hilly hinterland, for instance. Therefore, it is understandable if migrants from such poorer localities, even while raising their household income, cannot bring it up to the provincial average.

Estimated Effects of Migration on Income Growth of Rural Households

It should be recognized that the above comparisons are oversimplified, since the factors determining household income, in addition to labor force, include also land, production assets, and so forth. Besides, the huge regional disparities in rural China, the unbalanced development among different regions and the relatively independent fiscal policy of "linking expenditures to revenues" in individual provinces have all contributed to the formation of the income gaps.

In order to control for factors other than labor force, we estimate the effects of labor migration on household income growth, using a household income function. The income function of rural households includes land (divided into irrigated and nonirrigated land), production assets (in present values), and provincial dummy variables (to control for income differences arising from provincial location). Two different models are specified. In the first, the number of household out-migrant and nonmigrant workers are taken as two independent explanatory variables; their estimated coefficients can be interpreted as their marginal rates of contribution to household income. In the second model, while taking the total number of working members of the household as the explanatory variable, households with and those without out-migrant workers were introduced as dummy variables. The estimated results of the two models are presented in Table 13.6.

The results of model I show that the estimated coefficients of both out-migrant labor and nonmigrant labor are highly significant. The marginal contribution of out-migrant workers to total household income is higher, by about 10 percentage points, than that of nonmigrant workers. According to the 1995 survey data, household income came to 6,270 yuan in rural China, so our estimate implies that an average out-migrant worker earned about 600 yuan more than household members working locally. Therefore, we can conclude that there was a positive wage premium for being an out-migrant worker.

This conclusion is also supported strongly by the results of model II. When the presence of out-migrant workers is introduced into this model as a dummy variable, its estimated coefficient indicates that the marginal contribution to household income from having out-migrant members, compared to not having them, is 9.4 percentage points. The estimated coefficient was highly significant.

The results of the two models in Table 13.6 indicate that the rate of contribution to income of out-migrant workers was higher than that of nonmigrant workers. This is but one effect of rural migration on rural household income. In addition, rural migration is accompanied by a process of reallocation of production resources within households, and especially of labor. For households with surplus labor, out-migration would reduce the surplus and increase the marginal product of labor of the remaining members, especially those engaged in farming activities. This is another effect of rural migration on rural household income. If this effect exists, then the estimated coefficient of farm labor in the income function of MH should be higher than that for NMH.

To test our hypothesis, the income functions of MH and NMH are estimated separately. In the MH income function, the numbers of out-migrants and nonmigrant workers were introduced as explanatory variables along with other production variables and dummies; the NMH income function has the same specification, except that it excludes out-migrant workers. The difference in the estimated coef-

Table 13.6

Results of Income Function of Rural Households in China, 1995

Independent variables	Mean	Dependent variable: household income	
		Model 1	Model 2
Irrigated land (*mu*)	4.20	0.00009	0.00009
Nonirrigated land (*mu*)	3.35	−0.0064***	−0.0069***
Production assets (yuan)	2,727.8	0.00002***	0.000019***
Number of workers	2.45		0.108***
Migrant workers	0.265	0.170***	
Nonmigrant workers	2.185	0.076***	
Household with migrants (dummy)	0.21		0.094***
Household without migrants (dummy)	0.79		—
Province dummies			
Beijing		—	—
Hebei	0.062	−0.884***	−0.883***
Shanxi	0.035	−1.174***	−1.169***
Liaoning	0.035	−0.803***	−0.837***
Jilin	0.037	−0.905***	−0.917***
Jiangsu	0.063	−0.344***	−0.359***
Zhejiang	0.050	−0.411***	−0.430***
Anhui	0.057	−0.869***	−0.898***
Jiangxi	0.045	−0.802***	−0.823***
Shandong	0.088	−0.729***	−0.751***
Henan	0.087	−0.888***	−0.897***
Hubei	0.051	−0.916***	−0.935***
Hunan	0.062	−1.047***	−1.063***
Guangdong	0.063	−0.105	−0.127*
Sichuan	0.101	−1.188***	−1.213***
Guizhou	0.038	−1.147***	−1.166***
Yunnan	0.038	−1.107***	−1.132***
Shaanxi	0.038	−1.152***	−1.154***
Gansu	0.038	−1.282***	−1.299***
Intercept	1.000	9.345***	9.264***
Adj. R²		0.232	0.239
F-value		104.0	108.0
Mean of dependent		8.744	8.744
Observations		7825	7825

Source: 1995 Household Income Survey.

Notes: Migrant workers are those who worked outside their villages or left them to look for work for more than one month in 1995. Households with migrant workers were those having at least one migrant worker. In this and subsequent tables, *** denotes statistical significance at the 1 percent level, ** at the 5 percent and, * at the 10 percent level.

ficients of nonmigrant workers in the two functions reflects the difference in these workers' marginal rates of contribution to total income in the two types of households. It also reflects the difference in their marginal productivity, resulting from reallocation of labor within the household. Part of the estimated results were significant[5] and are given in Table 13.7.

Table 13.7

Income Functions of Rural Households with and without Migrant Workers

	Estimated coefficients				
	Migrant workers	Nonmigrant workers	Adj. R²	F-value	Obser-vations
Total sample					
Households with migrants (MH)	0.186***	0.099**	0.267	27.0	1,641
Households with no migrants (NMH)		0.069**	0.225	83.8	6,184
Anhui					
MH	0.420***	0.113	0.238	4.07	50
NMH		0.038	0.057	5.64	308
Henan					
MH	0.248**	0.113**	0.200	6.02	102
NMH		0.064**	0.129	22.5	580
Hunan					
MH	0.238**	0.130***	0.203	7.51	129
NMH		−0.014	0.034	4.18	358
Guangdong					
MH	0.214**	0.025	0.130	5.24	143
NMH		−0.032	0.092	9.75	347
Sichuan					
MH	0.339***	0.083**	0.111	6.93	238
NMH		0.061**	0.088	14.3	553
Guizhou					
MH	0.190	0.078*	0.125	3.25	80
NMH		0.040	0.014	1.76	217
Yunnan					
MH	0.272*	0.223**	0.335	4.02	31
NMH		0.029	0.124	10.28	264
Shaanxi					
MH	0.580**	0.147*	0.091	2.31	67
NMH		−0.0003	0.004	1.23	231
Gansu					
MH	0.035	0.128**	0.131	2.62	55
NMH		0.033	0.398	40.52	240

Sources: 1995 Household Income Survey.
Note: In the national and provincial regression models, control variables of land and production assets were introduced. Due to limited space, the coefficients of the control variables are not presented in this table.

The fit and estimated results of both functions for the entire rural sample—for households with and without out-migrant workers—are quite satisfactory statistically. The value of Adj.-R² means that more than 20 percent of the total variance in household disposable income is explained by the two models. In them, the estimated coefficients of the variables of both out-migrant workers and nonmigrant workers are highly significant. What is more interesting is that the coefficient on nonmigrant workers in the model for MH is 0.099, three percentage points higher than the corresponding figure, 0.069, in the model for NMH. This indicates that the marginal product of nonmigrant workers living in households having out-migrants is higher than that of workers in households with no out-migrant workers.[6] Such findings support our hypothesis that the rural migrant workers not only earn higher income outside their households but also raise the productivity of their stay-at-home relatives.

Perhaps a further question should be raised, however. If education is conducive to labor mobility, it is possible that MH have more human capital than NMH, and that this, rather than the posited reallocation of labor, is what explains the higher productivity of nonmigrant workers in MH. To answer this question, the average years of education of migrant and nonmigrant workers in the two types of households were compared. Although the average amount of education of out-migrants was 1.2 years more than that of nonmigrants in NMH (8.28 years compared with 7.04 years), in MH the average amount of education of nonmigrant workers was only 6.14 years in 1995. Thus, the higher productivity of nonmigrant workers in NMH than in MH was not due to more human capital. However, we cannot rule out spillover effects from the superior human capital of the out-migrant workers on the productivity of their nonmigrant relatives. It would be a very tough task to measure this!

Table 13.7 also presents estimates of the same income functions for nine provinces. Among the nineteen provinces in our survey, the estimated results were unsatisfactory for ten. Some of these had samples that were too small, and others had statistically insignificant labor coefficients. However, the regression results in the remaining nine provinces were significant. The estimated coefficients of nonmigrant workers in the income function of MH were higher than those of workers in NMH in all nine provinces, although some of them were not significant. These results further support our hypothesis that rural migration increases productivity of nonmigrant relatives.

Effects of Migration on Income Distribution

To what extent has rural migration impacted on the income distribution in rural China in the 1990s? Has it tended to widen or to narrow income inequality? Has it contributed to reducing the incidence of rural poverty, or has it had no significant role to play in poverty alleviation? Although all these issues have been touched upon in our theoretical discussion above, we need to see whether we can verify our theoretical hypotheses and also try through an empirical investigation to better understand the real situation, which is rather complicated.

The effect of migration on rural income distribution can be analyzed using two approaches. One is simply to examine the effect of income remitted back or brought home by out-migrant workers. Here, such remittances can be counted either as part of the total income of their households or as transfer income from other family members. Thus, the inequality measures can be compared for household income including and excluding remittances, and the effect of the remittances on rural income inequality can be precisely calculated. This approach is frequently seen in the current literature, and is even more applicable to developing countries, where labor mobility takes place through population migration and remittances become the main economic link between the out-migrants and their original families.

Another approach is based on estimating opportunity costs of the out-migrant workers. Knowing the opportunity costs, we can compare the actual income of households with their simulated income derived from substituting the opportunity cost of out-migrants (i.e., the estimated income they would have earned, had they not migrated) for their actual income, and therefore we can compute inequality measures for both the actual income and the simulated income. We have to assume, of course, that the out-migrant workers, had they remained in their home villages, would have earned only their opportunity cost—which is the income earned in home villages. The difference in some inequality measures, such as the Gini coefficient, between these two incomes, can be regarded as the change in income inequality caused by out-migration. Technically, the analysis required for this approach is more complicated, because the estimation of the opportunity cost of out-migrant workers requires a proper use of the production (income) functions of the rural households.

Fortunately, the 1995 rural household income survey data provide the possibility of attempting both approaches. Remittances from out-migrants were reported as a source of household income, and personal information was collected that can be used to distinguish permanent household members from nonpermanent members. Among the 7,998 rural households in the sample, 1,181 received remittances from out-migrant members, with the average amount being 2,190 yuan, accounting for 25.1 percent of total household income of those households receiving remittances. For all households in the sample, the average remittance came to 25 yuan, comprising 3.8 percent of household total income in 1995. The importance of remittances varied widely among the provinces. Table 13.8 shows the number of households receiving remittances, their proportions to all households, the size of remittances per household and other relevant information, for the entire sample and for each province in it. It is clear from the amount of regional variation that the impact of remittances on regional income differentials in rural China needs to be investigated, as well.

For the analysis of this, we make use of the Gini coefficients and decile distributions of rural personal disposable income, both including and excluding remittances (Table 13.9). The Gini coefficient shows how a commonly used aggregate measure of income inequality responds to remittances, while from the decile distribution we can see the changes in each decile group's share of total income due to remittances.

Table 13.9 shows that the Gini coefficient for personal disposable income in rural China as a whole in 1995 was 0.411. If the remittances sent back by the out-

Table 13.8

Remittances and their Shares in Household Income in Rural China, 1995

	Number of households receiving remittances	Percent of total house-hold	Average remittances (yuan)		Share of remittances in income	
			Receiving house-holds	All house-holds	Receiving house-holds	All house-holds
Total	1,182	14.8	2,190	324	25.1	3.8
Province						
Beijing	1	1.0	2,500	25	9.4	0.1
Hebei	50	10.0	2,073	208	28.3	2.8
Shanxi	46	15.3	1,374	211	27.4	4.2
Liaoning	7	2.3	1,695	40	24.0	0.5
Jilin	22	7.3	2,380	175	27.5	2.3
Jiangsu	21	4.2	3,807	160	27.4	1.2
Zhejiang	46	11.5	2,489	286	29.5	2.1
Anhui	132	29.3	2,061	604	28.6	8.6
Jiangxi	131	37.4	2,219	830	26.6	10.1
Shandong	64	9.1	2,221	203	17.7	2.0
Henan	63	9.0	1,641	148	18.3	2.0
Hubei	24	6.0	2,137	128	23.5	1.8
Hunan	117	23.4	1,864	436	29.3	7.3
Guangdong	118	23.6	4,045	955	23.0	5.0
Sichuan	198	24.8	2,097	520	27.8	9.1
Guizhou	43	14.3	965	138	16.1	2.4
Yunnan	30	10.0	1,347	135	24.6	2.2
Shaanxi	41	13.7	1,945	266	29.3	4.3
Gansu	28	9.3	1,023	95	21.1	1.9

Source: 1995 Household Income Survey.

migrant workers are deducted, the Gini coefficient would rise by 5 percent to 0.431. In other words, the presence of remittances lowers the Gini coefficient of rural personal disposable income by about 5 percent, suggesting that remittances were helpful in narrowing income differences.

The changes in the decile shares of income shown in Table 13.9 also support this conclusion. Remittances increased the respective shares of six of the seven lowest decile groups, all but the lowest, by 3 percentage points per decile group, on average. The share of the lowest income decile was reduced slightly by remittances, even though the remittances were responsible for a far higher share of this decile's total income (17.3 percent) than of any other decile's. This suggests that the *size* of remittances for this group was very small, relative to the size of remittances for other groups. Remittances lowered the shares of the richest three deciles. The expensive opportunity cost of migration for these well-off groups may have dampened their enthusiasm to move.

Table 13.10 shows the concentration ratios of personal income with and without remittances, and of remittances, themselves, as well as their respective shares

Table 13.9

Decile Shares of Income, with and without Remittances, Rural China, 1995

Decile (ascending order)	Personal income	Personal income after deducting remittances	Share of remittances in income (percent)
1	0.0227	0.0235	17.3
2	0.0394	0.0358	7.1
3	0.0485	0.0448	5.8
4	0.0577	0.0546	6.1
5	0.0676	0.0645	5.1
6	0.0792	0.0760	4.3
7	0.0931	0.0908	4.0
8	0.1114	0.1118	2.9
9	0.1461	0.1485	4.5
10	0.3343	0.3497	1.6
Gini coefficient	0.411	0.431	
Coefficient of variation	1.218	1.266	

Source: 1995 Household Income Survey.
Notes: There are 34,739 total individuals in the rural sample. Deciles are sorted in ascending order.

Table 13.10

Contribution of Remittances to Inequality of Rural Income: Decomposition Analysis

Type of income	Gini or concentration ratio	Shares of total income (percent)	Contribution to total inequality (percent)
Remittances	0.1702	3.8	1.57
Personal income after remittances	0.4207	96.2	98.43
Personal income	0.4113	100.0	100.0

Source: 1995 Household Income Survey.

in total income.[7] The concentration ratio of remittances was rather low, being 0.170 only, far smaller than the Gini coefficients for all income and for all income excluding remittances. Although the share of remittances in total income was 3.8 percent, their contribution to the inequality of total income was only 1.57 percent. Clearly, remittances are an "equalizing" source of rural income in the sense that, *ceteris paribus,* an increase in their share of total income would reduce the overall Gini coefficient.

Let us try a simple simulation analysis. Suppose the concentration ratios for the two income sources were unchanged, while the share of remittances in total income increased from the existing 3.8 percent to 10 percent and then to 20 percent. The Gini coefficient of total income would then decline, *ceteris paribus,* from the existing level of 0.411 to 0.396 and then to 0.371, decreasing by 3.7 percent and 9.7 percent, respectively. This suggests that encouraging more migration among low-income households would play a positive role in restraining the widening of income inequality in rural China.

The second approach is to estimate separately the income functions of MH and NMH. Then the marginal contributions of out-migrant workers and nonmigrant workers to household total income can be estimated. For the NMH, the income function includes only the number of nonmigrant workers as the labor variable, the coefficient of which is their marginal contribution to total household income. This can also be regarded as the opportunity cost of migrating. That is to say, if the migrating workers in a household were to stay at home, their marginal contribution to total household income would be equivalent to that of nonmigrant workers in NMH. The income function of MH can be expressed as

$$Y_n(L_m) = \beta_{m0} + \beta_{m1}L_m + \beta_{m2}L_n + \sum \beta_{mi}X_i + \varepsilon \tag{13.1}$$

Here Y_n is the total income of households; β_{m0} is intercept; β_{m1} is the marginal contribution of out-migrant workers to household income, and β_{m2} is that of the nonmigrant workers to household income; X_i is other production inputs and control variables; and ε is a random error term.

For NMH, the income function takes the form as follows:

$$Y_n(L_n) = \beta_{n0} + \beta_{n2}L_n + \sum \beta_{ni}X_i + \varepsilon \tag{13.2}$$

in which the explanations for the variables and parameters are basically the same as in equation (13.1). β_{n2} can be taken either as the marginal rate of contribution of workers to the income of their families, or as the opportunity cost of migration for out-migrant workers in MH. The latter interpretation stems from the assumption that if there were no out-migrants among MH, their income function would coincide with equation (13.2) and not equation (13.1).

So from our household income data, two sets of predicted incomes can be derived from the two formulas. One of the two sets, $Yp,$ is composed of the predicted incomes of the MH derived from equation (13.1) and the predicted incomes of NMH derived from equation (13.2). The other set, $Y_o,$ is composed of the predicted incomes of MH and NMH, both derived from equation (13.1). However, the predicted incomes of the MH here are actually the predicted opportunity costs to labor migration—that is, what those households would earn if their out-migrant workers stayed home. Table 13.11 also shows two inequality indexes of the two sets of predicted income for the whole rural sample, as well as for the samples for Guangdong and Sichuan provinces.[8]

In Table 13.11, the difference between the Gini coefficients for the two sets of

Table 13.11

Effects of Remittances on Lorenz Curves in Rural China: Income Function Approach

Deciles	Total sample Y_p	Y_o	Guangdong Y_p	Y_o	Sichuan Y_p	Y_o
1	0.0445	0.0445	0.0541	0.0551	0.0517	0.0580
2	0.1016	0.1015	0.1205	0.1219	0.1173	0.1298
3	0.1669	0.1669	0.1938	0.1944	0.1925	0.2108
4	0.2399	0.2395	0.2734	0.2721	0.2761	0.2983
5	0.3207	0.3200	0.3592	0.3584	0.3694	0.3913
6	0.4092	0.4089	0.4511	0.4442	0.4700	0.4969
7	0.5079	0.5079	0.5512	0.5446	0.5788	0.6054
8	0.6249	0.6231	0.6617	0.6564	0.6991	0.7201
9	0.7712	0.7680	0.7935	0.7898	0.8321	0.8505
10	1.0000	1.0000	1.0000	1.000	1.0000	1.0000
Gini	0.2686	0.2700	0.2134	0.2180	0.1856	0.1512
CV	0.7454	0.7624	0.4936	0.5479	0.3407	0.3452

Source: 1995 Household Income Survey.
Notes: The calculations are for individuals, not households. Y_p = Predicted personal income with income functions of households with and without migrant workers, respectively; Y_o = Predicted personal income of all households, using income function of households without out-migrants, thus assuming migrant workers make same contribution as nonmigrant workers. Province dummies were used in the household income functions for the total sample.

predicted incomes is very small, with inequality slightly higher for the second set of predicted incomes. That the Gini coefficients are so similar is in part due to a well-known deficiency of the Gini coefficient itself as an index of inequality, namely, that it is quite insensitive to income transfers among nonextreme groups.[9] The coefficient of variation (CV) in Table 13.11 registers a greater difference in inequality between the two sets of predicted income, with the CV of Y_o being 2.3 percent higher than that of Y_p. So we can conclude that, while the changes in inequality as measured by different indexes are different, the implications are basically similar, that is, if the out-migrant labor force had remained working at home, overall income inequality in rural China could have been somewhat higher than it was in 1995.

This conclusion, drawn from the analysis of the overall rural sample, may not hold for particular provinces with special conditions. Table 13.11 shows results for Guangdong and Sichuan provinces that basically tally with theoretical expectations. These expectations are that in more developed provinces (e.g., Guangdong), out-migrants tend to come from lower-income families; with strong feelings of relative deprivation, they have strong motivation to move out, as explained by

Stark (1984). The large difference between their expected income from migrating and the opportunity cost of migration promises to narrow the income gap between their families and high-income families. In the backward provinces (e.g., Sichuan), on the other hand, most out-migrant workers are from families with medium-level income and above, rather than those with the lowest incomes. This is mainly because of financial constraints facing the poorest families, who lack the means to travel, to bear risks, and to finance job searches. Migration thus tends to raise the incomes of middle-income families relative to low-income ones, which would widen income inequality in these areas.

For Guangdong Province, the Gini coefficient of Y_o is 2.2 percent higher than that of Y_p, while the coefficient of variation of Y_o is 11 percent higher than that of Y_p. This indicates that rural migration has narrowed income differences in rural Guangdong. However, for Sichuan, the results are just the opposite. Although the difference in coefficients of variation between Y_o and Y_p is very small, the 3.4 percent difference in Gini coefficients (that of Y_p being the higher) is rather substantial. In Sichuan, it seems, the outflow of rural labor has actually *increased* rural income inequality. Of course, these results obtain only for the two provinces concerned. Further research is needed before a general conclusion can be drawn that rural migration reduces income inequality in economically prosperous regions while increasing it in backward regions.[10]

Conclusions and Policy Implications

With the enormous gap, including the income gap, between urban and rural areas in China, the migration of rural workers looking for income-earning opportunities will be a long-term and continuing phenomenon. The results of our analysis indicate that rural migration makes a contribution to the growth of rural income, not only by raising labor productivity of migrant workers but also by permitting more efficient allocation of the remaining, nonmigrating workers. Faster growth of rural household income resulting from more rural workers moving into urban areas could narrow the urban-rural income gap.

From our two different approaches to estimating the contribution of rural migration to changes in rural income inequality, we can conclude that rural migration at least does not cause a deterioration in income distribution, and might improve it. Remittances from out-migrant workers have definitely played a role in reducing income differentials among rural households. Our simulation analysis also indicates that the distribution of rural household income in 1995 was more equal than it would have been in the absence of rural out-migration. However, at the provincial level, we find some evidence that rich and poor provinces experience quite different effects of rural migration on income inequality. In rich Guangdong rural migration reduces inequality, while in relatively backward Sichuan it appears to increase income inequality, mainly due (we suspect) to the lack of mobility of workers in very low-income households.

Given these conclusions, we draw a few policy implications. First and foremost, the present policy of separating the cities and the rural areas should be discontinued. Since the migration of the rural labor force toward the urban areas will be a drawn-out process, governments at all levels, especially the central government, should have a long-term perspective on the issue and work out correspondingly long-term strategies for dealing with it. Second, the integration of rural and urban labor markets should be encouraged. The urban labor market should be opened as widely as possible to rural migrant workers, the latter should be legally protected in pursuing employment opportunities, and they should not be discriminated against in the urban labor market. Governments should take more responsibility for the basic living conditions of the rural migrant work force, rather than putting more restrictions on their mobility and employment.

Third, it should be recognized that rural-urban migration will make cities more congested and create other problems. However, viewed from another angle this reflects the problem of lagging infrastructure construction in Chinese cities, which ought to be considered together with the issue of rural migration. For example, the method of *yigong daizhen* (providing work as a form of relief), used as a poverty alleviation technique in poor rural areas, might be employed as well for urban infrastructure projects. Under such an approach, contracts could be signed with immigrant workers fixing the duration of the work, three to five years, for instance. During the period of contract, the rural workers would earn a basic subsistence income, and on the expiration of the contract, they would receive an additional compensation package that they could use as they see fit. Such an arrangement would have the advantage described by the Chinese saying *yiju duode* (kill many birds with one stone): (1) The government could utilize in a massive way the rural labor surpluses through this contract arrangement, thus lessening its financial burden; (2) the backward urban infrastructure can be improved; (3) after the completion of the *yigong daizhen* contracts, the immigrant workers who chose to stay in the cities would bring about fewer social problems because they would have money for subsistence and investment.

And (4), once an integrated labor market is formed and the mechanism for free mobility of the labor force both in urban and rural China is established, the migration of the labor force itself can help the narrowing of the urban-rural income gap, and this in itself would eventually limit the scale and lower the speed of rural-urban migration. That is to say, the free mobility of people and labor between the cities and countryside can gradually become a mechanism for balanced development.

Notes

The author is grateful for comments from John Knight, Zuo Xuejin, and Zhu Ling. Wei Zhong made contributions to the computations in this report.

1. "Regulations on household registration of the People's Republic of China," adopted by the Standing Committee of the National People's Congress in January of 1958, enacted legal clauses concerning the range, reporting, nullification, and change of domicile regis-

trations. It was then, and through the household registration system, that overall control over migration, especially the migration of rural workers, began. In August of 1964 the State Council circulated regulations of the Ministry of Public Security on changes of registered permanent residences, and once again stressed the spirit of two "strict restrictions," that is, strict restriction on both migration of rural inhabitants to cities and towns, and migration of town residents to cities (Wang and Hu 1996).

2. These data underestimate the *total* number of rural migrants in cities because the objects of the survey included only the long-term floating population, that is, those migrants who had left their registered households for more than half a year. Short-term migrants away from their households for less than half a year were still treated as living at their original place of registration and so were not included in the survey.

3. It should be remembered that out-migrants include those *looking for work* as well as those working. Therefore, the average income per worker of households with out-migrants is lower than the average for those households whose out-migrant members actually found work.

4. Small sample sizes for some provinces, including poor provinces such as Yunnan and Gansu, increase the chance of sampling error. The results for these provinces should be regarded only as suggestive, at best.

5. Listed in Table 13.7 are the estimated results for nine provinces only. This is because most of the estimated coefficients of labor variables in these provinces passed the statistical test of significance, while those for other provinces were not statistically significant and so are not discussed further here.

6. Due to the very small difference in per capita income between the two groups of households, the absolute amount contributed by a nonmigrant worker in an MH is also higher than his (her) counterpart in an NMH.

7. We use here the formula for indirect decomposition of the Gini coefficient, which can be written as $G = \Sigma U_i * C_i$, in which U_i is the share of the ith source of income in total income and C_i is the *concentration ratio* of that income source. The concentration ratio is analogous to the Gini ratio, except that it measures the inequality in distribution of a given kind of income (e.g., wages) over all income recipients, not only recipients of that source (wage earners). For example, if wages were very high relative to other kinds of rural income, but distributed very equally among wage earners, they would have a very low Gini ratio but a very high concentration ratio. The relative contribution of an income source to the inequality of total income can be expressed as $R_i = U_i * C_i / G$. The R_i's for all income sources add up to the Gini ratio of total income. See Khan et al. 1992.

8. There are several reasons for choosing Guangdong and Sichuan as the provincial cases to examine. First, both provinces have high proportions of rural out-migrant workers, as shown in Table 13.3. Second, Guangdong is an economically prosperous province on the east coast, while Sichuan represents the underdeveloped west. Third, both provinces have large enough sample sizes, both with and without out-migrant workers, to permit the estimation of household income functions.

9. The changes in the Lorenz curve for the total rural sample in Table 13.11 show that, compared with Y_o, the income shares of the 2nd, 4th, and 5th decile groups of Y_p are higher. However, the reflection of these changes in the Gini coefficient is miniscule.

10. Similar estimates for all provinces in the 1995 household data were attempted in order to find the correlation between the difference in the Gini coefficients for Y_p and Y_o, on the one hand, and the income level of the provinces, on the other. However, small sample sizes and other problems led to unsatisfactory results.

References

Chai, H., Knight, J., Mo, R., and Song, L., 1996, "The Rural Labour Force Survey for China, 1994: The Main Results," unpublished paper.

Cooperative Research Team of Eight City Governments, 1993, *Labor Employment and Urban Development in the Large Chinese Cities* (in Chinese), Beijing, China Labor Press.

Corden, W., and Findlay, R., 1975, " Urban Unemployment, Intersectoral Capital Mobility and Development Policy," *Economica*, February.

Department of Population and Employment, SSB, 1996, *Key Data of 1995 One Percent National Population Sample Survey* (in Chinese), Beijing, China Statistical Publishing House.

Friedberg, R. M., and Hunt, J., 1995, "The Impact of Immigrants on Host Country Wages, Employment and Growth," *Journal of Economic Perspectives*, Spring.

Griffin. K., and Zhao Renwei (eds.), 1993, *The Distribution of Income in China*, London, Macmillan.

Gu Shengzu and Jian Xinhua (eds.), 1994, *Current Population Migration and Urbanization in China* (in Chinese), Wuhan, Wuhan University Press.

Guoqing, 1993, *Transition of Rural Surplus Labor in Modernization* (in Chinese), Beijing, Chinese Social Science Press.

Han Jun, 1994, *Inter-century Difficult Task—Transition of Chinese Agricultural Labor* (in Chinese), Taiyuan, Shanxi Economic Press.

Jin Dangsheng and Shaoqin, 1995, *The Situation and Management of Population Migration in China* (in Chinese), Beijing, China Population Press.

Katz, E., and Stark, O., 1986, "Labor Migration and Risk Aversion in Less-Developed Countries," *Journal of Labor Economics*.

Khan, Azizur, Keith Griffin, Carl Riskin, and Zhao Renwei, 1992, "Household Income and its Distribution in China," *China Quarterly* No. 132.

Knight, J., and Song, L., 1996, "Chinese Peasants Choices: Migration, Rural Industry or Farming," *Processing*.

Li Mengbai and Hu Xing, 1991, *Impact of Migrant Population on Development of Large Cities and Relevant Policy* (in Chinese), Beijing, Economic Daily Press.

Li Peilin (ed.), 1995, *Report of Class Stratification in New Period of China* (in Chinese), Shenyang, Liaoning People's Press.

Li Shi ,1997, *Rural Migration and Income Distribution in China*, Research report prepared for Washington Center for China Studies.

Office of the National Population Sample Survey, 1997, *Data of 1995 One Percent National Population Sample Survey* (in Chinese), Beijing, China Statistical Publishing House.

Perkins, Dwight H., 1988, " Reforming China's Economic System," *Journal of Economic Literature,* Vol. 26, June.

Project Team of Employment Department, Ministry of Labor, 1996, "Opportunity and Ability: Employment and Mobility of Rural Labor in China" (in Chinese), Discussion Paper.

Riskin, Carl, 1987, *China's Political Economy*, Oxford and New York, Oxford University Press.

Shorrocks, A.F., 1980, "The Class of Additively Decomposable Inequality Measures," *Econometrica,* 48.

Stark, O., 1984 "Rural-to-Urban Migration in LDCs: A Relative Deprivation Approach," *Economic Development and Cultural Change*, 32.

State Statistical Bureau, 1996a, *China's Regional Economy: 17 Years of Reform and Opening Up,* Beijing, China Statistical Press.

State Statistical Bureau, 1996b, *Statistical Yearbook of China, 1996,* Beijing, China Statistical Press.

Tang Ping, 1995, "Analysis of Income Level and Inequality of Rural Households in China" (in Chinese), *Management World*, No. 2.

Todaro, M., 1969, "A Model of Labor Migration and Urban Unemployment in Less Developed Countries," *American Economic Review*, 59.

Urban Investigation Team of Beijing, 1995, "Observing Mobility of Talented People in Beijing" (in Chinese), *Capital Economy*, October.

Wang Jianmin, and Hu Qi, 1996, *Migrant Population in China* (in Chinese), Shanghai, Shanghai Financial University Press.

World Bank, 1995, *World Development Report 1995: Workers in an Integrating World*, Oxford and New York, Oxford University Press.

World Bank, 1996, *World Development Report 1996: From Plan to Market* (Chinese version), Beijing, China Financial and Economic Press.

Zhao Renwei, 1992, "Some Special Phenomena of Income Distribution in Transitional China" (in Chinese), *Economic Research,* January.

Zhao Renwei and Li Shi, 1992, "Distribution of Personal Income in China: Urban, Rural, and Regional" (in Chinese), *Reform* No. 2.

14

Chinese Rural Poverty Inside and Outside the Poor Regions

Carl Riskin and Li Shi

Introduction

How is the transition to a market economy affecting the disposition of poverty in China? This chapter uses the data from the 1988 and 1995 national surveys of rural households to examine the characteristics of rural poverty as the transition progresses. While the extent of urban poverty increased in the nineties, it is still very much smaller than that of rural poverty and rather different in character and cause. We confine ourselves here to the rural poor.

Specifically, we seek to distinguish the poor population living within designated poor regions of China from that living in "normal" regions, and to compare relevant characteristics of the two subpopulations. This is an important question because China's poverty alleviation program has been aimed almost exclusively at the residents of poor counties. Poor people living elsewhere have not been the beneficiaries of any concerted antipoverty program, although there is an array of programs available to deal with particular causes of poverty, such as natural disasters. In 1995 China put forward a program to basically eliminate poverty by the end of the century. However, this commitment too was, until very recently, interpreted as applying to the poor rural areas only, as is now freely acknowledged. Poor people living outside these areas (as well as those in urban areas) are not targeted, although there are other policies available that are relevant to the situations of some of them.

Much rural poverty has been and still is concentrated in remote, ecologically disadvantaged areas of the northwest and southwest. Ecological disadvantage might be thought of as a "natural" cause of poverty rather than one stemming from bad policies. However, policies can contribute significantly, for example, by limiting population movement or preventing the affected population from taking action to improve their situation. Between 1978 and 1984 there was an enormous decline in the number of rural poor in poor regions (and elsewhere) because of benign changes in policy. Yet even when policy is constructive, the task of improving the welfare of people in remote areas with poor physical conditions is arduous. Much of the blame naturally falls on the conditions themselves.

As long as the focus of attention is entirely on regional poverty, then poverty can be ascribed to ecological adversity and location, if there are no important policy barriers to economic improvement in such areas. Ignored in this picture is the increase in poverty outside of these regions, in ordinary parts of China, including the towns and cities. The Chinese government has recently begun to recognize that poverty can be a predictable result of economic, social, and demographic forces in a market economy. Thus China's comprehensive plan for population, environment, and development, *China's Agenda 21 White Paper* (Zhongguo 1994), acknowledges the existence of a "new poverty stemming from setbacks in market competition"; while the government's *National Report to the 1995 World Summit on Social Development* (State Planning Commission 1995) recognizes the existence of urban poverty caused both by personal misfortune (disease, injury, etc.) and by social and economic factors such as unemployment and bankruptcy.

Even Beijing Municipality acknowledged that in 1994 some 300,000 of its residents were living below its poverty line. Indeed, urban poverty nationally was put at about 14 million in mid-1995, or 4.5 percent of urban residents. A study by the Institute of Nutrition and Food Hygiene of the Chinese Academy of Preventive Medicine, based on State Statistical Bureau sample data for six provinces and Beijing Municipality, found evidence of widespread malnutrition among children not only in remote Sichuan but even in Beijing and Guangdong. In Guangdong cities and towns, 26 percent of children in 1987 and 12 percent in 1990 were found to be significantly underweight. The figure was 4 percent for Beijing city in 1990 and 15 percent for its rural surroundings (Chen and Shao 1990). Similarly, the China Health and Nutrition Survey (CHNS), a collaborative longitudinal study of the nutritional impact of social change in China, based at the University of North Carolina, has found "an increase in underweight among those in the lowest income third, especially the low-income men" (Popkin 1994, p. 11) between 1989 and 1991. Clearly, poverty has remained a problem in China not just in the remote hinterland, and in some respects it might be a growing problem, emerging from the effects of marketization in the context of a big labor surplus.

There are two methods of distinguishing residents of poverty counties, based upon our survey instruments. One is subjective: it screens households according to their answer to the question "Do you live in a designated poor area?" The other is objective: it compares the survey counties with the list of almost 500 designated poor-counties as of 1988 and 592 for 1995, and places in the poor county category all sample households who live in one of the listed counties, regardless of how they answered the above question.

The finding that there are significant differences between rural poor households inside and outside of the poor areas holds up for both methods of identification, and with it some hypotheses about causal factors and policy consequences. However, we confine ourselves here to the objective method of designation, which we believe to be more reliable. We will discuss the characteristics of regional and nonregional poverty for 1988, and then for 1995, discussing significant changes between the two years.

Regional and Nonregional Poor in 1988

In the 1988 sample the rural poor population, roughly 1,100 households with 5,600 members, was identified by having household per capita disposable incomes lower than a specific poverty line, namely, 333 yuan in current prices. The rural poverty head-count rate, according to this threshold, was 12.7 percent. The poverty line used is a refinement of one devised by the State Statistical Bureau's rural survey team (Riskin 1993) and thus reflects Chinese government standards as to what constitutes absolute poverty in rural areas.[1] It would of course have been preferable, had the data permitted, to use measured incomes for several years rather than just one, in order to eliminate cases in which poverty or its absence was due to transitory factors. Having been identified, the poor population was then sorted by whether or not respondents were located in one of the approximately 700 rural counties officially designated as poverty counties by either the central government or the individual provinces. We refer to households identified as poor and located in a designated poverty area as "regional poor" (RP), and those residing outside of these areas as "nonregional poor" (NRP). Altogether, there were 563 NRP households in 1988, or 51.4 percent of all poor households in the sample, and 532 RP households (48.6 percent).

As would be expected, in 1988 the rural poor as a whole were overwhelmingly farmers—95 percent in nonpoor areas, 98 percent in the poor. This compares with a national average of 79 percent of the rural labor force in farming and related occupations in 1988 (State Statistical Bureau 1990, p. 128). As shown in Table 14.1, the poor were overwhelmingly self-employed (91 percent and 95 percent). Poor households in nonpoor regions actually had somewhat lower incomes (averaging 206 yuan) than their counterparts in poor areas (222 yuan). Yet NRP households were relatively better off in many of the characteristics measured, especially those concerned with education. They reported a much lower illiteracy rate (25 percent compared with 38 percent); 68 percent completed five years of education compared with 54 percent. As might be expected, a much smaller proportion had minority nationality status (3 percent compared with 21 percent). In NRP households, 83 percent had electricity, compared with only 61 percent of RP households. The former had slightly more (7 percent) cultivated land, but 60 percent more irrigated land. The advantages of the NRP pertain to human capital and economic and social infrastructure: education, irrigation, electrification. With respect to health, they spent 23 percent more on medical care, but went to the hospital or clinic less often—a combination suggesting that they faced more expensive medical facilities.[2]

Table 14.1

Characteristics of Poor Population in Poor and Nonpoor Regions, 1988

	(a) Nonpoor regions	(b) Poor regions	(c) Ratio a/b
Individual			
Income (yuan)	206	222	0.93
Completed 5 yrs of education (%)	68	54	1.26
Illiterate (self-reported) (%)	25	38	0.65
Minority nationality (%)	3	21	0.14
Primary occupation farming (%)	95	98	0.97
Ownership status: self-employed (%)	91	95	0.96
Household			
Total medical expenses (yuan)	14	11	1.23
Fixed productive assets (yuan)	506	618	0.82
Value of livestock (yuan)	256	379	0.67
Cultivated land (*mu*)	13.3	12.4	1.08
Irrigated land (*mu*)	1.8	1.1	1.60
Financial assets, incl. savings (yuan)	65	26	2.45
Outstanding debt (yuan)	162	115	1.40
For housing (yuan)	25	15	1.70
Annual production expenses (yuan)	961	744	1.29
Have electricity (%)	83	61	1.36
Went to hospital/clinic at least once (%)	48	57	0.86

The picture with regard to capital ownership was mixed: NRP had only 82 percent as much productive fixed assets per household, and only two-thirds the value of livestock, but 2.5 times the meager amount of financial assets (mostly savings deposits) held by RP. At the same time, they carried 40 percent more household debt, of which significantly more was for new housing.

The average per capita incomes of both poor groups were extremely low, less than 30 percent of the sample average for rural China, and only two-thirds or less of the poverty line itself. Moreover, the NRP would seem to be even poorer—with average incomes 7 percent lower—than their regional counterparts, despite superior human capital and infrastructural development.

Table 14.2, which shows the major components of personal income, provides some insight into the relative disadvantage of the nonregional poor. Wage-type income was a relatively minor item, contributing a little more to NRP than to RP incomes. By far the biggest component of income for all rural households, contributing almost three-quarters of total income, was household production (farming and subsidiary activities). Its relative contribution to poor households was even greater at more than four-fifths of total household income. The absolute level of per capita income from household production activities for poor households was only one-third the average for rural China as a whole. But that of the NRP was 10 percent lower than that of the RP. NRP households produced a larger *gross* value

Table 14.2

Composition of Household per Capita Income, Rural China and Poor Population, by Poor and Nonpoor Regions, 1988

	Rural China		Poor population			
			Nonpoor areas		Poor areas	
	Amount (Yuan)	Percent total income	Amount (Yuan)	Percent total income	Amount (Yuan)	Percent total income
Wages, etc.	85	11.1	10.1	5	6.4	3
Net income from farming and subsidiary activities cash and kind	564	74.2	169.50	82	185.9	84
Property income	1	0.2	0.30	0	0.02	0
Rental value of housing	73	9.7	27.9	14	18.8	8
Net fiscal transfer from state and collective	−14	−1.9	−15.3	−7.4	−6.8	−3
Other income (including private transfers)	51	6.7	13.6	7	17.5	8
Personal income per capita	760	100.0	206.1	100.0	222.1	100

of farm and subsidiary output, but this advantage was more than offset by cash production expenses that were 29 percent higher (Table 14.1). In other words, the NRP were significantly more dependent upon purchased inputs, and their net income from household production consequently suffered.

Two other kinds of expenses, contract payments to the state and collective and payments into the collective accumulation and welfare funds, are treated here as rent-type production expenses that are subtracted from gross income. The first, astonishingly, came to almost 4 times as much for the NRP as for the RP and exceeded even the rural average by 28 percent (Table 14.3). Similarly, NRP payments to collective funds, although smaller, were also 4 times as high as for the RP, which in turn paid more than the rural average. Like production expenses, these payments depressed the net income of NRP households both absolutely and relative to both the regional poor and the average rural household.[3]

Moreover, while only small numbers of households reported payments to collective funds, once again the NRP households bore by far the heaviest burden: 18 percent of them made such payments, twice as high as the proportion for the whole rural sample and 3 times that of the RP households. And the average size of payments by the NRP households that made such payments, 231 yuan, was 30 percent higher than the corresponding figure of 178 yuan for RP households, and 3 times the average (77 yuan) for all rural households. These facts suggest the hypothesis that high exactions by local authorities are a significant causal factor in generating nonregional poverty.

The contract fees and payments to collective funds are part of the fiscal inter-

Table 14.3

Household Income, Production Expenses, and Transfers to State and Collective, Rural China and Poor Population, by Nonpoor and Poor Regions, 1988

| | | Poor population | |
	Rural China	In nonpoor regions (NPR)	In poor regions (PR)
a. Net cash income from household production (yuan)	1,259	−16	20
b. Total production expenses (yuan)	1,043	1,099	777
Ordinary production expenses	970	961	743
Contract fees to state, collective	66	96	24
Contributions to collective funds	7	42	10
c. Gross value self-consumption	1,565	858	961
d. Gross value household production (a + b + c)	3,867	1,941	1,758
e. Net value household production (d − b)	2,824	842	981

actions between the local government or collective, on the one hand, and villagers, on the other. The evidently exorbitant burden they imposed on nonregional poor households suggests that we should also look into other aspects of the relationship between state/collective and household. The survey measured several other kinds of direct transfer to households, including relief payments, income from the collective welfare fund, relief grain valued at market prices, and medical expenses paid by the government or the collective; as well as transfers from the household in the form of direct taxes and miscellaneous fees paid to state and local governments and collective agencies. The algebraic sum of these various flows is only a partial measure of net direct subsidy/tax, embodying all of the direct transfers that we could identify. Subsidies that indirectly affect income are entirely excluded. Such exclusions include, for example, government infrastructural investments and subsidies to enterprises (such as tax relief programs for new township and village enterprises in poor areas), as well as price subsidies (e.g., on farm inputs). In particular, the indirect exaction on the rural economy in the form of quota purchases at low fixed prices, which was still very important in 1988, is not considered here. Moreover, there might have been other direct subsidies that are not identified or included.

The full relationship between households and the state/collective is therefore broader than the aspect of it measured by the survey. Omitted elements are important and of conflicting effects on the whole. Therefore, it is difficult to know whether a complete accounting would be more or less favorable to the household than the limited measure of direct tax/subsidy reported here. Nevertheless, it is worth noting that this measure was negative for rural households as a whole, transferring 1.9 percent of household average per capita income to the state/

collective. What is surprising is that the negative transfers take a substantially larger fraction of income for poor households in both types of regions, but especially in nonpoor regions. Transfers to the state claimed 2.6 percent of net income of RP households, and 7.4 percent for NRP households—almost four times the average rate for rural China.

NRP households on average got minimally more income per capita than did RP households from the collective welfare fund and from relief payments. However, they paid twice as high taxes (50 yuan compared with 27) and 4 times the level of miscellaneous fees to state and collective (27 yuan compared with 6). Indeed, the taxes and fees paid by poor households in nonpoor regions were as high as the average for all rural households in 1988. Thus the components of the state–household fiscal relationship examined here prove to be just as regressive as those treated as production expenses and reported above. It has long been known that China's tax system is regressive. Khan et al. (1993) in the summary paper on the results of the 1988 income survey emphasize the regressive nature of government fiscal intervention, as captured by this same measure, with respect to the national income distribution as a whole. Even so, the degree of regressiveness revealed here at the lowest level of income is somewhat surprising. Government and the collective seem to be major contributors to rural poverty in nonpoor regions. Their net extraction from income comes to over half of this population's "mean poverty gap" (i.e., difference between average income and poverty line) of 127 yuan. That is, if it were not for this negative component of income, the average poor household's income would rise over half the distance to the poverty line.

Among the rural poor, in general, wage income came to only a small fraction of household per capita income, but the fraction was higher for the NRP than for the RP (5 percent compared with 3 percent). Estimated rental value of housing came to 14 percent of income for the former and to only 8 percent for the latter. If we disregard this item as largely notional, the effect would be to reduce the income of the nonregional poor more than that of the regional poor, thus increasing the gap between their average incomes.

Regional and Nonregional Poverty in 1995

The estimates of incidence of rural poverty in 1995 and its distribution between designated poor and nonpoor regions, for several definitions of absolute poverty, are shown in Table 14.4. The official estimate of the poverty rate at the end of 1995 was 6 percent,[4] and the first thing to notice is that all of our poverty rates, including the 11.4 percent rate based upon the official poverty line itself, are far higher than this. They range from 11. 4 percent up to 30 percent.

Our estimate of the rural poverty head-count rate, based upon the official poverty threshold, is considerably higher than the official rate based on the same threshold. Part of the difference may be explained by our use of provincial price indexes to adjust household net income, rather than the national CPI. Since prices in the

Table 14.4

Incidences and Rates of Poverty Inside and Outside the Poor Regions, for Alternative Poverty Thresholds, 1995

	Poor region	Nonpoor region	Total
Official poverty line: 530 yuan			
Number of poor	1,324	2,909	4,233
Percent of poor population	31.3	68.7	100.0
Poverty incidence (%)	15.78	10.12	11.40
Adjusted poverty line: 570 yuan			
Number of poor	1,609	3,264	4,873
Percent of poor population	33.0	67.0	100.0
Poverty incidence (%)	19.17	11.36	13.12
Riskin poverty line: 662 yuan			
Number of poor	2,269	2,320	4,589
Percent of poor population	49.4	50.6	100.0
Poverty incidence (%)	27.04	8.07	12.36

Notes: The adjusted poverty line is derived by inflating the official poverty line for 1988, 260 yuan, using the national consumer price index for 1988–1995. Household incomes are adjusted to reflect each province's price behavior relative to the national CPI. The Riskin poverty line is based upon Riskin's poverty threshold of 301 yuan in 1988 (excluding rental value of housing), which is inflated using the provincial price indexes for 1988–1995. The sample is weighted by actual population in the poor counties and nonpoor counties. The total number of observations is 37,134 in the 1995 rural household survey. SSB's definition of net income is used together with SSB poverty lines, that is, 530 yuan and 570 yuan, as the official poverty line. Household disposable income per capita (excluding rental value of housing) is used in connection with the Riskin poverty line.

poor provinces rose faster than the national average, this procedure results in lower constant price incomes in those provinces and thus higher poverty rates. Using the national CPI, the overall poverty head-count rate would work out to 9.8 percent rather than 11.4 percent. Yet this is still much higher than the official rate of 6 percent based on the same poverty threshold. This remaining gap is unexplained; our data set derives from a subsample of the State Statistical Bureau's rural household sample (see the Introduction to this volume); the mean household disposable income for our subsample, using the SSB's definition of disposable income, is virtually identical to that derived from the parent sample. It is very unlikely, therefore, that sampling differences account for the disparity between the two poverty rates.

The inflation of the 1988 poverty line of 260 yuan into 1995 prices, using the official rural cost of living index, yields an "adjusted" line that is 7.5 percent higher than the official 1995 line of 530 yuan. Thus even on the basis of the official cost of living index, which Khan convincingly argues understates the actual rise in living costs of the rural poor, the official line for 1995 appears to represent a lower real income than in 1988. Moreover, the 7.5 percent increase in poverty threshold causes a 15 percent rise in poverty incidence, a result of the bunching of population at income levels close to the poverty line.

The head-count rate of poverty in 1995, according to the adjusted official poverty line—which represents an income with the same purchasing power as the 1988 official poverty line—is virtually identical with the head-count rate in 1988. Similarly, the Riskin poverty line yields a poverty incidence very close to that of 1988.[5] Thus, according to our findings, there was no perceptible decline in the rural poverty rate between the two years, and since the rural population grew, the absolute number of rural poor increased. This result contradicts the official figures on rural poverty, which indicate a substantial decline in the poverty rate over the same period, and the World Bank's conclusions, which similarly portray a decline. Our result is also in apparent conflict with Khan and Riskin (2001, Chapter 4), who find a reduction in the rural head-count poverty rate of between 13 and 28 percent, depending upon the definition of poverty and the CPI used. The reason for this is that our income and poverty line definitions exclude imputed rental value of private housing, whereas Khan and Riskin include it. Because we believe rental value of housing of poor households is probably overestimated and it also increased much faster than the CPI (see note 10), the effect of excluding it is to raise the incidence of poverty. If our approach is valid, the effect of it is to throw into doubt the widespread view that the incidence of rural poverty declined markedly between the late 1980s and the mid-1990s, and to strengthen the view, expressed by Khan and Riskin (2001), that sharply increasing inequality led to a very disappointing record of poverty reduction despite rapid economic growth during that period.

The distribution of the poor between poor and nonpoor regions is also striking: On the basis of the "official" poverty lines, the proportion of poor people living in designated poor areas is one-third or less. Using the "Riskin" poverty threshold and income definition, this proportion rises to 49 percent, about the same as in 1988.[6] This contrast in the regional distribution of poverty implies that the differences between the Survey and SSB enumerations of income are regionally sensitive. The Survey definition must include more income for items that are relatively important in nonpoor areas. For example, our enumeration of wage income is 46 percent greater than SSB's (Khan and Riskin 1998), and wage income is higher in the nonpoor than in the poor regions (see Table 14.6). However, in 1995 as in 1988, our measures indicate that a majority of the poor lived outside of official poverty regions and were thus largely ignored by national and regional poverty alleviation programs.

Characteristics of the poor in types of regions are shown in Table 14.5. Unlike in 1988, the average income of the regional poor was lower—by about 10 percent—than that of the nonregional poor. However, this change was due entirely to growth of rental value of housing. If this income source is excluded, the income of the RP would instead be 10 percent higher than that of the NRP. The adherence to farming as a primary occupation was only slightly less ubiquitous than in 1988. The representation of national minorities in the poor population of nonpoor regions increased from only 3 percent in 1988 to 14 percent in 1995.

Table 14.5

Characteristics of Poor Population in Poor and Nonpoor Regions, 1995

	(a) Nonpoor regions	(b) Poor regions	(c) Ratio: a/b
Individual			
Income (yuan)	543	495	1.10
Completed 5 years of education (%)	53	42	1.26
Illiterate (self-reported) (%)	27	37	0.73
Minority nationality (%)	14	25	0.56
Primary occupation farming (%)	92	93	0.99
Ownership status: self-employed (%)	93	93	1.00
Household			
Total medical expenses (yuan)	125	124	1.01
Fixed productive assets (yuan)	2,228	2,081	1.07
Value of livestock (yuan)	886	995	0.89
Cultivated land (*mu*)	12.9	11.9	1.08
Irrigated land (*mu*)	2.6	0.8	3.25
Financial assets, incl. savings (yuan)	2,648	1,020	2.60
Outstanding debt (yuan)	452	426	1.06
For housing (yuan)	89	73	1.21
Annual production expenses (yuan)	2,784	1,789	1.56
Have electricity (%)	96	91	1.05
Days of illness	3.4	6.9	0.49

A striking finding is that the educational attainments of the rural poor declined markedly between the two years. In nonpoor regions the percentage of poor people who completed five years of education fell from 68 to 53 percent; in poor regions, the fall was from 54 to 42 percent. The anecdotal evidence of poor villagers being unable to afford the proliferation of school fees, and the structural evidence of decline in fiscal redistribution to poor areas under the decentralized fiscal system, both lead to the conclusion that even primary education has been moving out of the reach of the rural poor. Our findings give concrete empirical support to this fear.

Another dramatic change between 1988 and 1995 occurred in medical expenditures. In 1988, the poor in both types of regions spent about 6 percent of their incomes on medical care; by 1995 this percentage had grown to 23 (NRP) and 25 (RP) percent, astonishingly high figures for people of such low income levels. The well-known decline in government commitment to public health and the consequent growth of out-of-pocket financing of health care are thus given rather startling quantitative dimensions here.[7] These results also suggest that illness may have been an important cause of poverty, although respondents reported missing only 3.4 (nonpoor regions) and 6.9 (poor regions) days of work on account of illness in 1995.

Poor people in the nonpoor regions remained at a relative disadvantage in livestock ownership, as in 1988, but now had a small advantage in other fixed productive assets. The comparison for the amount of cultivated land remained very much the same as in 1988, but there was a marked change in the crucial category of irrigated land. The NRP had access to three times as much irrigated land per capita as their RP counterparts, a much bigger relative advantage than in 1988. Moreover, the proportion of total cultivated land that was irrigated rose from 13 percent to 20 percent for the NRP, whereas it fell from 9 percent to 7 percent for the RP. Electrification had made progress in both types of regions, and only a small minority of villages were without electric power.[8]

It is not surprising that the rural poor, that is, those living at or below a relatively constant income poverty threshold, should have fallen farther behind the rest of the rural population, their average net income amounting to only about a quarter of that of rural China as a whole. If rental value of housing is left out of the reckoning, the relative position of the poor is worse still, their income coming to only 19–21 percent of rural average net income. As in 1988, the relative composition of income yields insights about the comparison between the two types of rural poor (Table 14.6). For the rural population as a whole, wages in 1995 had almost tripled their 1988 contribution of 10 percent of total income, but among the poor population in both kinds of areas they continued to contribute very small fractions of income—6 percent or less. Net income from farming and farm sidelines continued to supply the bulk of total income, its share having fallen only modestly—from over 80 percent in 1988 for both types of regions, to between 71 (NRP) and 76 (RP) percent in 1995. While there was virtually no gap between the two types of areas in this respect in 1988, a small one had opened by 1995.

A much larger gap existed for rental value of housing (33 percent of income for NRP, 19.3 percent for RP), no doubt due to the higher degree of commercialization in nonpoor regions, but this is a kind of income that is not really "bankable" in the absence of a developed real estate market. If rental value of housing were left out of the reckoning, the shares of net income from farming would actually be higher in nonpoor areas, where they would exceed total personal income![9] However, problems with the method of imputing rental value of housing make it unwise to put much weight on the apparent difference between RP and NRP in this source of income.[10]

The fiscal relationship between households, on the one hand, and the state and collectives, on the other, displayed the same regressive characteristics in 1995 as in 1988. The net fiscal transfer away from households came to 3.4 percent of income for rural China as a whole.[11] For the poor in nonpoor areas, however, the negative transfer was a much larger 15.7 percent of income, whereas for those in poor areas it was 5.6 percent of income. Thus the nonregional poor did considerably worse than the entire rural population, giving up a larger sum than the rural average, while the regional poor gave up a smaller sum but a larger percentage of income than the rural average. The major cause of the contrast in the fiscal burden between poor and nonpoor regions was the difference in their tax burdens (Table 14.7). While the poor in both regions received about the same amount of gross

Table 14.6

Composition of Household per Capita Income, Rural China and Poor Population, by Poor and Nonpoor Regions, 1995

	Rural China		Poor population			
			Nonpoor areas		Poor areas	
	Amount (yuan)	Percent total income	Amount (yuan)	Percent total income	Amount (yuan)	Percent total income
Wages, etc.	63.0	28.6	32.6	6.0	28.1	5.7
Net income from farming and subsidiary activities cash and kind	1,286.6	58.5	385.1	70.8	378.1	76.3
Property income	9.4	0.4	3.0	0.6	0.1	0.0
Rental value of housing	261.7	11.9	179.1	33.0	95.9	19.3
Net fiscal transfer from state and collective	−74.9	−3.4	−85.5	−15.7	−27.6	−5.6
Other income (including private transfers)	88.7	4.0	28.6	5.3	21.0	4.3
Personal income per capita	2,128.8	100.0	542.9	100.0	495.6	100.0
Personal income per capita (excluding rental value of housing)	1,867.1	—	363.8	—	399.7	—

Table 14.7

Distribution of Transfer Income of Poor and Nonpoor People in Poor and Nonpoor Regions in China, 1995

	Poor people		Nonpoor people	
	Mean (yuan)	As percentage of income (%)	Mean (yuan)	As percentage of income (%)
Net public transfer income				
Poor regions	−27.6	−5.6	−41.5	−3.0
Nonpoor regions	−85.5	−15.7	−85.6	−3.3
Gross public transfer income				
Poor regions	6.0	1.2	22.8	1.6
Nonpoor regions	6.1	1.1	19.2	0.7
Taxes and fees				
Poor regions	−33.5	−4.4	−64.1	−4.6
Nonpoor regions	−91.6	−14.6	−104.8	−4.0

Notes: In both tables income and its components are adjusted by difference of national CPI and provincial CPI for each province. Sample is weighted in accordance with the actual proportion of population in poor areas as the entire population in rural areas. In Table 14.6, personal income per capita is defined to include rental value of private housing.

Table 14.8

Household Income and Production Expenses of Rural China and the Poor Population by Nonpoor and Poor Regions, 1995

		Poor population	
	Rural China	Nonpoor areas	Poor areas
a. Net cash income from household production (yuan)	1,633.2	253.1	371.4
b. Total production expenses (yuan)	3,526.7	3,068.3	1,904.3
Ordinary production expenses	3,138.7	2,783.5	1,788.7
Contract fees to state, collective	221.7	164.1	81.2
Contributions to collective funds	166.3	120.7	34.4
c. Gross value of consumption in kind	4,812.0	1,591.6	1,887.4
d. Gross value household production (a + b + c)	9,971.9	4,912.9	4,163.1
e. Net value household production (d − b)	6,445.2	1,844.6	2,258.8

public transfer income, the NRP paid taxes and fees totaling more than three times the amounts paid by the RP. As a result, the net transfer away from the former (equal to gross transfer income minus taxes and fees) was three times as high. This finding, like the evidence about declining educational attainment by the poor, casts a spotlight on the fiscal decentralization and the resulting heightened regressive burden on the poor, perhaps especially in areas that are not targeted for poverty relief measures.

Expenses, other than taxes, are a large part of the explanation for the lower net incomes of the NRP, as shown in Table 14.8. As in 1988, the NRP had a larger gross value of household production than the RP, but this advantage was reversed by the larger production expenses of the former. The result was a net value of household production only 82 percent that of the RP households. Of these expenses, fees and contributions to the state and collective were 2.5 times as high for NRP as for RP. Although they were no longer actually higher than the rural average, as in 1988, they came to almost three-fourths of this average, despite a gross value of household production (GVHP) only 42 percent as high. Thus, as in 1988, the exactions of local authorities seem to be a contributing factor in nonregional poverty.

A greater contributor, however, was the differentially high ordinary production expenses of NRP households—some 56 percent higher than those of their RP counterparts. Indeed, these production expenses were almost 90 percent of the rural average. Thus, while ordinary production expenses claimed 35 percent of GVHP for rural China as a whole, the ratio was 57 percent for the NRP. This observation suggests that a substantial number of the latter may have suffered from crop failure because of flood, drought, insect infestation, or other natural disaster, after annual production expenses had already been incurred.[12]

Conclusion

Virtually all discussions of poverty in China have concluded that the head-count rate of poverty declined between the late 1980s and mid-1990s. Khan and Riskin (2001), for instance, using the same survey data on which this study is based, find that rural poverty fell by between 13 and 28 percent (depending on the poverty threshold and CPI used) from 1988 and 1995, a record they describe as disappointing, given the rapid growth in rural income per capita during that period. In this study we define income and the poverty threshold to exclude the rental value of private housing because of the likelihood that the estimate of this income component is overestimated for poor households. The resulting poverty estimates show *virtually no decline in the poverty rate between 1988 and 1995*. If the Khan/Riskin results are disappointing, the present ones are even more so; they imply that the reduction in poverty found by the former study came principally from increases in imputed income from housing services, some of which might be exaggerated and much of which is largely nominal in the absence of developed real estate markets.

We also find absolute head-count poverty rates in 1995 ranging from 11.4 to 13.1 percent of the rural population, substantially higher than the official rate of 6 percent, even when we measure using the official poverty threshold.

In 1988, slightly more than half (51.4 percent) of all poor rural households lived outside of officially designated poor areas, and were thus left out of the nexus of anti-poverty programs, all of which were focused on such areas. This distribution of poor population between poor and nonpoor areas remained virtually the same in 1995, by the measures closest to those used for 1988. Using official definitions of income and poverty line, however, the proportion of poor living outside of poor regions was much higher still, coming to over two-thirds of the total poor population.

In 1988 the average income of the poor population living in poor regions was higher than that of their counterparts in nonpoor regions. This remained the case in 1995, when income is defined to exclude rental value of housing. In both years, farming was overwhelmingly the primary occupation of the poor in both regions, but the representation of national minorities among the poor increased significantly.

The rapid growth of wage income in rural China, where the share of this income source had almost tripled in seven years, largely bypassed the poor, who got only about 6 percent of their income on average from wages. It appears that it has become more difficult and/or expensive for the poor to get basic social services, especially education and health. In both kinds of region, the percentage of poor people with five or more years of education dropped substantially, while the percentage of total income spent on medical care rose sharply to almost one-quarter, an extraordinarily high figure for very low-income people.

The fiscal relationship between the household and the state/collective displayed a sharply regressive character in both years. In 1995, the net outflow from households to state and collective came to 15.7 percent of income for nonregional poor households and 5.6 percent for those in poor regions, compared with 3.4 percent for rural China as a whole. The main reason for the difference in the net fiscal burden for the two kinds of region was the difference in the tax burden: The nonregional poor paid more than three times the amount of taxes and fees per capita than did the regional poor.

In both years the NRP had larger gross value of household production but smaller net value. The NRP thus had differentially high production expenses—virtually equal to the rural average in 1988 and almost 90 percent of this average in 1995. The NRP, for whom ordinary production expenses claimed 57 percent of gross household production value, seem to be much more heavily dependent upon purchased inputs than the regional poor (43 percent). It is possible that crop failure, injury, or other transient bad fortune, resulting in reduced output after expenses were already incurred, was a major explanation for nonregional poverty in 1995.

The large net outflow of income from the poor to the state and collective, the declining educational attainment of the poor, and the sharply increasing costs they face for health care, all cast spotlights on the fiscal decentralization of the reform era and the resulting heightened regressive burden on poor areas and poor people,[13] perhaps especially in areas not targeted for poverty relief measures. Greater fiscal resources for the poor population, wherever they live, and sharply increased investment in public schooling and health care, are needed core ingredients in a revitalized poverty reduction program for rural China.

Notes

1. A different method of estimation applied by Khan and Riskin (2001, ch. 4) resulted in 1988 rural poverty head-count rates ranging from 15.5 to 32.7 percent, depending upon the poverty threshold used.

2. The fact that extraordinarily large proportions of both groups of poor went to a hospital or clinic at least once during 1988—48 percent of the nonregional poor and 57 percent of the regional poor—suggests that ill health may be a major contributor to poverty in rural China.

3. Note that the poor population in nonpoor regions is listed as making *losses* averaging 16 yuan (Table 14.3). This figure, like the other net cash income figures, are an artificial result of our attributing all production expenses to output for cash sales, which was necessitated by our failure to collect information on the attribution of expenses between cash production and production for own consumption. See Khan et al. 1993.

4. This figure refers to the end of 1995, and is given in World Bank 1997b, p. 11, which presents this estimate as fact.

5. Both the Riskin poverty line and the measure of disposable income used in 1988 include estimated rental value of owned housing, whereas that component is omitted from both poverty threshold and income in 1995. Thus the poverty rates for the two years are not exactly comparable.

6. The reader is reminded that the "Riskin" poverty line is defined somewhat differently in 1995, to exclude rental value of housing. The reason this line, although higher than the other two, generates about the same total number of poor, is that the concept of income used with it results in a higher income than that used with the official poverty lines. See notes to Table 14.4.

7. See World Bank 1997a.

8. It should be recalled, however, that the most remote villages, which are probably also the poorest, are likely to have been undersampled. These undoubtedly also lack electricity.

9. This is because the negative fiscal transfer away from households in nonpoor regions exceeded the sum of all income sources other than farming and subsidiary activities.

10. We were obliged to estimate this item by using provincial average housing values per square foot, a procedure that obliterates intraprovincial variations in such values. Poor households in officially designated poor areas, as well as those in nonpoor areas, are likely to have housing whose value per square foot is well below the provincial average. Thus their rental value of housing is an overestimate, which may actually be more serious in nonpoor areas, where the (unmeasured) gap between the poor household's rental value and the provincial average is likely to be greater. In poor provinces, the provincial average may be closer to the poor household's rental value. One implication is that the inclusion of rental value of housing exaggerates poor household income, and may do so more in nonpoor than in poor areas.

11. This is higher than the estimate of –0.48 percent of rural income made by Khan and Riskin (1998). The main reason for the difference is the inclusion in net fiscal transfers of contract payments from farm households to the collective, which Khan/Riskin treat as a production cost.

12. If this conjecture is accurate, it implies that a substantial portion of NR poverty may be transitory in nature. By the same token, of course, a portion of the nonpoor are above the poverty line for transitory reasons. We are unable to examine this issue on the basis of data for a single year.

13. See Wong et al. (1997).

References

Chen, C., and Z. Shao (1990). *Food Nutrition and Health Status in China's Seven Provinces.* Beijing, China Statistics Press.

Khan, A.R., K. Griffin, C. Riskin, and R. Zhao (1993). "Household Income and Its Distribution in China," in *The Distribution of Income in China,* K. Griffin and R. Zhao, eds. London, Macmillan.

Khan, Azizur Rahman, and Carl Riskin (1998). "Income and Inequality in China: Composition, Distribution and Growth of Household Income, 1988 to 1995," *China Quarterly,* 154, June.

Khan, A.R., and C. Riskin (2001). *China: Income Distribution and Poverty in the Age of Globalization.* New York and London, Oxford University Press.

Popkin, B.M. (1994). "Social Change and its Nutritional Impact: The China Health and Nutrition Survey." *China Exchange News* 22, No. 2.

Riskin, C. (1993). "Income Distribution and Poverty in Rural China," in *The Distribution of Income in China.* K. Griffin and Zhao Renwei, eds. London, Macmillan.

State Planning Commission (1995). *National Report to the 1995 World Summit on Social Development.* Beijing.

State Statistical Bureau (1990). *China Statistical Yearbook 1990.* Beijing, China Statistics Press.

Wong, Christine, C. Heady, and L. West (1997). *Financing Local Development in the People's Republic of China.* Oxford and New York, Oxford University Press.

World Bank (1997a). *Financing Health Care: Issues and Options for China.* Washington, DC, The World Bank.

World Bank (1997b). *Sharing Rising Incomes: Disparities in China.* Washington, DC, The World Bank.

Zhongguo Guowu Yuan (1994). *Zhongguo 21 shiji yicheng, Zhongguo 21 shiji renkou, huanjing yu fazhan baipishu (China's Agenda 21, white paper on China's population, environment and development in the 21st century).* Beijing, China Environmental Sciences Press.

Index

Selected Studies of the East Asian Institute

Cadres and Corruption: The Organizational Involution of the Chinese Communist Party, by Xiaobo Lu. Stanford University Press, 2000

Japan's Imperial Diplomacy: Consuls, Treaty Ports, and War with China, 1895–1938, by Barbara Brooks. Honolulu: University of Hawai'i Press, 2000

Japan's Budget Politics: Balancing Domestic and International Interests, by Takaaki Suzuki. Lynne Rienner Publishers, 2000

Nation, Governance, and Modernity: Canton, 1900–1927, by Michael T.W. Tsin. Stanford: Stanford University Press, 1999

Assembled in Japan: Electrical Goods and the Making of the Japanese Consumer, by Simon Partner, University of California Press 1999

Civilization and Monsters: Spirits of Modernity in Meiji Japan, by Gerald Figal, Durham. NC: Duke University Press, 1999

The Logic of Japanese Politics: Leaders, Institutions, and the Limits of Change, by Gerald L. Curtis. New York: Columbia University Press, 1999

Driven by Growth: Political Change in the Asia-Pacific Region, Revised edition, edited by James W. Morley. Armonk, NY: M. E. Sharpe, 1999

Contesting Citizenship in Urban China: Peasant Migrants, the State and Logic of the Market, by Dorothy Solinger. Berkeley: University of California Press, 1999

Bicycle Citizens: The Political World of the Japanese Housewife, by Robin LeBlanc. Berkeley: University of California Press, 1999

Alignment Despite Antagonism: The United States, Japan, and Korea, by Victor Cha. Stanford: Stanford University Press, 1999

Trans-Pacific Racisms and the U.S. Occupation of Japan, by Yukiko Koshiro. New York: Columbia University Press, 1999

Chaos and Order in the Works of Natsume Sōseki, by Angela Yiu. Honolulu: University of Hawai'i Press, 1998

China's Transition, by Andrew J. Nathan. New York: Columbia University Press, 1997

The Origins of the Cultural Revolution, Vol. III, The Coming of the Cataclysm, 1961–1966, by Roderick Macfarquhar. New York: Columbia University Press, 1997

Japan's Total Empire: Manchuria and the Culture of Wartime Imperialism, by Louise Young. Berkeley: University of California Press, 1997

Honorable Merchants: Commerce and Self-Cultivation in Late Imperial China, by Richard Lufrano. Honolulu: University of Hawai'i Press, 1997

Print and Politics: 'Shibao' and the Culture of Reform in Late Qing China, by Joan Judge. Stanford: Stanford University Press, 1996

China in My Life: A Historian's Own History, by C. Martin Wilbur. Armonk, NY: M.E. Sharpe, 1996

China's Transition from Socialism: Statist Legacies and Market Reforms, 1980–1990, by Dorothy Solinger. Armonk, NY: M.E. Sharpe, 1993

Pollution, Politics and Foreign Investment in Taiwan: The Lukang Rebellion, by James Reardon-Anderson. Armonk, NY: M. E. Sharpe, 1993

Schoolhouse Politicians: Locality and State during the Chinese Republic, by Helen Chauncey. Honolulu: University of Hawai'i Press, 1992